Leonie Vierck | Pedro A. Villarreal
A. Katarina Weilert [eds.]

The Governance of Disease Outbreaks

International Health Law:
Lessons from the Ebola Crisis and Beyond

Nomos

PROTESTANT INSTITUTE
FOR INTERDISCIPLINARY
RESEARCH
F·E·S·T

MAX PLANCK INSTITUTE
FOR COMPARATIVE PUBLIC LAW
AND INTERNATIONAL LAW

Supported by:

Federal Ministry
of Health

on the basis of a decision
by the German Bundestag

NORMATIVE ORDERS
Cluster of Excellence at Goethe University Frankfurt/Main

The Deutsche Nationalbibliothek lists this publication in the Deutsche Nationalbibliografie; detailed bibliographic data are available on the Internet at http://dnb.d-nb.de

ISBN 978-3-8487-4328-5 (Print)
978-3-8452-8600-6 (ePDF)

British Library Cataloguing-in-Publication Data
A catalogue record for this book is available from the British Library.

ISBN 978-3-8487-4328-5 (Print)
978-3-8452-8600-6 (ePDF)

Library of Congress Cataloging-in-Publication Data
Vierck, Leonie / Villarreal, Pedro A. / Weilert, A. Katarina
The Governance of Disease Outbreaks
International Health Law: Lessons from the Ebola Crisis and Beyond
Leonie Vierck / Pedro A. Villarreal / A. Katarina Weilert (eds.)
393 p.
Includes bibliographic references.

ISBN 978-3-8487-4328-5 (Print)
978-3-8452-8600-6 (ePDF)

1st Edition 2017

Content

List of Abbreviations

AAAQ	Availability, Accessibility, Affordability, Quality
app.	application(s)
ASEAN	Association of Southeast Asian Nations
ASEOWA	African Union Support to the Ebola Outbreak in West Africa
AU	African Union
CDC	Centers for Disease Control and Prevention
CESCR	Committee on Economic, Social and Cultural Rights
doc.	document(s)
DSU	Dispute Settlement Understanding of the World Trade Organization
ECHR	European Convention of Human Rights
ECJ	European Court of Justice
ECOWAS	Economic Community of West African States
ECtHR	European Court of Human Rights
et al.	et alia/aliae/alii (and others)
et seq(q).	et sequentia/sequentes (and the following)
etc.	et cetera
ETU	Ebola Treatment Unit(s)
EU	European Union
EVD	Ebola Virus Disease
FCTC	Framework Convention on Tobacco Control
fn.	footnote(s)
G7	Group of 7
GC	General Comment (of the Committee on Economic, Social and Cultural Rights)
GHG	Global Health Governance
Global Fund	The Global Fund to Fight AIDS, Tuberculosis and Malaria
GOARN	World Health Organization's Global Outbreak Alert and Response Network
HIV/AIDS	Human Immunodeficiency Virus/Acquired Immunodeficiency Syndrome, correspondingly
IACHR	Inter-American Commission of Human Rights
IACtHR	Inter-American Court of Human Rights

IASC	Inter-Agency Standing Committee
ibid.	ibidem (in that same place)
ICAO	International Civil Aviation Organization
ICCPR	International Covenant on Civil and Political Rights
ICESCR	International Covenant on Economic, Social and Cultural Rights
ICH	International Conference on the Harmonisation of Technical Requirements for Registration of Pharmaceuticals for Human Use
ICJ	International Court of Justice
IHG	International Health Governance
IHL	International Humanitarian Law
IHR	International Health Regulations
ILC	International Law Commission
ILO	International Labour Organization
ILOAT	International Labour Organization Administrative Tribunal
IMF	International Monetary Fund
IO	International Organization(s)
IPA	International Public Authority
MDG	Millenium Development Goals
MERS	Middle East Respiratory Syndrome
MINUSTAH	United Nations Stabilization Mission in Haiti
MSF	Médecins Sans Frontières
NGO	Non-Governmental Organization(s)
no.	number(s)
NTD	Neglected Tropical Disease(s)
OCP	Onchocerciasis Control Programme
OECD	Organization for Economic Cooperation and Development
para.	paragraph(s)
PCA	Permanent Court of Arbitration
PEPFAR	US President's Emergency Plan for AIDS Relief
PHEIC	Public Health Emergency of International Concern
PPP	Public-private partnership(s)
R2P	Responsibility to Protect
RCDC	Regional Centre for Disease Control
SARS	Severe Acute Respiratory Syndrome

SDG	Sustainable Development Goal(s)
SP	Samaritan's Purse
TRIPs	Trade-Related Aspects of Intellectual Property Rights (TRIPs)
UDHR	Universal Declaration of Human Rights
UNAIDS	Joint United Nations Program on HIV/AIDS
UNDP	United Nations Development Programme
UN-HABITAT	United Nations Human Settlements Programme
UNICEF	United Nations Children's Emergency Fund
UNMEER	United Nations Mission for Ebola Emergency Response
UNMIL	United Nations Mission in Liberia
UNSC	United Nations Security Council
US	United States of America
USD	US-Dollar(s)
vol.	volume(s)
WAHO	West African Health Organisation
WB	World Bank
WHA	World Health Assembly
WHO	World Health Organization
WTO	World Trade Organization

Foreword

This edited volume entitled "The Governance of Disease Outbreaks - International Health Law: Lessons from the Ebola Crisis and Beyond" is a collaborative effort in many respects, and would not have been possible without the contributions of several persons involved. First, it is the product of an institutional collaboration between the Forschungsstätte der Evangelischen Studiengemeinschaft e.V./Protestant Institute for Interdisciplinary Research (FEST) and the Max Planck Institute for Comparative Public and International Law (MPIL), both located in Heidelberg, Germany. In 2014, the FEST and the MPIL identified a common research interest concerning "International Health Governance" (IHG) and formally set up their collaboration in 2015. The FEST had a particular research series on health responsibility on the public-private divide and the MPIL was framing health within the context of the "International Public Authority (IPA)"[1] approach in order to analyze international institutions. Health was quickly identified as a joint thematic area of interest within both institutions. While IHG has long been of interest to the discipline of public health with its roots in medicine, sociology of health, economics and political science, the field is still by and large under-researched in international law. In order to define a first concrete research field, the case of the then-ongoing Ebola crisis was chosen, and with it the international governance of disease outbreaks more generally. First and foremost, the editors wish to thank *Armin v. Bogdandy* (MPIL) and *Klaus Tanner* (FEST) as the responsible directors at the respective institutions for their support and trust in this project.

This edited volume has come to life through its collaborative contributions, which correspond with each other in many instances. Consequently, we wish to thank all contributors for their texts, engaged discussions, diligence, and patience. They are in alphabetical order: *Elif Askin*, *Susan L. Erikson*, *André den Exter*, *Robert Frau*, *Wolfgang Hein*, *Bonnie Kaiser*, *Hunter Keys*, *Michael Marx*, *Edefe Ojomo*, *Ilja Richard Pavone*, *Mateja*

1 For the latest lead publication of this project, see Bogdandy, A von, Goldmann, M & Venzke, I, "From Public International Law to International Public Law: Translating World Public Opinion into International Public Authority" (2017), 28 *EJIL*, 115.

Steinbrück Platise, and *Christian R. Thauer*. All contributors met in an earlier workshop in Heidelberg in March 2016 on the same topic. In this respect, we also would like to thank all funding institutions of both the workshop and the present edited volume for all their support, as well as the MPIL and the FEST: The German Federal Ministry of Health/Bundesministerium für Gesundheit (BMG), and the "Normative Orders" Cluster of Excellence at Goethe University Frankfurt/Main in Germany. Likewise, we wish to thank all workshop presenters for their insights and discussion: *Pia Acconci*, *Monica Cappelletti*, *Ali Aghahosseini Dehaghani*, *Eszter Kollár*, *Giuseppe Pascale*, and *Andra Le-Roux Kemp*. We also would like to thank all participants and thus engaged listeners of that workshop. The workshop could not have taken place without the staff support of *Margit Dagli*, and *Ute Emrich* (MPIL), as well as *Marie Bolster* and *Violetta Ritz* as student assistants.

Similar indispensable support throughout the publication process was provided by *Joel Maupin* for native speaker checks and *Simeon Prechtel* for unifying, proofreading and setting the proofs of all contributions, as well as the administrations of both MPIL and FEST, including *Nico Wiest* (MPIL). Directly after the workshop, presenters had the opportunity to post their initial articles in a symposium of the "Völkerrechtsblog (international law blog)" by the Working Group of Young Scholars in Public International Law (http://voelkerrechtsblog.org/international-health-governance-of-disease-outbreaks/). This was kindly made possible by our MPIL colleague *Raffaela Kunz*. Likewise, we acknowledge the instrumental support of *Berit Kieselbach* in obtaining visual data for one of the contributions. Last but not least, *Armin v. Bogdandy*'s MPIL researchers' colloquium, the Frankfurt "Normative Orders" International Graduate Programme (IGP) colloquium, and the FEST Kuratorium provided fora in which the entire project could be presented and discussed.

Heidelberg and Frankfurt/Main, June 2017

The editors: Leonie Vierck, Pedro A. Villarreal, and A. Katarina Weilert

The Concept of the Book

Leonie Vierck, Pedro A. Villarreal, and A. Katarina Weilert

The following pages introduce the present edited volume on "The Governance of Disease Outbreaks - International Health Law: Lessons from the Ebola Crisis and Beyond" and provide a concept of the book within the still under-researched and vaguely defined field of international health law. While the edited volume consists of several stand-alone contributions (and not chapters), these have been brought into correspondence with each other with a red thread described in the following lines. The reader will also be guided in detail by cross-references between the articles. Still, all authors bear responsibility for their contributions, and individual contributions do not necessarily reflect the view(s) of the editors. While the chosen title already makes clear that the angle of the book is international health law, this legal angle is, and has to be informed by other disciplines. This is reflected in contributions written from public health, political science, and anthropological perspectives. Of course, readers should be aware of the heterogeneous methodological choices within the contributions. We close this introduction with an outlook for future research questions in the area of international health law and governance.

I What is the Theme of the Book?

1 The Red Thread of the Book

Disease outbreaks occur regularly, and will present an even greater threat to humanity in the future; we know that major disease outbreaks will be increasing, but we do not know which ones and where exactly.[1] The Ebola

1 See the contribution of *Christian R. Thauer*, "The Governance of Infectious Diseases. An International Relations Perspective" in this volume showing how globalization increases demands for international health governance. Trade, investment, and travel allow infections to spread more easily. Population growth and urbanization are other highly important factors. All websites last accessed April 9, 2017.

crisis was unexpected in that previous Ebola disease outbreaks had never been that intense, as shown in *Michael Marx*'s contribution in this edited volume. Ebola could have become more globalized, but luckily the epidemic's peak is now over, even if additional cases have emerged afterwards.[2] Ebola especially hit those countries with extremely weakened health systems.[3] As a result, studying the Ebola crisis will ideally equip us with knowledge on managing future crises with similar potential. Ebola could serve as a wake-up call for the international community, but while reports on the Ebola response broadly agree on action plans concerning compliance with the International Health Regulations (IHR) and strengthened international institutions, preparedness is yet insufficient, as a very recent study indicates.[4] Next to Ebola, other major epidemics and pandemics include cholera, various influenza outbreaks, yellow fever, and the Zika virus in the Americas.[5] In 1980, the World Health Assembly (WHA) declared the eradication of smallpox following surveillance and vaccination campaigns[6] – a unique case. Ebola has been classified as either an epidemic referring to a disease outbreak rapidly spreading from one person to another, or even as a pandemic referring to a global disease outbreak.[7] However, Ebola was by and large contained within the West-African region. Those preferring to declare Ebola a pandemic disease outbreak usually wish

---

2 WHO Ebola Response Team, "After Ebola in West Africa – Unpredictable Risks, Preventable Epidemics" (2016), 375 *The New England Journal of Medicine*, 587 (593-594). See also Gates, B, "The Next Outbreak? We're not Ready" (March 2015), *TED Talks*, available at http://bit.ly/2sOc0rI.

3 In its World Health Report (WHR) 2000, the WHO comparatively ranked health system performance from 191 countries. Guinea was placed 161, Liberia 186, and Sierra Leone 191 of 191. The ranking was so controversial that it has not yet been repeated. Yet, single indicator data for individual countries could still lead to similar conclusions, see http://www.who.int/gho/en/ and http://www.who.int/healthinfo/indicators/en/.

4 See Moon, S, Leigh, J & Woskie, L et al., "Post-Ebola Reforms: ample analysis, inadequate action" (2017), 356:j280 *The British Medical Journal (BMJ)*.

5 See only for WHO's work on epidemic and pandemic diseases: http://www.who.int/csr/disease/en/.

6 See Resolution "Declaration of Global Eradication of Smallpox" WHA 33.3 of 1980, adopted at the 33rd WHA, available at http://apps.who.int/iris/handle/10665/155528.

7 See entries for "Epidemic" (339), "Epidemic Diseases" (339), and "Pandemic" (1082) in Kirch, W (ed.), *Encyclopedia of Public Health*, 2008; see also Morens, D, Folkers, G & Fauci, A, "What is a Pandemic?" (2009), 200 *The Journal of Infectious Diseases*, 1018 (1018-1020).

to emphasize the global factors shaping any disease outbreak currently.[8] In turn, the WHO declared Ebola to be a Public Health Emergency of International Concern (PHEIC), in light of its spread throughout several countries.[9] The Ebola crisis hit countries with highly unstable health systems particularly hard. Authors diverge in their opinion of classifying Ebola as either an epidemic or a pandemic, which can be considered as the result of an unclear distinction between both terms that emerges from long-lasting scientific debates.[10] Similar to this classification problem, the exact duration of the Ebola crisis is to an extent disputed. The WHO and also the Centers for Disease Control and Prevention of the United States (CDC) refer to the first relevant reported cases as occurring in March 2014.[11] However, some scientific articles refer to the year 2013 as the initial outbreak year.[12] The WHO officially declared the end of the Ebola crisis at different points of time for various countries: On November 7, 2015 for Sierra Leone; on December 25, 2015 and once again on June 1, 2016 for Guinea; and on June 9, 2016 for Liberia.[13] Consequently, and depending on how diverse factors are weighed, the end of the Ebola crisis is stated as occurring either in the year 2015 or 2016. Individual contributions in this edited volume mirror this diversity in interpreting scientific evidence and the factual issues related to the chronology of Ebola-related developments in West Africa.[14]

---

8 See for example Richardson, E, Bailor Barrie, M & Kellie, J et al., "Biosocial Approaches to the 2013-2016 Ebola Pandemic" (2015), 18 *Health and Human Rights Journal (HHR)*, 115 (115).

9 See WHO, *Statement on the 1st meeting of the IHR Emergency Committee on the 2014 Ebola outbreak in West Africa*, available at http://www.who.int/mediacentre/news/statements/2014/ebola-20140808/en/.
For a more detailed overview of the Ebola crisis' chronology, see WHO Ebola Response Team, "After Ebola in West Africa", above Fn. 2, 587-591.

10 Consequences of the lack of clarity in the use of terms during the 2009 H1N1 Influenza Pandemic are further discussed in Abeysinghe, S, *Pandemics, Science and Policy. H1N1 and the World Health Organization*, 2015, 7-16.

11 See WHO, *Ebola challenges West African countries as WHO ramps up response*, Note for media, available at http://www.who.int/mediacentre/news/notes/2014/ebola-response/en/ and CDC, *Outbreaks Chronology: Ebola Virus Disease*, available at https://www.cdc.gov/vhf/ebola/outbreaks/history/chronology.html.

12 See Richardson, Bailor Barrie & Kellie et al., "Biosocial Approaches", above Fn. 8, 115.

13 See an overview in *WHO Press Releases on Ebola*, available at http://www.who.int/mediacentre/news/ebola/press-releases/en/.

14 On this issue, the contribution of *Wolfgang Hein*, "The Response to the West African Ebola Outbreak (2014-2016): A Failure of Global Health Governance?" in this volume is of particular relevance. A series of subsequent facts leading to

The individual contributions in this book are inter-connected, clustered, and corresponding to the broader theme outlined. The book starts with introductory perspectives on the field of Ebola within the setting of international health law (*"Framing the Field"*). It continues with contributions on *"The Role of the Human Right to Health"* as a cornerstone of international health law generally, and infectious disease governance particularly. Afterwards, the role of *"International and Regional Organizations and the Securitization of Health"* is analyzed, also in light of the fact of their relevance in managing the Ebola crisis. The edited volume closes with contributions on *"Governance Beyond the Law"*.

The introductory contribution (*"Framing the Field"*) to this edited volume is given by *Marx* from a public health perspective. In his contribution titled "Ebola Epidemic 2014-2015: Taking Control or Being Trapped in the Logic of Failure – What Lessons Can Be learned?", he provides for an account of the Ebola crisis, regards the disease outbreak within the context of larger public health trends, and describes it as a wake-up call for the international community. Health systems strengthening (HSS) is at the core of his argument, also by taking stock of the new Sustainable Development Goals (SDGs). *Wolfgang Hein* responds to *Marx* as a scholar rooted in public health as well as political science with his contribution "The Response to the West African Ebola Outbreak (2014-2016): A Failure of Global Health Governance?". When characterizing the Ebola disease outbreak, and taking the complexities of the disease into consideration, he questions if the international response really can only be captured as a failure. After addressing *Marx*'s overview of the dire scenario of the national health systems most affected by Ebola as well as the lack of effective response by international stakeholders, *Hein* wonders how the final success in combating the regional disease outbreak can be adequately captured. The broader international background is then taken up by *Mateja Steinbrück Platise* in her contribution, "The Changing Structure of Global Health Governance". She scrutinizes how international organizations are increasingly sidelined in favor of alternative fora. This is reflected in debates on major trends such as privatization, fragmentation, and de-formalization. She seeks to analyze how international organizations could become more legitimate by incorporating diverging interests within a public space. *Steinbrück*'s findings are followed by *Leonie Vierck*, who examines "The Case Law of International

the Ebola crisis are quoted for assessing the dynamics and failures of the response by institutions, such as the WHO and the CDC, as part of the overall global health governance setting.

Health and Why its Scarcity is a Problem". In a first step, she takes stock of the fragmented body of case law existent in international infectious disease law, and shows in a second step how this is a phenomenon in international health law generally. In a third step, she enquires into the function of case law in legal systems, and argues that the virtual absence of coherent case law makes the legal argument too invisible with the governance system favoring empirical science arguments.

The second section of the book (*"The Role of the Human Right to Health"*) reflects on the role of the human right to health as entry to a broader system of international health governance. In her article titled "The Right to Health in International Law – Normative Foundations and Doctrinal Flaws", *A. Katarina Weilert* focuses on the human right to health, and explores its various dimensions, especially as concerns its complex legal interpretation. The contribution is innovative in exploring the tensions between individual health rights claims and public health policy – both dimensions are normatively enshrined in the right to health, and become especially pertinent during infectious disease outbreaks. The realization of the right to health, especially in its public health dimension, is exceeding a classical individual right and therefore is also seen as a policy strategy which asks for a broader approach of International Health Governance. In order to clarify in how far a human right to health can serve as a basis of obligations for states to engage beyond their territory, *Elif Askin* specifies the "Extraterritoral Human Rights Obligations of States in the Event of Disease Outbreaks". She argues that state obligations are not limited to the IHR, and presents a framework in order to understand if and under what conditions states, which are not the territorial states of right-holders, have legal duties *vis-à-vis* individual right bearers. *Askin* makes a strong claim that such obligations are not of a mere moral or political, but legal character. This is especially the case as concerns individual entitlements of rights holders in developing countries. One aspect of the right to health is often neglected, which is in this volume given special attention by *Hunter Keys*, *Bonnie Kaiser*, and *André den Exter* who present an interdisciplinary article on (the right to) mental healthcare, and the role of non-governmental organizations (NGOs) as healthcare providers. In their piece "The Real Versus the Ideal in NGO Governance: Enacting the Right to Mental Healthcare in Liberia During the 2014-2016 Ebola Epidemic", they mix anthropological and international law insights and provide a case study on international "soft law" guidelines such as the Inter-Agency Standing Committee (IASC)'s Guidelines on Mental Health and Psychosocial Support in Humanitarian Settings governing such NGO activities. Such guidelines can be traced back to the human right to health. They are brought alive and to their limits when testing their application – using anthropological methods – during their utilization.

The third section of this edited volume is reflecting upon *"International and Regional Organizations and the Securitization of Health"*. A particular emphasis is given to the legal analysis of the WHO's governance. In his article "The World Health Organization's Governance Framework in Disease Outbreaks: A Legal Perspective", *Pedro A. Villarreal* describes the institutional set-up of the WHO infectious disease governance framework, and explains the factors contributing to shortcomings when responding to the Ebola crisis. The WHO is often seen as a bureaucracy based on rational authority which, ultimately, exercises discretion when interpreting legal instruments such as the IHR. Initial questions on how it has exercised this authority in recent outbreaks could subsequently pave the way for normative debates in the future. When dealing with trans-border outbreaks of infectious diseases like Ebola in West Africa, regional organizations are also a part of the picture. *Edefe Ojomo* provides significant insights into "Fostering Regional Health Governance in West Africa: The Role of the WAHO". *Ojomo* does not only describe the institutional set-up of the West African Health Organisation (WAHO) as a specialized agency of the Economic Community of West African States (ECOWAS) in the case of the Ebola crisis, but also explains them against a backdrop of capacity and legitimacy concerns. She shows that regional institutions can support capacity building, and enhance the legitimacy of both national and global institutions. Next to the WHO and WAHO, which are already by their mandate concerned with an improvement of international health structures, another institution has come into focus on the occasion of the extreme dimensions of Ebola which gave rise to security concerns: *Ilja Richard Pavone* turns to the role of the United Nations (UN) Security Council in his article "Ebola and Securitization of Health: UN Security Council Resolution 2177/2014 and Its Limits". For the first time in history, this Resolution authoritatively qualified an infectious disease as a threat to international peace and security according to Article 39 of the UN Charter. *Pavone* wishes to understand whether this was an isolated decision or rather an indicator for the process of the securitization of health. He reflects on the underlying conceptual implications, especially in consideration of the concept of human security. *Pavone*'s considerations are also related to those by *Robert Frau,* who in his article "Combining the WHO's International Health Regulations (2005) with the UN Security Council's Powers: Does it Make Sense for Health Gover-nance?", connects the same Security Council Resolution with the

WHO's legal regime, particularly the IHR. *Frau* is convinced that rendering the IHR legally binding would not have a game-changing effect. However, con- necting the WHO legal framework to the Security Council, as has been evidenced for the first time during the Ebola crisis, would create legal impact – especially if combined with a human right to health approach in the interest of the individuals affected.

The fourth and last section of this book (*"Governance Beyond the Law"*) opens the floor for non-legal governance approaches which can at times even challenge a law oriented view. A specifically critical voice is included with *Susan L. Erikson's* article "The Limits of the International Health Regulations: Ebola Governance, Regulatory Breach, and the Non-Negotiable Necessity of National Healthcare". From an anthropological point of view, she questions the very idea of bindingness of the IHR in light of on-the-ground realities that considerably diverge from normative standards designed at the international level. *Erikson* refers to fieldwork done during the Ebola crisis in order to substantiate her thesis. She calls for shifting more attention towards national healthcare systems, particularly that of Sierra Leone, and not primarily to international instruments such as the IHR. Notably, she emphasizes how this need for strengthening health systems should pre-date promoting regulations deriving from the international community. Thus, her arguments aim towards framing the IHR as guidelines for other operational programs, instead of being legally binding regulations. Namely in this sense, her standpoint diverges from that of other contributions in this volume, including the current introductory chapter. Although not specifically mentioned, *Erikson*'s first-hand experiences are drawn from areas characterized by limited statehood. These areas pose a challenge to common law categories as law presupposes effective state-actors. Questions around this field are taken up by *Christian R. Thauer*, who closes the edited volume with his article "The Governance of Infectious Diseases: An International Relations Perspective". He scrutinizes global health governance in the context of limited statehood, especially in so-called developing countries. *Thauer* shows that limited statehood has been largely ignored as a contextual factor of international disease outbreaks, and especially suggests assigning new roles to non-state actors, including the private sector, in global health governance. His argument also builds upon prior research on the HIV/AIDS pandemic in South Africa.

2 The Development of the Book Project and the Broader Context

The IHG project is connected to the broader International Public Authority (IPA) framework. IPA provides a theoretical basis for analyzing the public authority exercised by international institutions. These institutions have been distinguished by world public opinion as ambivalent actors which are necessary, but raise serious legitimacy concerns at the same time. IPA proposes a theory of international public law, and not only public international law when identifying, reconstructing, and developing the law governing international institutions.[15] Earlier IPA works include publications on diverse international institutions,[16] and international courts as multifunctional judicial institutions.[17] While IPA is a theory-building contribution in order to scrutinize international institutions from an international law perspective, not all articles touch upon public international law theory building, and some are decidedly devoted to its practical application.

Also, IPA corresponds with other approaches such as Global Administrative Law (GAL).[18] *Ojomo* from New York University (NYU) adopts a typical GAL approach in her contribution within this volume. While contributions from other disciplines – public health, political science, and anthropology – inform the overall international public law methodology chosen for this edited volume, inter- or trans-disciplinary approaches were off limits for the explorative nature of the project. The IPA methodology as well as a specific interest in and knowledge of the system of the WHO from the MPIL's side merged with health-related research at the FEST. *Weilert* was leading an interdisciplinary working group at the FEST-Institute, which was centered around questions of responsibility for health within the national arena. Leading questions in this working group include "what is health and to what extent is the answer to this dependent on one's culture?", "what are the social determinants of health?", "how does the international human right to health relate to the national health system?",

---

15 See most recently Bogdandy, A von, Goldmann, M & Venzke, I, "From Public International Law to International Public Law: Translating World Public Opinion into International Public Authority" (2017), 28 *EJIL*, 115-116.

16 See especially Bogdandy, A von, Wolfrum, R & Bernstorff, J von et al. (eds.), *The Exercise of Public Authority by International Institutions: Advancing International Institutional Law*, 2010.

17 See most notably Bogdandy, A von & Venzke, I, *In Whose Name? A Public Law Theory of International Adjudication*, 2014, 8 et seq.

18 See Kingsbury, B, Krisch, N & Stewart, R B, "The Emergence of Global Administrative Law" (2005), 68 *Law and Contemporary Problems*, 15.

"how far does the health responsibility of the state extend and where is the individual responsibility of every person coming in?" and finally "is there a duty for a state to empower the individual in order to take over responsibility for one's health?". It became obvious that many questions arising in the national context needed further discussion in an international context. A few examples may illustrate this finding: While in the national context, the principle of solidarity can be seen as solidarity between the inhabitants of this country, in the international sphere the principle of solidarity plays a role between states. Also, unequal health opportunities are already a challenge within one country and even more so between the people of different states. Likewise, the question of whether states can restrict the freedom of the individual in order to improve health (and health security) can be seen as both an internal matter as well as an international problem. Broadly speaking, in the national context we are looking at the spheres of the state, private entities and the individual and query their responsibilities. In the international context, questions of responsibility also refer to the relationship of further international actors such as the community of states, international institutions (in particular international organizations), NGOs, transnational corporations and other private entities.

3 The West African Ebola Crisis as a Central Focus

Against the background of these research interests of the institutes involved and due to the failed international governance at the early stage of the Ebola outbreak, a workshop was set up (March 3-4, 2016) which identified many questions as to the state of international law in the context of international health governance. About 20 scholars from different parts of the world and different academic backgrounds were selected following a call for abstracts. The devastating effects of Ebola were reinforced not only by poor health systems and poor management of the affected states; the lack of organization to fight such an epidemic on the international level also became obvious. Epidemics control at the international level questions a traditional view of public international law in two ways: First, two different logics are at stake. On one hand, states feel challenged to fight Ebola for *security* reasons as epidemics easily transgress borders by people traveling all over the world. On the other hand, besides the concern for their own people, the idea of *development aid* has been growing since the 1970s due to an increasing sense of responsibility for other countries in a globalized world. This means that the same action can be rooted in the traditional idea of state security as well as being motivated by a human rights perspective.

Secondly, there is – as in many other fields of international law today – a great variety of actors and a confusion as to their roles, responsibilities and duties with regard to epidemics control. States are the main addressees of the right to health but their role is unclear if it comes to a cross-border situation. The WHO should fill in this gap, but seemed to suffer from several structural shortcomings which hindered a better handling of the situation. The WHO has a large administrative responsibility that affects individuals, private associations, public institutions and states. Its organs can enact binding regulations (such as the IHR) and more extensive non-binding regulations (such as recommendations, resolutions, and standards). The latter are often observed even though they are not legally binding. Therefore, the workshop partially pursued an actor-oriented approach. Such an approach is aimed at understanding the roles, responsibilities, legal duties and actions of states, international organizations (as the WHO or corresponding regional organizations) and non-state actors. The workshop consisted of the following components, which differed from the structure that later evolved for the present edited volume: In its first section, the Ebola crisis was analyzed and we primarily covered sustainable health and development policies. Policies and law are intertwined, yet distinct from each other. In international law, we face the fact that the rule of law is relatively fragile. The shortcomings in enforcing international law were especially referred to in Section II from different disciplinary perspectives. These ranged from a skeptical view towards norms over the particular challenges for the rule of law in areas of limited statehood to a mirror of ineffectiveness of the right to health under the African Charter on Human and People's Rights. However, new developments towards an even stronger international law were also discussed while reflecting upon the extraterritorial obligations of states in cases like Ebola. The potential of international law was further developed in Section III, which was dedicated to the role of two major players in international law: The WHO and the Security Council. Here, questions of international health governance directly met questions as to the development of international law. In its last section (IV), the workshop dealt with the role of regional organizations and private actors in disease outbreaks. The workshop made obvious that it is not easy to have a common language and common way of addressing the open questions in this field. Recognizing the considerable research deficit in this discipline, we decided to engage in the arduous work of publishing articles presented at the workshop not as they stood, but only after a thorough revision.

All articles provided by participants of the workshop were peer reviewed and commented upon, so that the authors could further develop their argumentation. The approach of this book is a legal one stemming from public international law and international public law, which is necessarily informed by other disciplines, but not generally interdisciplinary. In the future, developing a more advanced interdisciplinary approach could be a further step for intensifying the IHG project as such. As IHG is a very peculiar field of law, the edited volume mainly addresses the public international law community, including practitioners next to researchers, and especially those already concerned with phenomena of international administrations. If disciplines close to public international law, especially international relations, also find an interest in this publication, this would create an additional value. Given how legal obligations often collide with political and moral ones, it may be of some interest from the political theory audience, too. Last but not least, the international public health community is particularly important for obvious reasons – yet bridging the divide between predominantly empirical science and largely normative research is a challenge on its own.

II Conceptual Thematic Inputs

1 International Health Law and Infectious Disease Governance: What is it and why is it Important?

Discussing a specialized field for international health law evokes the idea of the fragmentation of international law.[19] It currently consists of a dispersed set of norms, standards and regulations which, strictly speaking, might not be limited to health issues. Although the WHO possesses the authority to create norms related to health,[20] it has only exceptionally been used.[21] And even health-specific legal instruments such as the IHR and the Framework Convention for Tobacco Control (FCTC) have considerable overlaps with fields such as trade and investment law, or even human rights

19 See the International Law Commission Report, *Fragmentation of International Law: Difficulties Arising from the Diversification and Expansion of International Law*, finalized by Martti Koskenniemi, A/CN.4/L.682, 2006.

20 Gostin, L, Sridhar, D & Hougendobler, D, *The normative authority of the World Health Organization*, 2015, 854 (856-857).

21 Burci, G L & Vignes, C H, *World Health Organization*, 2004, 141.

law. The rationale changes in each one, meaning that health arguments might enter into tension or even conflict with economic ones.

Due to the non-autonomous nature of international health law *vis-à-vis* other fields,[22] there is still a pending task of defining its contents without reference to another field. An ensuing consequence of its autonomy could be a growing group of specialized research addressing very specific topics, which means it would be directed at a particular audience.[23] But initially, the conceptual arguments for considering a legal field as autonomous would need to be convincing. This endeavor would extend beyond the scope of this edited volume, requiring a full-fledged textbook instead. Nevertheless, it is already possible to identify an ongoing academic discussion dealing with attempts to draw more concrete components of the field.[24] Whether or not this specialization will become entrenched throughout the academic community remains to be seen.[25]

In light of these unclear conceptual boundaries, suffice it to say that the control of the spread of infectious diseases has been at the core of international health ever since the first interstate meetings on this topic took place in the 19th Century. While the International Sanitary Conference of 1851 marked the first time in which twelve countries met for dealing with health matters, it did not give way to a lasting legal document.[26] Even after

---

22 An argument put forward by Fidler, D, "International Law and Global Public Health" (1999), 48 *The University of Kansas Law Review*, 1 (27-40).

23 Already a trend identified in the United States of America by Posner, R, "Legal Scholarship Today" (2002), 115 *Harvard Law Review*, 1314 (1319-1322).

24 See Toebes, B, "International health law: an emerging field of public international law" (2015), 55 *Indian Journal of International Law*, 299. By contrast, within international relations and political science the strand of "global health governance" has been developed to a larger extent, see Hein, W, "The New Dynamics of Global Health Governance" in Kickbusch, I, Lister, G & Told, M et al. (eds.), *Global Health Diplomacy: Concepts, Issues, Actors, Instruments, Fora and Cases*, 2013, 56-59.

25 For instance, recently an Interest Group on International Health Law has been founded at the European Society of International Law (ESIL). See http://www.inthealthlaw.com/. Another outstanding example is the O'Neill Institute for National and Global Health Law at Georgetown University, located in Washington, D.C., the existence of which already spans ten years. See http://www.law.george-town.edu/oneillinstitute/about/index.cfm.

26 For more on this event, see Goodman, N, *International Health Organizations and Their Work*, 1971, 46-51; likewise, see Kickbusch, I & Ivanova, M, "The History and Evolution of Global Health Diplomacy" in Kickbusch, Lister & Told et al. (eds.), *Global Health Diplomacy*, above Fn. 24, 12-13.

the adoption of the International Sanitary Convention of 1893, infectious disease epidemics control was addressed through *ad hoc* meetings and an overall "patchwork" legal process of updating lists of diseases subjected to quarantine procedures.[27]

After several reviews and iterations of the Sanitary Conventions, this inconsistent trend seemed to shift with the adoption of the Constitution of the WHO in 1946, particularly with the inclusion of extraordinary legal powers to the WHA for adopting regulations in the area of infectious disease outbreaks.[28] But throughout its first five decades and despite the creation of the International Sanitary Regulations in 1951 and the 1969 version of the IHR, these legal powers of the WHO were only rarely resorted to, leading some to consider them as "underutilized".[29]

In the same vein, the emergence of the 2005 version of the IHR was meant to explicitly address existing gaps in infectious disease epidemics control through an innovative governance framework for the WHO's authorities.[30] However, several years and outbreaks later, as this book's contents highlight, the shortcomings of this legal framework are evident on multiple levels. And, as seen also in several contributions in this edited volume, the role of law in global health governance is relatively limited in its reach, as states continuously resort to informal channels for addressing core issues of international health.[31]

Against this backdrop, events such as the 2014-2016 West African Ebola crisis or the 2016 Zika epidemic are health issues at the core, even if they also involve economic or human rights aspects. Under this assumption, a health-based legal framework would prevail over others. Yet, since there is

---

27 Fidler, D "From International Sanitary Conventions to Global Health Security: The New International Health Regulations" (2005), 4 *Chinese Journal of International Law*, 325 (329-333).

28 See also Lee, K, *World Health Organization (WHO)*, 2009, 16-18; others emphasize how this is one of the core issues where the WHO has an explicit mandate, as opposed to other institutions. See Ooms, G & Hammonds, R, "Global constitutionalism, applied to global health governance: uncovering legitimacy deficits and suggesting remedies" (2016), 12 *Globalization and Health*, 1 (11), available at http://europepmc.org/articles/PMC5135750.

29 Aginam, O, *Global Health Governance. International Law and Public Health in a Divided World*, 2005, 71.

30 Fidler, "From International Sanitary Conventions", above Fn. 27, 358 et seq.

31 See the contribution of *Mateja Steinbrück Platise*, "The Changing Structure of Global Health Governance" in this volume.

a scarcity of case-law related to these health issues, there is no data concerning the application of law to particular cases through adjudication, whether it is provisions from the IHR or other legal regimes that also deal with health issues.[32] Consequently, it is difficult to speak of a consistent legal field, which would encompass an ever-growing body of criteria for interpretation coupled with the consolidation of specialized professionals within epistemic communities.

For the sake of the thematic contributions and the legal perspective joining them, it is necessary to discuss the applicable law of international public health. How to define it? And what are the conceptual difficulties faced? International health law is not governed by any multilateral umbrella treaty, but builds upon an underlying concept ("international public health") across diverse public international law regimes.[33] International health law would rather be an example of a fragmented public international law regime. Some authors see international health law as an evolving body of law, especially fulfilling demands of so-called developing countries – an old attestation, which still holds true today.[34] Why then make it the focal point for considerations within public international law? There are different lines of argument. Globalization renders public health more international, and creates ever more pressing social needs – as can be evidenced above for infectious disease outbreaks. Law is one tool used in responding to these increasing needs – public health specialists, for example, advocated for the WHO FCTC as an important, multilateral treaty in the area.[35] In this edited volume, international health law can include legal norms and institutions concerned with international public health. There are diverging opinions whether or not these norms and institutions necessarily have to be geared towards the human right to health – also across the contributions. In this approach, we also consider actors that may not be subjects of international law (for example, NGOs and private businesses) to be important players if governed by public international law. The IPA approach can allow one to

32 See the contribution of *Leonie Vierck*, "The Case Law of International Public Health and Why its Scarcity is a Problem" in this volume.

33 Ibid.

34 See in particular Bélanger, M, "Une nouvelle branche du droit international: Le droit international de la santé" (1982), 13 *Études internationales*, 611 as an article written probably way ahead of its time, calling for a New International Economic and Health Order in the 1970s.

35 See Toebes, "International health law", above Fn. 24, 299. Toebes also makes the point for the intrinsic fragmentation of this wider field of law.

bypass many of these questions by centering the analysis on concrete authoritative actions. These are understood as actions which have an impact on others' freedom(s), either at an individual or at a collective level, by modifying a legal situation or even factually affecting persons or, considering the international level, even states.[36]

Additionally, some definitions of global health law include an ethical component, and result in a research agenda to increase social and global justice.[37] This clearly goes beyond a positivist approach to global or international health law. While law can be a tool to reach justice, an even broader domain for analyzing justice demands is political theory.[38] Another approach to define international public health law is a descriptive listing of relevant legal instruments (like treaties) according to issue areas (such as drug control or occupational health and safety).[39] While the relevance of legal instruments in specific areas of international public health law is undisputed, the general recognition of international health law as a special regime of public international law still has to be built. Research on international health law can play an important role in advancing legal concepts, which can eventually be taken up by practice.[40]

2 The Role of the Right to Health for Shaping the Field?

The right to health, as elaborated in the contribution of *Weilert*, comprises an individual right to health and an obligation to promote public health

---

36 Bogdandy, Goldmann & Venzke, "From Public International Law to International Public Law", above Fn. 15, 139-140.

37 See Gostin, L & Taylor, A, "Global Health Law: A Definition and Grand Challenges" (2008), 1 *Public Health Ethics*, 53 (55).

38 See for an introduction (on different philosophical streams) Prah Ruger, J, "Health and social justice" (2004), 364 *The Lancet*, 1075, and more specifically for example the "Special Issue: Health Justice and the capabilities approach: Essays on Sridhar Venkatapuram's work" (2016), 13 *Bioethics*, 1. The health justice approach is very rich, and in the international realm particularly relevant as concerns justice between the people of different states and in different areas of the world.

39 See for example Taylor, A, "International Law, and Public Health Policy" in Quah, S & Heggenhougen, K (eds.), *International Encyclopedia of Public Health*, 2008, 667 (668). For more detail see the discussion in the contribution of *Leonie Vierck*, "The Case Law of International Public Health and Why its Scarcity is a Problem" in this volume.

40 It should be noted this is not the only function of legal research. See Taekema, S, "Relative Autonomy. A Characterisation of the Discipline of Law" in Klink, B von & Taekema, S (eds.), *Law and Method*, 2011, 33 (37-39).

(standards). As an individual human right, the right to health should be perceived in a narrower sense focusing primarily on medical care. As an obligation to promote public (population) health, the human right to health can be seen in a broader context, embracing also the underlying determinants of health. The prevention and combat of epidemics is one of the main fields of public health. The most important source for the right to health is Article 12 International Covenant on Economic, Social and Cultural Rights (ICESCR). Thereby, states are obliged to respect, protect and (to a certain degree) fulfill the requirements under the right to health. In the well-known interpretation in General Comment 14, the Committee on Economic, Social and Cultural Rights (CESCR) stresses that the state's obligations are not restricted to the national context, but that

> "States parties should recognize the essential role of international cooperation and comply with their commitment to take joint and separate action to achieve the full realization of the right to health. In this regard, states parties are referred to the Alma-Ata Declaration which proclaims that the existing gross inequality in the health status of people, particularly between developed and developing countries, as well as within countries, is politically, socially and economically unacceptable and is, therefore, of common concern to all countries."[41]

Therefore, the right to health also has a transnational dimension of health justice and can be one catalyst for international public health and international health law. The commitment to the right to health is one reason (next to security and economic interests in health) for the motivation of states and other actors to enable health for everyone worldwide. As mentioned before, *Lawrence Gostin* defines global health law as encompassing all hard-law and soft-law instruments "that shapes norms, processes, and institutions to attain the highest attainable standard of physical and mental health for the world's population".[42] International public health and international health law imply a variety of actors and are not related merely to states and international organizations. In this respect, they go beyond the classic shape of the human right to health which is so far primarily state-based as they are the parties to the respective treaties.[43] However, the contents of the right to health as developed under Article 12 ICESCR is also

41 CESCR, *General Comment No. 14 on the right to the highest attainable standard of health E/C.12/2000/4*, para. 38.

42 Gostin, L, *Global Health Law*, 2014, 59.

43 Ibid., 61 et seq. Gostin sees the state-centric orientation of international law as a "serious limitation". Since international organizations and also individuals could be seen as subjects of international law, the shortcoming of international law especially refers to non-state actors.

referred to as a standard by other actors and serves as a driving force for the WHO[44] with its instruments, which can even be binding.[45] The human right to health can perhaps even be seen as a catalyst for the further development of WHO instruments. And the right to health might even serve as a "constitutional right" (not, of course, in its proper legal understanding, but more as a portrayal of the factual situation) in so far as it gives the broad picture and the threshold for other programs, institutions, actions, and (mainly soft-) law mechanisms. Without the underlying right to health as laid down in various treaties, international public health and international health law might only consist of policy concepts. Therefore, the right to health is a "vital aspect"[46] of international health law. On the downside, in international law, policy strategies and soft-law mechanisms are much more important than in national law due to the shortcomings of the limitations of treaty law (often only vague standards, lack of enforceability and no direct obligations for non-state actors).[47] Thus, a term like "international/global health law" needs to take into account the fact that international health governance is only somewhat law-related and partly follows a political agenda.

The response of the international community to the Ebola crisis also gave rise to question the role of ethics and ethical responsibilities. A prominent position to help in the affected countries was taken by Médecins Sans Frontières (MSF), an influential and well-financed NGO, who happened to be in the field early during the outbreak of Ebola. NGOs are not subject to international law and, therefore, are not bound by any treaties or customary rules. MSF's motivation to help is rooted in the "belief that all people should have access to healthcare regardless of gender, race, religion, creed or political affiliation, and that people's medical needs outweigh respect for national boundaries."[48] This is an ethical and political statement, but at the same time also an acknowledgement of a human right to health. Likewise, when states or the European Union provided bilateral or multilateral help to countries affected by Ebola, they did not solely act out of security interests or due to any international legal obligation, but also out of a sense of moral

44 It is also to be noted that the preamble of the Constitution of the WHO declares that the "enjoyment of the highest attainable standard of health" to be a fundamental right of every human being.

45 Compare Article 21 of the Constitution of the WHO.

46 Gostin, *Global Health Law*, above Fn. 42, 68.

47 Ibid., 64.

48 *MSF History*, available at http://www.msf.org/en/msf-history.

obligation.[49] Therefore, international health law is closely connected to the ethical conviction that powerful international entities (such as states, NGOs or other private actors) have a moral obligation to help others in need. The ICESCR has carefully maintained that this moral obligation of states is even a legal one in Article 2 para. 1, which is also read as a duty of the states to cooperate for the sake of human beings beyond their own borders.[50] The CESCR draws attention to the latter provision when fleshing out the right to health according to Article 12 ICESCR and asks State Parties to "recognize the essential role of international cooperation and comply with their commitment to take joint and separate action".[51] This is closely connected to the far reaching idea of international health justice,[52] a strong ethical claim. Although this is not the place to dwell on any theory concerning the relationship between ethics and international law,[53] a few observations can be made. Ethical claims can have a stronger impact within the international arena than in the national sphere. In the national realm, ethics can influence law-making processes (parliaments might enact a special law due to the prevailing ethical opinion of the majority). In international politics, ethical claims can also lead to binding treaty law. Ethical claims can, however, also be observed by states and other international actors. Since there are weaker mechanisms for enforcement in international law, ethical claims can have considerable weight compared to treaty law. Furthermore, the premises of human rights are based on strong ethical convictions about the position and worth of the individual human being after mankind had experienced the

---

49 EU Commissioner *Tonio Borg* spoke of a moral obligation of the EU to help Ebola-affected countries (September 3, 2014), available at http://bit.ly/2tcWhl7. The question was also raised at the 51st Munich Security Conference 2015, which took place along the theme of "collapsing order, reluctant guardians". Namely, whether or not states have a moral obligation to defend human rights (in a cross-border sense), also including multilateral aid against Ebola. See http://bit.ly/2rEa1F5.

50 Compare for a transnational legal obligation to help the contribution of *Elif Askin*, "Extraterritorial Human Rights Obligations of States in the Event of Disease Outbreaks" in this volume.

51 CESCR, *General Comment 14*, above Fn. 41, para. 38.

52 See already above Fn. 38.

53 Compare here Boldizar, A & Korhonen, O, "Ethics, Morals and International Law" (1999), 10 *EJIL*, 279-311; Jones, D, "Law, morality and international affairs" in Nardin, T & Mapel, D R (eds.), *Traditions of International Ethics*, 2008, 57 et seq.

consequences of two world wars in the first half of the 20th century. However, international law today is usually not consciously rooted in natural law thinking[54] anymore. Nevertheless, the far reaching and well received interpretation of the human right to health as put forward by the CESCR[55] shows that a strong ethical drive is having an impact on the development of international law.[56]

3 Why Use Governance as a Basis?

The idea of governance emerged as a possible frame for the contents of this book, in so far as it can contribute to open a space beyond the distinctions of what is considered "law" and what is not. The seminal work of *James Rosenau* on the topic can provide a starting point.[57] Although the post-Cold War world order in which the expression proliferated has been in continuous flux, its use still holds in many regards. The locus of authority at the international level is scattered beyond the nation-state, encompassing more than just governments and their actions.[58] The flexibility of the term governance allows for the inclusion of phenomena which would otherwise be lost under blunt binary distinctions of state vs. non-state, government vs. private actors, or legally binding vs. non-binding. It can also be noted, however, that this conceptual broadness has been the source of criticisms.[59] Its wide formulation can risk putting diverse actions under the same aegis, subsequently omitting important distinctions, for instance, between acts of authority from exclusively private acts.[60]

---

54 Compare Boyle, J, "Natural law and international ethics" in Nardin & Mapel (eds.), *Traditions of International Ethics*, above Fn. 53, 12 et seq.

55 CESCR, *General Comment 14*, above Fn. 41.

56 Compare the contribution of *A. Katarina Weilert*, "The Right to Health in International Law – Normative Foundations and Doctrinal Flaws" in this volume.

57 Rosenau, J, "Governance in the Twenty-first Century" (1995), 1 *Global Governance*, 13 (13).

58 Rosenau, J, "Governance, Order, and Change in World Politics" in Rosenau, J & Czempiel, E-O (eds.), *Governance Without Government: Order and Change in World Politics*, 1992, 4-5.

59 See already Finkelstein, L, "What is Global Governance?" (1995), 1 *Global Governance*, 367 (367-369).

60 This criticism of (global) governance is already made in Bogdandy, A von, Goldmann, M & Dann, P, "Developing the Publicness of Public International Law: Towards a Legal Framework for Global Governance Activities" in Bogdandy,

Nevertheless, given how the field of international health is highly fragmented, the term governance can, beyond its pitfalls, be suitable for analyzing phenomena that take place beyond the scope of states. The presence of both NGOs and even the private sector, requires a broader grasp that is not hindered by a state-centered approach. As the WHO is not alone in the international arena, rather acting in the field of health alongside other actors,[61] this requires a step forward from the institutional approach. Usually governance presupposes a certain degree of organization, authority and hierarchy. *Lawrence Gostin* describes governance as the "method by which organized society directs, influences, and coordinates the activities of multiple private and public actors to achieve collective goods".[62] However, there is no "organized society" in a strong sense in the international arena.

In addition, the idea of governance has a direct link to legal theory, as they both address an international order composed of states and other actors, as well as their relationships of power with individuals, i.e. their exercise of authority.[63] However, whereas the flexibility of the term governance further enables the analysis of a complex international arena, a positivist legal approach related namely to international law operates mostly on binary distinctions aimed precisely at reducing such complexity: either an act is legally binding, or it is not.[64] Consequently, a legal theory grounded on formal sources of (international) law cannot provide a comprehensive answer, whereas alternative proposals have to deal with problems of "relative" normativity.[65] By contrast, in so far as governance studies tend to focus on

---

Wolfrum & Bernstorff et al. (eds.), *The Exercise of Public Authority*, above Fn. 16, 10.

61 Already on the point of how the WHO has entered into partnerships with groups of non-state actors, see Burci, G, "Public/Private Partnerships in the Public Health Sector" (2009), 6 *International Organizations Law Review*, 359 (381-382). This circumstance is also referred to as marking the "golden era" of global health by Kickbusch, I & Cassar, M M, "A new governance space for health" (2014), 7 *Global Health Action*, available at https://www.globalhealthaction.net.

62 Gostin, *Global Health Law*, above Fn. 42, 72.

63 On the role of private actors as authorities through a governance perspective, see Sinclair, T J, "A private authority perspective on global governance" in Hoffmann, M & Ba, A D (eds.), *Contending Perspectives on Global Governance*, 2005, 179.

64 Although not every author would agree with this view. For an overview of the discussion dealing with this distinction, see Goldmann, M, "We Need to Cut Off the Head of the King: Past, Present and Future Approaches to International Soft Law" (2012), 25 *Leiden Journal of International Law*, 335 (341-346).

65 On the issue of the relationship between positivism and relative normativity in international law, see already the seminal work of Weil, P, "Towards Relative

continuous processes and not on identifying particular acts which may be legally relevant,[66] this means that there is a lack of direct translation between research on governance and legal theory. Similarly, the presence of actors of a varied background, as well as the formal and informal nature of their acts, have thus far not been framed under a comprehensive legal framework at the international level.[67] While this is also the case for the national level, absence is even more salient at the international level, with the lack of a central government[68] capable of issuing norms, regulations, administrative acts in an exclusive manner, or considering the uncertain legal personality of non-state actors at the international level as subjects of public international law, also with regards to their possible obligations.[69] Afterwards, the goal of making descriptive sense of this puzzle is followed by a need for devising normative answers. It is precisely at this point where there is a juncture between governance and law. Here, the IPA conceptual framework comes to the fore as an attempt to provide such answers, though it is by no means the only one.[70]

With the above in mind, the idea of governance for understanding the field of international health aims, firstly, at describing a very specific problem. Disease outbreaks such as the West African Ebola crisis of 2014-2016, or the more recent Zika epidemic of 2016, involve a mixed set of actors. International and regional organizations composed by Member States, such as the WHO or the West African Health Organisation, interact with non-

---

Normativity in International Law?" (1983), 77 *American Journal of International Law*, 413 (421).

66 Bogdandy, Goldmann & Venzke, "From Public International Law to International Public Law", above Fn. 15, 122-123.

67 The need for legal approaches capable of responding to this context is already put forward in Krisch, N, "Global governance as public authority: An introduction" (2012), 10 *ICON: International Journal of Constitutional Law*, 976 (982-983); see also the other articles comprising this special edition.

68 Taken from Frenk, J & Moon, S, "Governance Challenges in Global Health" (2013), 368 *The New England Journal of Medicine*, 936 (937).

69 For the case of multinational corporations, see Weilert, A K, "Taming the Untamable? Transnational Corporations in United Nations Law and Practice" (2010), 14 *Max Planck UNYB*, 445 (454 et seq.) and Weilert, A K, "Transnationale Unternehmen im rechtsfreien Raum? Geltung und Reichweite völkerrechtlicher Standards" (2009), 69 *Zeitschrift für ausländisches öffentliches Recht und Völkerrecht*, 883 (885, 915-916).

70 See notably Kingsbury, B, Krisch, N & Stewart, R B, "The Emergence of Global Administrative Law" (2005), 68 *Law and Contemporary Problems*, 15.

state actors such as NGOs (like MSF) and even the private sector (pharmaceutical companies). Although the role of each of them tends to be analyzed separately, they also engage in occasional partnerships.[71] Additionally, these actors within the field of health do not always issue legally binding acts, rather opting for informal arrangements and *ad hoc* political agreements. In fact, states themselves can resort to alternate venues with the explicit purpose of sidelining formal venues of international organizations.[72] Since they escape any attempt at binary classifications, facts within international health can be addressed through the idea of governance, particularly understood as a method by which "organized society directs, influences, and coordinates the activities of multiple private and public actors to achieve collective goods".[73] In this regard, governance in the field of international health is characterized by common goals of providing global public goods, one of which is the containment of the international spread of infectious diseases.[74] The notion of the "global", understood as a multi-level space, is fitting for describing the interactions between the national and the international sphere.[75] The conceptualization of global health governance has been explored with more detail elsewhere.[76] For this book, we decided to focus mostly on the international level, as there is currently no possibility to properly tackle the multi-level aspect with more depth. This does not imply there is a lack of realization of the analysis required for health issues. It is only meant to emphasize the relevance of both the inherent international

---

71 Notably, the recent development of an Ebola vaccine was done through a multi-partner collaboration between the WHO, governments (Guinea and Norway), NGOs (Médecins sans Frontières) and even private companies (Merck). It has been already deployed during a recent Ebola outbreak in the Democratic Republic of Congo. For journalistic reports on these issues, see McNeil, D G, "New Ebola Vaccine Gives 100 Percent Protection" (December 22, 2016), *The New York Times*, available at http://nyti.ms/2uchSOP; also, Pilling, D, "Congo to test experimental Ebola vaccine as disease re-emerges" (May 23, 2017), *The Financial Times*, available at http://on.ft.com/2rAPT9Y.

72 Benvenisti, E, *The Law of Global Governance*, 2014, 37.

73 Also espoused by Gostin, *Global Health Law*, above Fn. 42, 72.

74 Zacher, M W, "Global Epidemiological Surveillance. International Cooperation to Monitor Infectious Diseases" in Kaul, I, Grunberg, I & Stern, M (eds.), *Global public goods: International Cooperation in the 21st century*, 1999, 266-267.

75 Bogdandy, Goldmann & Dann, "Developing the Publicness of Public International Law", above Fn. 60, 7; also Zürn, M, "Global Governance as Multi-Level Governance" in Levi-Faur, D (ed.), *Oxford Handbook of Governance*, 2013, 731.

76 For a glimpse, see Kickbusch, I & Reddy, K S, "Global Health Governance - the next political revolution" (2015), 129 *Public Health*, 838 (839).

dimension of trans-border infectious disease outbreaks, as well as the ensuing response by entities that are not limited to the borders of a country.

Nevertheless, as will be seen in several contributions of this book, this choice of scope is not restrictive. The issue of the "global" is brought up as a topic for more specific analysis.[77] The emphasis on international health governance is, at this point, more of a guiding theme than a formal endorsement of a concept as opposed to others.

III What's Next?

The process that gave way to this book has yielded the realization that there is still a need for more general textbooks on the field of international health law. Tackling the conceptual challenges requires extensive argumentation, which ranges beyond the scope of this piece. Some of the works on the subject matter adopt the idea of an expansive "global" approach, since viewing it in a stricter sense would entail that the field would be quite "sparse" if it was limited only to legally binding instruments.[78] However, as it is recognized that there are other binding sources of health-related issues, the way in which health law is understood will also determine which other legal fields that hinge upon health would be included under its aegis.[79] This way, for instance, trade and environmental law would also be addressed by the area of health law. Whereas stand-alone book chapters and research articles have also dealt with this issue, they have argued for the autonomous nature of this legal field up to a certain degree.[80] It remains unclear how and why a health approach may lead to different outcomes than one focused on trade law, environmental protection, illicit drug regulation, etc. Even though health matters are explicitly incorporated into the provisions of these fields, it remains to be discussed whether a parallel health-law field would lead to different decisions or normative conclusions.

---

77 See particularly the contributions of *Mateja Steinbrück Platise*, "The Changing Structure of Global Health Governance" and *Christian R. Thauer*, "The Governance of Infectious Diseases. An International Relations Perspective" in this volume.

78 Such approach can be seen, mainly, in Gostin, *Global Health Law*, above Fn. 42, 60.

79 Ibid., 69.

80 Gostin & Taylor, "Global Health Law", above Fn. 37, 55-56; Toebes, "International health law", above Fn. 24, 301-302.

Despite these possible objections, we believe there is still a need for more research on the topic of why there can be international health law as a particular field of law. Even though literature on global health law exists, and considering the copious contributions on global health governance, there nevertheless remains a gap in legal works. Of course, speaking of approaches with a focus on law do not entail adopting a "pure", i.e. positivistic theory[81] that casts other disciplines aside. Due to requirements imposed by the interpretation of vague health-related provisions, interdisciplinary insights are necessary for making sense of the substantive health-related claims. Problems with an overarching health dimension such as those related to tobacco control or non-communicable diseases (NCDs) in general, drug policy, and others, can already be addressed through a health-centered mindset. This means that, even if they do take aspects of trade law or even criminal law into consideration, the interpretation of the purposes of instruments and provisions would focus on the (public) health perspective. For instance, the legal assessment of whether a particular measure is justified or not touches upon matters that directly fall under the distinct fields of medicine and public health. Notwithstanding the central position of public health, the IHR provide a yardstick with which acts by the WHO, such as declarations of a PHEIC as in the case of the West African Ebola crisis, or of a pandemic in the case of H1N1 Influenza, cannot be assessed by resorting exclusively to medical criteria. Their consequences are also economic and social in nature. While not without nuances and disagreements, this is also recognized by the literature in public health.[82]

In the same sense, the broad set of interests and stakeholders needs to be provided with a legal response. Some authors deal with the limits of several approaches of international institutional law, particularly those found within a functionalist strand.[83] As long as a focus on the sources of international law prevails,[84] such limitations will continue to represent a gap in legal debates. As a result, lawyers may continue to be "left out of the equation" due to this constrained normative vision. However, since there is an existing

81 The classical formulation in this sense is by Kelsen, H, *Reine Rechtslehre*, 1960, 1-2.

82 For a list of objectives, see also the Rio Political Declaration on Social Determinants of Health, adopted at the 65th WHA in 2012 through resolution WHA65.8.

83 Notably Klabbers, J, "The EJIL Foreword: The Transformation of International Organizations Law" (2015), 26 *EJIL*, 9 (79-80).

84 Generally, to those deriving from Article 38 of the Statute of the International Court of Justice.

(international) legal framework that begins with the Constitution of the WHO and also includes the IHR, this entails that there is room for input by legal scholarship. Whether the answer is in the sense of emphasizing the potentials of reform,[85] or rather to the limits of arguments centered in international law,[86] the inclusion of discussions on law can yield insights on how to understand the role of legal norms.

As for the WHO's role in international health governance, special mention can be made of the recent WHO Director-General election, which took place in May 2017.[87] The incoming head of the WHO's Secretariat faces a post-Ebola juncture in which many of the questions addressed in this book linger on the role of the organization in exercising its legal mandate regarding disease outbreaks. Given the authority that the WHO Director-General holds with regard to the IHR, discretion exercised by officials cannot be overlooked. Although this book is not devoted to an assessment of specific officials, the responsiveness of the whole organization – a recurring criticism of the handling of the West African Ebola crisis – depends to a large extent on the Director-General's willingness to declare a PHEIC or not. Therefore, the "new administration" is also tasked with exercising authority amidst infectious disease outbreaks that spread beyond geographical borders. Furthermore, as the spread of Zika unfolded during the stage of editing this book, there is a pending task of contrasting its emergence – mostly in Brazil – with the context of the West African Ebola crisis. There is still much to be said about the underlying conditions within which this epidemic spread, as well as how the actors of global health governance – whether international organizations, states, private companies, NGOs or even individuals – contributed to the response. For starters, both the Ebola and Zika outbreaks took place within social contexts mired with economic hardship, systemic institutional deficiencies at the international and national levels, as well as overall shortcomings of the rule of law. Thus, although future work on this matter requires broader interdisciplinary perspectives incorporating insights beyond law, legal approaches are still pertinent as to the role

---

85 Gostin, L, Friedman, E & Buse, K et al., "Towards a framework convention on global health" (2013), 91 *Bulletin of the World Health Organization*, 790 (790-792), available at http://dx.doi.org/10.2471/BLT.12.114447.

86 See also the contribution of *Leonie Vierck*, "The Case Law of International Public Health and Why its Scarcity is a Problem" in this volume.

87 At the 70th WHA, which took place in May 2017, former Minister of Health of Ethiopia, *Tedros Adhanom Ghebreyesus*, was elected as the successor of *Margaret Chan* for a period of five years. He would have the possibility of running for re-election for another term in 2022.

of the legal and institutional framework for disease outbreak preparedness and response. The arguments put forward in this book could be contrasted alongside a comparative view, all the while keeping the substantive differences in mind. As mentioned earlier, a comparative view is of high relevance in international infectious disease governance, because we do not know when exactly and which particular infectious disease will spread in the future – but we know that it will cost many lives in times of population growth. Identifying common patterns between infectious diseases in research is thus important for dealing with them.

Another major pending issue that requires deeper research is the notorious role of non-state actors – NGOs and private companies alike. Firstly, the question arises as to whether they would each need to have a different standing in international law in light of their different purposes.[88] Secondly, the growing presence of private entities, such as the Bill and Melinda Gates Foundation,[89] as important financer of – and, therefore, stakeholders within – the WHO merits a closer inspection at the very least.[90] The preference given to earmarked funds for "pet projects" raises concerns as to the autonomy with which said organization can have leeway in determining its own agenda.[91]

Last but not least, in parallel to the focus on infectious disease throughout this publication, the growing challenges stemming from NCDs also need to be taken into consideration. A sensible appraisal of current epidemiological patterns yields insights of how NCDs constitute an ever-growing cause of

---

88 The need to distinguish between for-profit and not-for-profit actors is also mentioned in Hanrieder, T & Kamradt-Scott, A, "Introduction. Same, Same But Different: Reforming the World Health Organization in an Age of Public Scrutiny and Global Complexity" (2017), IX *Global Health Governance*, 4 (4), available at http://bit.ly/2tcBdeE.

89 The contributions of the Bill and Melinda Gates Foundation to the WHO's finances through the Voluntary Fund for Health Promotion are sketched out, for example in the organization's Financial Reports for the year 2004. See http://bit.ly/2rYCDxO.

90 For instance, in the financial year of 2016, contributions to the WHO by non-state actors amounted to circa 37 % of the organization's total budget. See the 70th WHA document entitled *WHO Mid-Term Programmatic and Financial Report for 2016-2017, including audited financial statements for 2016*, Provisional Agenda Item 20.1, A70/40, 132-133, available at http://bit.ly/2tWbEiL.

91 The trend dates back to the 1980s. See Hanrieder, T, *International Organization in Time. Fragmentation and Reform*, 2015, 9-11.

death within the global burden of disease.[92] Therefore, it is not possible to ignore the necessity of addressing the underlying issues that contribute to explain this fact, whether it is tobacco consumption, physical inactivity, alcohol abuse or inadequate nutrition.[93] Despite this overall trend towards the rise of NCDs, infectious diseases do not cease to be a factor of concern; to the contrary, both of these problems coexist and contribute in complicating the landscape of public health.[94] As the emergencies declared in the West African Ebola and Zika epidemics remind, the dangers posed by infectious diseases should not be underestimated, given how these are still threats requiring a global rather than a local or regional response.[95] Therefore, a comprehensive approach capable of taking this complexity into consideration seems as necessary as ever.

92 While there are nuances in how this rate diverges across age groups depending on regions, the growing incidence of NCDs as a cause of death seems to be clear. See the detailed data in the study by the Global Burden of Disease 2015 Mortality and Causes of Death Collaborators, "Global, regional, and national life expectancy, all-cause mortality, and cause-specific mortality for 249 causes of death, 1980-2015: a systematic analysis for the Global Burden of Disease Study 2015" (2016), 388 *The Lancet*, 1459 (1482-1492).

93 See WHO, "Major NCDs and their risk factors", available at http://www.who.int/ncds/introduction/en/.

94 Frenk, J & Moon, S, "Governance Challenges in Global Health" (2013), 368 *The New England Journal of Medicine*, 936 (936).

95 Also in this sense, Heesterbeek, H, Anderson, R M & Andreasen, V et al., "Modeling infectious disease dynamics in the complex landscape of global health" (2015), 347 *Science*, aaa4339-1 (aaa4339-7).

Framing The Field

Ebola Epidemic 2014-2015: Taking Control or Being Trapped in the Logic of Failure – What Lessons Can Be Learned?

Michael Marx*

Abstract[1]

The Ebola outbreak 2014-2015 in West Africa – declared a pandemic by the World Health Organization – was the first in the sub-region and the largest ever recorded with more than 28,639 people affected by the Ebola Virus Disease (EVD) and resulting in 11,316 casualties. EVD stretched local health care systems as well as International Organizations in an unprecedented manner. The outbreak revealed fundamental structural deficiencies of the respective health systems and failures in establishing consistent health policies. In the aftermath of the outbreak, health system strengthening is seen as determinant for countries to meet the Sustainable Development Goals and to better prepare for the threats of pandemics in the future. The EVD is a wake-up call for higher efficiency, rationality and evidence in the health policy of partner countries and the development policy of donors.

---

* The author (MD, PhD) is professor for International Public Health at the Institute of Public Health of the University of Heidelberg. He is a medical doctor, specialized in internal medicine, tropical medicine and public health. As general background literature, especially for lawyers unfamiliar with the public health discipline, he recommends the following three textbooks: Detels, R, Beaglehole, R & Lansang M A et al., *Oxford Textbook of Public Health*, 2009; Schwartz, F W, *Public Health: Gesundheit und Gesundheitswesen*, 2003, and Razum, O, Zeeb, H & Laaser, U, *Globalisierung-Gerechtigkeit-Gesundheit. Einführung in International Public Health*, 2006. All websites last accessed January 14, 2017.

1 Important parts of the manuscript are drawn from an editorial of The European Journal of Health Economics by Flessa, S & Marx, M, "Ebola fever epidemic 2014: a call for sustainable health and development policies" (2016), 17 *The European Journal of Health Economics*, 1.

I. Introduction

The Ebola outbreak 2014-2015 in West Africa was the first in the sub-region and the largest ever recorded. It first struck Guinea, Liberia and Sierra Leone – fragile, post-conflict nations in the midst of reconstruction. From December 2013 onwards the Ebola epidemic emerged and exceeded any previous Ebola epidemic with regard to incidence and prevalence.[2] According to estimates of the World Health Organization (WHO) more than 28,639 people worldwide suffered from Ebola Virus Disease (EVD) until February 2016. About 40.6 % (11,316) of them died. The extent of this epidemic took many experts by surprise and it was declared a pandemic by WHO as it crossed country borders and the boundaries of a continent. EVD stretched local health care systems as well as International Organizations excessively when a coordinated response was required. This outbreak can serve as a multifaceted case study revealing fundamental structural deficiencies of the respective health systems (HS) and failures in establishing consistent health policies within those countries, structural weaknesses of regional governance institutions, as well as challenges in development policies of the so-called donor countries.[3]

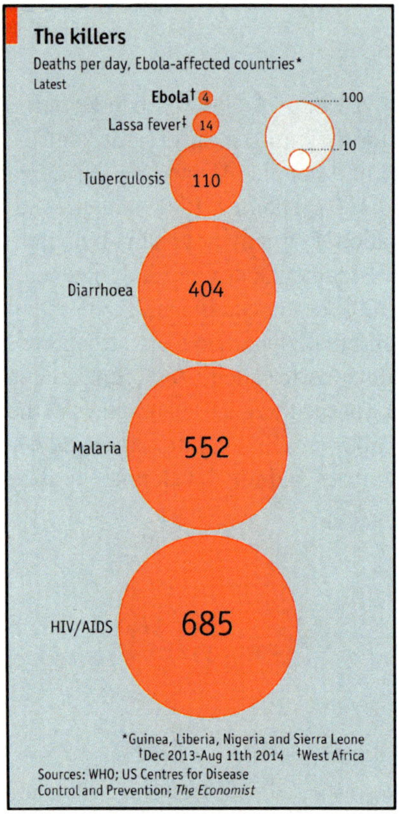

Figure 1: Number of deaths per day (diarrhea, malaria, HIV/AIDS), The Economist, "Ebola. Fever rising" (August 15, 2014), available at http://econ.st/1pix7ME.

2 Benton, A & Dionne, K Y, "International Political Economy and the 2014 West African Ebola Outbreak" (2015), 58 *African Studies Review*, 223.

3 De Cock, K M, Mbori-Ngacha, D & Marum, E, "Shadow on the Continent: Public Health and HIV/AIDS in Africa in the 21st century" (2002), 360 *The Lancet*, 67.

II Key Features of Ebola Virus Disease (EVD)

The Ebola virus causes a hemorrhagic fever with multi-organ failure and a case fatality rate between 25-90 %. The transmission of this highly infectious virus is possible via any kind of body fluids, and the smallest amount of virus is sufficient to trigger the disease. The disease was first identified in 1976 and takes its name from the location of the first outbreak (Ebola River, Democratic Republic of Congo). The fruit bat, whose habitat is tropical rain forests, is a natural reservoir of the Ebola virus. Since then, about 35 outbreaks have been registered with the highest number of cases of one single outbreak totaling 425 in Uganda in 2001. Therefore, the epidemic in 2014-2015 was of a completely unknown dimension.[4] Before 2014, the outbreaks were locally restricted, primarily situated in rural areas, and seemed to self-regulate in that they spontaneously came to a halt after a comparatively short period of time. The eradication of Ebola is thus extremely unlikely in the foreseeable future.

The Ebola epidemic of 2014-2015 stands out significantly from previous epidemics with regard to intensity and dynamics. This is primarily due to the fact that this epidemic expanded to the urban population as well as across borders, for instance, in cross-border trade between Guinea, Sierra Leone and Liberia, which traditionally has been very intensive.[5] In addition to cross-border migration facilitating the rapid spread of disease, the deficiency or absence of social structures in urban settings lowered the social and medical control in case of illness. Ritual washing of the dead, which is common in large parts of Africa, further contributed to the risk of virus transmission.[6] These two factors exacerbated the spread of EVD and resulted in the overburdening of already weak health care systems.

From a public health point of view, it is striking that there were a lot of "collateral damages" caused by Ebola, for example declining vaccination coverage in the population, declining consultations, untreated malaria, diarrhea, pneumonia as well as a decline of HIV prevention and treatment

---

4 Flessa, S, "Basic Health-Care Package without Antiretroviral Therapy?" (2008), 16 *Journal of Public Health*, 145.

5 Omonzejele, P F, "Ethical Challenges Posed by the Ebola Virus Epidemic in West Africa" (2014), 11 *Journal of Bioethical Inquiry*, 417.

6 Levin-Sparenberg, E, Gicquelais, R, & Blanco, N et al., "Ebola: The Natural and Human History of a Deadly Virus By David Quammen" (2015), 181 *American Journal of Epidemiology*, 151.

activities.[7] In 2014, utilization of consultations and hospitalizations decreased by 50 % compared to 2013. In the same time, there was an almost 50 % reduction in the number of children vaccinated and the number of reported malaria cases dropped by 40 %, likely due to fear of health facilities.

In the three countries most affected by Ebola, the fear of getting infected was spreading very fast among the population, which prompted many health workers to leave health facilities. This led to an acute shortage of staff in hospitals and health centers. After a short period, local health care systems literally collapsed. Other vital sectors, such as agriculture, were severely affected. There, the fear of infection from working alongside others in the fields in parallel with the installment of travel restrictions led to a severe labor shortage. This also resulted in massive declines in the gross national product of the respective countries (estimates differ between US $6.2 and $25), in food shortages and the (almost) complete exodus of foreign professionals (also from neighboring countries) who held key positions in the economy.

The course of the disease demonstrates that although treatment of patients is a medical challenge of highest complexity, the epidemic as such was not primarily a medical problem. The intensity and dynamics of dispersal occurred in the context of health care systems that are following a strongly curative strategy. Factors include access to education and information, participation in and the strengthening of self-responsibility of individuals, as well as social practices within the local community which – as a study object – have received very little attention to date.

III What Was the Response to this Pandemic Threat?

After a much criticized delay at the outset, there was an unprecedented response to the pandemic. The mass media disseminated the news effectively across the globe. The fear of EVD becoming a global pandemic played an important driving force, and resulted in a massive donor commitment and deployment of huge funds in a short time. By Mid-2014, external aid for the three overburdened countries started. About the same time, in August 2014, the WHO provided an estimated budget of US $500 million, and in September *Ban Ki-Moon* already called for US $1 billion. At the end of

7 Ndawinz, J D A, Cissé, M & Diallo, M et al., "Prevention of HIV Spread During the Ebola Outbreak in Guinea" (2015), 385 *The Lancet*, 1393 et seqq.

October 2015, donors had pledged a total of US $8.9 billion to address the Ebola outbreak. As of October 2015, US $5.9 billion has been disbursed until then.[8] Indeed, in contrast to other catastrophes, the majority of funds were paid right away. This was mainly as a reaction to news in the mass media and the fear of industrialized countries being threatened by Ebola.[9] These amounts are a multiple of national health budgets (Guinea: US $98 million per annum; Sierra Leone: US $81 million per annum; Liberia: US $112 million per annum) as well as health-related development aid that the affected countries have received in recent years.[10] Although the mobilization of the donor community and International Organizations helped affected countries, the lack of leadership of WHO, as well as poor inter-state cooperation and flaws at the local level revealed the need for the reform of HS at large.[11]

1 Global and International Responses

When it comes to global health governance and leadership, WHO officially holds a prime position. In the course of the of the Ebola pandemic, WHO was much criticized for its late response. Its role has been weakening over the last two decades due to lacking capacities and funding resulting from the rise of other influential organizations partially taking over the same tasks as WHO, such as the World Bank (WB) and the European Union and Global Health Initiatives (GHI).

However, there have been efforts by the WHO to come up with a response system in case of health emergencies. To address the complexity of a pandemic, in 2005 the WHO issued the International Health Regulations (IHR).[12] They provide a framework for epidemic alert and rapid response activities to be implemented in collaboration with countries to control inter-

8 Office of the United Nations Special Envoy on Ebola, *Resources for Results V*, October 31, 2015, available at http://bit.ly/2kViHmP.

9 Flessa & Marx, „Ebola Fever Epidemic 2014", above Fn. 1.

10 World Bank, *Health Expenditure, total (1996–2014)*, available at http://data.worldbank.org/indicator/SH.XPD.TOTL.ZS/countries.

11 World Bank Group, *The Economic Impact of the 2014 Ebola Outbreak. Short- and Medium-Term Estimates for West Africa*, 2014, available at http://bit.ly/2mi4p0H.

12 Moon, S, Sridhar, D & Pate, M A et al., "Will Ebola change the game? Ten essential reforms before the next pandemic. The report of the Harvard-LSHTM Independent Panel on the Global Response to Ebola" (2015), 386 *The Lancet*, 2204.

national outbreaks and to strengthen international public health security. Member States are obliged to issue a national IHR focal point in order to inform WHO about public health risks that can cause the spread of diseases across borders.[13] Unfortunately, the IHR were not implemented on time, an effective communication network was not yet established and risk assessment and risk communication failed, which contributed to a late response and a lack of coordination. As to the legitimacy of IHR, it is certainly a major challenge to effectively implement this multifaceted global agreement.

2 Regional Responses

At the regional level, the community of states was not well enough prepared to rapidly detect and identify infectious diseases nor to combat them. There are regional political and economic structures such as the Economic Community of West African States (ECOWAS) and the African Union (AU), as well as specialist public health institutions such as the West African Health Organisation (WAHO) as part of ECOWAS. The Ebola epidemic has at least increased the visibility of WAHO and underlined the organization's important functions and mandate, thus acting as a catalyst for a change process. However, communication structures, processes and tools are still insufficient to address the new challenges to respond efficiently and adequately to epidemic threats at regional level in a concerted manner. The Heads of States of the ECOWAS region decided to create a Regional Centre for Disease Control (RCDC) under the auspices of WAHO.[14] This may change the landscape of the region with regard to pandemic and epidemic preparedness and response. The massive increase of engagement and commitment of donors calls for better communication, strategic planning and coordination of implementation measures. The reform process in ECOWAS is ongoing and presents opportunities and risks for the future regarding the institutional environment. A further challenge concerns the coordination of stakeholders and their willingness to cooperate with one another.

---

13 WHO, *International Health Regulations (2005)*, available at http://www.who.int/ihr/about/en/.

14 See Gyang, J B, "Nigeria inaugurates Board Of ECOWAS Centre for Disease Control" (June 30, 2016), *Today*, available at https://www.today.ng/news/nigeria/145435/nigeria-inaugurates-board-ecowas-centre-disease-control.

The enormous influx of funds into WAHO and RCDC, and the capacity of the region and other organizations to absorb these funds should be addressed by donors and recipients. ECOWAS and WAHO, holding political power over the Member States, should take into account the IHR 2005 and their required core capacities and create the necessary technical environment that allows for implementing the regulations. Risk assessment and risk communication will be paramount in close collaboration with the countries and across the region.[15] Thus, ECOWAS-WAHO jointly with WHO's Regional Office for Africa could consolidate the overall public health architecture in the region.

3 National Responses by Affected Countries

On a national level, the first major challenge arose from the fact that in the beginning, symptoms were not recognized and associated with Ebola. The HS of these countries lacked the necessary infrastructure for pandemic preparedness and response. In this respect a major determinant was a chronic shortage of skilled personnel, especially in rural areas. In addition, poor hygienic working conditions, the absence of essential drugs and personal protection to prevent staff from infections further contributed to the spread and the magnitude of the epidemic. Laboratory confirmation was late, with the first test declared positive by the *Pasteur Institute* in France more than three months after the first case. Only then were diagnostic and treatment centers established by Non-Governmental Organizations, like Médecins sans Frontières, which was among the first International Organizations to take action as of March 2014.

The second challenge concerned the lack of an effective risk communication system in place between governments and affected communities. Consequently, the already low level of trust in national governments was further weakened by the initial response measures, which were inadequately attuned to the cultural and traditional practices of the population. Health promotion and prevention measures were successful only after religious

15 ECOWAS-WAHO, *Report on ECOWAS Meeting with Technical and Financial Partners to Discuss Implementation of the ECOWAS Regional Centre for Disease Control and Prevention (ECOWAS-RCDC)*, June 16-17, 2015 in Dakar, Senegal.

leaders took the floor in allowing an adaptation of funeral rites.[16] The traditional washing of the dead body by the family needed to be replaced by a rite that would meet cultural and religious obligations but prevented family members from acquiring the virus. Moreover, obsolete practices such as the re-use of inadequately sterilized materials in health services, as well as virus transmission through unprotected contacts and funeral rites are evidence not only of underfunding, but also of neglecting the education of professionals and the general public for a long time. In the context of the EVD outbreak in West Africa, the weakness of HS mirrors the shortcomings of international and national health policy. WHO defines a HS as

> "the people, institutions and resources, arranged together in accordance with established policies, to improve the health of the population they serve, while responding to people's legitimate expectations and protecting them against the cost of ill-health through a variety of activities whose primary intent is to improve health".[17]

This definition calls for a holistic approach which takes into account the various components of a HS as well as the interdependency of those parts.

However, according to the WHO definition of a HS, it is worth noting that a HS is not built by the health sector alone. Among the above mentioned six building blocks, other sectors also form important components of a HS, such as education, agriculture and social policy.

For almost half a century, there has been a constant struggle over concepts and approaches used to fight life-threatening diseases and to cope more effectively with the numerous challenges in health care. One of the milestones of international health policy was the International WHO conference in Alma Ata in 1978 where the concept of Primary Health Care (PHC) was declared as the most adequate response to ensure access to essential health care for all populations on the planet by the year 2000. The Alma Ata Declaration does not entail hard law obligations, but it is one of the most outstanding milestones in international public health. PHC is a holistic concept that includes access to health services, a clean environment and health-related behavior. It consists of eight elements: basic health care, health promotion and prevention, nutrition, water supply and sanitation, family planning, immunization, control of local endemic diseases, and es-

---

16 Frieden, T R, Damon, I & Bell, B P et al., "Ebola 2014 – new challenges, new global response and responsibility" (2014), 371 *New England Journal of Medicine*, 177.

17 See WHO, *Health Systems Strengthening Glossary – Health System*, available at http://www.who.int/healthsystems/hss_glossary/en/index5.html.

sential drugs; and seven principles including: integration of promotive, preventive and curative care in HS and rural development, community participation, needs orientation and cooperation with local human resources and a multi-sectoral approach.
It is worth mentioning that in the early 1990s, Guinea, together with Mali and Benin, was one of the spearheads among countries implementing PHC and the Bamako Initiative, the latter being an initiative for implementing and financing PHC in Sub-Saharan Africa following a 1987 Conference convened by WHO. At that time, the HS and health indicators of Guinea were far better than today. Unfortunately Guinea's success story lies 25

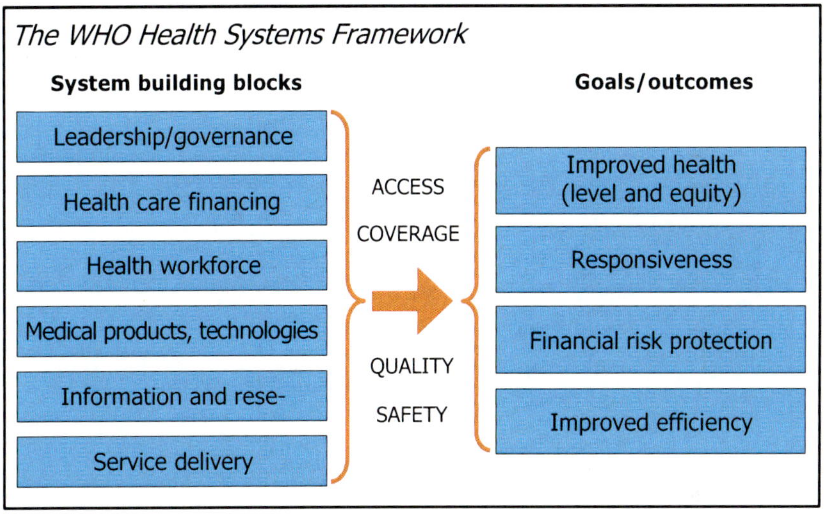

Figure 2: Adapted from WHO publication: The WHO Health Systems Framework, available at http://bit.ly/2mDOURK.

years in the past, and little remains from community participation and PHC today. The reasons for this decline and weakening of the HS can be attributed to the instability and erosion of the political system on one hand, and to inconsistency and discontinuity of international health policy on the other.

It turns out that there is little criticism and coherence among the international stakeholders, but rather a frenzied search for quick wins with magic recipes, with donors and health politics stumbling from one concept to another. The rapid abandonment of the PHC approach has triggered a number of new strategies, initiatives and attempts to quickly resolve priority problems in the last 20 years. The almost frantic search for new concepts was also initiated and nurtured by an increasing pressure by donor countries and their development organizations to justify the allocation of funds and to prove the effectiveness of development cooperation. A critical reflection and analysis of failed approaches actually never happened. Especially contextual factors, hypotheses, and the assumptions under which strategies and concepts were implemented were not sufficiently analyzed.[18]

To date, there is general consensus that sustainable improvement of the health situation is only achievable through consistent policies of HS and health system strengthening (HSS). As important as these measures are, they unfortunately cover only partial components of a HS. Community work, as well as education, were neglected. As soon as an epidemic is under control, integration of disease control activities into health services of all levels is paramount.

18 Marx, M & Benn, C, "Viewpoint: Primary Health care and the Global Health Initiatives – Contradictions or Opportunities for Health Systems?" (2010), 5 *Präventive Gesundheitsfragen*, 37.

IV Identification of Major Challenges of Health Systems (HS)

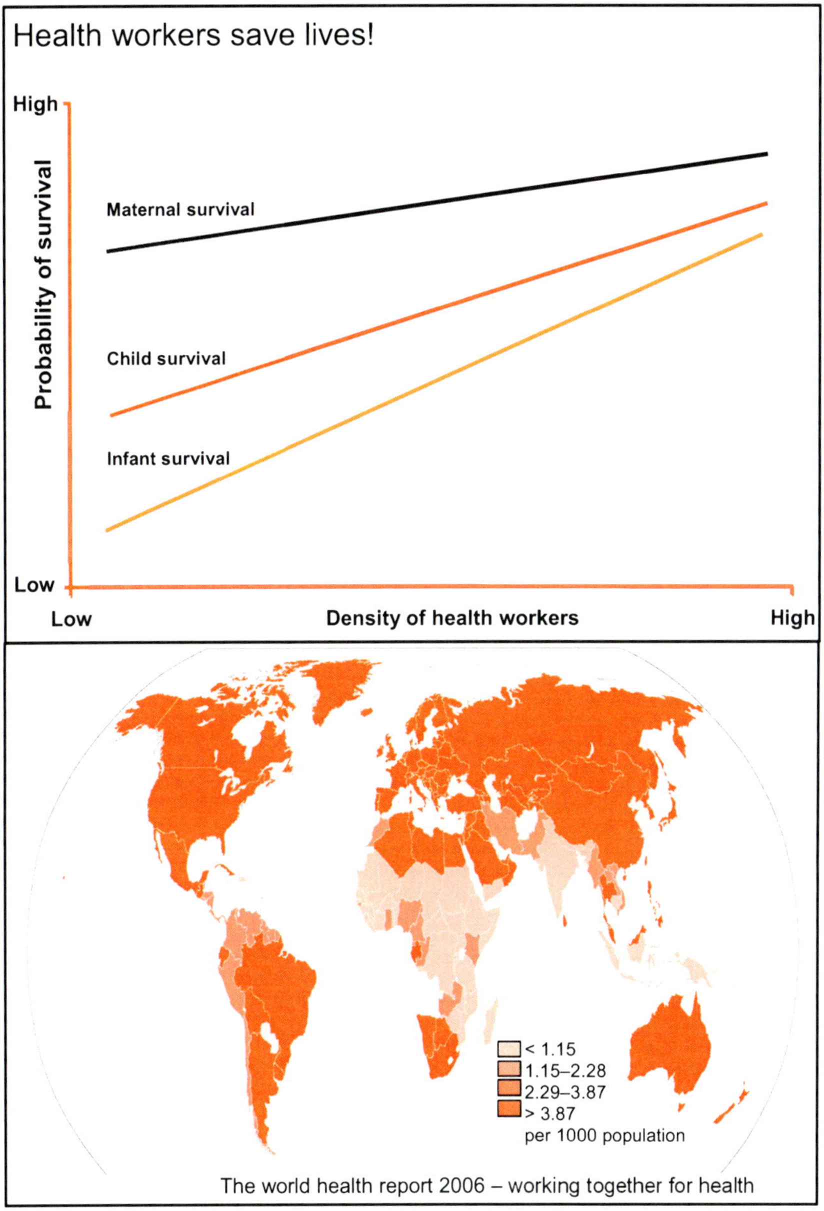

Figure 3: Adapted from WHO publication: The World Health Report 2006, available at http://bit.ly/2lxW0qb.

The EVD epidemic revealed a tremendous weakness of the HS caused by a lack of health workers. A shortage of health workers has evolved in many Sub-Saharan African countries over the last two decades and existed in Guinea already before EVD hit the country. The WHO defines skills shortage with the indicator of professionals density (physicians, nurses, midwives) per 1,000 people of the population. All countries under the threshold of 2,3/1000 – as defined by the WHO – are likely to not have the necessary human resources for health to offer acceptable health services to their population. A certain neglect of the "human resources arena" had contributed to the lack of strategic workforce planning and under-investment in developing capacities of health staff.[19] Contributory factors also include early retirements, poor job conditions and losses due to brain drain, which means the emigration of highly skilled workers, within and outside developing countries.[20] Brain drain commonly refers to the loss of qualified health workers to high income countries, whereas it can also be defined more broadly as migration motivated by the search for greener pastures such as a higher quality of life, increased salaries or more stable environment.[21] In the general context of health worker migration, there are two important questions that remain unanswered today: Can the right to emigrate be restricted and on what legal grounds? What are legitimate means to restrict migration?[22]

In the WHO's World Health Report 2006 – Working Together for Health, the following factors are cited:

> "[...] production capacity as a result of years of poor planning and underinvestment in health education and training institutions, especially in many developing countries. Often, training outputs are poorly aligned with the health needs of the population. There are also 'push' and 'pull' factors that affect workforce retention and may encourage health service providers to leave their workplaces, including those

19 Kolehmainen-Aitken, R L, "Decentralization Impact on the Health Workforce: Perspectives of Managers, Workers and National Leaders" (2004), 2 *Human Resources for Health*, 5.

20 Chen, L, Evans, T & Anand, S et al., "Human Resources for Health: Overcoming the Crisis" (2004), 364 *The Lancet*, 984.

21 Dodani, S & Laporte, R E, "Brain Drain from Developing Countries: How Can Brain Drain Be Converted Into Wisdom Gain?" (2005), 98 *Journal of Social Medicine*, 487.

22 Kollar, E, "Symposium on Brain Drain: The Merits and Limits of Furthering Normative Solutions in Source Countries 2016" (2016), 3 *Moral Philosophy and Politics*, 1.

> related to unsatisfactory working conditions, poor remuneration and career opportunities, and other labor market pressures."[23]

Among the push and pull factors, international development cooperation continues to play an important role. Yet, it shows that on the downside, well-trained health workers who migrate abroad, cause a major hemorrhage to the HS at home. Moreover, there is evidence from several countries that health professionals increasingly work in internationally funded programs, so-called GHI.[24] A study by the Center for Global Development on programs of the World Bank (WB), the Global Fund and the US "President's Emergency Plan for AIDS Relief" (PEPFAR) illustrated how in these programs health workers were recruited from the public sector, leaving gaps in the public system that could not be filled afterwards.

This issue was finally picked up by Member States of the 69th World Health Assembly in May 2016 when they addressed Universal Health Coverage (UHC) and the shortage of human resources for health in unanimously adopting a landmark resolution.[25] WHO estimates that around 40 million new health sector jobs need to be created by 2030 globally, mostly in low and middle income countries (LMIC). But due to the above mentioned push and pull factors, there will probably be a projected shortage of 18 million health workers needed to achieve the Sustainable Development Goals (SDGs) in LMIC.

V Alternatives: Global Health Initiatives – Objectives and Assessment

GHI aim at the establishment of new institutional forms of cooperation. They mobilize and invest substantial funds and resources for the development of new products and services to support broader health programs. Today, GHI represent an important part of the global architecture in international development cooperation. It is increasingly difficult to overlook

---

23 WHO, *The World Health Report 2006. Working Together for Health*, 2006, available at http://www.who.int/whr/2006/en/.

24 Oomman, N, Berstein, M & Rosenzweig, S, *Seizing the Opportunity on AIDS and Health Systems*, 2008, available at http://www.cgdev.org/publication/seizing-opportunity-aids-and-health-systems.

25 WHO, *Global strategy on human resources for health: workforce 2030 (WHA69.19)*, available at http://apps.who.int/gb/ebwha/pdf_files/WHA69/A69_R19-en.pdf.

the numerous international donors, implementing organizations and initiatives and to understand how they operate. There are now more than 40 bilateral organizations of development cooperation, 26 United Nations (UN) organizations, 20 global and regional financial organizations and agencies, and over 100 GHI.[26] However, these initiatives vary greatly in their financial capacity, global alignment and legitimacy by international institutions.

Speaking of national and global health governance structures and processes, this epidemic revealed enormous national shortcomings, especially in the three most affected countries, whereas countries like Senegal and Nigeria managed to contain the epidemic. At the same time, ECOWAS-WAHO jointly with WHO's Regional Office for Africa was able to consolidate the overall public health architecture in the region.[27] These budgets are a multiple of national health budgets and health-related development aid that the affected countries have received in recent years.[28]

> "Thereby, Ebola caught up with a group of 'exceptional diseases' which are of international interest, while other equally relevant diseases and HS needs are often ignored by politics."[29]

Over the past decade, most funds were allocated to vertical programs to combat three diseases only (malaria, the acquired immune deficiency syndrome (AIDS) and tuberculosis) while the most significant "killers" (for example diarrhea) have been almost completely ignored.[30] For this purpose, objectives and programs of development cooperation need to be defined and operationalized clearly and in the long-term. Funding security beyond the usual two to three year cycle of projects is important. This also implies that the choice of funding resources has to be reconsidered. The tendency towards highly focused GHI has been called into question. This conclusion can be drawn from international responses to non-epidemic situations, where the focus on such vertical programs combating individual diseases resulted in parallel structures, increased costs, inefficiency and inequity.

---

26 Paris Declaration on Aid Effectiveness (2005), available at http://www.oecd.org/dac/effectiveness/34428351.pdf.

27 Ndawinz, Cissé & Diallo et al., "Prevention of HIV spread during the Ebola outbreak in Guinea", above Fn. 7.

28 World Bank, *Health Expenditure*, above Fn. 10.

29 Flessa & Marx, "Ebola Fever Epidemic 2014", above Fn. 1, 2; see also WHO, *The World Health Report 2008: Primary Health Care – Now more than ever*, 2008, available at http://www.who.int/whr/2008/en/.

30 Dieleman, J L, Graves, C & Johnson, E et al., "Sources and Focus of Health Development Assistance, 1990-2014" (2015), 313 *Journal of the American Medical Association*, 2361.

Disease-specific programs in particular have led to a collapse of community-based education programs, since these only engaged in, for example, bed nets and condoms instead of general health promotion. This can also be seen as a result of mushrooming GHI, such as The Global Fund to Fight AIDS, Tuberculosis and Malaria (GFATM), PEPFAR, the Bill & Melinda Gates Foundation, and the vaccine alliance Gavi. The more than 150 GHI in existence today are still a powerful driver of the international health agenda.

The response to the Ebola epidemic points to the need for deliberate allocation of resources beyond political agendas or media preferences. This also applies to new epidemic threats such as the Zika virus. To date, Ebola apparently has a high priority in national and international health and development policies. As important and appropriate as this is, we must not repeat the mistakes of the past. Ebola cannot simply be added to a few target diseases, but the structures and approaches of control programs have to be reconsidered fundamentally.[31] We need sustainable health and development policies obliged to long-term objectives. Hence, in 2015 the UN launched the new Sustainable Development Goals (SDG) as successor of the Millennium Development Goals (MDGs).[32] Among the 17 SGDs, the third one ("Ensure healthy lives and promote wellbeing for all at all ages") addresses key challenges in health with nine targets. Target 3.3 reads "by 2030, end

31 Mid-2015, WHO's Secretary-General announced the creation of an advisory group to reform the present emergency system in case of disease outbreaks, reports of the group, available at http://bit.ly/2mi1LYM.

32 WHO, *UN Development Summit 2015*, September 25-27, 2015, summary available at http://bit.ly/2mi7Cxs.

the epidemics of AIDS, tuberculosis, malaria and neglected tropical diseases and combat hepatitis, water-borne diseases and other communicable disease".[33]

Figure 4: Sustainable Development Goals, available at http://bit.ly/1IqICxS.

Based on the SDGs, international development policy promotes the establishment of health care systems being able to function on a long-term basis. We need a holistic approach to HS strengthening. Reflecting the key elements and principles of PHC, horizontal basic health care systems need to be promoted in order to enable the building of stable societies, health awareness in the population, as well as participation of community and other important decision-makers outside politics. In particular, the development of community-based HS, primary and secondary prevention, as well as the participation of the respective population and the national ownership of development processes have proven to be a conveyor of sustainability. Strengthening primary health services, education, and basic health groups, as well as the training of community health workers have to be primary goals of development partnership and policies. In this context, the shortage of skilled workers is a crucial issue. Health has to remain a focus of inter-

---

33 Sustainable Development Goals, available at https://sustainabledevelopment.un.org/sdgs.

national development cooperation. But the selection of programs and projects should rather be based on efficiency and effectiveness in the long run, rather than on short-term opinions.[34]

Efficient allocation of resources is needed beyond political and media preferences. The allocation of resources for development cooperation in partnering countries, sectors, regions, diseases and levels of health care has to be a rational process. For this purpose, objectives and programs of development cooperation need to be defined and operationalized clearly and in the long-term.

The intensity and dynamics of the Ebola epidemic took many experts by surprise. This is partly due to a lack of reliable early warning systems and forecasting models for epidemics. In the coming years, such systems need to be designed and installed not only for Ebola but for other infectious diseases as well. In particular, mathematical models of disease dynamics need to be developed and validated by international groups of experts. Their results should be included in development policies of donor countries. The continuous collection and analysis of solid epidemiological data as well as high-quality system indicators are also essential to early warning systems. The Centre for Disease Control (CDC) in Atlanta has set up branches in Guinea, Liberia, and Sierra Leone to support the ministries of health to better prepare for epidemics in the future. A close collaboration with the RCDC in Abudja/Nigeria needs to be established.[35]

VI Conclusion

In the aftermath of the Ebola outbreak, the strong regional and international momentum and leadership to strengthen resilient HS offer a unique window of opportunity to improve and mainstream disease control programs at national, regional and international levels.

HSS is seen as determinant for countries to meet the SDGs, while being able to better prepare for the threats of pandemics in the context of global health. More implementation research is needed to better understand the influential factors of HSS and quality improvement, for example, and how to implement HSS effectively from the communities upwards in the context

34 Marx & Benn, "Viewpoint: Primary Health Care and Global Health Initiatives", above Fn. 18, 37.

35 See Gyang, "Nigeria inaugurates Board Of ECOWAS Centre for Disease Control", above Fn. 14.

of emergencies. The Ebola fever epidemic is a wake-up call for demanding higher efficiency, rationality and evidence in the health policy of partner countries and the development policy of donors. If we fail to learn the necessary lessons from this epidemic, it can be expected that similar or graver outbreaks of Ebola or other infectious diseases will occur in upcoming years accompanied by highly negative economic and humane consequences.

The Response to the West African Ebola Outbreak (2014-2016): A Failure of Global Health Governance?

*Wolfgang Hein**

Abstract

This article provides an overview and characterizes the events of the 2014 West African Ebola outbreak as they unfolded, as well as the response of the international community to this outbreak. On this background, the harsh criticisms of the alleged failure of the international community and the key recommendations for the improvement of disease outbreak response are scrutinized. Critique in retrospect has to be taken with caution, as each outbreak has its specific features. It is important to distinguish between (a) the potential for flexible short-term responses to hitherto unknown features of a specific outbreak; (b) general improvements of international emergency response facilities; and (c) long-term structural improvements needed to develop the core capacity requirements for surveillance and response. In contrast to early critical assessments, many reports published in late 2015 and early 2016 had a strikingly different tone, stressing the final success in combating the regional outbreak. The article closes with some concerns regarding the consistency with which the far-ranging recommendations will be pursued.

I Introduction

The international response to the Ebola epidemic in West Africa has been broadly criticized by many authors, and, partly as a form of self-criticism,

---

* Senior research fellow at the German Institute of Global and Area Studies, Hamburg and professor at the University of Hamburg in the field of International Relations and Development Studies, working primarily on Global Health and Environmental Governance.
I thank the participants of the Heidelberg Workshop on "International Health Governance of Disease Outbreaks" and in particular *Michael Marx* and *Pedro A. Villarreal* for valuable comments and references. All websites last accessed November 30, 2016.

by many actors of Global Health Governance (GHG). This criticism refers in particular to the first months of a reluctant reaction by the World Health Organization (WHO) and other top international health actors, such as the United States Centers for Disease Control and Prevention (CDC). Thus a report by a panel from the Harvard Global Health Institute and London School of Health and Tropical Medicine (LSHTM) stated:

> "The west African Ebola epidemic that began in 2013 exposed deep inadequacies in the national and international institutions responsible for protecting the public from the far-reaching human, social, economic, and political consequences of infectious disease outbreaks."[1]

And the WHO Ebola Interim Assessment Panel criticized:

> "Given WHO's extensive experience with outbreaks, health promotion and social mobilization, it is surprising that it took until August or September 2014 to recognize that Ebola transmission would be brought under control only when surveillance, community mobilization and the delivery of appropriate health care to affected communities were all put in place simultaneously."[2]

Pierre Rollin, Ebola expert from the CDC, talked of a "missed opportunity", as "without a robust and coordinated response, an invisible epidemic was allowed to thrive alongside the one assumed to be contained".[3] It is only after the declaration of a public health emergency of international concern (PHEIC) that the beginning of a "global response" is recognized.

As a starting point, this article will focus on clarifying the sequence of events around the Ebola outbreak, document the rather slow development of international cooperation and put this process into context. This might help to explain the governance failures during the first months of the outbreak, as well as the more long-term aspects of local problems and international surveillance of infectious diseases which resulted in the catastrophic spread of Ebola in the second half of 2014.

Most of the more local and regional factors impeding an early containment of the Ebola outbreak are discussed in the contribution by *Michael Marx* in this volume, which focuses primarily on the deplorable state of the health systems and of state institutions in general in the three main affected

---

1 Moon, S, Sridhar, D & Pate, M A et al., "Will Ebola change the game? Ten essential reforms before the next pandemic. The report of the Harvard-LSHTM Independent Panel on the Global Response to Ebola" (2015), 386 *The Lancet*, 2204 (2204).

2 WHO, 68th World Health Assembly, Document A68/25, *Annex "Ebola Interim Assessment Panel" 3*, available at http://apps.who.int/gb/ebwha/pdf_files/WHA68/A68_25-en.pdf?ua=1.

3 Sack, K, Fink, S & Belluck, P et al., "How Ebola Roared Back" (December 30, 2014), *New York Times*, D1, available at http://www.nytimes.com/2014/12/30/health/how-ebola-roared-back.html?_r=0.

countries after a decade of devastating warfare, and on cultural elements, such as burial customs, etc. Considering the discourse on the failure of the international community in general, and WHO in particular, this contribution presents a short overview of the West African Ebola outbreak and the early responses to it and then refers in some detail to the systems of international emergency response to outbreaks of infectious diseases. This will refer not only to WHO, its regional organizations, and the International Health Regulations (IHR 2005), but also to the entire system of GHG, defined by *David Fidler* as "the use of formal and informal institutions, rules, and processes by states, intergovernmental organizations, and non-state actors to deal with challenges to health that require cross-border collective action to address effectively".[4] An interesting comparison of nine different assessments and recommendations has been published in the paper "Global Response to Health Crisis", and will be discussed in more detail in Section III.[5]

In fighting the Ebola outbreak, a large variety of GHG actors such as Médecins Sans Frontières (MSF) and other Non-Governmental Organizations (NGOs), philanthropic organizations, important health research and policy centers (CDC etc.), other intergovernmental organizations in the field from regional organizations such as the West African Health Organisation (WAHO), which is a specialized institution of the Economic Community of West African States (ECOWAS), and even up to the UN Security Council participated.

---

4 Fidler, D P, *The challenges of global health governance, Council on Foreign Relations Working Paper*, 2010, 3. Besides the text by *Fidler*, there is now a huge body of literature on GHG, starting with Dodgson, R, Lee, K & Drager, N, "Global Health Governance. A Conceptual Review" (2002), *Discussion Paper No. 1*; Buse, K, Hein, W & Drager, N (eds.), *Making Sense of Global Health Governance. A policy Perspective*, 2009; Moon, S, Szlezák, N A & Michaud, C M et al., "The global health system: Lessons for a stronger institutional framework" (2010), 7 *PLOS Medicine*, 1; (article in a four-part series on the global health system in *Plos Medicine*); Schrecker, T (ed.), *The Ashgate Research Companion to the Globalization of Health*, 2012; Kickbusch, I & Cassar Szabo, M M, "A new governance space for health" (2014), 7 *Global Health Action*, 23507, available at http://dx.doi.org/10.3402/gha.v7.23507.

5 Global Response to Health Crisis, *A Comparison of Expert Recommendations following the Ebola-Outbreak in West Africa*, available at http://www.thinkglobalhealth.de/Inform/ (website by *Mathias B. Bonk*). The assessments dealt with in more detail will be quoted below.

In the final part of this article, some observations on the limitations of emergency operations are added, trying to determine important governance failures without forgetting that they have been identified in an ex-post analysis. If these failures are linked to structural problems (for example lack of support for surveillance systems in poor countries), reform policies can be embarked on; if they are based on false expectations about characteristics of a disease, this is a matter of methods of foresight.

II Timeline of the West African Ebola Outbreak and Responses

An exact timeline of the outbreak and the main dates of intervention (diagnosis, medicines and vaccines development, treatment regimes)[6] helps in understanding the dynamics and failures of outbreak control. Here, emphasis is placed on the early phase of the outbreak until full international engagement was reached in September 2014, and also the last phase with various declarations on the "end of the outbreak", as those are most important concerning the discourse on the "failure of the international community".

The data shows clearly distinguishable phases of the development of the outbreak. About three months passed before the disease was identified as Ebola:

- December 2013: Two-year-old boy dies of Ebola (presumed first fatality of the outbreak, according to information published in the New England Journal of Medicine in May 2014).[7]
- February 2014: Guinean sources talked about a "strange disease" (see below), initially suspected to be caused by Lassa virus.

---

6 The dates of this timelime have been compiled from various sources: WHO, *Ebola situation reports*, available at http://www.who.int/csr/disease/ebola/situation-reports/archive/en/ (starting August 29, 2014); WHO, *Emergencies Preparedness, Response*, available at http://www.who.int/csr/don/archive/year/2014/en/; WHO, *A year of the Ebola response "at a glance"*; WHO, *Ebola response activities 2014-2015*, available at http://www.who.int/csr/disease/ebola/who-activities-report/en/; United States Centers for Disease Control and Prevention, *Outbreak updates (now: "previous outbreak updates")*, available at http://www.cdc.gov/vhf/ebola/outbreaks/2014-west-africa/previous-updates.html; MSF, *MSF reports on Ebola*, available at http://www.msf.org/en/search?keyword=Ebola. For other references, see the following footnotes.

7 Baize, S, Pannetier, D & Oestereich, L et al., "Emergence of Zaire Ebola Virus Disease in Guinea" (2014), 371 *New England Journal of Medicine*, 1418 (1418).

- March 10, 2014: Hospitals and public health services in Guéckédou and Macenta alerted the Ministry of Health of Guinea and – 2 days later – Médecins sans Frontières in Guinea about clusters of a mysterious disease characterized by fever, severe diarrhea, vomiting, and an apparent high fatality rate.
- March 13, 2014: First formal report from WHO Country office in Guinea into the Emergency.[8]
- March 14, 2014: Xinhua, the Chinese news agency reports: "A disease whose nature has not yet been identified caused the death of eight people in the prefecture of Macenta, in south-eastern Guinea, Thursday revealed Dr Sakoba Keita, Director of the Division prevention of diseases in the Department of Health".
- March 14, 2014: MSF is asked by the Guinean Ministry of Health to investigate an "unidentified" disease[9] and launches an emergency response.
- March 15, 2014: Guinéenews (interviewing Sakoba Keita) reports about a "strange disease that *has been raging for the month of February* in the Forest Region, killed 9 of 15 reported cases".[10]

After the Ebola virus had been confirmed as the cause of that "strange disease", for approximately two months the expectation prevailed that the outbreak would have had a limited impact comparable to previous outbreaks of the disease in Central Africa:[11]

- March 21, 2014: Laboratory tests confirm Ebola in Guinea.
- March 22, 2014: Ebola outbreak officially declared by the Guinean Ministry of Health.
- March 22, 2014: First contribution to Ebola Funding through WHO by EU Humanitarian AID Office.
- March 25, 2014: First CDC report on outbreak in Guinea (86 suspected cases, including 59 deaths) and references to suspected cases in Liberia and Sierra Leone (CDC 25 March).
- March 31, 2014: MSF "declared that the outbreak was 'unprecedented' in terms of its geographic spread" (first cases in the capital Conakry and in Liberia).

---

8 For a more detailed information on WHO actions until the declaration of PHEIC, see: WHO, *Review Committee on the Role of the IHR (2005) in the Ebola Outbreak and Response*, Implementation of the International Health Regulations (2005), A69/21, May 13, 2016.

9 Richter, S, "What went wrong in Ebola response?" (2015), 21 *Rural*, 9.

10 See the following website FluTracker, http://bit.ly/2mcuXBc.

11 The previous most severe outbreaks were in Zaire (1976: 318 cases/280 deaths) and in Uganda (2000/2001: 425 cases/224 deaths), see: CDC, *Outbreaks Chronology*, available at http://www.cdc.gov/vhf/ebola/outbreaks/history/chronology.html.

- April 1, 2014: Early WHO health supplies arrived.
- Emergency measures by other NGOs, medical research institutes, bi-national cooperation and WHO were intensifying since early April 2014.
- May 26, 2014: government of Sierra Leone officially declares an Ebola outbreak.

In June and July 2014, Ebola cases and deaths in the three countries were rapidly rising and surpassed the dimensions of previous outbreaks, but the WHO was still hesitant to declare a public health emergency of international concern (PHEIC).

- Ebola cases/deaths on May 27: 281/186; rapidly rising in June and July; June 18: 528/337; July 12: 964/603; July 30: 1,440/826, all of them in 2014.
- July 2-3, 2014: WHO called an emergency sub-regional ministerial meeting in Accra (Ghana).
- July 31, 2014: Sierra Leone declares state of emergency.
- August 6, 2014: Liberia declares state of emergency.

Finally, in August 2014, WHO declared a PHEIC and the respective IHR mechanisms were activated, followed by UN activities in September. This marked the starting-point of coordinated measures within the UN system.

- August 8, 2014: WHO/IHR: Declaration of a public health emergency of international concern (PHEIC).
- September 18, 2014: UN Security Council declares the outbreak "a threat to peace" and establishes the UN Mission for Ebola Emergency Response (UNMEER).
- September 30, 2014: The description of a public event on Ebola organized by the British Overseas Development Institute (ODI) talked about "some predicting that more than 500,000 could be infected by the end of January (2015)".[12]

Since early 2015, the intervention of the international community appeared to be successful. The number of cases declined, and by the end of April 2015 there were no cases in Liberia for the preceding 21 days. According to WHO criteria, after a 42 days observation period and additional 90 days

12 See ODI, *Ebola: What more can be done?*, available at https://www.odi.org/events/4033-ebola-more-can-be-done. CDC estimated in September 2014: "Without additional interventions or changes in community behavior, CDC estimates that by January 20, 2015, there will be a total of approximately 550,000 Ebola cases in Liberia and Sierra Leone or 1.4 million if corrections for underreporting are made.", see CDC, *Questions and Answers: Estimating the Future Number of Cases in the Ebola Epidemic—Liberia and Sierra Leone, 2014–2015*, available at http://www.cdc.gov/vhf/ebola/outbreaks/2014-west-africa/qa-mmwr-estimating-future-cases.html.

of enhanced surveillance since the last observed virus transmission, the outbreak is declared to "have ended".[13] Nevertheless, there were a few small outbreaks after that.

- January/February 2015: Rapid decline of cases (October 29, 2014: 2966; November 26, 2014: 2032; January 7, 2015: 1314; February 25, 2015: 397); April 29, 2015: 101 (Liberia: 0).
- May 9, 2015: WHO declared Liberia free of Ebola virus transmission for the first time.
- September 3, 2015: WHO declares end of Ebola outbreak in Liberia.
- November 7, 2015: WHO declares end of Ebola outbreak in Sierra Leone.
- December 29, 2015: WHO declares the end of Ebola outbreak in the Republic of Guinea.
- March 29, 2016: WHO terminated the Public Health Emergency of International Concern (PHEIC).
- April 2016: Three new cases of Ebola in Liberia.
- April 13, 2016: Updated cases/deaths: 28,652/11,325.[14]
- May 2, 2016: Liberia and Guinea discharge final Ebola patients in latest flare-up and begin 42 days of heightened surveillance.

III Has the International Community Failed?

As the timeline shows, it took more than *ten weeks* from the emergence of the disease until the Guinean health system recognized that they needed help in identifying the character of a "strange disease" that in fact has been internationally known for several decades. Considering the breakdown of the health systems during the wars in all three countries between 1989 and 2003 and the extremely small number of medical personnel,[15] such problems of diagnosis of uncommon diseases in remote regions are not really

---

13 WHO, *Criteria for declaring the end of the Ebola outbreak in Guinea, Liberia or Sierra Leone*, available at http://www.who.int/csr/disease/ebola/declaration-ebola-end/en/.

14 These data include cases in Italy, Mali, Nigeria, Senegal, Spain, UK and the USA, see CDC, *2014 Ebola Outbreak in West Africa - Case Counts,* available at http://www.cdc.gov/vhf/ebola/outbreaks/2014-west-africa/case-counts.html.

15 Ulbert, C, "Die Ebola-Epidemie als Herausforderung für staatliches und internationales Handeln: Diagnose und Lehren" in Kursawe, J, Johannsen, M & Baumgart-Ochse, C et al. (eds.), *Friedensgutachten 2015*, 2015, 215 (218) (based on WHO data).

surprising. NGOs frequently working to support health care in remote regions can be in a favorable position for an early reaction to outbreaks of infectious diseases as was recognized by the CDC in their Outbreak Update on March 31, 2014:

> "Médecins sans Frontières (MSF/Doctors without Borders) is helping the Ministry of Health of Guinea in establishing Ebola treatment centers in the epicenter of the outbreak. In Liberia, several international organizations including the International Red Cross (IRC), Pentecostal Mission Unlimited (PMU)-Liberia, and Samaritan's Purse (SP) Liberia are aiding the Ministry of Health of Liberia by supporting awareness campaigns and providing personal protective equipment (PPE) for healthcare workers."[16]

In fact, support for Ebola treatment in Guinea started in late March and, because of the later spread of the disease, a few weeks later in Liberia and Sierra Leone. Since April, WHO activities had been relatively strong.[17] Then, however, about four more months passed until a coordinated international response was pushed by the decision of WHO to declare a PHEIC according to the International Health Regulations (IHR).

It has to be taken into account, however, that between the 15th and the 20th week in 2014 (mid-April to mid-May) the number of newly reported cases in Guinea was considerably lower than during the weeks before, and that until the beginning of June there were very few new cases in Liberia (none between April 9 and May 27) and Sierra Leone. On May 27, the total cumulative number in the three countries stood at 281 (186 deaths).[18] Therefore, at that time, the quantitative dimension of the outbreak did not surpass a number of former Ebola outbreaks, which always disappeared after a period of a few weeks, because of the tendency of the virus to kill its host before many other people could be infected, and that it does not stay alive very long in surviving people. Ebola had been seen as a "self-limiting" disease.[19] On the other hand, MSF was right calling the outbreak "unprecedented" because of its geographic spread and the inclusion of large cities.

---

16 See CDC, *Ebola (Ebola Virus Disease)*, http://www.cdc.gov/vhf/ebola/outbreaks/2014-west-africa/previous-updates.html.

17 See the WHO's report, *A year of the Ebola response "at a glance"*, available at www.who.int/csr/disease/ebola/who-activities-report/en/; see also Kamradt-Scott, A, "WHO's to blame? The World Health Organization and the 2014 Ebola outbreak in West Africa" (2016), 37 *Third World Quarterly*, 1 (4 et seq.).

18 See WHO Regional Office for Africa, *Epidemic and Pandemic Alert and Response,* available at http://bit.ly/2lID0Im.

19 This characterization can be found in many publications. See for example Nave, A, "Ebola" in Gates, H L & Appiah, K A (eds.), *Encyclopedia of Africa* (Oxford

Thus, it is at the same time understandable why nobody expected an outbreak of the dimension it reached a few months later,[20] but on the other hand it has to be considered an incident of insufficient foresight not to have taken those specific characteristics of the West African Ebola epidemic stressed by MSF seriously enough.

The failure of an early and strong reaction to the Ebola outbreak in Guinea that could have prevented the catastrophic turn of events some months later has been the topic of critical assessments and recommendations by many actors in global public health which cannot be discussed in a rather short contribution. Frequently, WHO is held responsible for this failure.[21]

An interesting comparison of nine different assessments commissioned by various actors and group of actors in GHG has been published under the title "Global Response to Health Crisis".[22] There is not sufficient space to discuss all the points raised in more detail. All recommendations refer to the role of WHO and the IHR (which will be taken up further below) and have drawn conclusions linking the Ebola crisis to many aspects of global health. These are very well systematized in the Harvard-LSHTM paper[23] which presents the following rather concrete recommendations:

- Develop a global strategy to invest in, monitor, and sustain national core capacities.
- Strengthen incentives for early reporting of outbreaks.
- Create a unified WHO Centre for Emergency Preparedness and Response.
- Emergency declarations by a transparent, politically protected Standing Emergency Committee.
- Create an independent Accountability Commission for Disease Outbreak Prevention and Response.
- Develop a framework of rules to ensure access to the benefits of research.
- Establish a global facility to finance, accelerate, and prioritize R&D.

Reference, online version 2010), also Flessa, S & Marx, M, "Ebola fever epidemic 2014: a call for sustainable health and development policies" (2015), 17 *The European Journal of Health Economics*, 1 (1).

20 See Interview with Bausch, D, "Glimmers of hope on the Ebola front" (2014), 92 *Bulletin of the World Health Organization*, 704 (704 et seq.).

21 See for example Ulbert, "Die Ebola-Epidemie als Herausforderung für staatliches und internationales Handeln", above Fn. 15; see also Moon, Sridhar & Pate et al., "Will Ebola change the game?", above Fn. 1, 2206.

22 Global response to health crisis, *A Comparison of Expert Recommendations*, above Fn. 5.

23 Moon, Sridhar & Pate et al., "Will Ebola change the game?", above Fn. 1.

The "Commission on Creating a Global Health Risk Framework for the Future" puts strong emphasis on the role of public health systems as "the first line of defence" against pandemics, to be supplemented by "strengthening the global and regional system for outbreak preparedness, alert and response" and "accelerating research and development to counter the threat of infectious diseases".[24] A group of scholars from the University of Sydney, the LSHTM and the Queen Mary University of London stresses the importance of civil-military relations in the case of Ebola outbreak and demands an "independent research program to systematically investigate the roles and functions that military-based actors can perform".[25] Other reports deal with the role of the G7[26] and the European Union, which besides the general demands to improve global governance and coordination mechanisms (based on the WHO and the IHR) and to strengthen health systems, call for improving "EU preparation to tackle future outbreaks, including increasing cooperation among its Member States".[27]

The author of the comparative report points[28] to a neglect of socio-cultural and political dimensions in the assessment reports presented. In my contribution, the main focus will be on the character of global health governance as a complex system within the "international community" reacting to various types of health challenges in a flexible, but not necessarily optimal way. This has to be seen in relation to the difficulties to anticipate the course a particular outbreak will take, which depends on the specific socio-cultural and political context in which an outbreak occurs.[29]

---

24 See Sands, P, Mundaca-Shah, C & Dzau, V J, "The Neglected Dimension of Global Security – A Framework for Countering Infectious Diseases" (2016), 374 *The New England Journal of Medicine*, 1281 (1283).

25 See Kamradt-Scott, A, Harman, S & Wenham, C et al., *Saving Lives: The civil-military response to the 2014 Ebola outbreak in West Africa*, 2015, 2.

26 See Declaration of the G7 Health Ministers, *Think Ahead. Act Together*, October 8-9, 2015, available at http://bit.ly/2kPrwnl.

27 See (a) Conference Report, available at http://ec.europa.eu/health/preparedness_response/docs/ev_20151012_sr_en.pdf and (b) (for the quote): Council Conclusion, available at http://bit.ly/2kPlcMj.

28 Presumably *Mathias B. Bonk*, the organizer of the website Think Global Health, above Fn. 5.

29 Flessa & Marx, "Ebola fever epidemic 2014", above Fn. 19, refer to various factors in West Africa which favored a rapid spread of the epidemic (funeral rites, weak health care systems after two decades of civil war and rather high mobility between rural and urban population); see also the contribution of *Michael Marx*, "Ebola Epidemic 2014-2015: Taking Control or Being Trapped in the Logic of Failure – What Lessons Can Be Learned?" in this volume.

1 Multi-actor Character of GHG

GHG is characterized by a complex interaction of quite different types of actors pursuing the aim of improving health at different spatial levels and in different fields.[30] The multiplicity of actors has created problems of co-ordination frequently referred to, but it also implies advantages of a great flexibility. While state actors might be hampered by bureaucratic hurdles, and international governmental organizations might have problems to reach consensus before taking large-scale actions, many NGOs are in a position to respond swiftly and to raise international public attention – although in most cases they are restrained by their financial means.

The multi-actor character of GHG played an important role in the early phase: MSF, as the most important NGO during this outbreak, played an outstanding role, particularly in the early phase; other agencies have already been referred to. In addition to WHO's activities, the advantages of GHG's multi-actor activities – including Humanitarian Aid from many states, International Organizations (like the UN Office for the Coordination of Humanitarian Affairs), health NGOs and philanthropies – have been confirmed since the end of March 2014, and considerable amounts of resources in the fight against Ebola were mobilized. MSF alone spent nearly US$ 113.7 million from March 2014 to December 2015[31] and was the first organization to fully react to the Ebola outbreak in Guinea in March. On the whole, the international community did react in a rather broad way to the situation in West Africa, but these activities could not make up for a coordinated, much better financed "emergency response" after the declaration of a PHEIC. The contribution of sub-regional organizations, the West African Health Organisation (WAHO) and the ECOWAS commission, to the concrete fight against the outbreak, was close to negligible.[32]

---

30 On GHG see the texts quoted below, above Fn. 6.

31 MSF, *Ebola 2014-2015 Facts & Figures. Key financial data on MSF's response to the Ebola epidemic in West Africa*, 2, available at http://www.msf.org/sites/msf.org/files/ebola_accountability_report_low_res.pdf. US$ 91.1 million were raised from private donations, US$ 22.6 million from public institutional funders (8). Data are converted into US$ at the exchange rate of December 31, 2015.

32 See the contribution of *Edefe Ojomo*, "Fostering Regional Health Governance in West Africa: The Role of the WAHO" in this volume; Nsoedo, E E, "The Ebola Crisis in the West African Region: Should It Have Been So Severe?" (2014), 2 *Open Journal of Social Sciences*, 98.

2 WHO Responses and the Late Declaration of a PHEIC

There was a prompt reaction by WHO to the Ebola Outbreak in Guinea. The first team drawn from institutional partners in the WHO Global Outbreak Alert and Response Network (GOARN) travelled to Guinea on March 28, 2014; on the same day, WHO stated that the Emerging and Dangerous Pathogens Laboratory Network was coordinating international reference laboratory support, sent clinical teams, provided advice and training to local health institutions, and developed contact-tracing activities, among others.[33] *Kamradt-Scott* stressed that the WHO secretariat had deployed 113 experts to West Africa within six weeks of the outbreak being confirmed (significantly more than in the case of earlier outbreaks of Ebola), which "suggests that the IO's initial response was at least reasonable and arguably defensible".[34] Until January 2016, WHO had deployed nearly 4.000 technical experts (including Ebola vaccination teams) and 45 laboratories.[35]
In reaction to rising numbers of Ebola cases in June, on July 2-3, 2014, WHO summoned an emergency sub-regional Ministerial meeting in Accra, Ghana, and a Sub-regional Ebola Outbreak Coordination Centre (SEOCC) was established in Conakry with a number of partners – GOARN, CDC, MSF, UNICEF, IFRC, Institute Pasteur of Dakar, Save the Children, Plan Guinea, and others.[36] In the Communiqué[37] Governments were asked to "continue to build and strengthen IHR core capacities, especially those needed to respond to serious public health events". Additionally, "the ministers of health agreed that the current situation poses a serious threat to all countries in the sub-region and beyond and therefore called for immediate action", which can be seen as a call for the declaration of a PHEIC.

For emergency operations, WHO depends on extraordinary funds[38]: Certainly the declaration of a PHEIC constitutes an important instrument to

---

33 On early WHO activities in West Africa, see http://www.who.int/features/2014/preventing-ebola/en/. Also, http://who.int/csr/disease/ebola/en/.

34 Kamradt-Scott, "WHO's to blame?", above Fn. 17, 5.

35 See WHO, *Progress in the Ebola response,* available at http://www.who.int/csr/disease/ebola/response/infographic/en/.

36 See WHO, *Ebola virus disease, West Africa - update,* available at http://www.who.int/csr/don/2014_07_31_ebola/en/.

37 WHO-Afro, *Communiqué (3 July 2014)*, available http://bit.ly/2lbIVCM.

38 That is one of the main points of the WHO Report of the Ebola Interim Assessment Panel, available at http://www.who.int/csr/resources/publications/ebola/report-by-panel.pdf?ua=1, 16 et seq.; see also further below. See also WHO, *Review*

mobilize international support. Thus, it is not surprising that donations for "Ebola Response Funding" went up considerably after August 8, 2014. Nevertheless, while the monthly average between August 2014 and the end of December 2015 was around US $24 million, it had previously reached (from March 22 to August 7) an average of about US $11 million. WHO (and the international community in providing funds) in fact responded strongly – in correspondence to its limited financial means – already in the months before August 8.[39]

Nevertheless, WHO took over its full coordination role[40] only after the declaration of a PHEIC in August. Later on, coordination was additionally strengthened by the UN Security Council Meeting on September 18 and the establishment of UNMEER, which took over the task of overall planning and coordination, directing the efforts of the UN agencies, national governments, and other humanitarian actors to the areas where they were most needed.

The question remains: why was the PHEIC declared only 4 ½ months after Guinea's declaration of an Ebola outbreak, and about 2 months after case numbers began to grow rapidly? A PHEIC is defined by Article 1 of the International Health Regulations as

> "an extraordinary event which is determined to [...] constitute a public health risk to other States through the international spread of disease and [...] to potentially require a coordinated international response".[41]

Annex 1 of the IHR determines the "Core Capacity Requirements for Surveillance and Response" which all State Parties have to meet, which include (at "the local community level and/or primary public health response level") "clinical descriptions, laboratory results, sources and type of risk, numbers of human cases and deaths, conditions affecting the spread of the disease and the health measures employed". According to Article 44(2) IHR, WHO should collaborate "in the provision or facilitation of technical cooperation and logistical support to States Parties"; and "the mobilization of financial resources to support developing countries in building, strengthening and maintaining the capacities provided for in Annex 1". Guinea, Liberia, and

---

Committee on the Role of the IHR (2005) in the Ebola Outbreak and Response, above Fn. 8, para. 160.

39 Own calculation from WHO, *Ebola response funding*, available at http://www.who.int/csr/disease/ebola/funding/en/.

40 According to Article 2(a) of its Constitution: "WHO is the directing and co-ordinating authority on international health work".

41 WHO, *International Health Regulations*, 3rd edition, 2016, available at http://www.who.int/ihr/publications/9789241580496/en/.

Sierra Leone were far from disposing of these capacities. For example, national IHR focal points should have been developed in each Member State; while the IHR focal point in Nigeria had been involved in information about the first suspected case of Ebola in the country at the end of July 2014, no comparable information on focal points in Guinea, Liberia and Sierra Leone could be found. However, in July, as mentioned before, WHO had established the SEOCC.

Nevertheless, taking into account the first appearance of Ebola in a big city like Conakry with about 2 million inhabitants and severe infrastructure problems, and (from early June onwards) the rising number of confirmed cases in Liberia and Sierra Leone, it is surprising that the IHR system did not react earlier to the Ebola threat. There have been many reproaches that such an action could have helped to prevent the explosive growth of the Ebola epidemics in the second half of 2015. This has also been pointed out by the WHO Ebola Interim Assessment Panel.[42]

During its special session on Ebola in January 2015, the WHO Executive Board requested an interim assessment by an independent expert panel "on all aspects on WHO's response to the Ebola outbreak". The Report of the Panel[43] referred to the following factors delaying the declaration of a PHEIC:

> "A late understanding of the context and nature of this Ebola outbreak, which was different from previous outbreaks; unreliable reporting on the spread of the virus; problems with information flow and decision-making within WHO; and difficult negotiations with countries." (Paragraph 22, Box)[44]

The Panel also pointed out that WHO had been criticized for declaring a PHEIC for pandemic influenza H1N1 ("swine flu"). The "swine flu" turned out to be a rather mild form of flu, but this declaration rapidly led to a stockpiling of anti-viral medicines (such as Tamiflu) and thus resulted in considerable revenues for the respective pharmaceutical corporations.[45]

---

42 WHO, *Report of the Ebola Interim Assessment Panel*, above Fn. 2, para. 10.

43 Ibid. The following quotes are from the indicated paragraphs of this Report.

44 It is surprising that the difference from previous outbreaks was understood by MSF already in late March.

45 WHO, *Report of the Ebola Interim Assessment Panel*, above Fn. 2, para. 22, Box. See for more details WHO, *Review Committee on the Role of the IHR (2005) in the Ebola Outbreak and Response*, above Fn. 8. Feinberg, H V (chair), *Report of the Review Committee on the Functioning of the International Health Regulations (2005) in relation to Pandemic (H1N1)*, 2009.

The Panel also noted the problem that the IHR only allows for "binary decisions": Either a PHEIC is declared or it is not. It recommended to "consider the possibility of an intermediate level that would alert and engage the wider international community at an earlier stage in a health crisis".[46] Furthermore, the Panel proposed to improve WHO's emergency response capacity in particular "in situations involving fragile states"[47] and recommended setting up a unified "WHO Centre for Health Emergency Preparedness and Response".[48] To finance such a center, the World Health Assembly (WHA) should reconsider its zero nominal growth policy with respect to assessed contributions, hence the proposal to increase this amount by 5 %.[49] In addition, a contingency fund to finance WHO's initial response to an emergency should be set up as decided by WHA 2015, based on voluntary contributions with a target capitalization of US $100 million (Paragraph 37).[50]

Assessments refer to the importance of regional organizations, but mostly to the role of the WHO Regional Office for Africa. Critique has to take into account that the core team for outbreaks and emergencies consists of fewer than ten people for the whole region (Paragraph 45).[51] WAHO/ECOWAS, as a sub-regional organization for health, is not even mentioned in most reports.

IV The International Community, Global Health Care and Emergency Response

To better understand the role of GHG in the context of infectious disease outbreaks, three factors with varying time scales are important to consider.

(1) A broad scope of actors in GHG (such as: NGOs, philanthropic organizations, medical research institutes) act at rapid notice, are present in

---

46 WHO, *Report of the Ebola Interim Assessment Panel*, above Fn. 2, para. 23.

47 Ibid., para. 30.

48 Ibid., para. 31-34. See also the Report by the Director-General to the World Health Assembly, A 69/30, May 2016, especially para. 5-7.

49 WHO, *Report of the Ebola Interim Assessment Panel*, above Fn. 2, para. 36. See also WHO, *Review Committee on the Role of the IHR (2005) in the Ebola Outbreak and Response*, above Fn. 8, para. 160, demanding "an increase in assessed contributions to the WHO budget".

50 WHO, *Report of the Ebola Interim Assessment Panel*, above Fn. 2, para. 37, and WHO, *Review Committee on the Role of the IHR (2005) in the Ebola Outbreak and Response*, above Fn. 8, para. 128.

51 WHO, *Report of the Ebola Interim Assessment Panel*, above Fn. 2, para. 45.

many regions, have growing resources at their disposal, act with a high degree of compassion, but are not in a position to successfully fight an extended emergency like the Ebola outbreak by themselves. As in the case of Guinea, NGOs such as MSF can substitute for a lack of expertise among national public health institutions, and mobilize partners among global health actors.

(2) As for international emergency mechanisms such as the IHR, it would be interesting to have a closer look at declarations of PHEICs related to the IHR's 2005 version by comparing the decisions on other outbreaks, such as the Severe Acute Respiratory Syndrome (SARS) (in anticipation of the rules of IHR 2005, which in 2003 were not yet fully negotiated); the "Swine Flu" (Influenza H1N1); the Wild Poliovirus; the Zika Virus, and the Middle East Respiratory Syndrome (MERS) (the subject of various discussions in the IHR Emergency Committee, but not "accepted" as a PHEIC).[52] The cases at hand leave the impression that a PHEIC is only mobilized if an outbreak is seen to produce risks for developed countries – this could explain why MERS, for example, has not been declared a PHEIC and the declaration of Ebola was delayed.[53] Improving transparency in the working of the Emergency Committee could disperse such suspicions. The declaration of a PHEIC ought to be independent from Member States' interests as it rests on the authority and responsibility of the Director General of WHO and is based on recommendations of an ad-hoc Emergency Committee, convened by him or her from a list of independent experts. The Harvard-LSHTM Panel recommends the creation of a Standing Emergency Committee with the mandate to declare a PHEIC. The Committee's first members should be appointed by the Director General following an open call for nominations. The Committee would periodically vote-in new members, and would publish minutes and votes immediately after each meeting to guarantee transparency.[54] The IHR Review Committee took over the idea of a

52 See for more details the contribution of *Pedro A. Villarreal*, "The World Health Organization's Governance Framework in Disease Outbreaks: A Legal Perspective" in this volume.

53 See the attention paid in the US on three cases of imported Ebola in nurses (where one of them was infected in the US) that occurred in September/October, which left the impression that averting the risk of infections in the US was an equally serious task as controlling Ebola in West Africa. See news reports in October 2014, for example CBS, "Obama acknowledges Ebola missteps" (October 16, 2014), available at http://cbsn.ws/2lynsVF.

54 Moon, Sridhar & Pate et al., "Will Ebola change the game?", above Fn. 1, 2212.

standing committee, but in the form of a standing *advisory* committee, leaving the authority to declare a PHEIC with the WHO Director General. This committee would also have an important advisory role to declare an intermediate level of alert, an "International Public Health Alert" (IPHA). The purpose and criteria for IPHAs and PHEICs should be defined by WHO "in a publicly accessible manual" which also ought to define "the operational and financial consequences they trigger".[55]

(3) Problems of developing countries' health systems have to be addressed with more urgency. The provisions in the IHR 2005 on supporting emergency surveillance and reaction capacities in developing countries have not materialized so far. In addition, infectious diseases which primarily affect Least Developed Countries (LDCs) are frequently treated as "business as usual", such as Malaria, Tuberculosis and other tropical diseases.[56] However, an effective "emergency response" depends on capacities of health systems all over the world. A functioning primary health care system in Guinea could have considerably accelerated the diagnosis of Ebola to a point where the virus could have been contained before it had reached Conakry – taking into account that there were reports on Ebola ("strange disease") in remote regions in February 2014, but in Conakry only in the second half of March,[57] and furthermore the "self-limiting" character of the disease.[58] It could have also helped to gain more confidence in emergency interventions among the local population and to reduce problems of coordination of many actors.

The improvement of mechanisms to detect and confirm emergencies, and in particular capacities to fight diseases, are dependent upon functioning health systems. If there are no capacities (knowledge, physical facilities and financial means) to deal with ongoing health problems, the pre-conditions for effective emergency responses are also missing. This is a global task, not only because many infectious diseases constitute a global threat, but

---

55 WHO, *Review Committee on the Role of the IHR (2005) in the Ebola Outbreak and Response*, above Fn. 8, Recommendation 6 (quotes from 6.2).

56 There are a number of health partnerships supporting the fight against these diseases, such as Roll Back Malaria and Stop TB, which are dealing with them as persistent problems and do not reach a similarly high level of public attention as emergency responses.

57 See Rico, A, Brody, D & Coronado, F et al., "Epidemiology of Epidemic Ebola Virus Disease in Conakry and Surrounding Prefectures, Guinea, 2014–2015" (2016), 22 *Emerging Infectious Diseases*, 178 (180), available at http://wwwnc.cdc.gov/eid/article/22/2/15-1304_article.

58 See above section III.

also because we are living in "globalizing societies". Providing Global Public Goods[59] (such as an internationally guaranteed minimum standard of health care or an effective control of infectious diseases) is costly and produces conflicts with national politics, national elites and local cultures. In the face of various severe global problems, we can observe a greater readiness to share resources, but the impact depends on a broad consensus about the role of actors and institutions in global politics on the one hand, and processes of social and political change in the countries concerned on the other. Global society and global institutions should facilitate an improvement of national health systems. Likewise, in order to prevent such processes getting stuck in conflicts and corruption at the national level and also to pool regional resources, sub-regional institutions[60] such as WAHO and ECOWAS might be suitable mediating points – even though their capacity to actively intervene in the West African Ebola crisis had been very limited.[61] It remains to be seen whether this last circumstance will change with the recent creation of the ECOWAS Regional Centre for Disease Control (RCDC), which includes an active participation by WAHO officials in its decision-making processes.[62] Along the same lines, the African Union has developed an African Centre for Disease Control in Abudja/Nigeria, with its own Regional Collaborating Centers in Kenya, Nigeria, Gabon, Egypt and Zambia.[63]

---

59 See for example Smith, R, Beaglehole, R & Woodward, D et al. (eds.), *Global Public Goods for Health. Health economic and public health perspective*, 2003; Smith, R D, Woodward, D & Acharya, A et al., "Communicable Disease Control: a 'Global Public Good' perspective" (2004), 19 *Health Policy and Planning*, 271.

60 In the UN system "regional" institutions are those on a continental scale (such as WHO AFRO).

61 See the contribution of *Edefe Ojomo*, "Fostering Regional Health Governance in West Africa: The Role of the WAHO" in this volume.

62 WAHO Director-General also acts as Chairman of the Governing Board of the ECOWAS RCDC. For instance, see WAHO, "Prof Nasidi heads ECOWAS Centre for Disease Control", *Latest News*, available at http://www.wahooas.org/spip.php?article1318&lang=en. Also Federal Ministry of Health of Nigeria, *FG Inaugurates Governing Board of the ECOWAS Regional Centre for Disease Control (RCDC)*, available at http://bit.ly/2l2PuGZ.

63 A director in charge of the AU Commission for Social Affairs declared in March 2016: "We are satisfied with our findings that Nigeria can be able to take on the triple responsibility of running the Nigeria-CDC, the Regional-CDC and African-CDC", see Audu, O, "AU approves Nigeria's Centre for Disease Control as regional hub" (March 13, 2016), *Premium Times*, available at http://bit.ly/1Ufo9jL; see also African Union, "1st Governing Board Meeting of the Africa Center for

What could be the role of WHO in such a process? In spite of its foundation as the "directing and co-ordinating authority on international health work", WHO is (like other intergovernmental organizations) not an independent actor, insofar as it is dependent on finance from Member States, its decision-making processes are based on Member States' positions and it is not a financing institution (as the World Bank is).[64] Its effectiveness depends to a large degree on the cooperation of Member States, which has been rather unstable during recent decades.[65] We have to take into account that global capacities for emergency responses and the attainment of minimum standards in international health care are interdependent. Working to improve health care standards, however, cannot substitute for a system of emergency response (a) because of the different time-horizons of realizing both goals and (b) because of the need to overcome national egoisms in preventing the global spread of diseases.[66]

V All is Well that Ends Well?

Reconsidering the sequence of events around the Ebola outbreak, the sometimes devastating criticisms on the apparently slow reaction of the international community to the West African Ebola outbreak seem to be misleading. In this contribution, it was argued that due to the unprecedented

---

Disease Control and Prevention Endorses Five Regional Collaborating Centers", *Press Release of May 13, 2016*, available at http://bit.ly/2kPo7oo.

64 Taking-up its role as a financing institution, the World Bank launched in May 2016 the Pandemic Emergency Facility as an insurance for poor countries in cases of an pandemic outbreak (providing coverage of about US $500 million), in cooperation with WHO and reinsurance companies. See Tyson, J, "Inside the World Bank's Pandemic Emergency Facility" (May 23, 2016), *Devex Newswire*, available at http://bit.ly/1Rk49pw.

65 Hein, W, "A United Nations Global Health Panel for Global Health Governance: A commentary on Mackey" (2013), 76 *Social Science & Medicine*, 18; Kickbusch, I, Hein, W & Silberschmidt, G, "Addressing Global Health Governance Challenges through a New Mechanism: The Proposal for a Committee C of the World Health Assembly" (2010), 38 *Journal of Law, Medicine & Ethics*, 550.

66 See Global response to health crisis, *A Comparison of Expert Recommendations following the Ebola-Outbreak in West Africa*, above Fn. 5; one of the concluding questions asked by the author (15) is: "Who is WHO? […] It needs to be re-emphasized that WHO consists not only of a group of people at the Geneva headquarters, but also of 194 Member States, 34 board members, 6 Regional and 150 Country offices."

character of this epidemic and the disastrous state of local health systems, it was in fact difficult to anticipate the scale of the outbreak at an early stage, despite MSF's alert that the outbreak could expand (spread over a larger region than earlier Ebola outbreaks, in particular into large cities).

On the other hand, rather early after the declaration of the PHEIC and the UN Security Council meeting, voices appeared – in particular in the US – praising the comprehensive effort to fight the disease, among others in a Fact Sheet by the White House,[67] and the "unprecedented coordination" which succeeded in controlling the outbreak.[68] The CDC commented in a document on the eventual control of the outbreak: "Not only has this epidemic been unprecedented, but so has the public health response launched by CDC and its partners."[69] The 2014 Health Security Report of CDC included no (self-)critical comments concerning the slow start of a strong response to the outbreak in its section on the "2014 Ebola Response".[70] Similarly, WHO statements in 2016 – after the end of the PHEIC had been declared – praised the success of international cooperation. In its updated version (of January 2016), the web page "Ebola Response in Action" takes July 2014 as a starting-point and simply ignores the "lost months" before:

> "Since July 2014 unparalleled progress has been made in establishing systems and tools that allowed us to respond rapidly and effectively. Thanks to the diligence and dedication of tens of thousands of responders, scientists, researchers, developers, volunteers, and manufacturers, we now have diagnostics, a vaccine, registered foreign medical teams, and thousands of trained responders who can rapidly deploy to outbreaks."[71]

There could be a certain risk that political attention to all the recommendations made in response to the Health Crisis will decline again due to the final success of controlling the outbreak – after nearly two years and after

67 The White House. Office of the Press Secretary, *Fact Sheet: U.S. Response to the Ebola Epidemic in West Africa*, September 16, 2014, available at http://bit.ly/2mfkyVx.

68 USAID, "Unprecedented Coordination Helped Turn the Tide of an Unprecedented Outbreak", statement posted by Pendarvis, J, *Impact Blog on Emerging Infectious Diseases*, December 15, 2015, available at http://bit.ly/1Ou0UM0.

69 CDC, *The Road to Zero: CDC's Response to the West African Ebola Epidemic*, 2014-2015, available at http://www.cdc.gov/about/pdf/ebola/ebola-photobook-070915.pdf.

70 CDC, *2014 Health Security Report. 2014 Ebola Response*, July 31, 2015, available at http://www.cdc.gov/about/report/2014/2014-ebola-response.html.

71 WHO, *Ebola Response in Action*, January 2016, available at http://apps.who.int/ebola/our-work/achievements.

more than 10.000 deaths. It would not be the first case of "pandemic fatigue", leading to a loss of momentum, when "the memory of what happened will fade".[72] Nevertheless, for the time being, the global health community continues discussing large number of reviews and critical assessments of the response of the international community to the West African Ebola outbreak presented by the diverse actors in GHG and (quite incompletely) referred to in section III.[73] A certain tendency to focus on "health security" can be observed. In an article on the treatment of health in the 2015 G7 meeting, *Garrett W. Brown* commented "that there has been little movement to rectify the lack of global preparedness since the Ebola outbreak", and criticized that most of the G7 discussions and commitments centered on the Global Health Security agenda.

> "[…] the securitization of health by the G7 might do little to address the key determinants of health that often cause mass scale epidemics, since security approaches often focus on symptoms rather than causes and reduce health system strengthening to issues of containment rather than tackling the root causes of epidemics associated with weak health systems."[74]

Those recommendations, however, require long negotiations and a sustained readiness among high-income countries, which had not been directly affected by the epidemics, to support the Global Public Good of "infectious disease control" through financial support, training and sharing knowledge.

Can we expect that after "learning the lessons" of the human catastrophe of the West African Ebola outbreak a similar event will not occur again? Certainly, the international community has learnt that nature is presenting us with ever new challenges concerning the appearance of pathogens and ways of transmission henceforth unknown. However, the problems of health system development, lack of research and development in the field of most infectious diseases (including anti-microbial resistance) and an extremely unequal access to the benefits of research, are man-made. During the last two decades, they have played an important role in global health discourses but have only led to quite limited achievements. The improvement of emergency mechanisms and emergency funds in response to the Ebola epidemic should be able to strengthen preparedness in the case of

---

72 Dumiak, M, "Push needed for pandemic planning" (2012), 90 *Bulletin of the World Health Organization*, 800 (800 et seq.).

73 See website Think Global Health, above Fn. 5; an even larger list of 45 reviews is published by the WHO, *WHO evaluation department*, available at http://bit.ly/2maJiS9.

74 Brown, G W, "The 2015 G7 summit: A missed opportunity for global health leadership" (2015), *Global policy/Global Leadership Initiative,* June 9, 2015, available at http://bit.ly/2m884lR.

further outbreaks. However, a sustained commitment not only by the epistemic and political community, but also by the larger public is needed to raise sufficient financial means and to reach an equitable distribution of these means to strengthen the foundations of global health.

The Changing Structure of Global Health Governance

Mateja Steinbrück Platise[*]

Abstract

This article examines whether and how certain trends in global health governance, such as privatization, fragmentation and de-formalization, change the governance structure and modify the legal framework in which the right to health is protected. Particular attention is given to the role played by International Organizations, in order to show how a specific nature and functioning of certain organizations has been one of the reasons for failures of global health regulation in addressing global health crises, which prompted structural changes in global health governance.

However, the article also shows that recent structural changes and in particular the emergence of new actors, policies and instruments of global health regulation results in a selective, fragmented and donor-driven regulation, produces structural deficiencies and escapes some of the most essential standards for an effective and legitimate governance. The article therefore analyzes how diverse powers, obligations and responsibilities of the more prominent actors in the health sector relate to each other, and explores both the risks and potentials of the present global health governance.

Thereby, it shows that while International Organizations can indeed be considered as part of the problem that prompted structural changes in global health governance, they can, under certain conditions, also offer a solution to the systemic deficiencies that now arise from the new governance structure. That would require, however, that governance by International Organizations becomes more inclusive in order for them to cope with global health risks in a more effective and legitimate way.

---

* Ph.D (Ljubljana), M.Jur (Oxford); Senior Research Fellow at the Max Planck Institute for Comparative Public Law and International Law. All websites last accessed January 19, 2017.

I Introduction

Some of the recent global health crises, in particular the outbreak of epidemics such as HIV/AIDS, SARS, Ebola and Zika, revealed challenges and limitations in global health regulation and its inability to cope with large-scale risks and global problems that adversely affect health. At the forefront of the critique have been International Organizations (IOs) like the World Health Organization (WHO) and some other UN agencies, which increasingly need to compete with new global governance actors for financial and human resources, expertise and novel regulatory instruments. Many of these new governance actors belong to the private sector or feature public-private partnerships (PPPs), such as The Global Fund to Fight AIDS, Tuberculosis and Malaria (Global Fund).[1] While sociologists, medical experts, political scientists and many other scholars have already addressed the interplay between the changing structure of global health governance, on the one hand, and insufficient protection and promotion of the right to health, on the other hand, legal scholarship still lacks more comprehensive research on that topic.[2]

The present paper therefore aims to contribute to that discussion by examining whether and how certain trends in global health governance, such as privatization, fragmentation and de-formalization, change the governance structure and modify the legal framework in which the right to health is protected. A specific nature and functioning of certain IOs has been one of the reasons for the failures of global health regulation in coping with global risks that adversely affect health and for prompting structural changes in global health governance, but that IOs might also offer a solution to the systemic deficiencies that now arise from the new governance structure.

For the purposes of the present paper, the term "global" health governance is used in order to a) analyze an increase of intergovernmental as well as transnational actors and activities in the health sector, the latter being carried out by civil society and private sector; b) to address an increase of non-formal instruments that these various actors deploy, which generally do not amount to legal instruments that are subject to regulation by inter-

1 For further examples see Section III of this paper.

2 For an analysis of the belayed discussion on the link between health and human rights as well as for an introduction into some fundamental international legal aspects of the right to health see Tobin, J, *The Right to Health in International Law*, 2011.

national or domestic law; and to c) underline interdependence of different legal systems and different governance levels in the health sector.

In order to explore some of the elements of the present global health governance and to examine the role that IOs have played in that respect, Section II examines the structural changes that have occurred in the past decades, the extent to which these changes have been part of broader developments in global governance, and the aspects in which they could have been prompted by the failures of IOs. In Section III, these insights are used to show how new governance actors and their goals lead to an increased contestation of the normative content of the right to health, why competing instruments of the multitude of actors result in selective regulation and structural defects of global health governance, and how diverse powers, obligations and responsibilities of the more prominent actors in the health sector relate to each other, especially those of states and IOs. Section IV aims to address general risks and potentials of the present governance structure, especially the trend of privatization of the health sector,[3] which weakens certain IOs, but also pressures the respective IOs to become more inclusive, thus acting as proper global public institutions that have been given the formal mandate to engage in global health regulation. Section V summarizes some of my main findings.

II The Fall of International Organizations

1 Structural Changes in Global Governance

In recent decades, traditional governance mechanisms of the nation state have lost their dominance as new government arrangements have emerged. The changes in governance have occurred at the local, regional, national, transnational and international levels, and have transformed decision-making, implementation, supervision and enforcement mechanisms. Vertically, an increased shift in the exercise of public authority has first taken place from the nation state to international and supranational organizations, such as the United Nations (UN), the World Trade Organization (WTO) and the

---

3 See also the contribution of *Christian R. Thauer*, "The Governance of Infectious Diseases. An International Relations Perspective" in this volume.

European Union (EU).[4] That shift of governance from the state to international and supranational organizations has been visible in most, if not all policy sectors, but also within particular branches of government, giving rise to global administration[5] and boosting international adjudication.[6]

Somewhat less attention has been given to the increased downward vertical shift of public authority from the national to sub-national and regional levels, resulting in empowerment of regional and local communities. The downward shift has also taken place at the international and supranational level, in that organizations commonly entrust tasks and powers to lower governance levels and rely not merely on states, but also increasingly on regional and local communities to implement and enforce their acts.[7]

The exercise of public authority has also been re-allocated horizontally. The shifts from the legislature to the executive have been prompted in particular by increased international cooperation by states: Since the executive has traditionally represented the state at the international level, the increased exercise of public authority at these governance levels commonly strengthens the executive at the expense of the domestic legislature.[8] More recently, the judiciary has likewise gained a more prominent role vis-à-vis legislature and the executive, especially due to increasing juridification of social relations.[9]

---

4 Sarooshi, D, *International Organizations and their Exercise of Sovereign Powers*, 2005.

5 Kingsbury, B, Krisch, N & Steward, R B, "The Emergence of Global Administrative Law" (2005), 68 *Law and Contemporary Problems*, 15.

6 Bogdandy, A von & Venzke, I, *In Wessen Namen? Internationale Gerichte in Zeiten globalen Regierens*, 2014, Introduction.

7 That shift has been most visible in the European context, where the so-called principle of subsidiarity of the powers exercised by the EU institutions and by the European Court of Human Rights (ECHR), respectively, has found its place in the founding treaties; for the EU, see Article 5(3) of the Treaty on European Union and Protocol No. 2 on the application of the principles of subsidiarity and proportionality; for the ECHR, see Article 1 of Protocol No. 15 amending the Convention on the Protection of Human Rights and Fundamental Freedoms (adopted in 2013, not yet in force); compare also with the West-African regional structures described by the contribution of *Edefe Ojomo*, "Fostering Regional Health Governance in West Africa: The Role of the WAHO" in this volume.

8 See for the critique of that trend Wheatley, S, *The Democratic Legitimacy of International Law*, 2010, 23-31.

9 For identifying the trend by a comparative analysis, see Tate, C N & Vallinder, T, *The Global Expansion of Judicial Power*, 1995.

Particular attention in the present paper is given to the re-allocation of the exercise of public authority away from public institutions towards semi-public and private entities. As decision-making, implementation, supervision and enforcement become more complex and require ever greater expertise, the reasons of efficiency and effectiveness demand greater specialization and delegation of particular tasks to expert bodies, market agents and other agencies of public-private and private character. In fact, the tendency towards functional specialization because of the need for technical expertise has been seen as one of the main reasons for the proliferation of governance actors on national and international levels.[10]

Thus, an increasing number of states as well as international and supranational organizations establish PPPs with private actors, thereby allowing such actors to take part in the exercise of public authority in the respective policy field. Examples include agencies regulating areas as diverse as environmental protection, social security, telecommunication and security.[11] Most examples of PPPs, however, are found in the health sector and, more specifically, in the context of regulating the production of drugs, where partnerships have been established with the pharmaceutical industry.[12]

Some critics have termed that phenomenon as "the flight from international governmental organizations"[13] and warned against global governance being increasingly entrusted to the private sector, or to informal international or transnational institutions, whose regulation escapes some of the

10 Wessel, R A & Wouters, J, "The Phenomenon of Multilevel Regulations: Interactions between Global, EU and National Regulatory Spheres" (2007), 4 *International Organizations Law Review*, 257; for the critique of that shift see Koskenniemi, M, "The Fate of Public International Law: Between Technique and Politics" (2007), 70 *The Modern Law Review*, 1.

11 Dickinson, L A, "Public Law Values in a Privatised World" (2006), 31 *The Yale Journal of International Law*, 367; for the specific features of that trend in the developing countries see Leadership and Social Transformation in the Public Sector, *Moving from Challenges to Solutions, Public Administration, the United Nations*, 2003.

12 Benvenisti, E, *The Law of Global Governance*, 2014, 55; for a critical assessment of that trend see also Börzel, T A & Risse, T, "Public-Private Partnerships: Effective and Legitimate Tools of International Governance?" in Grande, E & Pauly, L W (eds.), *Complex Sovereignty. Reconstituting Political Authority in the Twenty-First Century*, 2005, 195.

13 Benvenisti, *The Law of Global Governance*, above Fn. 12, 37 et seqq.

most essential standards for a legitimate governing, including certain basic human rights and the rule of law standards.[14]

2 The Specific Nature of Global Health Governance

While privatization of governance can be analyzed as a general trend that transcends individual states, institutions, and policy areas, there is scarcely any other field where the new governance forms have gained comparable significance as in the public health sector.[15] One important reason for that tendency has been subscribed to the traditional engagement of non-state actors in health affairs, ranging from private physicians, insurances, pharmaceutical companies, to church-related organizations, charity and relief organizations like the Red Cross Federation.[16]

Many actors of global health governance are thus rooted in the private sector, including professional associations, such as Médecins Sans Frontières (MSF), PPPs, such as the International Conference on the Harmonisation of Technical Requirements for Registration of Pharmaceuticals for Human Use (ICH), or the Global Fund as well as certain global human rights organizations, such as Amnesty International. That strong presence of private actors in health affairs might be closely related to the ethical pressure that underlies the concern for ill and vulnerable people, which in the last decades gained prominence in light of the growing awareness of widespread poverty-related diseases.[17] On the other hand, the trend of privatization has been subject to market forces, including the interests of pharmaceutical companies and healthcare providers in selling their products and services, thereby pursuing their own business models.

14 Pauwelyn, J, Wessel, R A & Wouters, J, "When Structures Become Shackles: Stagnation and Dynamics in International Law" (2014), 25 *European Journal of International Law*, 733 (752).

15 Hein, W & Kohlmorgen, L, "Global Health Governance: Conflicts on Global Social Rights" (2008), 8 *Global Social Policy*, 80 (84).

16 Kohlmorgen, L, "International Organisations and Global Health Governance. The Role of the World Health Organization, World Bank and UNAIDS" in Hein, W, Bartsch, S & Kohlmorgen, L (eds.), *Global Health Governance and the Fight Against HIV/AIDS*, 2007, 119.

17 For the historical account of that feature see Riedel, E, "The Human Right to Health – Conceptual Foundations" in Clapham, A (ed.), *Realising the Right to Health*, 2009, in particular at 21.

The health sector has been marked in a specific way by the four global crises: Climate change as well as economic, food and epidemic crises have all adversely affected health and thereby revealed limitations in global health regulation to cope with large-scale political, economic and environmental problems. For example, the outbreak of pandemic influenza A (H1N1) led the WHO to acknowledge the lack of a "global framework" that would ensure equitable access to the influenza vaccines.[18] The global economic crisis has reportedly undermined efforts to achieve the Millennium Development Goals (MDGs), most of which concern health problems or address policy areas affecting health.[19] Thereby, the four crises exposed the economic, social and environmental determinants of health and showed that global health regulation required a stronger cross-sectoral approach.[20]

However, not only socio-economic factors have become acknowledged as some of the determinants of health. Health has also become, in turn, defined as one of determinants of social and economic development.[21] That new understanding of health can be identified in particular in more recent policies aiming at poverty reduction, whose agendas increasingly integrate strategies for combating infectious diseases that are commonly referred to as "diseases of the poor".[22] Moreover, the normative content of the right to health seems to have overstepped the confines of the economic and social rights, and has become part of a more general human rights discourse, including the civil and political rights discourse.[23]

---

18 Fidler, D P, "Negotiating Equitable Access to Influenza Vaccines: Global Health Diplomacy and the Controversies Surrounding Avian Influenza H5N1 and Pandemic Influenza H1N1" (2010), 7 *PLoS Medicine*, 1.

19 Benatar, S R, Gill, S & Bakker, I, "Global Health and the Economic Crisis" (2011), 101 *American Journal of Public Health*, 646; see also for the impact of financial crises Ruckert, A & Labonté, R, "The financial crisis and global health: the International Monetary Fund's (IMF) policy response" (2013), 28 *Health Promotion International*, 357 (357), with further references.

20 For the impact of the climate change, see Luber, G & Lemery, J, *Global Climate Change and Human Health: From Science to Practice*, 2015.

21 See also the contribution of *Michael Marx*, "Ebola Epidemic 2014-2015: Taking Control or Being Trapped in the Logic of Failure – What Lessons Can Be Learned?" in this volume.

22 See for example WHO, *Global Report for Research on Infectious Diseases of Poverty*, 2012.

23 That development has been importantly influenced by the case law of the ECHR on health-related issues; see Council of Europe, *Thematic Report on Health-related issues in the case law of the European Court of Human Rights*, 2015.

Most importantly, health risks in the form of the global spread of infectious diseases, but also health threats in the area of biological terrorism, have resulted in global health being defined also in terms of national and security interests. That insight has pushed health issues up to the level of high politics, foreign policy goals and even the UN Security Council agenda.[24] Such broader understanding of the notion of health and its implications for national and global security requires a new legal framework, which gives rise to new global health actors and instruments, including those of the UN Security Council.[25] Quite tellingly, such a paradigmatic turn in conceptualizing global health governance has been considered in political science as nothing less than "a political revolution".[26]

3 The Flaws of International Organizations in the Health Sector

As the global crises exposed a too narrow approach in seeking to secure global health, they have also revealed the inability of IOs and the WHO in particular to respond adequately to global health threats, which required a more holistic approach and development of strategies that would reach far beyond the health sector. The lack of flexibility to react to the new challenges of globalization and undergo necessary reforms particularly hampered the WHO in retaining the central role in securing global health. Its decline can be subscribed to factors internal as well as external to the organization and relate, *inter alia*, to the WTO's institutional setting, the growing influence of non-state actors as well as other UN agencies in the

---

24 The UN Security Council took up for the first time the HIV/AIDS issue in 2000, when it adopted a resolution recognizing the potential of the epidemic, if unchecked, to pose a risk to stability and security; see Resolution 1308 (2000) on the Responsibility of the Security Council in the Maintenance of International Peace and Security: HIV/AIDS and International Peace-keeping Operations, S/RES/1308 (2000); for the health securitization debate see also the contributions of *Robert Frau*, "Combining the WHO's International Health Regulations (2005) with the UN Security Council's Powers: Does it Make Sense for Health Governance?" and *Ilja Richard Pavone*, "Ebola and Securitization of Health: UN Security Council Resolution 2177/2014 and its Limits" in this volume.

25 For the distinction between high and low politics in political science see for example Jackson, R H & Sørensen, G, *Introduction to International Relations: Theories and Approaches*, 6th edition, 2015, 105.

26 Kickbusch, I & Reddy, K S, "Global health governance – the next political revolution" (2015), 129 *Public Health*, 840 (840 et seq.).

health sector and the interest of certain countries to shift health regulation towards other actors.[27]

There are thus several more or less related reasons for the failures of IOs in governing global health. Some reasons seem to be organization-specific and relate to the mandate and management of the respective IOs, in particular some UN organizations, which rely on very formalized decision-making processes and procedures involving all Member States. Their regulation tends to be highly bureaucratic and slow, complicated, and not best suited to react effectively to crises that demand swift response.[28] The proposals to reform their mandates, structure and functions themselves initiate lengthy and complex decision-making processes, that may be protracted by the IO's inertia as well as by the Member States themselves.[29]

In addition, by ensuring a voice and a vote to all Member States, IOs with a universal membership function to a large extent on behalf of the interests of developing countries, which do not always reflect the interests of industrialized countries.[30] The latter are, however, likely to be the main contributors or donors to the IO's budget, as the examples of the WHO and some other universal IOs show. That asymmetry prompted some of the powerful states to pursue their agendas rather within the IOs such as the World Bank, where higher financial contributions provide for greater voting powers.[31]

The interest of powerful actors in retaining control over the expenditure has also manifested itself in the shift from IOs towards the private sector. Thus, while the WHO has been severely obstructed by a freeze of contributions to its budgets,[32] an increased number of PPPs in the field of global

---

27 Lidén, J, "The World Health Organization and Global Health Governance: post-1990" (2014), 128 *Public Health*, 141.

28 These features have been identified as one of the main reasons for certain states to favor informal cooperation to cooperation within International Organizations; see for example Pauwelyn, Wessel & Wouters, "When Structures Become Shackles", above Fn. 14, 25 et seqq.

29 Kickbusch & Reddy, "Global health governance", above Fn. 26, 838.

30 Benvenisti, E & Downs, G W, "The Empire's New Clothes: Political Economy and the Fragmentation of International Law" (2007), 60 *Stanford Law Review*, 595.

31 The World Bank has however also been subject to criticism due to financial mismanagement; see for example Garret, L, "The Challenge of Global Health" (2007), 86 *Foreign Affairs*, 14.

32 Brown, T M, Cueto, M & Fee, E, "The World Health Organization and the Transition from 'International' to 'Global' Health" in Bashford, A (ed.), *Medicine at the Border: Disease, Globalisation and Security*, 2014, 76.

health governance evidences the rise in financial and other resources given at disposal to the private sector. A telling example is the Global Fund, which was established in 2002 in close collaboration with the G8 countries. While it has been labelled as a PPP, its financial structure discloses that the majority of its funds are provided by states, making it function as a multilateral funding mechanism rather than a semi-private actor.[33]

The comparison in the functioning and influence between some social policy oriented IOs such as the WHO, on the one hand, and PPPs, private actors, but also some governmental global economic institutions, on the other hand, also suggests that the rise of global economy increases competition in regulation among various actors in the field of global health and advances those actors whose power is based on financial resources. Thus, among IOs, the World Bank has become almost undisputedly the most important IO of global health governance, exercising its public authority by lending and granting activities and winning the status of being the greatest single donor in the field of health.[34] In the private sector, the lead has been taken over by financially heavily buttressed philanthropic foundations such as the Bill and Melinda Gates Foundation, which has been reported as becoming one of the most prominent funders in promoting global health.[35]

But global health governance has not been restructured merely under the demands of the global market. Its development seems to reflect also the need for new governance modes and instruments, which have been promoted as more flexible, context-oriented and inclusive, and therefore more effective in attaining global health than those traditionally employed by IOs. That assumption will be examined in the following section.

---

33 For the latest figures see Pledges and Contributions, available at www.theglobalfund.org/en/financials/.

34 The World Bank has been considered as one of the most powerful actors in global health governance according to different indicators; compare Abasi, K, "The World Bank and World Health: Changing Sides" (1999), 318 *British Medical Journal*, 865; Thomas, C & Weber, M, "The Politics of Global Health Governance: Whatever Happened to Health for All by the Year 2000?" (2004), 10 *Global Governance*, 187; Ruger, J P, "The Changing Role of the World Bank in Global Health" (2005), 95 *Am J Public Health*, 50.

35 Dodgson, R, Lee, K & Drager, N, "Global Health Governance, A Conceptual Review" (2002), *Discussion Paper No. 1 Department of Health & Development WHO*, 22.

III The New Legal and Political Architecture

1 New Actors, Instruments and Policies

The current structure of global health governance demonstrates an increase in the quantity and diversity of actors engaged in global health issues and manifests the preference for private actors established under domestic private law and for informal instruments of regulation, which escape the traditional public law domain. However these two phenomena are only partly related. The present section will first address the relationship between the emergence of new actors and new types of regulatory instruments that they employ in pursuing their particular policies. Afterwards, the new regulatory instruments that are not necessarily adopted by these new actors, but by traditional actors that have changed their governance mode will be examined.

New actors in the field of health governance include a variety of civil society organizations, ranging from private foundations and professional associations to business actors such as multinational corporations. Some of the larger civil society organizations, such as Oxfam and MSF, have gained a more prominent role since the 90's, by campaigning for social rights in general and for global health in particular. They are using a wide variety of instruments to co-determine the regulation of public health, including lobbying, issuing recommendations, or organizing protests. Their political weight can be well illustrated by the Nobel Peace Prize that was awarded to the MSF in 1999.

Furthermore, large foundations such as the Gates Foundation, the Rockefeller Foundation and the Ford Foundation play an ever more important role, based primarily on their extensive resource-based power.[36] Their main regulatory instrument is their funding activity, which enables them to co-determine the health policies that shall be fostered, the people that shall be subject to health care programs and other goals of health governance. The scope and relevance of their instruments transpires from the

36 For a critical assessment of that trend see Stuckler, D, Basu S & McKee, M, "Global Health Philanthropy and Institutional Relationships: How Should Conflicts of Interest Be Addressed?" (2011), 8 *PLoS Medicine*, 1.

reports stating that today national and global health programs are becoming largely funded by private actors.[37]

Certain private business actors likewise continue to gain importance in the field, especially transnational pharmaceutical companies from some of the most developed countries, who have managed to develop most PPPs with states.[38] For example, the ICH was established in 1991 by drug regulatory authorities from the US, the EU and Japan, as well as by associations of domestic pharmaceutical companies from these countries, with the aim to harmonize technical requirements for ensuring the quality, efficacy and safety of drugs. Their main regulatory instruments are the issued guidelines, which have become *de facto* global standards, since they have been adopted by its members as well as by non-member countries and companies.[39]

The establishment of the Global Fund, which was inspired by the G-8 summit in 2000, similarly reveals the emergence of new actors conceived by cooperation of states with private actors. Its structure aims at greater inclusiveness of the private sector and provides for the main organ of the Fund (the Foundation Board) to consist of seven representatives from donor states, seven from developing states and five members representing civil society organizations and the private sector. The primary instrument used by the Fund is disbursement of funds, which is regulated by individual grant agreements implementing international law and the Trade-Related Aspects of Intellectual Property Rights (TRIPs) in particular. Such instruments amount to very effective regulatory mechanisms and enable business actors to significantly shape the policies concerning public health.[40]

However, despite such a shift from public to private forums, IOs remain among the central actors of the new legal and political architecture, although they have been affected by structural changes in global governance in several ways. Universal IOs, such as the UN, the WHO, the World Bank, the International Labour Organization (ILO), the United Nations Children's

---

37 Buissonniere, M, "The New Realities of Global Health: Dynamics and Obstacles" in Carbonnier, G (ed.), *Aid, Emerging Economies and Global Policies*, 2012, 60.

38 Benvenisti, *The Law of Global Governance*, above Fn. 12, 53.

39 Berman, A, "Informal International Lawmaking in Medical Products" in Berman, A, Duquet, S & Pauwelyn, J et al. (eds.), *Informal International Law-Making: Case Studies*, 2012, 353.

40 For the critique of that development see Berman, A, "The Role of Domestic Administrative Law in the Accountability of IN-LAW: The Case of the ICH" in Pauwelyn, J, Wessel, R & Wouters, J (eds.), *Informal International Lawmaking*, 2012, 468.

Emergency Fund (UNICEF) and the WTO, as well as regional IOs, such as the Organization for Economic Cooperation and Development (OECD), the EU, the African Union and the Association of Southeast Asian Nations (ASEAN), are becoming increasingly prominent as venues for negotiation and coordination among the multiple global health governance actors. Many of them cooperate with a wide range of stakeholders, securing their voice in the IO's own decision-making processes and procedures. The establishment of the Joint United Nations Program on HIV/AIDS (UNAIDS) may serve as a prime example for such negotiation and coordination efforts at the international level, whereas the EU boosts a number of mechanisms for ensuring inclusive health governance at a regional level.[41] Moreover, some IOs rely on particularly effective instruments of regulation, with the World Bank providing an example of applying conditionality of structural adjustment policies as a means of fostering the IO's goals in the field of public health.[42]

The new instruments and modes of governance are therefore also used by IOs and states in particular. Their shift towards public-private networks and their concessions to the private sector suggests that certain states increasingly favor informal governmental regulation. First, they prefer to transfer the regulation on less formal international and transnational institutions, and second, they prefer informal and private instruments to broad, integrative international agreements.[43] That tendency has been identified especially with the most developed states, some of which explicitly adhered to the strategy of adopting informal non-binding instruments as a matter of their national policy.[44] While that shift is part of a general trend in global

---

41 For the EU strategy see Communication from the Commission to the Council, the European Parliament, the European Economic and Social Committee and the Committee of the Regions, *The EU Role in Global Health*, COM(2010)128 final, under 4.1; for a comparative account see Lamy, M & Hong, P K, "Southeast Asian cooperation in health: A comparative perspective on regional health governance in ASEAN and the EU" (2012), 10 *Asia Europe Journal*, 233.

42 See however for controversies surrounding the bank's structural adjustment programs in Breman, A & Shelton, C, "Structural Adjustment Programs and Health" in Kawachi, I & Wamala, S (eds.), *Globalisation and Health*, 2007, 219.

43 For the controversial legal nature of these instruments see Ruiter, D W P & Wessel, R, "The Legal Nature of Informal International Law: A Legal Theoretical Exercise" in Pauwelyn, J, Wessel, R & Wouters, J (eds.), *Informal International Lawmaking*, 2012, 162.

44 For examples of national policy statements and their comparative analysis see Benvenisti, *The Law of Global Governance*, above Fn. 12, 37 et seqq.

governance, it is particularly evident in the field of health regulation.[45] Ever since the most developed states identified global health risks as their own national security risks, they increasingly engage in so-called strategic health diplomacy and afford development assistance.[46] The US President's Emergency Plan for AIDS Relief (PEPFAR), launched in 2004, thereby counts among the most noted foreign aid programs and has made the US one of the biggest donor states.[47]

2 Structural Deficits in Ensuring the Right to Health

The developments discussed above manifest the trend of privatization of health governance, which may lead to the weakening of IOs and thus to a decline of those global public institutions that have been given the formal mandate to engage in global health regulation. While more general concerns about the legitimacy of the present system are discussed in Section IV, the present section seeks to show, first, that those who are ultimately affected by the present trends are developing countries and other weaker global actors, such as less organized civil society groups.[48] That deprivation follows in particular from the shifting of the forums of decision-making from traditional universal IOs, in which developing countries seek to minimize the power disparities, to the forums, in which developing countries have less of a voice and a vote – if they can participate in them at all. Less formal structures, processes and forums may likewise affect those non-profit civil society organizations, whose inclusion into the decision-making procedures is put at the discretion of the more powerful actors, thus those actors who

---

45 Examples include also cooperation between national governments, International Organizations and private actors, such as the Global Alliance for Vaccines and Immunisation (GAVI), established in Davos in 2000.

46 Brown, M D, Mackey, T K & Shapiro, C N et al., "Bridging Public Health and Foreign Affairs: The Tradecraft of Global Health Diplomacy and the Role of Health Attachés" (2014), 3 *Science and Diplomacy*, available at http://bit.ly/213lhas.

47 Fidler, D P, "The Challenges of Global Health Governance", (2010) *Council on Foreign Relations, International Institutions and Global Governance Program*, 10.

48 On the problem of underrepresented groups and individuals in global governance see Steward, R B, "Remedying Disregard in Global Regulatory Governance: Accountability, Participation and Responsiveness" (2014), 108 *American Journal of International Law*, 211.

might least be interested in the participation of the weaker actors in the global governance structures. Circumvention of some of the traditional IOs can therefore result in insulation of weaker actors, in particular developing countries and their populations – indeed those who are suffering most from poor health standards.

Second, the functioning of some of the present actors and instruments results in a donor-driven development, as most technical assistance, grants and loans that are provided for the health sector need to comply with donors' priorities, goals, values and policies, and not with those of the receiving countries or communities.[49] Since donor funding is often determined by donors' preferences, which tend to be disease- and program-specific, it may fail to address broader socio-economic determinants of health or weak institutional capacity in the country.[50] At the same time, these trends shift the focus of global health governance from primary health care to fighting specific diseases, in particular infectious diseases that have been considered by the powerful countries as a risk to the health of their own population.[51] That leads towards reducing the protection of the right to health as a universal right to the fighting of infectious diseases, or, even narrowly, towards the "fighting the diseases of the poor".[52]

Third, the multiplication of actors, instruments and policies can lead to fragmentation in global health governance, lacking general and universal norms, effective coordinating actors and comprehensive solutions addressing the overall health standard in countries. Instead, the present system faces overlapping mandates, competition and duplication of health activities, conflicting standards on the global and national level, and forces recipient

49 Certain PEPFAR funding conditions have even been found by the US Supreme Court to be contrary the US Constitution; see *Agency for International Development et al. v Alliance for Open Society International, Inc, et al.* 570 U. S. (2013).

50 Walt, G & Buse, G, "Global Cooperation in International Public Health" in Merson, M, Black, R & Mills, A (eds.), *International Public Health: Diseases, Programmes, Systems and Policies*, 2nd edition, 2006, 649.

51 For an example as to how infectious diseases are perceived as a national security threat to a powerful state see the 1992 Report of US Institute of Medicine "Emerging Infections: Microbial Threads to Health in the United States", cited in Feldbaum, H, *US Global Health and National Security Policy, A Report of the CSIS Global Health Policy Center*, 2009.

52 See also Section II.2.

countries and actors to struggle with demands of multiple donors.[53] Ultimately, the present system of global health governance risks becoming ineffective, being impaired by diverging norms and conflicting goals.

3 Competing Goals, Shared Responsibilities

The multiple actors that take part in global health governance are driven by diverse interests, which these actors seek to translate into the normative framework of public health regulation. Particular actors may thereby pursue several, more or less interdependent goals, which may possibly complement or conflict with the interests of other actors. For example, states and certain IOs can regulate the health sector *inter alia* with human rights objectives, recognizing the right to health as one of the fundamental human rights and a common public good. Under this normative framework, they meet the goals pursued by a number of civil society organizations, such as human rights Non-Governmental Organizations (NGOs), charity and humanitarian relief organizations.

But states, IOs and other non-state actors pursue other goals as well. Once health has become recognized as a determinant for economic and social development, states started to protect health more distinctively with the goal of reaching social and political stability and have focused on eradication of poverty-related diseases. Moreover, when the right to health became defined as a determinant for global economy and for fully functioning global markets, the focus was further modified towards the prevention of international spread of infectious diseases.[54] Under the global economy paradigm, the goals of states, especially those of the most powerful ones, can meet the goals of other powerful global economic actors, including certain international economic IOs, such as the WTO, and transnational corporations, such as pharmaceutical companies, that seek to secure their profits by selling drugs. However, since a pricey medicine inhibits accessibility to that medicine, these goals often conflict with the goal of securing health for all

53 Brugha, R, Donoghue, M & Starling, M et al., "The Global Fund: Managing Great Expectations" (2004), 364 *Lancet*, 95.

54 The 2005 WHO International Health Regulations thus provide in Article 2 (Purpose and scope): "The purpose and scope of these Regulations are to prevent, protect against, control and provide a public health response to the international spread of disease in ways that are commensurate with and restricted to public health risks, and which avoid unnecessary interference with international traffic and trade."

and undermine the right to health as a universal human right, as promoted by some other actors.

In addition to economic interests, security interests also play a role in defining the goals of global health governance actors. Thus, in the most recent and comprehensive understanding, global health has been considered as being a matter of national and international security. The recent global health challenges, posed by epidemics such as HIV/AIDS, SARS, Ebola and Zika, that have arisen in developing countries and speedily spread in developed countries, lead to infectious diseases being defined by developed states and some IOs as a new threat to international peace and security. That understanding has further modified the normative framework under which global health is regulated and triggered the powers of the UN Security Council, which for the first time in history acted under Article 39 of the UN Charter in order to promote and protect the right to health.[55]

The diversity of goals pursued in global health governance and multiplicity of actors operating in this field thereby produce continuous contestations as to how the right to health is to be understood, which values it ultimately protects, how it should be regulated and the goals of which actors should be given priority in the global regulation.[56] The above discussion suggests that states have the capacity to endorse the widest range of goals, values and purposes implied in the right to health, while non-state actors, including IOs, commonly pursue only specific goals. That state capacity to entertain a wide range of social goals and values is based on the state's general competence in regulating social relations and on its fundamental function to govern different interests and values. The distinctive character of the states vis-à-vis non-state actors such as IOs, which function according to the so-called principle of specialization, was well expressed by the International Court of Justice (ICJ) in the WHO Advisory Opinion by the statement that "[u]nlike states, which have a general competence to act, an International Organization can only act where it has been entrusted by the states with the power to act".[57]

55 UN Security Council Resolution 2177(2014); for more details see the contribution of *Robert Frau*, "Combining the WHO's International Health Regulations (2005) with the UN Security Council's Powers: Does it Make Sense for Health Governance?" in this volume.

56 See the contribution of *A. Katarina Weilert*, "The Right to Health in International Law – Normative Foundations and Doctrinal Flaws" in this volume.

57 ICJ Reports, *The Legality of the Use by a State of Nuclear Weapons in Armed Conflict*, 1996, 78-89, para. 25.

Moreover, the state is also the actor who carries the primary obligation to promote and protect the right to health, being bound by human rights treaties and customary international law. Thus, every state is bound by at least one treaty containing a provision on the right to health, and is subject to customary human rights norms, including Article 25 of the Universal Declaration of Human Rights.[58] That primary obligation of the state continues even when the state entrusts non-state actors with the mandate to act in the relevant field, as analyzed in the first sections of this paper. Therefore, despite such re-allocation of the exercise of public authority, the state does not escape its obligations under international law but remains bound by them, including by its obligations relating to the right to health.[59]

The obligations of non-state actors in the health sector, in particular those of IOs and PPPs, are therefore subsidiary to the state obligations under international law.[60] As regards private actors such as companies and NGOs, on the other hand, there are at present no binding rules governing their obligations under international law.[61] In that case, the applicable obligations under international law are merely those of the state and involve state duty to protect against abuses of human rights by third parties.[62] The obligations of non-state actors are thus defined in relation to the scope of the state's powers, competences and limits to promote and protect the right to health, and in relation to the scope of transfer of such powers to other actors, including IOs.[63]

---

58 Marks, S P, "The Emergence and Scope of the Human Right to Health" in Zuniga, J M, Marks, S P & Gostin, L O, *Advancing the Human Right to Health*, 2013, 2 (20).

59 See in that respect Article 61 of the UN ILC Draft Articles on the Responsibility of International Organizations, in particular the references to the case law of the ECHR; Report of the International Law Commission, 63rd Session, April 26 - June 3 and July 4 - August 12, 2011 GAOR 66th Session, Suppl. No. 10 (A/66/10 and Add. 1).

60 For the obligations of these actors and their relationships see Clarke, L, *Public-Private Partnerships and Responsibility under International Law. A Global Health Perspective*, 2014.

61 Alston, P (ed.), *Non-State Actors and Human Rights*, 2005.

62 See, however Guiding Principles on Business and Human Rights, Implementing the United Nations "Protect, Respect and Remedy" Framework; Ruggie, J, Special Representative of the Secretary-General Human Rights Council, UN Doc A/HRC/17/31 (2011).

63 For implied powers, see the Reparations for Injuries Suffered In the Service of the United Nations, Advisory Opinion, ICJ Reports (1949), (at 182-183): "Under International law, the Organization must be deemed to have those powers, which

The obligations of IOs – be they in the health sector or any other policy field – thus necessarily depend on the nature and scope of the mandate, powers and competences of each particular IO, and are to be determined in accordance with the principle of specialty and subsidiarity.[64] Consequently, the state cannot escape its obligations relating to the right to health by delegating tasks to IOs or other non-state actors.[65] However, IOs are also themselves bound to promote and protect public health to the extent provided for by their mandate, the rules of the IO, and other applicable norms and thus share with states the responsibilities in the health sector.[66]

In that context, it is important to note that regulatory instruments adopted by an IO, even if non-binding vis-à-vis its members, may have binding effect within the IO. For example, the standards and regulations on health and safety adopted by the International Atomic Energy Agency (IAEA) are recommendations vis-à-vis the members. Under the Agency's Statute, however, they are binding with regard to its own operations.[67] In the next section, some of the features of the emerging normative framework under which IOs may, and should, participate in global health governance will be sketched.

IV The Rise of International Organizations?

1 Organizations as Public Forums

If the potential of the state rests in its general competence to regulate social relations in the country and to manage diverse interests, goals and values of

---

though not expressly provided for in the Charter, are conferred upon it by necessary implication as being essential to the performance of its duties."

64 For the principle of subsidiarity see Feichtner, I, "Subsidiarity" in Wolfrum, R (ed.), *The Max Planck Encyclopedia of Public International Law*, 2007, available at http://opil.ouplaw.com/home/EPIL.

65 See also Benvenisti, E, "Sovereigns as Trustees of Humanity: On the Accountability of States to Foreign Stakeholders" (2013), 107 *The American Journal of International Law*, 295.

66 On the exercise of public powers by international institutions see Bogdandy A von, Wolfrum, R & Bernstorff, J von et al. (eds.), *The Exercise of Public Authority by International Institutions: Advancing International Institutional Law*, 2009.

67 Schermers, H G & Blokker, N M, *International Institutional Law*, 5th edition, 2011, 766, 780 and 792.

the various *national* actors, the potential of IOs seems to lay in their potential to host diverse *global* actors, serving them as a public forum for discourse and organization, by giving them a formal voice, or in the case of membership even a vote, at the international level. With the multiplication of actors in global health governance, diversification of the goals and purposes pursued in the name of the right to health, and the more complex and competitive environment in which these actors operate, IOs become prominent as possible venues for inclusion, contestation, negotiation and co-operation. In that capacity, they can offer an important counterpart to the regulation of the health sector by the global market and can moderate the privatization of global health governance, in particular by including private actors into the decision-making processes and procedures of particular IOs.[68] On the other hand, private actors, once participating in the decision-making structures of an IO as a public forum, are not subjected anymore merely to market competition, but also to deliberative processes and normative constrains of legitimate exercise of public authority by the respective IO.

In that respect, the WHO as a public health IO has never been more important. Having been confronted with the loss of its significance, in particular in relation to some new actors such as the Global Fund and PEPFAR, the WHO started to engage itself in forms of hybrid regulation and cooperation with private actors, for example by launching its own HIV/AIDS strategy, which is defined as a movement initiated and coordinated by the WHO, in cooperation with national authorities, UN agencies, multilateral agencies, foundations, non-governmental, religious and community organizations, private sector, labor unions and people living with HIV/AIDS.[69]

An even clearer attempt to coordinate fragmented activities and to embrace new forms of governance may be found in the establishment of the UNAIDS, which has been set up by the UN and its eleven agencies, including the WHO, the World Bank and the United Nations Development Program (UNDP), with an aim to coordinate the response of the UN system to the HIV/AIDS epidemic. Besides these IOs, delegates of 22 governments

---

68 For the initiatives taken in this respect by the WTO see Hein & Kohlmorgen, "Global Health Governance", above Fn. 15, 97.

69 For the so-called 3 by 5 Initiative see WHO, *Treating 3 Million by 2005, Making it Happen, The WHO Strategy*, 2003.

from all geographic regions and five NGOs (including associations of people living with HIV) are members of the governing body of the UNAIDS.[70] Due to its coordinating function and the inclusion of civil society organizations, UNAIDS is often seen as an example for a promising UN reform that could minimize ineffectiveness and duplication of structures in global health governance.[71]

Other IOs, whose core mandate is not to promote global health but other objectives, have also adapted themselves to the emergence of new actors, powers and structures in the field of global health governance. The World Bank, which has been charged with global economic development and only indirectly with social rights, has been at the forefront of promoting PPPs, for example by conditioning the financing of health services with the inclusion of private actors into public health structures.[72] Similarly, the WTO's objective has been to regulate and facilitate world trade, rather than global welfare, and yet, free trade has been promoted on the assumption that expanding trade has a generally positive impact on all participants. The preamble of the Agreement Establishing the World Trade Organization thus refers to the goals supporting development and improving standards of living.[73] The WTO has accordingly responded and adapted itself to the new governance actors, and developed a number of mechanisms for inclusion of and interaction with these actors, including with civil society groups.[74]

---

70 For its coordinating function, see Article 1 (Objectives) and Article 2 (Functions) of the WHO.

71 See, however, for a skeptical view Bartsch, S, "The Global Fund to Fight AIDS, Tuberculosis and Malaria" in Hein, W, Bartsch, S & Kohlmorgen, L (eds.), *Global Health Governance and the Fight Against HIV/AIDS*, 2007, 146.

72 World Bank Group, *Strategic Framework for Mainstreaming Citizen Engagement in World Bank Group Operations*, 2014.

73 The first paragraph of the Preamble states, *inter alia*: "The Parties to this Agreement, recognizing that their relations in the field of trade and economic endeavor should be conducted with a view to raising standards of living, ensuring full employment and a large and steadily growing volume of real income and effective demand, and expanding the production of and trade in goods and services, […]."

74 For the variety of mechanisms see Grasstek, C van, *The History and Future of the World Trade Organization (WTO)*, 2013, 180 et seqq.

2 International Organizations as Autonomous Actors

While IOs can play an important role in serving as public forums to other actors operating in the field of global health, they function also as autonomous actors and can be charged with promoting health in their own right, as noted in Section III.3. In that respect, IOs function also as independent international bureaucracies, pursuing their own goals, policies and interests, which is particularly evident in the organs and bodies of IOs not composed of state officials, but organization's members of staff.[75]

For example, the WHO was established as a classical intergovernmental IO with states as its members, all of them being represented in the World Health Assembly and 34 of them being represented also in the Executive Board. In that regard, the WHO functions as a forum for intergovernmental discourse and cooperation. Yet, the WHO's Secretariat can be considered as enjoying a semi-autonomous status, being actively engaged in shaping the WHO's strategies, standards and policies.[76] Similarly, the World Bank cannot be described merely as a venue for hosting a discourse among states, as it is functioning as a development bank, aiming at the fight against poverty in poor countries. Capital contribution and shares of course give economically stronger countries greater voting power; nevertheless, the bank's overall decision-making processes and procedures, its internal structure and its mandate to provide for financial resources grant the bank an autonomous position, distinct from the legal and economic position of any particular Member State.

Due to their relatively autonomous position in relation to their Member States, IOs are capable of possessing their own legal personality under international and national law and can acquire rights and obligations of their own, independent from the rights and obligations of their members. They can also institute legal proceedings against other actors, negotiate and conclude international agreements in their own name, or become members of other IOs.[77] IOs can also partner with the private sector in their own right, the way the WHO, World Bank and UNAIDS became non-voting members of the hybrid Global Fund.

---

75 Venzke, I, "International Bureaucracies from a Political Science Perspective – Agency, Authority and International Institutional Law" (2008), 9 *German Law Journal*, 1401, in particular 1410 et seqq.

76 See also the contribution of *Pedro A. Villarreal*, "The World Health Organization's Governance Framework in Disease Outbreaks: A Legal Perspective" in this volume.

77 Brownlie, I, *Principles of Public International Law*, 6th edition, 2003, 57.

As autonomous actors, IOs are obliged to protect and promote the right to health in their own right and as their own obligation. That obligation is to be carried out in accordance with their mandate, powers and competences, and goes beyond providing a mere forum for inclusion, coordination and contestation by other actors, and implies – depending on the mandate – an active support of, and participation in, decision-making, implementation, dispute settlement or even enforcement of global health standards. IOs, although serving a subsidiary role in promoting and protecting the right to health, represent the community of their members and as such by definition cannot function merely in the service of national interests of any individual country, but are required to act in the interest of all their members and their populations and to pursue their aims on the regional or even global scale.

By acquiring rights and obligations under international law vis-à-vis their members as well as third parties, such as non-Member States, other IOs and private parties, IOs can also acquire rights and obligations towards individuals. In the field of public health, these may include obligations towards the sick, poor and other individuals exposed to health risks. However, commitments of IOs are often formulated as declarative and programmatic norms, guidelines and standards, rather than rules with clearly defined obligations for the IO and its members. Moreover, many obligations are defined as obligations of conduct, rather than obligations of result, leaving a broad scope for interpretation of IOs' responsibilities.[78] Furthermore, in case an IO breaches its obligations, the affected party might have difficulties in enforcing the claim against it, in particular due to the lack of dispute settlement mechanisms that would entertain claims against IOs and award a remedy to the affected party.[79] Obligations of IOs, either arising directly from their mandate, from their contractual obligations, or from their actions in tort, are therefore often hard to enforce, especially by individuals – indeed those ultimately affected by IOs activities.[80]

---

78 For a comparative analysis, see Clapham, A, *Human Rights Obligations of Non-State Actors*, 2006, Ch. 4 and 5, addressing the obligations of the UN, the WTO and the EU.

79 Wellens, K, *Remedies against International Organisations*, 2002.

80 For the immunities that International Organizations enjoy before domestic courts see Reinisch, A, *International Organizations Before National Courts*, 2004, 278; for the position of individuals see Bogdandy, A von & Steinbrück Platise, M, "ARIO and Human Rights" (2012), 9 *IOLR*, 67.

One of the recent examples includes the dispute involving cholera outbreak in Haiti, where the United Nations Stabilization Mission in Haiti (MINUSTAH) has been claimed responsible for causing the outbreak. The outbreak has been attributed to poor construction of the sanitation system in the UN base, which resulted in contamination of the primary water source of Haitian residents.[81] The claim by the NGOs representing thousands of victims before the US courts has been rejected by the first- and second-instance courts, which both recognized UN immunity in the domestic proceedings.[82] Thus, even when the failure to protect the human right to health could be attributed to an IO, and could even amount to an epidemic, the obligation of the IO to remedy the situation will be hard to enforce.[83]

However, the existence of obligations of IOs should clearly be distinguished from the lack of monitoring and enforcement mechanisms that could ensure compliance of IOs with their obligations, and from the lack of possibility of third parties, including individuals, to enforce these obligations. That distinction is based on the fundamental difference between primary and secondary rules of international law, whereby the primary rules concern the substantive rights and obligations binding upon IOs, whereas the secondary rules determine when an IO is responsible for a breach of primary obligations and what are the means of redress.[84] Difficulties in *enforcing* the right to health against an IO do not therefore affect the *existence* of the corresponding IO's obligation to protect that right.

3 The Risks and Potentials

The new legal and political landscape in global health governance that was analyzed in the previous sections opens a number of risks, but also potentials for an effective and legitimate governance of the health sector in which

---

81 Cravioto, A, Lanata, C F & Lantagne, D S et al., *Final Report of the Independent Panel of Experts on the Cholera Outbreak in Haiti*, 2011, 29, available at www.un.org/News/dh/infocus/haiti/UN-cholera-report-final.pdf.

82 *Delama Georges et al. v. The United Nations et al.*, 13-cv-7146 (JPO), opinion and order of January 9, 2015; for the decision on the appeal see *Delama Georges et al. v. The United Nations et al.*, No. 15-455-cv (2nd Cir 2016), decision of August 18, 2016.

83 See also the contribution of *Leonie Vierck*, "The Case Law of International Public Health and Why its Scarcity is a Problem" in this volume.

84 For the distinction see the Draft Articles on the Responsibility of International Organizations with commentary, above Fn. 59, General Commentary para. 3, 2.

IOs could play a prominent role. Some of the current structural deficits in health governance, described in Section III, are due to the multiplication of actors with overlapping mandates, duplication of work, competition and lack of coordination of their activities in the health sector. Such a deficiency results in selective regulation of specific diseases, rather than in a comprehensive promotion and protection of health worldwide, and primary health care in particular.[85] Proliferation of actors with overlapping mandates, coupled with poor coordination, also leads to duplication of governance structures and can produce conflicting priorities, standards and policies. The current structure of global health governance therefore risks ever-greater institutional and regulatory fragmentation.

More importantly, fragmented governance structures, strategies and norms hamper effectiveness of global health governance. Some observers therefore criticize the current governance patchwork as incapable of producing a convergence of interests, resources and strategies, and warn that it prevents in particular developing countries from effective participation.[86] Instead of pooling available resources and knowledge to address health risks as collective action problems, various actors need to compete for financial and human resources. Such competition especially weakens those actors whose functioning is not market-oriented, such as the WHO and some other UN agencies. Moreover, the actors' success and effectiveness in their functioning is measured against organizational criteria, such as the number of loans dispersed or amount of funding provided, rather than in terms of their ultimate impact on health and disease control.[87]

If duplication of tasks, confusing priorities and poor coordination impede effectiveness of global health governance and thereby its *output* legitimacy, the exercise of public authority by some of the most powerful actors, which lack democratic governance structure, puts into question also the *input* legitimacy of global health governance. According to this distinction, the input legitimacy of an actor is secured in particular by democratic guarantees such as participation, representation and transparency in the actor's deci-

---

85 For the critique concerning the World Bank and the Global Fund see UNAIDS, *The Global Task Team on Improving AIDS Coordination Among Multilateral Institutions and International Donors (Final Report)*, June 14, 2005, 15.

86 Fidler, "The Challenges of Global Health Governance", above Fn. 47, 12 et seq.

87 Brooks, A, Cutts, F T & Justice, J et al., *Policy Study of Factors Influencing the Adoption of New and Underutilized Vaccines in Developing Countries, CVI and USAID*, 1999, 33 et seqq.

sion-making, whereas the output legitimacy concerns the actor's performance and is obtained in particular by providing effective solutions to collective problems.[88]

The concern for the input legitimacy has been raised especially with respect to private actors, who dominate and control resource allocation in the health sector and determine health policies in accordance with their own preferences, goals and interests. In particular, the involvement of the pharmaceutical industry in the regulation and standard-setting has been harshly criticized in that it has been too prone to engage in merely profit-oriented activities, as the decision-making of private business actors necessarily follows their own private interests and cost-benefit analysis, rather than health needs and interests of larger communities or indeed of the international community.[89] Moreover, many not-for-profit NGOs have been considered as representing merely themselves and their own interests, thus not representing their constituencies in any formal, accountable or participatory way.[90] This observation is relevant also for a number of actors of a public-private character, including the Global Fund, whose national-level mechanisms such as the Country Coordinating System do not represent the constituencies in which they operate.[91] The new forms of governance like self-regulation and hybrid regulation therefore lack external and internal accountability mechanisms, yet they increasingly compete with the public and – more or less – democratically legitimized IOs.

Indeed, IOs have likewise been criticized for lacking legitimacy, in particular for failing to meet many of the standards of democratic decision-

---

88 For the notion of input and output legitimacy of International Organizations, see Steffek, J, "The Output Legitimacy of International Organizations and the Global Public Interest" (2015), 7 *International Theory*, 263 (263 et seqq.); see also Bexell, M, "Global Governance, Legitimacy and (De)Legitimation" (2014), 11 *Globalizations*, 289 (291 et seqq.).

89 Benvenisti, *The Law of Global Governance*, above Fn. 12, 54, with further references.

90 See also the contribution of *Hunter Keys*, *Bonnie Kaiser* & *André den Exter*, "The Real Versus the Ideal in NGO Governance: Enacting the Right to Mental Healthcare in Liberia During the 2014-2016 Ebola Epidemic" in this volume.

91 Kageni, A, Mwangi, L & Mugyenyi, C et al., *Representation and Participation of Key Populations on Country Coordinating Systems in Six Countries in Southern Africa*, Final Report, AIDSPAN, 2015.

making[92] and for giving greater regard to the interests of some actors, especially powerful states and well-organized economic actors, and lesser regard to the interests of more weakly organized groups and vulnerable individuals.[93] Nevertheless, due to their dual capacity to serve as public forums for other governance actors and as autonomous actors, they may carry, first of all, the potential for inclusion and integration of diverse actors and interests, especially those of weaker countries, less represented peoples and marginalized groups and individuals. The inclusion of state and non-state actors, NGOs, business actors, local organizations and other stake-holders can enable political processes that are closer to the needs of the affected individuals and communities, and can therefore increase the legitimacy of the respective IO, and of global health governance more generally.

Second, due to their public nature, IOs are well endowed with powers and competences for addressing collective action problems. They are *the* actors that have been entrusted with protecting global common goods and given the mandate for promoting and protecting the right to health on the international level, for coordinating international response to health risks and for regulating the health sector in the interest of global population. They are the actors who are competent for pooling available resources, skills and knowledge and who are charged with facilitating integrative agreements. The establishment of the UNAIDS and the WHO's launching of its own initiative to fight HIV/AIDS may therefore be seen as an attempt towards a better inclusion of underrepresented stakeholders, prevention of further privatization of global health governance, and coordination and cooperation in the fight against certain infectious diseases through a public – and thus more legitimate – international forum.

Third, if IOs will be able to embrace the private sector, engage more actively in forming partnerships and networks with other actors, including business actors and not-for-profit NGOs, and enable them to participate in the IOs' own decision making processes and procedures, IOs may not only gain higher input legitimacy, but also higher acceptance and thus better implementation of their policies and decisions on the national and local level,

92 Compare Wheatley, S, *The Democratic Legitimacy of International Law*, 2010; Wouters, J, Braeckman, A & Lievens, M et al. (eds.), *Global Governance and Democracy, A Multidisciplinary Analysis*, 2015; Klabbers, J, Peters, A & Ulfstein, G, *The Constitutionalization of International Law*, 2009.

93 Particularly forceful Stewart, R B, "Remedying Disregard in Global Regulatory Governance: Accountability, Participation and Responsiveness" (2014), 108 *The American Journal of International Law*, 211.

which could improve their effectiveness. Such changes, however, require reforms of institutional structures, instruments and policies within each IO.

Thereby, it seems that apart from an IO's inertia, one of the greatest challenges to successful reforms might be the hesitance of powerful states and powerful private actors to support such changes, as they seem to prefer bilateral and informal agreements to the broader collective actions. Still, IOs such as the WHO show that also international public institutions – precisely because they are public – have the potential to accommodate diverse competing interests, enhance cooperation between public and private actors and build networks with and between them, thereby contributing towards greater legitimacy and effectiveness of the global health sector.

V Conclusion

In recent decades, several structural changes have occurred in global health governance, in which traditional regulation by international governmental organizations has increasingly been replaced by new government modes and structures, in particular by bilateral arrangements, PPPs and less formal instruments.[94] The shift of governance away from IOs has been prompted by different factors, including by certain failures of IOs such as the WHO, which to a large extent have been lacking flexible, context-oriented and inclusive governance modes and instruments, and were unable to respond swiftly and adequately to some of the recent global crises. On the other hand, the decline of IOs has been part of a more general trend of shifting the exercise of public authority towards informal international or transnational institutions and entrusting global governance to the private sector, whereby the health sector has manifested more examples of PPPs than any other policy sector. However, the new global health governance architecture produces a number of structural deficiencies, such as selective and donor-driven regulation, fragmentation and ineffectiveness of the global health sector. In addition, the regulation by some of the most powerful global actors, such as those dominated by pharmaceutical companies, escapes some of the most essential standards of legitimate governance, including certain basic democratic, human rights and the rule of law standards. What is more, informal governance arrangements, be they adopted by state or

94 See also Pauwelyn, J, "Is it International Law or Not and Does it Even Matter?" in Pauwelyn, J, Wessel, R & Wouters, J (eds.), *Informal International Lawmaking*, 2012, 125.

non-state actors, remain below the threshold of legally binding instruments and can therefore escape the requirements for a legitimate exercise of public authority. In view of such structural deficiencies, IOs carry the potential to redress the lack of effectiveness and legitimacy of global health governance, in that they could more prominently use their dual character of public forums and of autonomous actors, by hosting – and moderating – the contestation, negotiation and cooperation between multiple actors, goals, interests and values. Thereby, they have the potential to bring public governance back to public forums and subjecting the global health governance to the normative framework for a legitimate and effective exercise of public authority. That would require, however, that governance by IOs becomes more inclusive, if in the future IOs are to prevent global health risks in a more coordinated, effective and legitimate way.

The Case Law of International Public Health and Why its Scarcity is a Problem

Leonie Vierck[*]

Abstract

This systematizing article spotlights the virtually absent case law in international infectious disease governance. In a first step, it describes the phenomenon and inventories the scarce and scattered case law. This small body of case law consists of rulings tackling international infectious disease governance using the entry doors of the law governing international public servants, international aviation law, and some regional human rights law. Yet, no coherent body of case law appears. The article continues to show that the phenomenon of virtually absent case law is a common feature of international public health law more generally. In a second step, it analyses the functional loss that international public health law generates without coherent case law against the backdrop of restatements of current legal theory. Especially highly scientific disciplines such as public health, which is dominated by empirical methodology, are prone to natural fallacy arguments,

* Currently, the author is research fellow at the Max Planck Institute for Comparative Public Law and International Law (MPIL) in Heidelberg, and affiliated with the Cluster of Excellence "Normative Orders" at Goethe University, Frankfurt/Main, Germany. Prior to joining the MPIL, she worked for several years in the German aid system, including the health sector. In broad association, this article builds upon thoughts expressed in an earlier blog entry: Vierck, L & Böckenförde, M, "Research questions arising from practice of law" (December 4, 2015), *Völkerrechtsblog (international law blog)*, available at http://voelkerrechtsblog.org/research-questions-arising-from-practice-of-law/. Many thanks are owed to the entire researchers colloquium of Professor *Armin v. Bogdandy* at the MPIL, the International Graduate Programme (IGP) colloquium of the "Normative Orders" cluster, the co-editors of this edited volume, *Ingo Venzke*, and *Allain Zysset* for their constructive feedback and remarks, and to *Evelyne Asaala* and *Conrad M. Bosire* for their orientation in Kenyan law. All websites last accessed March 9, 2017.

i.e. deducing normative reasoning from facts.[1] An established judicial discourse would counter-balance such tendencies. Vice versa, judicial application of the law to concrete facts would filter relevant empirical scenarios for international lawyers. While commenting on the dormant International Health Regulations (IHR) dispute settlement, the article also promotes several doctrinal proposals, especially to interpret the wording of the IHR in analogy to the World Trade Organization Dispute Settlement Understanding.

I Introduction

Between 1974 and 1978 *Joseph Toa Ba*, who was born in 1952, served as a so-called "blackfly collector" with the United Nations (UN) World Health Organization (WHO) in Côte d'Ivoire. Blackflies are the vector for onchocerciasis, a neglected tropical disease (NTD) also known as river blindness. This skin and eye disease, which can even lead to permanent blindness, is caused by a parasitic worm, whose larvae are transmitted to humans by the bites of infected blackflies. It can take many months until the symptoms develop, i.e. when the larvae have developed into worms in their human host.[2] In the 1970s, river blindness affected up to 50 % of adults in some Western African areas, and economic losses were estimated at US $30 million. In 2015, 11 million persons worldwide were still in need of onchocerciasis drug treatment.[3] International efforts to control onchocerciasis can briefly be summarized as follows: WHO and the World Bank initiated the Onchocerciasis Control Program (OCP), which lasted between 1975 and 2002. OCP was succeeded by the African Program for Onchocerciasis

1 Petersen, N, "Avoiding the common-wisdom fallacy: The role of social sciences in constitutional adjudication" (2013), 11 *International Journal of Constitutional Law (I-Con)*, 294 (296).

2 For more disease-specific information see for example Taylor, M, Hoerauf, A & Bockarie, M, "Lymphatic filariasis and onchocerciasis" (2010), 376 *The Lancet*, 1175.

3 The information stems from the most recent WHO factsheet and online information covering onchocerciasis (last updated in October 2016, and available at http://www.who.int/mediacentre/factsheets/fs374/en/ next to http://www.who.int/apoc/onchocerciasis/disease/en/). For a scientific public health introduction to onchocerciasis see for example Richards, F, Boatin, B & Sauerbrey, M et al., "Control of onchocerciasis today: status and challenges" (2001), 17 *Trends in Parasitology*, 558.

Control (APOC). APOC ran between 1995 and 2015, and was supported by the (non-binding) 2006 Yaoundé Declaration on Onchocerciasis Control by African Ministers of Health. Since 2016, onchocerciasis control is part of the WHO Expanded Special Project for the Elimination of NTDs in Africa (ESPEN).[4] Back to *Joseph Toa Ba* who continued to work as local staff in international health projects until 1994, when weakening eyesight made him incapable of working. Today he is considered seriously disabled. His communication in 1994 already revealed that he believes he contracted his illness during his time as blackfly collector. A complex series of internal WHO proceedings was kick-started. And because international labor law disputes are exceptionally justiciable within international administrations generally and international public health law specifically, he could seek judicial recourse to the competent International Labour Organization Administrative Tribunal (ILOAT) on several occasions.[5] In 2016, the ILOAT sentenced WHO to pay the plaintiff's medical expenses plus potential interests as well as compensation amounting to US $30,000. WHO also had already paid him 10,000 Swiss francs for the length of proceedings. All four relatively short judgments leave many questions open: Facts were difficult to establish in the course of decades, and documents not well archived (see for example the claims in section D. of Judgment No. 3012). The plaintiff had difficulties in understanding procedural steps (Judgments No. 2017 and 2434), but he was also not correctly instructed on his rights of appeal (§ 6 of the Considerations in Judgment No. 3012). Further, the dilemma of NTDs (the main public health argument is in a nutshell that they receive

4 See again the WHO factsheet, above Fn. 3.

5 In chronological order these are Judgments No. 2017 *In Re Toa Ba* (January 31, 2001), No. 2434 (July 6, 2005), No. 3012 (July 6, 2011), and No. 3689 *T. B. (No. 4) v. WHO* (July 6, 2016). ILOAT judgments are final and without appeal pursuant to Article VI, para. 1 of the Statute and Rules of the Administrative Tribunal. In light of the fact that all legally contentious procedural and substantial issues have now been addressed by the ILOAT, the series of cases should be closed. The WHO is recognizing the jurisdiction of the Administrative Tribunal of the International Labour Organization (ILOAT) with currently 461 judgments available in total. See http://www.ilo.org/dyn/triblex/triblexmain.showlist. For an overview of such procedures more generally see Thévenot-Werner, A, *Le droit des argents internationaux à un recours effectif: Vers un droit commun de la procédure administrative internationale*, 2016 and Ziadé, N (ed.), *Problems of International Administrative Law – On the Occasion of the Twentieth Anniversary of the World Bank Administrative Tribunal*, 2008 as well as Amerasinghe, C, "International Administrative Tribunals" in Romano, C, Alter, K & Shany, Y (eds.), *The Oxford Handbook of International Judicialization*, 2013, 316.

disproportionately little attention, because they only affect the world's poorest populations)[6] seems to materialize: Expert knowledge was needed, but experts were difficult to find, and the impartiality of one of the few available experts was questionable (§ 3 of the Considerations in Judgment No. 2434). Beyond this fog of open questions the main legal question to answer was: Was *Joseph Toa Ba*'s weakened eyesight caused by onchocerciasis contracted during his performance in the 1970s as a blackfly collector, and thus legally attributable to WHO? WHO Staff Rule 730 entitles staff members to compensation for illness attributable to the performance of official duties on behalf of WHO. Broadly speaking, the internal WHO review mechanisms distinguish between two tiers: Staff decisions can either be challenged on medical grounds, or as breach of administrative rules. So far, *Joseph Toa Ba* had to present his claims only before medical experts, because empirical causality had to be determined (§ 6 of the Considerations in Judgment No. 2017). In its most recent judgment, the ILOAT points out that it cannot substitute its own opinions for those of medical experts (§ 3 of the Considerations in Judgment No. 3689). Yet, when confronted with diverging medical opinions, the Tribunal can judicially balance spheres of responsibility. It ruled that the existence of an empirical link was more probable than not (ibid.), especially in light of the fact that *Joseph Toa Ba* was instructed not to wear protective clothing. On the contrary, he was asked to wait until the blackflies settled on his body, so he could better catch them, which exposed him to a high risk of contracting river blindness (§ 5 of the Considerations in Judgment No. 3689). This concrete case is an exception, because few cases can be found tackling the international governance of infectious diseases, i.e. there is no developed judicial discourse. This shows that the proliferation of international courts and tribunals has not (yet?) led to a thorough judicialization of public international law,[7] to the degree that areas of international administrative law are scarcely justiciable. The introductory case also serves to introduce various abstract aspects of this article: First, it demonstrates that there are hidden areas of neglected case law in international public health. Second, the clash between the empirical determination of facts and their normative evaluation is the key issue of this case: Whether and how judges are competent in handling empirical evidence, although they are neither medical nor public health experts? And third, the

6 For an introduction to NTDs see for example Feasey, N, Wansbrough-Jones, M & Mabey, D, "Neglected tropical diseases" (2010), 93 *British Medical Bulletin*, 179.

7 Alvarez, J, "The New Dispute Settlers: (Half) Truths and Consequences" (2003), 38 *Texas International Law Journal*, 405 (411 et seq., especially 413).

case constellation is not specific to onchocerciasis but can be transferred to virtually any infectious disease. It can then function as precedent providing a pattern for ruling on disease control projects generally. The international health personnel meant to control infectious diseases are always themselves at high risk of contracting them; this is an important issue for the Ebola case study of this edited volume, too.[8]

This article will highlight the absence of a coherent body of case law within the sub-field of the international public health law governing infectious disease control – as an example for the wider field of international public health law. Particular attention will initially be paid to commenting on the dormant dispute settlement mechanism contained in the (revised) IHR, which were adopted by the WHA in 2005.[9] This mechanism currently has no practical relevance, while there are scholarly and practice calls for its activation.[10] To found its claim and describe the phenomenon, the article then continues to take stock of existing case law in the field. A relatively eccentric case collection surfaces from the peripheries of public inter-

---

8 In this respect, community workers during the Ebola crisis adhered to the motto "Do or die", see Jung, A, "Cured but not in good shape" (2016), 8 *D+C (Development and Cooperation) e-Paper*, 23, available at http://bit.ly/2m2qAHM. A recent presentation on "Aid Worker Safety in the Context of Health Crisis: The Example of the Ebola Pandemic in Liberia and Sierra Leonie" by *Joachim Gardemann* shed additional light on the subject. The presentation was part of the conference "Protecting the Unprotected – Humanitarian Action and Human Rights after the WHS", which took place between September 21 & 22, 2016 at the Institute for International Law of Peace and Armed Conflict (IFHV) at the Ruhr University.

9 For an introduction to the IHR and its contextual relevance during the Ebola crisis see the contribution of *Pedro A. Villarreal*, "The World Health Organization's Governance Framework in Disease Outbreaks: A Legal Perspective" in this volume. The contributions of *Mateja Steinbrück Platiše*, "The Changing Structure of Global Health Governance", *Robert Frau*, "Combining the WHO's International Health Regulations (2005) with the UN Security Council's Powers: Does it Make Sense for Health Governance?" and *Ilja Richard Pavone*, "Ebola and Securitization of Health: UN Security Council Resolution 2177/2014 and its Limits" analyze additional links to international public health security. For a comparative perspective on domestic laws governing infectious diseases see Koyuncu, A, "Infectious Disease Control Law" in Kirch, W (ed.), *Encyclopedia of Public Health*, 2008, 770.

10 Gostin, L, DeBartolo, M & Friedman, E, "The International Health Regulations 10 years on: the governing framework for global health security" (2015), 386 *The Lancet*, 2225. In this line also again note the call for effective IHR sanctions in the *WHO Final Report of the Ebola Interim Assessment Panel* (July 2015).

national case law. It consists of rare, hidden, and unconnected judicial components. This shows that the fragmentation or domain specialization of public international law is institutionally mirrored by a fragmented or decentralized arrangement of (quasi-)judicial bodies.[11] While the international law governing infectious disease control can be analyzed in greater depth, this phenomenon is pertinent to international public health law more generally. The primary focus on case law is also not to deny non-judicial enforcement mechanisms, which will loom in the background of this article. It is rather to collect the rare instances of case law, and understand the function of the virtual absence of an established judicial discourse.

By analyzing positive law and practice at its core, the article is rooted in doctrinal constructivism as far as it lists judicial mechanisms and systematizes them, while no new legal concepts are introduced.[12] Although it understands that the law is embedded in a social reality beyond it, it does not blur the positivistic line between facts and the law.[13] It does not construe public international law from the State perspective, but understands that governance activities by international institutions can be exercises of international public authority (IPA) in need of legitimacy determined by internal legal approaches.[14] When later looking at the function of international adjudication, this article does not engage in theory building, but enquires into

11 Oellers-Frahm, K, "Multiplication of International Courts and Tribunals and Conflicting Jurisdiction – Problems and Possible Solutions" (2001), 5 *Max Planck Yearbook of United Nations Law (UNYB)*, 67 (75).

12 For an accessible introduction to the method see Bogdandy, A von, "The past and promise of doctrinal constructivism: A strategy for responding to the challenges facing constitutional scholarship in Europe" (2009), 7 *I-Con*, 364.

13 On today's debate of positivism in international law see recently Kammerhofer, J & D'Aspremont, J, *International Legal Positivism in a Post-Modern World*, 2014.

14 For an introduction to IPA see Bogdandy, A von, Wolfrum, R & Bernstorff, J von et al. (eds.), *The Exercise of Public Authority by International Institutions: Advancing International Institutional Law*, 2010. For parallel research streams also concerned with international administrative authority, see Krisch, N & Kingsbury, B, "Introduction: Global Governance and Global Administrative Law in the International Legal Order" (2006), 17 *The European Journal of International Law*, 1, and the contribution of *Edefe Ojomo*, "Fostering Regional Health Governance in West Africa: The Role of the WAHO" in this volume for an application of the Global Administrative Law (GAL) approach. For the Italian comparative administrative approach see Napolitano, G & Cassese, S (eds.), *Diritto amministrativo comparato*, 2007.

the functional loss of coherent case law in international public health.[15] Building upon the concrete regime at hand, the idea is thus rather to restate theory, and test it as appropriate. The phenomenon of scarce case law is also regime specific - due to the technicality of the field, the discourse is limited to public health and medical experts who dominate international public health bureaucracies.[16] The introductory case for example illustrates how the Tribunal needs to justify its entering into a discourse which so far was labeled as strictly medical or empirical, and not administrative or legal.

The case referred to is the Ebola crisis as the case study selected for this edited volume.[17] Next to the factual descriptions provided by *Marx* and *Hein* in this edited volume, this article builds upon the *WHO Final Report of the Ebola Interim Assessment Panel* (July 2015) and the *WHO Secretariat response* to it dating from August 2015 and the *Report of the Review Committee on the Role of the IHR (2005) in the Ebola Outbreak and Response* (May 2016) as authoritative sources.[18] The executive summary of the first report already mentioned flags three major and continuous shortcomings: Member State incapacities (1), travel bans and especially trade-restrictive measures exceeding WHO recommendations under the IHR by 25 % (2), and significant and unjustifiable delays (3). The report notably calls for an IHR review as concerns sanction mechanisms drawing comparisons to the World Trade Organization (WTO) system (marginal numbers 17 and 19). The WHO response specifically welcomes potential IHR revisions in this respect (marginal number 8). The report also notably calls for an institutional re-arrangement for dealing with public health emergencies (marginal number 26). It is relatively easy to imagine hypothetical case

15 For theory-building of full-fledged systems of international adjudication see Bogdandy, A von & Venzke, I, *In Whose Name?: A Public Law Theory of International Adjudication*, 2014.

16 See Stein, E, "International Integration and Democracy: No Love at First Sight" (2001), 95 *The American Journal of International Law (AJIL)*, 489 (499). Note that this article is outdated as concerns WHO's use of legal instruments. Following this thought further could lead to anthropological analysis of bureaucracies, see for example Douglas, M, *How Institutions Think*, 1986.

17 For a more comprehensive conception of the broader policy and (project) management issues of the Ebola crisis see Halabi, S, Gostin, L & Crowley, J (eds.), *Global Management of Infectious Disease Control after Ebola*, 2016.

18 For a critique on the Interim Assessment Panel documents see for example Fidler, D, "Ebola Report Misses Mark on International Health Regulations" (July 17, 2015), *Chatham House Expert Comment*, available at http://bit.ly/2lSS2Yk. *Fidler* especially dismisses any institutional analogy to the WTO system from a legal standpoint.

scenarios for example as regards travel bans between States, but also involving private air carriers and affected travelers.

II Case Law in International Public Health Governance is Scarce and Scattered

Now, the article will provide an assessment of the scarce, scattered islands of case law in international public health governance. With a view to the Ebola case, the focus will rest on the international governance of infectious disease control. However, the broader field of international public health governance will quickly be screened in order to demonstrate that the finding ("adjudication is scarce, scattered, and generally off the beaten track, which results in a lack of established judicial discourse") is by and large the same. The selection criteria for this inventory can be presented as follows: In a first step, the dormant IHR dispute settlement mechanism is commented upon, because it is the judicial mechanism originally foreseen for international infectious disease governance. In a second step, borrowed judicial mechanisms are screened. They are borrowed, because they are primarily established in a different international legal regime, but can connect to international infectious disease governance. The introductory case for example deals with an issue of the employment law governing international public servants, but substantially covers an issue of international infectious disease governance. The case selection is also limited to the Ebola case study chosen as a common theme for this edited volume, and thus to the West-African region. Also note that the interest of this article rests on describing the judicial review of the international infectious disease governance structure. In terms of a conceptual clarification however, the legal regime governing international infectious diseases does not distinguish between bilateral and multilateral disputes. For instance, the IHR dispute settlement mechanism treats disputes between Member States and disputes between (a) Member State(s) and the WHO alike. When transferring the argument that no coherent body of case law appears in international infectious disease governance to the wider field of international public health, this article is confronted with the fact that is not governed by a single and clearly recognizable set of public international law treaties. Applicable international norms are rather bound together by a conceptual definition. The article thus rests on a leading scholarly contribution by *Allyn Taylor* defining this particular field of public international law in order to screen dispute mechanisms.[19]

1 Systems of WHO Adjudication and Dispute Settlement Under the IHR

a The Wider Field of WHO Adjudication

Although originally rooted in the international public law governing the United Nations UN WHO and the multilateral treaties negotiated within the WHO system,[20] international public health law can largely be characterized as a fragmented body of public international law inclusive of WHO law, but also reaching beyond it. It spans across diverse regimes of public international law, and consists of many "soft law" sources next to several, often highly technical treaties.[21] Multilateral cooperation in infectious disease control is a particularly old concern of diplomacy and public international

19 Taylor, A, "International Law, and Public Health Policy" in Quah, S & Heggenhougen, K (eds.), *International Encyclopedia of Public Health*, 2008, 667 (668).

20 Article 19 of the WHO Constitution grants the World Health Assembly (WHA) representing the WHO Member States the authority to adopt conventions by 2/3 majority concerning any matter within WHO competence. Disagreeing Member States can furnish statements of non-acceptance to the Director-General pursuant to Article 20. Article 21 proceeds to grant the WHA the specific authority to adopt regulations in matters of international disease control, disease nomenclatures, diagnostic standards, medical product standards, and advertising and labeling of products of public health relevance. Member States can again notify the Director-General of rejections or reservations pursuant to Article 22. In order to capture the difference between constitutive and regulative legal rules, the social philosopher *John Searle* provides a catchy definition for distinction: Only constitutive rules contain social status function declarations following the pattern "X counts as Y in the context C". In very short terms, societies impose functions on objects and people independent of their physical structure. By contrast, regulation covers action that can exist independently of the rule. Here, the logical pattern is "Do X". Searle, J, *Making the Social World: The Structure of Human Civilization*, 2010, 9-10. The mentioned articles provide for good examples of this distinction. Here, Article 20 sets constitutive rules and is visibly distinguished from Article 21 on regulations.

21 For a similar assessment see Taylor, A & Bettcher, D, "Editorials: International law and public health" (2002), 80 *Bulletin of the World Health Organization*, 923. *Matthias Goldmann* shows how "soft law" by creating normative expectations can be legally construed beyond the classical sources canon contained in Article 38 para. 1 ICJ Statute: *Internationale öffentliche Gewalt: Handlunsgformen internationaler Institutionen im Zeitalter der Globalisierung*, 2015, 3 & 4, 387 et seq.

law, and the IHR can be traced back to the first International Sanitary Conference in Paris in 1851 following a European cholera crisis. According to Article 75, the WHO Constitution refers dispute settlement to the International Court of Justice (ICJ) if negotiation fails and no other mode of settlement is agreed upon. In analogy to similar provisions in the constituent documents of other international institutions, such referral to the ICJ or arbitration is not interpreted as determining the (in-)validity of acts of an organ of an international institution beyond interstate disputes.[22] Article 76 stipulates that the WHO may also request ICJ advisory opinions with the Director-General representing the WHO before the Court (Article 77). However, the two readily available advisory opinions initiated by the WHA bear political or institutional character,[23] and do not substantially engage with international public health law. In terms of sanction regimes, this article leaves aside the connection with Chapter VII UN Charter resolutions by the Security Council (SC, in the case of Ebola *Resolution 2177 (September 18, 2014)*).[24]

b The Dormant IHR Dispute Settlement

The IHR provides for a dispute settlement mechanism, which is basically unrecognized in practice.[25] The contribution of this article is the commentary on the mechanisms, which has not yet produced any case law. Like

---

22 Vos, J., *The Function of Public International Law*, 2013, 234 with further references and within the context of a classical understanding of international institutional authority stemming from Member State powers solely. Else, the book is a peculiar theoretical endeavor on the multi-polarity of public international law between classical and critical theory – but also a solitaire, because it does not integrate into a school of thought, and challenges school leaders such as Lauterpacht, H, *The Function of Law in the International Community*, 2011 (first published in 1933) already in its title.

23 These are Legality of the Use by a State of Nuclear Weapons in Armed Conflict, (1996) ICJ Reports 66 (July 8), and Interpretation of the Agreement of March 25, 1951 between the WHO and Egypt, (1980) ICJ Reports 73 (December 20) on the possible transfer of a WHO regional office.

24 The conceptualization of infectious disease outbreak as a threat to international peace and security is extensively dealt with by *Frau* and *Pavone* in this edited volume.

25 See Fidler, D, "Return of the Fourth Horseman: Emerging Infectious Diseases and International Law" (1997), 81 *Minnesota Law Review*, 847-849 with a reference

many recent UN instruments, the 2005 IHR take a principal international arbitration approach when it comes to compulsory jurisdiction.[26] This fosters a trend within the UN system of proliferating judicial institutions beyond the ICJ.[27] Consensual means of dispute settlement grant special roles to the Director-General of the WHO and the WHA. Article 56 is the applicable norm dealing with the settlement of disputes, and provides for a relatively complex system.[28] Legal action is the last resort. According to the newly introduced para. 1, State Parties are first meant to settle any dispute concerning the IHR interpretation through peaceful means of their choice. The State Parties shall also re-enter bilateral dispute settlement, even if it failed the first time. The non-exhaustive list provided includes negotiation, good offices, mediation, or conciliation. Negotiation understood as the direct bilateral discussion between the parties is substituted by good offices, mediation, or conciliation involving a third party on different degrees.[29] The latter are the same instruments as listed in Article 5 of the Dispute

to Roelsgaard, E, "Health Regulations and International Travel" (1974), 28 *WHO Chronicle*, 265 (266).

26 Notably see the difference with the 1946 WHO Constitution, which refers contentious cases to the ICJ. And indeed Article 93 para. 3 of the former IHR 1969 ultimately referred cases to the ICJ. For another arbitration example in the founding documents of a UN entity see Article XVIII of the *Agreement between the UN and the Food and Agriculture Organization (FAO) of the UN on the one part and the Government of the Italian Republic on the other part regarding the Headquarters for the World Food Programme (WFP)* from 1991. Interestingly, the ICJ plays a second-tier role, here: The WFP and Italy would both select an arbitrator, and these two arbitrators would agree on the nomination of a third one. Should they fail to agree within six months, the President of the ICJ would appoint the third arbitrator. Of course, these examples are of doctrinal, and systemic interest, and not relevant in international administrative practice, which is not shaped by a vivid legal discourse.

27 Kingsbury, B, "Foreword: Is the Proliferation of International Courts and Tribunals a Systemic Problem?" (1999), 31 *International Law and Politics*, 679 (693 & 694). For details see above Fn. 26.

28 Article 93 of the IHR 1969 as the preceding rule created a simpler system with the Director-General being entrusted with an initial responsibility. If settlement was not reached, the Director-General or a State concerned could refer the case to any committee or organ within the WHO, thus rendering the dispute more technical. However, the ultimate responsibility of the ICJ would entail a full-fledged judicial solution.

29 This resembles a slow handing over of control as a demarcation line between negotiation and adjudication. Merrills, J, *International Dispute Settlement*, 2011, 16.

Settlement Understanding (DSU) of the WTO. Their specific legal interpretation can thus follow the distinctions of the DSU by analogy (with only a slight difference in the sequencing of the list). Good offices then are a traditional diplomatic instrument with a third party involved that facilitates negotiations without substantial interference.[30] UN good offices can mean involving the capacity of the UN Secretary General especially with a view to convening power in settling the dispute.[31] Sometimes, such decisions can come close to adjudication.[32] Conciliation involves direct interference by the third party, while a mediator may even go further and propose a concrete solution to end the dispute between the parties.[33] Second, the State Parties can refer the case to the WHO Director-General according to para. 2. In the case of disputes between the WHO and Member States, the quasi-judicial function moves to the WHA as the plenary body, which makes sense because the Director-General represents the WHO as its executive body, and thus cannot be deemed sufficiently neutral. It is, however, questionable if the WHA is sufficiently neutral based on the political power of Member States to conceptually fulfill this function. Rather, this power should have been assigned to a body within the wider UN system such as the Secretary General. Interestingly, as a result of this system, the executive and decision-making functions of both the Director-General of WHO and the WHA are complemented by quasi-judicial functions in the black letter law. Para. 3 then proceeds to regulate arbitration. Legal action can be sought for dispute over the interpretation or application of the IHR or for specific disputes between two States. Concerning proceedings, Permanent Court of Arbitration (PCA) rules are applicable.[34] The WHA is granted a discretionary right to information, which also means that arbitration proceedings cannot remain

---

30 Schorkopf, F, "Article 5 DSU" in Wolfrum, R, Stoll, P & Kaiser, K (eds.), *WTO Institutions and Dispute Settlement*, 2006, 331 (332).

31 Traditionally, the role of the Secretary-General's good offices lies in peacemaking, see http://www.peacemaker.un.org/peacemaking-mandate/secretary-general, and Franck, T, "The Secretary-General's Role in Conflict Resolution: Past, Present and Pure Conjecture" (1995), 6 *The European Journal of International Law (EJIL)*, 1. However, an extension into the field of human rights and humanitarian action have become an established field of the Secretary-General's mandate for a long time, see Ramcharan, B, "The Good Offices of the United Nations Secretary-General in the Field of Human Rights" (1982), 76 *AJIL*, 130.

32 Alvarez, "The New Dispute Settlers", above Fn. 7, 413.

33 Schorkopf, F, "Article 5 DSU", above Fn. 30, 332.

34 For an introduction see Daly, B, "Permanent Court of Arbitration" in Giorgetti, C (ed.), *The Rules, Practice, and Jurisprudence of International Courts and Tribunals*, 2012, 37 (42 et seq.).

completely confidential. With a view to institutional fragmentation, para. 4 states that State Parties can resolve their dispute by resorting to dispute settlement mechanisms of other intergovernmental organizations or established under any international agreement. The IHR thus create an open system for dispute settlement, which lists offers to the parties, but does not restrict them in their choice. The paramount interest seems to be that the conflict should be solved at any cost. This also explains the detailed introduction of peaceful means of dispute settlement. IHR dispute settlement has until now almost no visible relevance as law in practice (see *Appendix III* of the *WHO 2016 Ebola Review Committee Report* noting that the mechanism has not been formally invoked yet), adding to the partial confidentiality of proceedings. However, leading scholars in the field call upon States to consider dispute settlement through the Director-General or international arbitration.[35] The motivation behind this call is to push compliance by precedent, especially with a view to economic losses caused by IHR travel or trade restrictions or IHR non-compliance also amounting to human rights violations.[36] In order to illustrate the latter aspect in the case of Ebola, one can for example turn to the delays in WHO notification, which were a factor for the unchecked spread of Ebola (*Report of the Review Committee on the Role of the IHR (2005) in the Ebola Outbreak and Response (May 2016)*, §§ 56-62, suggesting to tie aid flows to IHR notification). This could amount to a violation of the obligation to respect the right to control of diseases as enshrined for example in Article 12 §2 (c) of the International Covenant on Economic, Social and Cultural Rights (ICESCR) in parallel to a potential non-compliance with Article 6 §1 IHR laying down notification requirements. Beyond hypothetical legal review as established in Article 56, the IHR also contain a reporting mechanism to the WHA by both, States and the WHO Director-General in Article 54 para. 1.[37]

This article does not deal with the classical debate resulting from the fragmented order of public international law, of whether WTO dispute settlement could piggyback international health law, and equip it with partial

---

35 Above Fn. 10.

36 Ibid.

37 In the broader picture, such IHR mechanisms have been described as increasingly transparent in terms of WHO political accountability and distinguishing it from its former technical medical role: Bruemmer, E & Taylor, A, "Institutional Transparency in Global Health Law-making: The World Health Organization and the Implementation of the International Health Regulations" in Bianchi, A & Peters, A (eds.), *Transparency in International Law*, 2013, 271 (292 & 293).

jurisdictional mechanisms. While the limited jurisdiction of WTO panels is not contested, the applicable law "[...] is not to be read in clinical isolation from public international law".[38] In other words, WTO law is substantially not a self-contained regime.[39] Procedurally, the WTO legal system is described elsewhere as a fine example of potential use for other special legal regimes, especially international environmental law.[40] However, it is likewise a clear result of the differing legal opinions surrounding this matter that the legal claims as such will follow the particular regime, in this case the covered WTO agreements and not claims based on international public health law. By and large, the IHR try to correspond with the WTO system judging from WHO policy documents exploring this direction, but this is still seen as a one-way street with the WTO not adopting the IHR – they are still parallel legal systems.[41] The WTO Appellate Body case *Brazil –*

---

38 See WTO Appellate Body, *United States – Standard for Reformulated and Conventional Gasoline* (complainants: Venezuela and Brazil), WT/DS2/9, May 10, 1996, 17. This was the first case actually reported by the Appellate Body.

39 Generally, while including an evaluation of the WTO see Simma, B & Pulkowski, D, "Of Planets and the Universe: Self-Contained Regimes in International Law" (2006), 17 *European Journal of International Law*, 483. This raises the additional question of state responsibility in case of breach of international public health norms. This - until now largely hypothetical – substantial question is beyond the scope of this article focusing on (the absence of) international judicial settings. For some evaluation see the contribution of *Elif Askin*, "Extraterritorial Human Rights Obligations of States in the Event of Disease Outbreaks" in this volume.

40 See UN International Law Commission Report (finalized by Koskenniemi, M), *Fragmentation of International Law: Difficulties Arising from the Diversification and Expansion of International Law*, A/CN.4/L.682 (April 13, 2006) §§ 165 et seq. Fragmentation as a phenomenon is understood as "[...] the emergence of specialized and relatively autonomous spheres of social action and structure." (§ 7) *Koskenniemi* distinguishes three types of conflict between general and special laws: (1) the conflict between the general law, and a particularly unorthodox interpretation of it, (2) the conflict between the general law, and a special law as an exception to it, and (3) the conflict between special laws. (§ 47) Here, types (2) and (3) are in play, and especially type (3) with a view to conflict between international economic and environmental law.

41 See also the restatement of the main conclusions of the *WHO Final Report of the Ebola Interim Assessment Panel* (July 2015) above Fn. 10 and further strong calls in the *WHO 2016 Review Committee Report* favoring WTO dispute settlement over an activation of the consensual IHR dispute settlement (marginal number 84 and its Appendix III). The focus on international trade and the role of the private sector in international public health law is too complex to fully cover within the cut of this article, but potential jurisdictional points of convergence with international economic law can briefly be sketched. Rich literature exists on inter-

Measures Affecting Imports of Retreaded Tyres (complainant: European Communities), WT/DS332/AB/R, December 3, 2007, is illustrative in this respect. The import restriction was justified as a public health necessity, because waste tires are *inter alia* breeding grounds for mosquitos transmitting dengue, yellow fever, and malaria (§ 153). Yet no reference is made to international public health sources. Also, note that eventually, the import ban was not upheld for a different reason, namely arbitrary Mercado Común del Sur (MERCOSUR) exemptions.

---

national trade law and public health focusing on domestic regulative restrictions of trade liberalization. For an overview see WHO & WTO, *WTO Agreements & Public Health: A joint study by the WHO and the WTO Secretariat*, 2002, and the critical scholarly appraisal by Howse, R, "The WHO/WTO Study on Trade and Public Health: A Critical Assessment" (2004), 24 *Journal of Risk Analysis*, 501. A relatively low-threshold introduction is provided by Labonte, R & Sanger, M, "Glossary of the World Trade Organisation and public health: parts 1 & 2" (2006), 60 *Journal of Epidemiology & Community Health,* 655 & 738. With a view to infectious diseases the prime entry point is the WTO Agreement on the Application of Sanitary and Phytosanitary Measures (SPS Agreement) whereby trade-restricting public health measures such as travel bans must meet justification. For a description of this link and the IHR connection to WTO law more generally see Fidler, D, "From International Sanitary Conventions to Global Health Security: The New International Health Regulations" (2005), 4 *Chinese Journal of International Law*, 325. *Fidler* makes a clear point in demonstrating how the WHO takes in WTO references, but the WTO by and large ignores the IHR regime (see especially 341). WTO law also protects intellectual property rights. Here, international WTO governance overlaps with the World Intellectual Property Organization (WIPO). For the latter aspect, see Abbott, F, "Distributed governance at the WTO-WIPO: an evolving model for open-architecture integrated governance" (2000), 3 *Journal of International Economic Law*, 63. For the substantial law see for example Mitchell, A & Voon, T, "Patents and Public Health in the WTO, FTAs and Beyond: Tension and Conflict in International Law" (2009), 43 *Journal of World Trade*, 571 and Abbott, F & Reichman, J, "The Doha Round's Public Health Legacy: Strategies for the Production and Diffusion of Patent Medicines under the Amended TRIPS Provisions" (2007), 10 *Journal of International Economic Law*, 921. For a focus on non-communicable diseases see for example McGrady, B, *Trade and Public Health: The WTO, Tobacco, Alcohol, and Diet*, 2011. Interestingly, the connection between international public health law and investment law and arbitration has not yet received as much attention. For an in-depth exception see Vadi, V, *Public Health in International Investment Law and Arbitration*, 2013. Case types especially include tobacco control regulation, and intellectual property rights. See Mercurio, B, "International investment agreements and public health: neutralizing a threat through treaty drafting" (2014), 92 *Bulletin of the World Health Organization*, 520.

2 Human Rights Case Law in the Context of the Ebola Crisis

As concerns international human rights protection, the respective UN treaty bodies offer quasi-judicial proceedings for individual complaints, which result in so called "considerations". The database for these considerations does not include any on a human right to health complaint from the West-African region (where Ebola's impact was greatest, providing the case study of this edited volume).[42] While the health security nexus is dealt with in other contributions of this edited volume, it should be quickly mentioned that the discourse around UN human rights accountability particularly centers on peacekeeping missions, and can correlate with infectious disease outbreak, although no case law is yet particularly pertinent.[43] As concerns the African Court on Human and People's Rights (within the African Union system), no relevant case law on the merits exists.[44] Next to it, the sub-regional Community Court of Justice (CCJ) of the Economic Community of West African States (ECOWAS) was originally only designed as a pure

---

42 UN treaty body jurisprudence is searchable at http://juris.ohchr.org/. However, even beyond legal consideration human rights fact-finding (also as an advocacy tool) is gaining attention in legal scholarship: Alston, P & Knuckey, S (eds.), *The Transformation of Human Rights Fact-Finding*, 2016. Especially see the contribution from Mégret, F, "Do Facts Exist, Can They Be 'Found', and Does it Matter?" in Alston, P & Knuckey, S (eds.), *The Transformation of Human Rights Fact-Finding*, 2016, 27 critically challenging the notion of facts as existing, and assessing (strategic) productions of truth.

43 See especially the contribution of *Mateja Steinbrück Platiše*, "The Changing Structure of Global Health Governance" in this volume detailing the allegation that the UN Stabilization Mission in Haiti (MINUSTAH) based on UN SC Resolution 1542 (April 30, 2004) is responsible for a 2010 cholera outbreak. US courts rejected claims due to immunity. For an overview to the complex human rights accountability of peacekeeping troops see Dannenbaum, T, "Translating the Standard of Effective Control into a System of Effective Accountability: How Liability Should be Apportioned for Violations of Human Rights by Member State Troop Contingents Serving as United Nations Peacekeepers" (2010), 51 *Harvard International Law Journal*, 113.

44 However, see the Decision of the Application No. 005/2011 in the matter of *Daniel Amare and Mulugeta Amare v. Republic of Mozambique and Mozambique Airlines* on claims concerning alleged hardships following a 26 days' flight delay, which the Court had to dismiss on procedural grounds, because Mozambique had not yet recognized the Court's jurisdiction. For an introduction to the matter see Ssenyonjo, M (ed.), *The African Regional Human Rights System: 30 Years after the African Charter on Human and Peoples' Rights*, 2012.

regional economic integration court, but later incorporated human rights jurisdiction through case law and a 2005 Protocol (apparently struggling with the European Court of Justice (ECJ) in its judicial discourse).[45] The CCJ case ECW/CCJ/APP/01/07 *Emmanuel Akpo & Anor v. G77 South-South Healthcare Delivery Programme & Anor* (October 16, 2008) is a curious case in many respects, although it does not rule on the merits. In it, two medical doctors seek access to court following termination of their employment contracts subjected to arbitration (this is common practice, and also *Joseph Toa Ba*'s last WHO 1993 and 1994 service contract in the introductory case was subjected to arbitration only, and thus beyond the ILOAT's jurisdiction, see § 2 of the Considerations in Judgment No. 2017). The G77 as a non-formal institution (and the counter to the G7 from the global South) is the employer within the context of a health development project. It is rare to have a court deal at all with questions of development administration. This is due to lack of fora and diplomatic privileges and immunities in multilateral development cooperation and the fact that bilateral development cooperation is mediated through the recipient state for those individuals affected, while taxpayers usually lack standing *vis-à-vis* their donor states,[46] or even legal standards can be difficult to determine like in Germany where development cooperation is not based on a parliamentary law.[47] Through an extensive argumentation, the CCJ finally reaches the conclusion that contractual arbitration clauses as such do not exclude its jurisdiction, because the complaint alleges human rights violations (§ 63), which cannot be sub-

45 See Alter, K, Helfer, L & McAllister, J, "A New International Human Rights Court for West Africa: The ECOWAS Community Court of Justice" (2013), 107 *The American Journal of International Law*, 737. On the governance of regional African institutions during the Ebola crisis see also the contribution of *Edefe Ojomo*, "Fostering Regional Health Governance in West Africa: The Role of the WAHO" in this volume. Despite the existence of these regional African protection mechanisms, the adherence to the public international rule of law is described as only skin-deep for the African elites in power, see Romano, C, "The Shadow Zones of International Judicialization" in Romano, C, Alter, K & Shany, Y (eds.), *The Oxford Handbook of International Judicialization*, 2013, 90 (99).

46 A notable popular action exception is the British case *R v Secretary of State for Foreign and Commonwealth Affairs, ex p World Development Movement Ltd* (November 10, 1994) where a Non-Governmental Organization (NGO) was granted spending in order to review an extraordinarily expensive dam funding in Malaysia without sufficient prove of socioeconomic impact.

47 See Dann, P, *The Law of Development Cooperation – A Comparative Analysis of the World Bank, the EU and Germany*, 2013, 341 et seq.

jected to (diplomatic) arbitration (§ 89). However, the relief sought for termination of contract and access to a Court concerns the application of the principle of rule of law but not human rights in the view of the court (§ 95).[48] The CCJ only has jurisdiction over employment contracts with ECOWAS (§ 93). This last point illustrates again that contentious issues of international health governance can be justiciable, if they constitute a conflict over an international employment contract (in this variation in form of the preliminary human rights question of access to court).

3 International Aviation Private Law

With a view to the Ebola crisis as the concrete case at hand, and the IHR more generally, one could also take into account the body of international

48 By means of comparative regional human rights law, it is interesting to note that the European Court of Human Rights (ECtHR) currently interprets the right to fair trial as enshrined in Article 6 of the 1950 Convention of the European Convention of Human Rights (ECHR) covering access to court as well. For a right to access to court in the case of civil proceedings this interpretation is built on case law stemming from the decision *Golder v. The United Kingdom*, ECtHR February 21, 1975. The case concerned a prisoner, Mr. *Golder*, who wished to initiate civil proceedings against an officer, but was not permitted to contact a solicitor. Mr. *Golder* believed that the officer had wrongly accused him of participating in a serious disturbance in the prison recreation area one evening, which had led to additional proceedings against him. In its Article 6 para. 1, sentence 1 the ECHR specifically grants a fair, and public hearing within a reasonable time by an independent and impartial tribunal established by law for determining civil rights. The ECtHR consequently asks if access to court is one factor or aspect of these rights? (§§ 27 & 28) The ECtHR develops a lengthy argumentation comparing language versions, international human rights law, and is particularly struggling with the fact that the ECHR preamble does not explicitly reference the rule of law principle. However, it then contextually demonstrates how the signatory governments to the ECHR embraced the rule of law principle. The final sentence of § 34 follows this line of reasoning: "And in civil matters one can scarcely conceive of the rule of law without there being a possibility of having access to the courts." In his separate opinion, it is *Alfred Verdross* himself attacking exactly this line of reasoning by underlining the selective ECHR approach in granting human rights – next to similar separate opinions by judges *Mehmed Zeika*, and *Sir Gerald Fitzmaurice*. The ECtHR finally arrives at the conclusion that access to court must also be an inherent right of Article 6 with regard to its context and object and purpose as a law-making treaty (§ 36).

aviation law, which is described as a legal labyrinth.[49] Any domestic private liability lawsuit issued by individuals against airlines[50] would ultimately follow substantial rules defined in international public law conventions creating private transnational rights and obligations, and interpreted by civil courts across diverse legal traditions.[51] During a public health emergency, attribution of damages to the carriers would be an obvious difficulty but interesting in cases of State travel bans exceeding WHO recommendations under the IHR.[52] It is impossible to screen all West-African domestic jurisdictions for the purposes of this article, and the article also leaves aside a potential supra-regional applicability of air passenger rights as contained in EU Regulation (EC) No 889/2002. However, for the substantial international law regulating damages due to delay see for example Article 19 of the Montreal Convention. Here, the carrier is not liable for damages if it

---

49 Havel, B & Sanchez, G, *The Principles and Practice of International Aviation Law*, 2014, 3. Besides, the author speaks out against the notion of the distinction between private and public international law (13) following a new trend to render this classical distinction obsolete. See for example Muir Watt, H, "Private International Law Beyond the Schism" (2011), 2 *Transnational Legal Theory*, 347. Through the prominent ICJ ruling *Case concerning Questions of Interpretation and Application of the 1971 Montreal Convention arising from the Aerial Incident at Lockerbie (Libyan Arab Jamahiriya v. United States of America)*, 1992 ICJ Reports 114 (April 14) the basic entanglement between both fields in international aviation law became highly visible. Yet, it remains a blind spot. For a perspective from international private law see Weller, M-P, Rentsch, B & Thomale, C, "Schmerzensgeld nach Flugzeugunglücken" (2015), 27 *Neue Juristische Wochenschrift*, 1909, and for an expanded English version Thomale, C, "Harmonization over Maximization: European choice of law solutions to aviation accidents" (2015), XIV *The Aviation & Space Journal*, 2.

50 Reported airlines affected by Ebola were Air France, Arik Air, Asky Airlines, British Airways, Emirates Airlines, Gambia Bird, Kenya Airways, Korean Air, and Senegal Airlines according to Geier, B, "Which airlines have been affected by Ebola?" (October 27, 2014), *Fortune*, available at http://for.tn/2m33EIp. Emirates Airlines was for example the first international airline to shut down a route to West Africa completely, see Withnall, A, "Ebola outbreak: Emirates becomes first major international airline to suspend all flights to virus-affected region" (August 3, 2014), *The Independent*, available at http://ind.pn/2n9Oxih. A huge expert debate surfaced on the pros and cons of flight bans, see for example Berenson, T, "Why Airlines and the CDC Oppose Ebola Flight Bans" (October 17, 2014), *Time*, available at http://www.time.com/3517197/ebola-frieden-travel-ban/.

51 Havel & Sanchez, *The Principles and Practice of International Aviation Law*, above Fn. 49, 12-14, 22 & 23. Relevant conventions are especially the 1929 Warsaw and the 1999 Montreal Conventions.

52 See above Fn. 17.

proves to take all measure that could reasonably be required to avoid. The "unavoidability" criterion is implicitly interpreted as a *force majeure* clause, thus potentially covering public health emergencies: If a carrier is not liable when having taken all reasonable measures, this must be true *a fortiori* when any such measure is senseless in the first place. Air carriers can also exculpate themselves when an independent third party was responsible for the loss, and the air carrier had no means of influence on them.[53] Hypothetical liability for death or injury due to transmission from one passenger to another would follow for example Article 17 of the Montreal Convention, but is unlikely with a view to the burden of proof and because it would be difficult to legally qualify such a transmission as an "accident".[54] In terms of actual cases for example the Kenyan Consumer Federation reportedly went against Kenya Airways before Court in order to cut off flights to Nigeria during the Ebola crisis for public health reasons, although they were in line with WHO recommendations under the IHR.[55] It seems that the case has not been concluded yet according to Kenyan lawyers. The complainant might have withdrawn the case.

The Chicago Convention which established the International Civil Aviation Organization (ICAO) within the UN system responsible for codification and standardization in the field also knows of an interstate dispute settlement body, which has been largely dormant until recently.[56] Other intersections with international public health are not visible apart from the international trade association IATA (International Air Transport Association) collaborating with WHO and ICAO.[57]

---

53 See Schmid, R, "Article 19 – Delay" in Giemulla, E & Schmid, R (eds.), *Commentary on the Montreal Convention*, 1999, 2008, 15.

54 See Masutti, A & Laconi, A, "Ebola Outbreak: Are Air Carriers Liable?" (November 23, 2014), *Mondaq*, available at http://bit.ly/2na3Asf.

55 See Thome, W, "Consumer organization goes to court to stop Nigeria flights" (August 19, 2014), *eTN – Global Travel Industry News*, available at http://bit.ly/2mKi70e.

56 Havel & Sanchez, *The Principles and Practice of International Aviation Law*, above Fn. 49, 22.

57 See IATA, *Air Transport & Communicable Diseases*, available at http://www.iata.org/whatwedo/safety/health/Pages/diseases.aspx. These actors also formed the informal Travel and Transport Task Force on Ebola virus disease outbreak in West Africa, also including the UN World Tourism Organization (UN WTO), the Airports Council International (ACI), and the World Travel and Tourism Council (WTTC), see Masutti & Laconi, "Ebola Outbreak", above Fn. 54.

4 Conclusion: The Absence of Established Judicial Discourse is a Phenomenon Common to International Public Health Governance

Focusing on international infectious disease governance with a view to the Ebola case study underlying this edited volume means dealing with a relatively small body of law. Nevertheless, this sub-thematic field of international public health governance is by no means an exception to the rule. The absence of coherent case law is a phenomenon common to international public health governance, and potentially international administrative law in general. In order to substantiate this claim, adjudication in other subfields of international public health governance needs to be analyzed. How is international public health law then defined? This body of law is extremely fragmented and scattered with no umbrella treaty, but rather a concept ("international public health") at its core.[58] In order to structure the legal data, this article departs from a 2008 article by *Allyn Taylor* allocating international agreements to categories of public health concern in its "Table 1".[59] Next to communicable disease control, these are: disability, global tobacco control, human rights, arms control, environmental health, international narcotic drug control, occupational health and safety, and international trade law. Human rights mechanisms including the quasi-judicial UN bodies, and among them the Committee on the Rights of Persons with Disabilities have been tackled above. The same is true for international trade law. For occupational health and safety,[60] the relevant umbrella legislation is especially the International Labour Organization (ILO) Occupational Safety and Health Convention (C155) from 1981. Articles 26 through 34 of the ILO Convention install a formal complaint mechanism, which can be triggered by ILO Member States, its tripartite Governing

58 For broader conceptualization of the fragmented body of international public health law in the context of globalization see Toebes, B, "International health law: an emerging field of public international law" (2016), 55 *Indian Journal of International Law*, 299. The lack of coherence and the absence of a meaningful dispute settlement mechanism in global health law are addressed by Gostin, L & Taylor, A, "Global Health Law: A Definition and Grand Challenges", 1 *Public Health Ethics*, 53 (59). The authors, however, flag that the IHR are an important case of concrete normative standards for national epidemiological surveillance (ibid.).

59 See Taylor, "International Law, and Public Health Policy", above Fn. 19.

60 Apart from such legal aspects, *Christian R. Thauer* deals with a South-African case illustrating the role of the private sector in workplace health in this edited volume.

Body, or any Conference delegate (thus allowing employer or worker representatives the same right). None of the several complaints has yet dealt with C155.[61] As concerns global tobacco control, the 2003 WHO Framework Convention on Tobacco Control (FCTC) provides for a dispute settlement mechanism similar to the IHR in its Article 27, which has met almost no State acceptance yet.[62] Likewise, the refined dispute settlement mechanisms provided in Article 32 of the UN Convention against Illicit Traffic in Narcotic Drugs and Psychotropic Substances granting a potentially prominent role to the ICJ has not been accepted by States in practice.[63] The category of environmental health leads to the international environmental law, but international environmental adjudication usually takes place before borrowed fora.[64] Last but not least, it is necessary to highlight the specific intersection between international public health law, and the regimes of international humanitarian and international criminal law, often integrating standards of medical ethics. Here, individual criminal prosecution of medical war crimes is a real option.[65]

Next to the categories *Taylor* uses, there are still more technical areas of high importance in international public health practice, for example food safety. Here technical standardization can be fairly legalistic, and adjudicated through WTO dispute settlement.[66] *Taylor* also does not distinguish

---

61 By comparison and in terms of broader reporting obligations, which do not tackle concrete cases, the ILO Committee of Experts on the Application of Conventions and Recommendations, comprised of jurists, has so far issued 27 recommendations on matters of occupational safety and health.

62 Jarmann, H, *The Politics of Trade and Tobacco Control*, 2015. At the same time, the FCTC monitoring mechanism has been characterized as strengthening surveillance, but not compliance. See Taylor, A & Thorpe, J, "Strengthening the Framework Convention on Tobacco Control's Monitoring Mechanism: An Agenda for Reform" (2014), *Report on behalf of the O'Neill Institute for National and Global Health Law at the Georgetown University Law Center*.

63 Gurulé, J, "The 1988 U.N. Convention against Illicit Traffic in Narcotic Drugs and Psychotropic Substances – A Ten Year Perspective: Is International Cooperation Merely Illusory?"(1998), 22 *Fordham International Law Journal*, 74 (117).

64 Dupuy, P-M & Viñuales, J, *International Environmental Law*, 2015, 243 et seq. (especially 247). This subject is not dealt with in depth, because it essentially concerns another highly complex area of public international law.

65 For an overview see Mehring, S, *First Do No Harm: Medical Ethics in International Humanitarian Law*, 2014, 148-175.

66 See Pereira, R, "Why Would International Administrative Activity Be Any Less Legitimate? – A Study of the Codex Alimentarius Commission" (2008), 9 *German Law Journal*, 1693.

the important practitioner field of sexual and reproductive health and rights, which is not highly legalized despite its wording.[67]

Note that this categorization builds upon substantial public international law regimes. Another way of structuring the positive law material would be to categorize according to institutions. This would allow highlighting issues such as the proliferation of international institutions beyond the WHO involving innovative governance structures across public and private, international and national categories.[68] Their legal status can change flexibly,[69] and any adjudication is often limited to complaints from individuals with a contractual relation to the institution.[70] Yet, nowhere will we find a comprehensive system of adjudication in the forefront of international public health governance.

---

67 For an introduction see Gebhard, J & Trimiño Mora, D, "Reproductive Rights, International Regulation" in Lachenmann, F & Wolfrum, R (eds.), *The Max Planck Encyclopedia of public international law*, 2013, available at http://opil.ouplaw.com/home/EPIL. On the distinct practical nature of human rights based approaches (here with a view to the notion of sexual and reproductive rights) to be distinguished from the normative sphere see later Fn. 85.

68 On the competitive institutional pressures that the WHO is facing see Hanrieder, T, "Die Weltgesundheitsorganisation unter Wettbewerbsdruck: Auswirkungen der Vermarktlichung globaler Gesundheitspolitik" in Dingwerth, K, Krewer, D & Nölke, A (eds.), *Die organisierte Welt – Internationale Beziehungen und Organisationsforschung*, 2009, 165. For a comparative institutional study of the WHO by the same author see *International Organization in Time: Fragmentation and Reform*, 2015. From a legal perspective see Clarke, L, *Public-Private Partnerships and Responsibility under International Law: A Global Health Perspective*, 2014.

69 See for example Triponel, A, "Global Fund to Fight AIDS, Tuberculosis and Malaria: A New Legal and Conceptual Framework for Providing International Development Aid" (2009), 35 *North Carolina Journal of International Law*, 101, describing how the Global Fund (GFATM) was founded as a Swiss foundation first administratively hosted by WHO, and then expanded its status as a quasi-International Organization, especially through negotiating privileges and immunities equal to an International Organization.

70 See for example the GFATM's recognition of the jurisdiction of the ILOAT pursuant to its Governing Body decision GB.303/11/2, 303rd session (2008), Reports of the Programme, Financial and Administrative Committee, marginal numbers 45-48 following the decision memo GB.303/PFA/15/2 (2008). The ILOAT case-law database indicates sixteen judgments as of September 1, 2016, available at http://www.ilo.org/dyn/triblex/triblexmain.showList?p_lang=en&p_org_id=83.

III What Does the Absence of Coherent Case Law Mean?

The thrust of this article rests on the description of the phenomenon that no thorough judicial discourse has yet been established in international public health. At the same time, the absence of a coherent body of international case law in the technical field of international disease control, and the fragmented body of international public health law more generally requires one to investigate its function and meaning. Here the article now proceeds to restate some theoretical frameworks – while being aware that an in-depth theoretical contribution is beyond its means. It cannot contribute to the foundational tension between law and facts in legal theory, let alone given the fact that international adjudication is a challenging subject for legal philosophy.[71] Instead, it departs from the concrete phenomenon just described, namely the virtual absence of case law in international public health law.[72] In order to do so it is important to preliminarily remark that this article does not disqualify the legal nature of public international law, because of this incoherent enforcement structure.[73] International (health) law might well be described as "inherently imperfect"[74] – but there is no better coordination mechanism currently. This is why it is more interesting to enquire into the

71 Besson, S, "Legal Philosophical Issues of International Adjudication" in Romano, C, Alter, K & Shany, Y (eds.), *The Oxford Handbook of International Judicialization*, 2013, 413 (416). For further overview see Kammerhofer & D'Aspremont, *International Legal Positivism*, above Fn. 13.

72 Another factor in the case of the Ebola crisis could be that access to adjudication is *per se* limited in and for developing countries. For a case study see for example Romano, C, "International Justice and Developing Countries: A Quantitative Analysis" (2002), 1 *The Law and Practice of International Courts and Tribunals*, 367.

73 For an introduction to the debate between international relations and law see Koh, H, "Why Do Nations Obey International Law?" (1997), 106 *The Yale Law Journal*, 2599. At the extreme, the anthropologist, *Susan L. Erikson* strikes down the quality of international health law as such in this edited volume, because of the highly visible absence of a coherent enforcement mechanism. Suffice it to add that post-colonial theory goes one step further, and questions the substantial foundations of public international law in any development context. For a review essay see Riegner, M, "How universal are international law and development? Engaging with postcolonial and Third World scholarship from the perspective of its Other" (2012), 45 *Verfassung und Recht in Übersee (VRÜ) / Law and Politics in Africa, Asia and Latin America*, 232. For a postcolonial account from a medical perspective see Chakrabarti, P, *Medicine and Empire 1600-1960*, 2013.

74 Taylor, "International Law, and Public Health Policy", above Fn. 19, 672.

function of adjudication. As concerns the theories offered, this article adheres to a constructivist perspective, but will also recognize more radical voices from empirical and critical legal theories. With a view to the application to the international legal public health system, the article will point out the type of communication that is missing between technical experts and lawyers prior to the establishment of a coherent judicial discourse, and the underlying threat to subjective rights in the absence of case law.

In order to find a constructivist response, the multi-functional understanding of international judicial institutions exercising international authority by, and not limiting it to the single function of adjudication proposed by *Armin von Bogdandy* and *Ingo Venzke* gives first clues. They distinguish the following functions: dispute settlement or adjudication in individual cases (1), stabilization of normative expectations (2), law making (3), and control and legitimation (4). A single-function understanding of adjudication focuses on the classical promise of international Courts to bring about peace between States in a concrete case.[75] A multifunctional understanding of international adjudication can be able to embrace international administrative adjudication beyond interstate adjudication, and systematically embed it into its social context. Adjudication then also serves to reconstruct social realities by establishing the facts of a concrete case. International administrative processes are difficult to understand, especially in highly technical areas such as international public health. Coherent case law would make it easier to understand central issues for lawyers by delivering critical facts.

Acknowledging the communication between the spheres of international law and empirics must not blur their lines. However, there are more radical approaches calling to blend law with empirical findings. Empirical legal studies are for example a popular approach in the US.[76] Another, related

---

75 Bogdandy & Venzke, *In Whose Name?*, above Fn. 15, 5-19. Note that also this dimension can be conceptually extrapolated, for example to assigning the international judicial system as a whole the functions "[…] to provide an institutional framework for cooperation, to promote compliance with international law, and to reinforce rights-respecting democracy on the national level." Martinez, J, "Towards an International Judicial System" (2003), 56 *Stanford Law Review*, 429 (463). The latter article is a liberal call for a coherent international judicial system, and provides an analytical framework.

76 For public international law see for example Chilton, A & Tingley, D, "Why the Study of International Law Needs Experiments" (2013), 52 *Columbia Journal of Transnational Law*, 173. On the different legal cultures in the US and Germany see Towfigh, E, "Empirical arguments in public law doctrine: Should empirical

approach is the new legal realism advocated for by *Andrew Lang*.[77] He describes the clash of the "relative objectivities" of both legal formalism and scientific empiricism. Applying his approach to WTO disputes, he shows how much this clash can be about control: Are empirical findings applied within the controlling framework of legal concepts or vice versa?[78] The result is a complicated "mode of mixed legal-scientific techno-governance".[79] Without buying into the foundations of empirical legal approaches, this description fits with the struggle in the introductory case of this article to acknowledge medical causality and legal qualifications of causality alike.

In critical legal studies, the objectivity of law as such is refused. Law is instead described as pure fiction. The function of the law is the fictional but necessary re-construction of a social conflict in order to handle this conflict, which is perceived as beyond the control of the real world. The resource of this legal production machinery would be the passion to fight by the parties before an independent umpire.[80]

While upholding the distinction between the legal and the empirical sphere, this article argues that case law is key to understanding the fragmented field of international public health law. It processes factual accounts and helps lawyers to shape their argumentation. The mere existence of dispute settlement mechanisms is practically insufficient as long as they are

---

legal studies make a 'doctrinal turn'?" (2014), 12 *I-Con*, 670. On infusing law with the specific empirics of (behavioral) economics and psychology see Aaken, A, "Behavioral International Law and Economics" (2014), 55 *Harvard International Law Journal*, 421.

77 Lang, A, "New Legal Realism, Empiricism, and Scientism: The Relative Objectivity of Law and Social Science" (2015), 28 *Leiden Journal of International Law*, 231.

78 Ibid., 248 & 254.

79 Ibid., 241.

80 These are thoughts from the article "Rechtsentfremdungen: Zum gesellschaftlichen Mehrwert des zwölften Kamels"/"Alienating Justice: On the Social Surplus Value of the Twelth Camel" by *Gunther Teubner & Peer Zumbansen*. The German version was published in (2000), 21 *Zeitschrift für Rechtssoziologie/The German Journal of Law and Society*, 189. The English translation can be found in Nelken, D & Pribán, J (eds.), *Law's New Boundaries: Consequences of Legal Autopoiesis*, 2001, 21. I am leaning on the German original. *Teubner & Zumbansen* build on an essay by *Niklas Luhmann* narrating the inheritance battle of three sons over their dead father's camel. Essentially, one camel is missing, which blocks the sons from managing their conflict. Finally, a kadi guides them to controlling the situation by providing for a twelfth camel, which is as real as it is fictional in serving as a necessary projection for the sons in the very process.

dormant: The example of the IHG has just been mentioned above. The legal argument becomes vivid and strong when there are actual cases.[81] Case law would create what is labeled as "judicial governance" entailing a system-building function in the fragmented international legal order by stabilizing expectations.[82] Judicial decisions can have what is labeled as interpretative authority beyond mere decisional authority.[83] This is not a formal claim for the common law doctrine of precedent in the international legal order, but for recognition of the function of case law. Case law also makes the normative sphere visible for natural and social scientists. Public health is a discipline rooted in medical science as a foremost natural, empirical science, and reaches out to social science methods as well acknowledging the "social determinants of health".[84] It is prone to natural fallacy arguments when normative statements are inferred from descriptive statements: If publications are concerned with international norms, they consequently tend to capture the normative sphere with quantitative and/or qualitative social science methodological sets, often without being aware of the normative argument as such. For example when public international law treaties are only understood as a "type of global intervention" from this perspective meant to create impact.[85] At the same time, there are relevant voices in the international

---

81 Jacobs, M, "Precedents: Lawmaking Through International Adjudication" in Bogdandy, A von & Venzke, I (eds.), *International Judicial Lawmaking – On Public Authority and Democratic Legitimation in Global Governance*, 2012, 35 (43).

82 Ibid., 49 & 51.

83 Besson, "Legal Philosophical Issues of International Adjudication", above Fn. 71, 420.

84 For an account of the disciplinary development see for example Rosen, G, *A History of Public Health*, 1993, and more tailored to the case study at hand Rhodes, J, *The End of Plagues: The Global Battle against Infectious Disease*, 2013. In Germany, the 19th century physician *Rudolf Virchow* was one of the founders of "social medicine", see Ackerknecht, E, *Rudolf Virchow: Doctor, Statesman, Anthropologist*, 1953. For an introduction to the discipline as such see Detels, R, Gulliford, M & Karim, Q A et al., *Oxford Textbook of Global Public Health*, 6th edition, 2015.

85 See for example Hoffman, S & Røttingen, J, "Assessing the Expected Impact of Global Health Treaties: Evidence From 90 Quantitative Evaluations" (2015), 105 *American Journal of Public Health*, 26. According to these authors, publications on the subject-matter are still few, while they perceive an international policy-making trend in international public health treaty negotiation. They contrast potential policy and economic impact to missing social impact. Their approach is described as a qualitative summary of quantitative impact, and is proposed to be extended in detail according to Hoffman, S, Hughsam, M & Randhawa, H et al.,

public health community now highlighting this gap between empirical evidence, and a (conscious) normative position, and calling for improved dialogue.[86] Other voices attribute the infrequent use of any WHO dispute settlement in part to its domination by personnel trained in public health and medicine only.[87] This leads to the conclusion that the technocratic nature of international public health administration is a strong factor in explaining the domain-specific absence of established judicial discourse.

This article does not offer a contribution to legal theory on its own. However, within the sketched field of diverse approaches that legal theory offers, this article can take a position. While it does not argue for blending the normative and the empirical sphere, the virtual absence of case law results in a loss of a filtering mechanism for facts. The absence of coherent case law in international public health, and specifically as concerns disease control, shows how this supportive function of case law is missing. Arguably,

---

"International law's effects on health and its social determinants: protocol for a systematic review, meta-analysis, and meta-regression analysis", 5 *Systematic Reviews*, 64. Note that international human rights protection as a public international law regime is similarly contrasted by a human rights-based approach in health (and even more generally in international development aid and humanitarian assistance). For an introduction to the normative analysis of the human right to health see the contributions of *A. Katarina Weilert*, "The Right to Health in International Law – Normative Foundations and Doctrinal Flaws" and *Elif Askin*, "Extraterritorial Human Rights Obligations of States in the Event of Disease Outbreaks" in this volume. By contrast, Risse, T, Ropp, S & Sikkink, K (eds.), *The Power of Human Rights: International Norms and Domestic Change*, 1999 manage to bridge human rights advocacy and the normative sphere. Again in this edited volume, *Christian R. Thauer* references their work, and *Hunter Keys, André den Exter & Bonnie Kaiser* deal with specific questions involving NGOs.

86 In particular, see the contribution by Ooms, G, "From international health to global health: how to foster a better dialogue between empirical and normative disciplines" (2014), *14 BMC International Health and Human Rights*, 36. For *Ooms*, public health should inter-disciplinarily be able to comprise both, the empirical and the normative level. His main concern is, how to improve fruitful dialogue between different disciplinary backgrounds. In a nutshell, he argues that empirical researchers are to reflect their normative assumptions, and normative researchers are to consider more standardized paper structures in order to translate their line of reasoning. For a splendid (because it is as short as it is correct) overview on how to carry out inter-disciplinary research from a legal perspective see Taekema, S & Klink, B van, "On the Border. Limits and Possibility of Interdisciplinary Research" in Klink, B van & Taekema, S (eds.), *Law and Method. Interdisciplinary Research into Law*, 2011, 7.

87 Stein, "International Integration and Democracy", above Fn. 16, 499.

adjudication can function as a transmission belt between both spheres. Normative decisions predispose a basic understanding of facts.[88] In the case of adjudication, these facts are to an extent brought to the lawyer. The court or tribunal is a place where the facts and the norms must meet. Questions of legality often do not form in the abstract alone, but rely on empirical assumptions.[89] *Sabino Cassese* points to a different, individual dimension of the absence of case law: With the absence of an international rule of law, he argues, and global governance phenomena thus little structured by coherent international case law, individual procedural rights and obligations such as participation come under threat.[90]

IV Conclusions

Case law in matters of international public health law can be described as scarce and scattered, summing up the cursory inventory provided within this article. In terms of the international public health law governing infectious disease control, and particularly the Ebola crisis, the following picture evolves: The IHR provide a dispute settlement mechanism, which is by and large unused and forgotten. The WTO dispute settlement does not piggyback international public health law governing infectious disease control. Borrowed fora for the international law governing infectious disease control exist for employment contract claims of international public servants, human rights case law, and international private aviation law (substantial assessment of damage claims issued against aircraft carriers would principally stem from public international law conventions). This picture does not differ drastically from other areas of international public health law.

The article also includes a proposal to legally interpret the wording of IHR dispute settlement in analogy to the WTO DSU. In commenting on the IHR dispute settlement mechanism, it argues that the WHO Director-General and the WHA are assigned a quasi-judicial function. However, in the cases foreseen for the WHA concerning contentious disputes with the WHO itself, the drafters of the 2005 IHR should have placed this function in the wider UN system, for example with the Secretary General. The article does

88 Petersen, N, "Braucht die Rechtswissenschaft eine empirische Wende?" (2010), 49 *Der Staat*, 435 (437).

89 Petersen, "Avoiding the common wisdom fallacy", above Fn. 1, 304 et seq.

90 Cassese, S, *Chi governa il mondo?*, 2012, 92-96.

not entail a legal policy call to increase litigation. However, dormant dispute settlement mechanisms such as the one provided by the IHR should not pass by unnoticed, and thus become a real policy option for actors concerned.[91]

The described virtual absence of a coherent body of case law demonstrates that the proliferation of international courts and tribunals is regime-specific. In fields such as international public health law, which are highly driven by empirical science, this leads to increased invisibility of the legal argument and natural fallacy arguments. Functionally, lawyers lack a mechanism opening the door to relevant empirical data at the same time: Case law can filter facts and co-condition legality decisions – even while upholding the separating lines between the normative and the factual spheres. In the absence of case law, lawyers cannot develop a basic understanding of the empirical sphere through the facts as established in (leading) cases. Instead, lawyers need to develop a basic understanding of the discipline of public health in order to apply the law to hypothetically relevant case scenarios.

91 See above Fn. 10.

The Role of the Human Right to Health

The Right to Health in International Law – Normative Foundations and Doctrinal Flaws

*A. Katarina Weilert**

Abstract

The human right to health is a highly complex right. The broad conception of health as devised in the preamble of the Constitution of the World Health Organization amounts to a moral and political claim, but cannot form the basis of a legal right to health. This contribution briefly introduces different sources of the right to health and identifies Article 12 of the International Covenant on Economic, Social and Cultural Rights as the central norm, which is examined in greater detail. The structure of the right to health is challenging in various dimensions: First, the right to health, although considered amongst social rights, combines aspects from all three generations of human rights. Second, it often serves as an umbrella right and loses its distinctiveness as virtually everything can have an impact on a person's health. Third, the right to health is a hybrid right combining elements of both an individual's as well as a public health approach. When it comes to infectious diseases, the individual's rights can clash with a public health-strategy. In this contribution, it is argued that the different aspects of the right to health should be better distinguished. As an individual human right, the right to health should be perceived in a narrower sense focusing primarily on medical care. As an obligation to promote public health, the human right to health can be seen in a broader context, embracing also the underlying determinants of health. Combatting infectious diseases is one of the main tasks within the obligations of states to promote public health. Public health cannot be measured in terms of the feasibility of individual legal actions, but should primarily be seen as a policy strategy (with different accountability structures), embracing national and international actors who need to be coordinated in terms of International Health Governance.

---

* Dr. (Freie Universität, Berlin), LL.M. (University College London), Senior Research Fellow at the FEST (Forschungsstätte der Evangelischen Studiengemeinschaft e.V., Protestant Institute for Interdisciplinary Research, Heidelberg). All websites last accessed on January 10, 2017.

I The Complexity of the Right to Health

International Health Governance (IHG) presupposes that the protection and promotion of health is not solely an issue of the internal affairs of a person's state of residence, but has a strong cross-border dimension. Out of the necessity to view health in international terms, two streams of reasoning prevail – the first arguing for health as a security issue and the second relating to health as a human right or moral obligation. Infectious diseases do not stop at borders and states and other actors have an interest to ensure that international traffic and trade, key features of the globalized world, are safe. Therefore, the first reason to consider health as an international issue is rooted in the interest of states concerning their security.[1] The second stream of reasoning, the human rights approach, focuses on the individual or on specific groups of human beings or the population as such, and thus establishes a moral, political and legal responsibility to promote the health of human beings within and across national borders.[2] This contribution provides an overview of the sources, content, inner structure and actual state of the right to health. Although in recent times literature and documents released by international institutions (such as the World Health Organization (WHO) and the United Nations Special Rapporteurs on the right to health) have increased on this topic, there are many open questions. To date, there is no unambiguous definition of health and the scope of a universal right to health. Furthermore, there is an intense debate on how to promote a legal

---

1 Compare the contributions of *Robert Frau*, "Combining the WHO's International Health Regulations (2005) with the UN Security Council's Powers: Does it Make Sense for Health Governance?" and *Ilja Richard Pavone*, "Ebola and Securitization of Health" in this volume. Toebes, B, "International health law: an emerging field of public international law" (2015), 55 *Indian Journal of International Law*, 299 (312 et seqq.) divides the scope of international health law into three categories as she considers "health and international trade" to be separate from "health security threats". Gostin, L O, "Global Health and the Law" (2014), 370 *New England Journal of Medicine*, 1732 (1732) speaks of "multiple spheres, ranging from national security, economic prosperity, and sustainable development to human rights and social justice".

2 Compare Ruger, J P, "Normative Foundations of Global Health Law" (2007-2008), 96 *Georgetown Law Journal*, 423 et seqq. which addresses legal, political and moral aspects of global health law; Hunt, P & Backmann, G, "Health Systems and the Right to the Highest Attainable Standard of Health" in Clapham, A & Robinson, M (eds.), *Realizing the Right to Health*, 2009, 40 (57) maintaining that the right to health "is the only perspective that is both underpinned by universally recognized moral values and reinforced by legal obligations".

and effective right to health instead of a mere political ideal. Moreover, there is no clear distinction of public (in the sense of population[3]) health strategies and an individual right to health.[4]

Despite its uncontested significance, for a long time health has not been perceived as a human right.[5] *Mahesh S. Poudel* notes that conventionally, people used to see health as being part of the private and not the public realm.[6] It seems that many people have not been used to the thought that there can be human rights claims and international responsibilities with regard to health.[7] There is also nearly unanimous agreement that there is no "right to be healthy", as health is dependent on many factors that are out of reach of a state or any other entity (for example genetic predispositions).[8] As health is most important for an individual's well-being and is the basis for pursuing other aims, it is a precondition for the enjoyment of other human rights.[9] If health is severely affected (as it was during the epidemic of

---

3 Compare Toebes, B, "Human rights and public health: towards a balanced relationship" (2015), 19 *International Journal of Human Rights*, 488. See also Tobin, J, *The Right to Health in International Law*, 2012, 54 ("[…] a level of moral agreement – not merely legal or political – still exists and is reflected in the social process that leads to the recognition of a particular interest, such as the highest attainable standard of health, as a human right").

4 Compare for the concepts of "individual rights" *ICJ LaGrand Case (Germany v. United States of America)*, ICJ Reports 2001, 466 para. 76 et seq. ("individual rights").

5 Bielefeldt, H, "Der Menschenrechtsansatz im Gesundheitswesen" in Frewer, A & Bielefeldt, H (eds.), *Das Menschenrecht auf Gesundheit*, 2016, 19 (20), speaks of a "Wahrnehmungsdefizit" (deficit of perception) with regard to the right to health; Poudel, M S, "Right to Health and Its Jurisprudence: An Overview" (2011), 5 *National Judical Academy Law Journal*, 215 (220): "The right to health is unquestionable part of international human rights law, but still many people do not grasp that it is a fundamental human right."

6 Poudel, "The Right to health", above Fn. 5, 218; compare also Riedel, E, *Right to Health, MPEPIL*, 2016, para. 1: Historically private entities (families, churches, charities) were predominantly responsible for fighting diseases, however, with respect to epidemics, state institutions were actively engaged.

7 Bielefeldt, "Menschenrechtsansatz", above Fn. 5, 51.

8 Bielefeldt, "Menschenrechtsansatz", above Fn. 5, 22 ("Kann es einen Rechtsanspruch auf Gesundheit im eigentlichen Sinne überhaupt geben und wer soll ihn garantieren?"); Riedel, E, "The Human Right to Health: Conceptual Foundations" in Clapham, A & Robinson, M (eds.), *Swiss Human Rights Book Vol. 3, Realising the Right to Health*, 2012, 21 (28); CESCR, *General Comment No. 14 on the right to the highest attainable standard of health E/C.12/2000/4*, para. 8.

9 CESCR, *General Comment 14*, above Fn. 8, para. 1; Riedel, E, "The Human Right to Health" in Clapham, A & Robinson, M (eds.), *Realizing the Right to Health*,

the deadly Ebola virus in West Africa from 2014-2016), the right to health can have overlaps with the fundamental right to life.

Human rights are usually divided into three so-called "generations":[10] (1) liberty rights and rights to participate in political life, (2) economic, social and cultural rights and (3) – debatable – group rights. The third category is only "emerging" and many questions are unsolved, for example whether a group can be a rights-holder at all.[11] Usually, the right to health is perceived to fall into the second category. However, the right to health combines – as will be shown later – aspects of all three generations as it includes freedoms and entitlements as well as a protection for vulnerable groups and the underlying determinants of health.[12] This adds to the non-specific structure of the right to health and forms part of its impediment to make the right more effective.

The right to health is framed as part of a catalogue of universal and fundamental rights. This means that generally every human being can refer to this right and that this right does not depend on any qualification of the individual or preliminary behavior or social role.[13] Since the right to health

---

2009, 21: "Health is a fundamental human right, indispensable for the exercise of many other human rights, and necessary for living a life in dignity." See also: Oldring, L & Jerbi, S, "Advancing a Human Rights Approach on the Global Health Agenda" in Clapham, A & Robinson, M (eds.), *Realizing the Right to Health*, 2009, 102: "There is broad agreement that health policies, programmes and practices can have a direct bearing on the enjoyment of human rights [...]"; Poudel, "The Right to health", above Fn. 5, 220: "Health is a fundamental human right which is indispensable for the exercise of other human rights."

10 Today many authors claim that the difference between civil and political rights on the on hand and economic and social rights on the other hand is artificial, compare Kumar, C R, "Human Rights Crisis of Public Health Policy" (2012), 52 *Indian Journal of Int. Law*, 351 (355, 386).

11 The existence of group rights is highly disputed in international law as this dimension of rights faces many flaws. Compare for a general discussion Bisaz, C, *The Concept of Group Rights in International Law*, 2012; Bronwlie, I, *Principles of Public International Law*, 7th edition, 2008, 567. Compare for group rights in the "Banjul-Charta": Schaarschmidt, J, "Gruppenrechte als Menschenrechte? – Erkenntnisse aus dem afrikanischen Völkerrecht" in Junge Wissenschaft im öffentlichen Recht e.V. (ed.), *Kollektivität*, 2012, 97 et seqq. She maintains that group rights can be individual rights – individuals having a right as being part of the group – as well as group rights as such (113).

12 Compare Akhvlediani, M, "Right to Health Care in International Law" (2008), 1 *Saertášoriso samartlis žurnali*, 236 (244).

13 Bielefeldt, "Menschenrechtsansatz", above Fn. 5, 25.

not only includes freedoms, but also entitlements to prevent diseases, restore health and provide for the underlying factors of health, the right to health has been criticized as being a mere political ideal. The tension between the claim of health as a universal and fundamental right and the notion that only (if at all) a basic protection can be provided for all people, is one of the great challenges and unsolved problems which will be dealt with in this contribution.

A further challenge of any legal framing of the human right to health is the problem that "health" itself is an imprecise term.[14] The well-known and manifoldly criticized[15] definition of the preamble of the WHO Constitution reads: "Health is a state of complete physical, mental and social well-being and not merely the absence of disease or infirmity."[16] This broad and controversial conception of health emphatically removes it from a mere medical connotation and views it in a larger social context.[17] There is an extended discussion among philosophers and social scientists around the definition of health, which cannot be mapped out here.[18] In international human rights law, health is usually conceived as a concept not being restricted to physical health, but also embracing mental health and furthermore being related to a "healthy" social and ecological environment. It is persuading to look at

---

14 Compare Akhvlediani, "Right to Health Care", above Fn. 12, 242.

15 Compare for a discussion on the definition of "health" Toebes, B, *The Right to Health as a Human Right in International Law*, 1999, 21 et seqq. (she suggests to abstain from any clear definition of "health" within the right to health).

16 Constitution of the World Health Organization, Preamble. The Constitution was adopted by the International Health Conference held in New York from June 19 to July 22, 1946, signed on July 22, 1946 by the representatives of 61 states (Off. Rec. Wld Hlth Org., 2, 100), and entered into force on April 7, 1948.

17 Compare for a discussion of the WHO definition of health: Toebes, "International health law", above Fn. 1, 303. See also Marmot, M, "Social Causes of Social Inequalities in Health" in Anand, S, Peter, F & Sen, A (eds.), *Public Health, Ethics, and Equity*, 2006, 37-61; Wikler, D, "Personal and Social Responsibility for Health" in Anand, S, Peter, F & Sen, A (eds.), *Public Health, Ethics, and Equity*, 2006, 109-134.

18 Huber, M et al., "How Should we Define Health" (2011), 343 *British Medical Journal*, d4163; Nussbaum, M, *Creating Capabilities: The Human Development Approach*, 2011; Sen, A, *Development as Freedom*, 1999; Venkatapuram, S, *Health Justice: An Argument for the Capabilities Approach*, 2011; Siegrist, J, "Gesundheitsverständnis und Verantwortung für die Gesundheit" in Weilert, A K (ed.), *Gesundheitsverantwortung zwischen Markt und Staat*, 2015, 53; Rothhaar, M, "Ansätze zur philosophischen Rechtfertigung eines Rechts auf solidarische Gesundheitsversorgung" in Weilert, A K (ed.), *Gesundheitsverantwortung zwischen Markt und Staat*, 2015, 243, 245 et seqq.

health in this comprehensive way. However, if it comes to the concept of a human right which creates clear legal obligations and shall ideally be enforceable, this conception of health causes great difficulties. The vast majority of people could likely be considered to be "not healthy" if they refer to the WHO definition as a model with which they compare their actual life. In addition to that, the full protection of human health is factually and legally impossible as "virtually every activity has some implications for human health".[19] Thus, this broad definition can be used as a political aspiration and as an ideal, but not as the basis of international obligations.[20]

The problems around the right to health as sketched in this introduction shall in the following be further examined by recalling the sources of the right to health and the content attributed to them (II), analyzing the tension of the individual's right to health and the collective right to public health (III), as well as a reflection on the content of the right to health (IV).

II Sources of the Right to Health

The right to health has been widely acknowledged in multilateral contracts and further international documents.[21] This contribution concentrates on the most important sources. It does not include regional instruments and conventions to maintain and improve health, such as Article 16 African Charter on Human and People's Rights ("Banjul Charter"), Article 11 and 13 Revised European Social Charter, Article 35 European Union Charter of

19 Tomaeševski, K, "Health Rights" in Eide, A, Krause, C & Rosas, A (eds.), *Economic, Social and Cultural Rights*, 1995, 125, 127.

20 The WHO preamble is not legally binding, see Krennerich, M, "Das Menschenrecht auf Gesundheit. Grundzüge eines komplexen Rechts" in Frewer, A & Bielefeldt, H (eds.), *Das Menschenrecht auf Gesundheit*, 2016, 57 (59); Hestermeyer, H, *Human Rights and the WTO. The Case of Patents and Access to Medicines*, 2007, 113 (with further references). Under another view, the WHO preamble should be regarded as binding law, Toebes, *The Right to Health as a Human Right*, above Fn. 15, 33.

21 For a comprehensive overview see: Toebes, *The Right to Health as a Human Right*, above Fn. 15, 27 et seqq.; a shorter overview is provided by Riedel, "Human Right to Health", above Fn. 9, 22 et seqq.; Riedel, "The Human Right to Health: Conceptual Foundations", above Fn. 8, 22 et seqq.; Riedel, *Right to Health*, above Fn. 6, para. 6 et seqq.; Krennerich, "Menschenrecht auf Gesundheit", above Fn. 20, 58 et seqq. Compare for the question whether the right to health belongs to customary international law: Hestermeyer, *Human Rights and the WTO*, above Fn. 2120, 127.

Fundamental Rights and Article 10 Additional Protocol to the American Convention on Human Rights in the Area of Economic, Social and Cultural Rights ("Protocol of San Salvador").[22] Rather, it focuses on the development of the universal human right to health and its content.

1 Origins at the United Nations and World Health Organization

The Universal Declaration of Human Rights (UDHR) of 1948[23], not legally binding in itself but largely accepted as part of international customary law,[24] does not provide for a separate right to health. Rather, "health" is included in the right to an adequate standard of living.[25] The Charter of the United Nations (UN Charter), which has been in force since October 1945, already addresses health, but not in the specific shape of a human right: The States Parties transferred to the United Nations (UN) the very general task to promote solutions of health problems within the chapter on international economic and social co-operation (Article 55 lit. b).[26] Article 57 UN Charter provides for a specialized agency in the area of health and thus laid the foundation for the WHO which was established in 1948.[27] The preamble of the Constitution of the WHO declares the "enjoyment of the highest attainable standard of health" to be a fundamental right of every human being. Although the preamble is not binding in a legal sense,[28] it gained much po-

22 For an overview of the right to health in documents of regional human rights organizations: Toebes, *The Right to Health as a Human Right*, above Fn. 15, 62 et seqq.

23 Universal Declaration of Human Rights adopted by the United Nations General Assembly resolution on December 10, 1948 (A/RES/3/217 A).

24 Bernstorff, J von, "The Changing Fortunes of the Universal Declaration of Human Rights" (2008), 19 *EJIL*, 903 (913); Krennerich, "Menschenrecht auf Gesundheit", above Fn. 20, 57.

25 Article 25 (1) UDHR: Everyone has the right to a standard of living adequate for the health and well-being of himself and of his family, including food, clothing, housing and medical care and necessary social services, and the right to security in the event of unemployment, sickness, disability, widowhood, old age or other lack of livelihood in circumstances beyond his control.

26 Further mentioning of "health" in Article 57 (Specialized Agencies) and Article 62 (Functions and Powers of the Economic and Social Council) of the UN-Charter.

27 WHO-Constitution adopted by the International Health Conference in 1946 and signed by the representatives of 61 States; entered into force on April 7, 1948.

28 Compare above Fn. 20.

litical attention and for the first time expressly acknowledged health as human right.[29] The mandate resulting from this proposition[30] raised high and unrealistic expectations. The WHO is guided primarily by a "policy oriented approach"[31], although it is also entrusted with a set of legal tools.[32] About 30 years after its foundation, in September 1978 the WHO organized a universal conference in Alma-Ata (then the capital of Kazakhstan) on primary health care which was attended by representatives of 134 states and 67 International Organizations. This widespread participation led to the historical meaning of the so-called Alma-Ata-Declaration, although it is not binding in a legal sense. The Declaration, which sees primary health care[33] as the key tool[34] for a *health for all*, reaffirms that health in the sense of a "complete physical, mental and social wellbeing" is a "fundamental human right". It is noteworthy, though, that the "highest possible level of health" is not directly mentioned as part of the human right to health as such, but as a "most important world-wide social goal". Primary health care is defined and outlined in seven points.[35] In addition to "promotive, preventive, curative and rehabilitative services" health care is also seen in the broad context of health education as well as safe food and water. The Declaration further

29 It is not known whether the drafters were aware of the legal claims going on with a "right to health", see Toebes, *The Right to Health as a Human Right*, above Fn. 15, 32.

30 Compare also Article 1 WHO-Constitution.

31 Riedel, "The Human Right to Health: Conceptual Foundations", above Fn. 8, 23.

32 For a short overview of the standard-setting instruments of the WHO compare Toebes, "International health law", above Fn. 1, 305 et seqq.; see also Gostin, "Global Health", above Fn. 1, 1733 et seq.

33 Compare for a description of primary health care also CESCR, *General Comment 14*, above Fn. 8, footnote 9: "primary health care typically deals with common and relatively minor illnesses and is provided by health professionals and/or generally trained doctors working within the community at relatively low cost".

34 Compare Poudel, "The Right to health", above Fn. 5, 219: "The Declaration of Alma-Ata had a significant role with respect to the development of a right to health. The Declaration developed the bases for implementing primary health care systems."

35 The concept of "primary health care" as stated in Alma-Ata has been criticized as "elusive" (for example Tobin, *Right to Health in International Law*, above Fn. 3, 264). Tobin also points to the fact that primary health care was a concept "in response to the ineffectiveness of the dominant Western model of medical or institutional based health care in developing countries". There is to-date no uniform definition of primary health care except for certain core principles (see, for example the WHO's *World Health Report*, 2003, 106-107, available at http://www.who.int/whr/2003/en/).

recognizes that the "people have a right and duty to participate individually and collectively in the planning and implementation of their health care". The latter assertion as well as other statements in the Declaration show that the right to health is conceived as going beyond an individual human right. After the Alma-Ata-Declaration, a series of global conferences on health promotion followed, the last having taken place in Shanghai (China) in November 2016.[36] All these conferences on health promotion ended with an official statement, the earliest being the well-known Ottawa-Charter (1986).

2 The Right to Health within the International Covenant on Economic, Social and Cultural Rights

Besides the system of the WHO, a major step of the development of the human right to health was its inclusion in the International Covenant on Economic, Social and Cultural Rights (ICESCR) in 1966.
Article 12 ICESCR reads as follows:

> "1. The States Parties to the present Covenant recognize the right of everyone to the enjoyment of the highest attainable standard of physical and mental health.
> 2. The steps to be taken by the States Parties to the present Covenant to achieve the full realization of this right shall include those necessary for:
> (a) The provision for the reduction of the stillbirth-rate and of infant mortality and for the healthy development of the child;
> (b) The improvement of all aspects of environmental and industrial hygiene;
> (c) The prevention, treatment and control of epidemic, endemic, occupational and other diseases;
> (d) The creation of conditions which would assure to all medical service and medical attention in the event of sickness."

Article 12 ICESCR acknowledges the "enjoyment of the highest attainable standard of physical and mental health" as a human right, followed by a non-exhaustive enumeration as to its specific content. The ICESCR does not define health as such,[37] but makes clear that both physical and mental health are comprised.[38] The provision encompasses an ambitious statement

---

36 For an overview see WHO, *Global Health Promotion Conferences*, available at http://www.who.int/healthpromotion/conferences/en/.

37 CESCR, *General Comment 14*, above Fn. 8, para. 4; Toebes, *The Right to Health as a Human Right*, above Fn. 15, 43, 47 et seq., 51.

38 Initiatives to stretch the right to health by definition to the "social wellbeing" or even "moral wellbeing" were dismissed during the drafting period of Article 12 ICESCR (Krennerich, "Menschenrecht auf Gesundheit", above Fn. 20, 60).

as to the scope of health, namely that it grants the people a right to the "highest attainable standard". Article 12 ICESCR is to be viewed in light of its context. Article 2 para. 1 ICESCR reads:

> "Each State Party to the present Covenant undertakes to take steps, individually and through international assistance and co-operation, especially economic and technical, to the maximum of its *available resources*, with a view to achieving *progressively* the full realization of the rights recognized in the present Covenant by all appropriate means, including particularly the adoption of legislative measures." (emphasis by author)

This clause tries to bridge between the ambitious aims of the single provisions of the Covenant and the insight that states are not economically developed and equipped in the same manner and therefore cannot provide for the same standards of social, economical and cultural rights. The clause is admitting that the aims of the treaty provisions, such as the "highest attainable" standard of health, cannot be an immediate binding obligation because *impossibilium nulla obligatio*. The inclusion of obligations that are more aspirational in nature demonstrates that, in international law, binding treaties can also display a mixed character as a policy-oriented approach and a legal basis for claims. Therefore, Article 2 para. 1 ICESCR is the essential link to uphold a legal character of the whole covenant. At the same time, this clause reveals that the lack of resources is not an argument in itself, but that a state needs to make efforts to strive for further progress ("progressively"). Thus it is widely assumed that states can have different obligations under the ICESCR.

In the tension between political aspirations and legally binding obligations, the Committee on Economic, Social and Cultural Rights (CESCR) has developed the concept of "minimum core obligations".[39] The Committee has specified these core obligations also with regard to the "right to the highest attainable standard of health" in its General Comment No. 14 dating from 2000.[40] Although the interpretations of the treaty provisions by the CESCR are not legally binding, the General Comments are treated as being authoritative.[41] They are not undisputed however, because the

39 CESCR, *General Comment No. 3 (The Nature of States Parties' Obligations)*, para. 10; *General Comment 14*, above Fn. 8, para. 43 et seq.

40 CESCR, *General Comment 14*, above Fn. 8, para. 43 et seqq. The core obligations are discussed below under IV 1.

41 See Nieada-Avshalom, L, "Some scepticism on the right to health: the case of the provision of medicines" (2015), 19 *The International Journal of Human Rights*, 527 (529), who recognizes that the CESCR comments are not binding and at the

CESCR is at times transgressing the path of interpretation and instead legislating.[42]

The CESCR describes the normative content of the right to health of Article 12 ICESCR as embracing freedoms and entitlements. "Freedoms" entail claims as to be free from (state) interference such as "the right to control one's health and body" and the right to be free from "non-consensual medical treatment and experimentation". The entitlements are, broadly speaking, focused on "the right to a system of health protection".[43] The Committee is further interpreting the right to health as

> "an inclusive right extending not only to […] health care but also to the underlying determinants of health, such as access to safe and potable water and adequate sanitation, and adequate supply of safe food, nutrition and housing, healthy occupational and environmental conditions, and access to health-related education and information".[44]

The CESCR identifies the so-called "AAAQs", standing for "availability", "accessibility", "acceptability" and "quality",[45] which are interrelated and subject to the particular conditions in a State Party.[46] Thus, health care and other health-related elements (such as potable drinking water) have to be *available* in sufficient quantity. *Accessibility* is seen in four dimensions, namely (1) non-discriminatory accessibility (accessible also for vulnerable and marginalized groups), (2) physical accessibility ("health facilities […] must be within safe physical reach" for all persons), (3) economic accessibility (in the sense of "affordability"), and (4) accessibility of information (relating to health issues). With "acceptability" the CESCR relates to a respect for medical ethics and cultural backgrounds. The notion of "quality" means that services must be "scientifically and medically appropriate". Besides the idea of the AAAQs, the CESCR also uses the concept of the threefold obligations to "respect, protect and fulfil".[47] The obligation to *respect*

---

same time acknowledges that they are "authoritative interpretations"; Toebes, "International health law", above Fn. 1, 309.

42 Riedel, "Human Right to Health", above Fn. 9, 27.

43 CESCR, *General Comment 14*, above Fn. 8, para. 8.

44 Ibid., para. 11. This broad concept has been widely accepted, compare only Wilson, B, "Social Determinants of Health from a Rights-Based Approach" in Clapham, A & Robinson, M (eds.), *Realizing the Right to Health*, 2009, 60 et seqq.

45 The AAAQ´s are often quoted and further elaborated in the academic literature, see only Riedel, "Human Right to Health", above Fn. 9, 28 et seqq.

46 CESCR, *General Comment 14*, above Fn. 8, para. 12.

47 Ibid., para. 33. For further explanation see also Riedel, "Human Right to Health", above Fn. 9, 26 et seqq. and Krennerich, "Menschenrecht auf Gesundheit", above Fn. 20, 68 et seqq.

"requires states to refrain from interfering directly or indirectly with the enjoyment of the right to health".[48] The obligation to *protect* is of a horizontal dimension whereby the state has to protect the people (or individual) from possible harm brought about by third parties (like private insurance companies, private suppliers of medical equipment and medicines and health professionals). The states need to control their quality and make sure that these private actors do not "constitute a threat to the availability, accessibility, acceptability and quality of health facilities, goods and services".[49] The obligation to *fulfil* goes one step further in that the states need to adopt appropriate measures (especially legislative) in order to bring about the full realization of the right to health (for example "immunization programmes against the major infectious diseases"[50]). Also, states are obliged to "create, maintain and restore the health" for individuals or a group if they cannot "for reasons beyond their control" realize this themselves.[51]

Besides this, the CESCR clarifies that the "highest attainable standard" is a reference as well to the "individual's biological" as well as the "social-economic preconditions and a State's available resources".[52] With this finding, the CESCR aims at preventing the right to health from turning into a mere unrealistic utopia. Further, the Committee identifies obligations of immediate effect in order to avoid Article 12 ICESCR from becoming a mere political target.[53] Namely these are the duty to guarantee that the right to health is "exercised without discrimination" and the "obligation to take steps towards the full realization of article 12". These duties are, however, still considerably broad and flexible and thus are not providing enough clout to claim any rights on this basis. As mentioned already, the Committee has also defined more specific core obligations. Surprisingly, the CESCR did not expressly declare that these core obligations are those which are of immediate effect.

The right to health as established by Article 12 ICESCR has also been further interpreted by the UN Special Rapporteurs on the right to health.[54]

48 CESCR, *General Comment 14*, above Fn. 8, para. 33.
49 Ibid., para. 35.
50 Ibid., para. 36.
51 Ibid., para. 37.
52 Ibid., para. 9.
53 Ibid., para. 30.
54 The first Special Rapporteur was appointed by the Commission on Human Rights in April 2002. The mandate was later endorsed and extended by the Human Rights

In their reports, the UN Special Rapporteurs deal with certain specific aspects of the right to health. Recent topics have included unhealthy food and non-communicable diseases,[55] the right to health in conflict situations[56] and access to medicines.[57] The Reports also focus on certain groups such as migrant workers[58] and older persons.[59]

3 The Right to Health for Specific Groups and Marginalized Individuals

Human Rights Law has specifically focused on vulnerable groups or marginalized individuals in order to improve their situation.[60] In this context, health is addressed in specific conventions on women,[61] children,[62] migrant workers,[63] employees,[64] and disabled persons.[65] These specific groups and individuals have special needs which are considered in the respective international treaties and other soft law instruments. As poor health is very often related to a weak socioeconomic background of the respective people or

---

Council (last in October, 2013). For a detailed overview of the different mandates see http://bit.ly/2kTASyn.

55 Report of the Special Rapporteur on the right of everyone to the enjoyment of the highest attainable standard of physical and mental health, A/HRC/26/31 of 2014.

56 A/68/297 of 2013.

57 A/HRC/23/42 of 2013; A/HRC/17/43 of 2011; A/65/255 of 2010; A/HRC/11/12 of 2009.

58 A/HRC/23/41 of 2013.

59 A/HRC/18/37 of 2011.

60 For an overview of the right to health with regard to special groups see for example Krennerich, "Menschenrecht auf Gesundheit", above Fn. 20, 61 et seqq.

61 Convention on the Elimination of All Forms of Discrimination against Women (adopted by General Assembly resolution on December 18, 1979, A/RES/34/180, entry into force September 3, 1981): Article 12 (see further Article 10 lit. h; Article 11 para. 1 lit. f; Article 14 para. 2 lit. b).

62 Convention on the Rights of the Child (adopted by General Assembly resolution on November 20, 1989, A/RES/44/25, entry into force September 2, 1990): Article 24 (see further Article 3 para. 3; Article 23 para. 3 and 4; Article 25; Article 32 para. 1).

63 International Convention on the Protection of the Rights of All Migrant Workers and Members of Their Families (adopted by General Assembly resolution on December 18, 1990, A/RES/45/158, entry into force July 1, 2003) Article 28 (see further Article 25 para. 1 lit. a; Article 43 para. 1 lit. e; Article 45 para. 1 lit. c; Article 70).

64 The ILO conventions contain numerous provisions related to health.

65 Convention on the Rights of Persons with Disabilities, Article 25.

individuals, it is of particular importance that international human rights law addresses health not only as a general matter, but also as a special need of these groups and persons who cannot in the same manner care for themselves or afford to have access to medical treatment.

III The Right-Holders of the Right to Health: Individual Right, Collective Right or Mere Standard?

1 The Different Dimensions

The right to health is ambiguous as to its structure and rights holders. It could possibly be perceived, as an individual right (either in the sense of a "liberty right" or a "social right"), as a collective (group) right[66] (if it is assumed that a group can be a right-holder) or, as a mere standard (as an "objective" obligation of the state) to promote public health. In other words, the right to health is not restricted to the individual's dimension, but also contains an obligation to promote public ("population") health which connotes either a collective (group) right or a mere "objective" obligation of the state without corresponding individual rights. In this contribution, "objective obligations" are meant to embrace all legal obligations, while individual rights are restricted to those obligations which endow the individual with a right (claim). Thus an "objective obligation without a corresponding individual right" is a "standard" which is to be followed by a state without giving the individual (or a "group") a right to legally claim it.

Historically, the public health approach preceded the notion of a right to health as individual right.[67] Under the manifold definitions and descriptions of public health, only one shall be quoted here, stemming from the American Public Health Association: "Public health is the practice of preventing disease and promoting good health within groups of people, from small communities to entire countries."[68] Public health is concerned with the population, the "people", "groups" and lastly "numbers" and not individual patients. It is a policy-oriented approach which deals with maintain-

66 As to the debated existence of group rights, see above Fn. 11.
67 Murphy, T, *Health and Human Rights*, 2013, 30.
68 American Public Health Association, *What is Public Health? Our Commitment to Safe, Healthy Communities*, available at https://www.apha.org/~/media/files/pdf/factsheets/whatisph.ashx.

ing the health of the people in a comprehensive and interdisciplinary perspective, also including the arrangement of socioeconomic and environmental conditions for the promotion and maintenance of health. If it comes to legal terms, the focus lies primarily on the "objective" obligation of the state (or other actors) to arrange for a setting which allows the maximum health for the whole population. The individual right to health, on the other hand, is starting from a "subjective" point of view. It considers what an individual person needs to become or stay healthy.

2 Approach of the CESCR and the UN Special Rapporteur on the Right to Health

In order to examine whether Article 12 ICESCR is seen primarily as an obligation to promote public health or as an individual human right, the interpretations of the CESCR and the UN Special Rapporteur on the Right to health are of high relevance. In its general comment, the CESCR starts with a clear human rights perspective:

> "Health is a fundamental human right indispensable for the exercise of other human rights. Every human being is entitled to the enjoyment of the highest attainable standard of health conducive to living a life in dignity."[69]

On the other hand, the CESCR recalls on a number of occasions that the promotion of health is not confined to medical care, but embraces the "underlying determinants of health, such as food and nutrition, housing, access to safe and potable water and adequate sanitation, safe and healthy working conditions, and a healthy environment".[70] This reflects a public health approach that is an integrative concept and also includes elements, such as a "healthy environment", which are in the first instance more a political strategy than an individual right. When the CESCR is elaborating on the "normative content" of Article 12 ICESCR,[71] it combines both concepts. The "freedoms" of the right to health are clearly of an individual nature. If we regard freedoms such as "to control one's health and body" or freedom from "non-consensual medical treatment and experimentation", those freedoms do not only entitle the individual, but also show that – for example with regard to particular research interests – the conflict of interests is resolved

69 CESCR, *General Comment 14*, above Fn. 8, para. 1.
70 Ibid., para. 4. See also para. 10, 11 and 36, 40.
71 Ibid., para. 7 et seqq.

in favor of the individual[72] (while "population health" would benefit best if many people took part in clinical trials, the individual only takes advantage of its participation if the chances for healing outweigh the possible damages). Turning to the entitlements, the CESCR states that these "include the right to a system of health protection".[73] A system of health protection is clearly not enforceable as such, only specific elements might be part of an individual's claim before a court. Therefore, the AAAQs (see above), which break down the general notion of a right to a proper health system, again display both the elements of individual and public health. The CESCR's reference to certain vulnerable groups (maternal and child health, healthy workplace, older persons, persons with disabilities, indigenous peoples, etc.) are primarily part of a public health approach in order to grant the particular group the same rights or even special attention as to their special needs. However, it can also be read as an obligation to provide legal rights for the individuals of these groups. In its section on the implementation at the national level, the CESCR seems to break down population health to individual claims when stating: "Any person or group victim of a violation of the right to health should have access to effective judicial or other appropriate remedies at both national and international levels."[74] The Committee further explains that "States parties are bound by both the collective and individual dimensions of article 12".[75] According to the CESCR, Article 12 ICESCR obliges the State Parties to

> "give sufficient recognition to the right to health in the national political and legal systems, preferably by way of legislative implementation, and to adopt a national health policy with a detailed plan for realizing the right to health".[76]

This shows that some aspects of the right to health remain in the political sphere, while others shall be framed as (national) legal rights.

The reports of the UN Special Rapporteurs on the right to health also display both a reference to the individual right to health and a public health approach. In the first annual report, the UN Special Rapporteur saw his work being guided

72 Compare also Article 3 of the Universal Declaration on Bioethics and Human Rights (adopted by UNESCO's General Conference on October 19, 2005).

73 CESCR, *General Comment 14*, above Fn. 8, para. 8.

74 Ibid., para. 59.

75 Ibid., footnote 30.

76 Ibid., para. 36.

> "by the fundamental principle that international human rights law, including the right to health, should be consistently and coherently applied across all relevant national and international policy-making processes."[77]

Over the years, the Special Rapporteurs have focused on different "groups" rather than the individual (for example reports being on the right to health of adolescents[78] and early childhood[79]). Then again, in its recent report of 2014, the Special Rapporteur was dealing in detail with the "justifiability of the right to health"[80] and the "enforcement"[81] and thus brought the right to health into the legal realm of individual claims. Health is seen as a precondition for the "individual's ability to live with dignity".[82] The Special Rapporteur aims at strengthening the domestic justifiability of the right to health in its three dimensions (respect, protect, fulfil) in order to "fulfil the right to health of individuals".[83] Also the report on informed consent[84] is in the first place an expression of the individual's right to health. However, it is often not entirely clear whether the emphasis lies on the individual's right to health or a public health perspective.[85]

3 The Necessity to Differentiate Between the Dimensions

In many writings on the international right to health, both the individual right to health and the concept of public health are not differentiated. This is striking not only because public health is of a different nature than an individual right to health, but also because both can compete with each other. Very obviously this is the case when it comes to epidemics control.[86]

77 E/CN. 4/2003/58 (February 13, 2003), para. 8.

78 Report of the Special Rapporteur on the right of everyone to the enjoyment of the highest attainable standard of physical and mental health, A/HRC/32/32 of 2016.

79 A 70/213 of 2015.

80 A/69/299 (August 11, 2014), para. 5 et seqq.

81 Ibid., para. 30 et seqq.

82 Ibid., para. 71; for a critical view see Tobin, *Right to Health in International Law*, above Fn. 3, 56.

83 A/69/299 (August 11, 2014), para. 72.

84 A/64/272 (August 10, 2009).

85 Compare only A/HRC/7/11 (January 31, 2008), para. 38: Health system should focus on the "well-being of individuals, communities and populations".

86 See also the International Health Regulations (IHR) which try to balance individual rights and a public right to health, compare Zidar, A, "WHO International Health Regulations and human rights" (2015), 19 *The International Journal of Human Rights*, 505.

From an individual's perspective, each person who is infected needs medical treatment, even if the person is terminally ill. From a public health perspective, the medical resources should be distributed in the way that saves the life of most. Certainly, individual rights can be limited due to the rights of others, but as a matter of principle, the structure of an individual right is all about the health of a person (and that the person is entitled to claim this right) while public health is all about the health of a population. Both concepts merge together in that the public right to health ultimately serves human beings. But while public health is all about numbers and groups and fair distribution of resources, the individual right to health involves granting a right to an individual person. Thus, if it comes to an individual right, a person ideally needs the possibility of recourse to a legal action if his right is violated. A public health approach can do without such individual legal action and becomes effective by diverse political and legal monitoring systems. If it comes to the fair distribution of limited resources, a public health strategy is most effective if based on a utilitarian ethic[87], while an individual's rights approach is effective if the individual can enforce its right to health irrespective of utilitarian arguments.

Katarina Tomaeševski[88] has already addressed the issue in 1995, before the release of the CESCR's general comment on the right to health. Under the title "Balancing Public Health and Human Rights"[89] she shows how both concepts can clash. With examples such as "immunizations" which are only effective if at least 80 % of a particular population participate, she underpins her argument that public health necessities can infringe individual rights.

> "Many public health measures may deny individual rights and justify this by the need to protect society. With epidemics, the objective of public health measures is to identify and isolate the affected persons. Such persons lose their identity, privacy, dignity, their individuality, and become merely 'carriers' of a disease."[90]

Tomaeševski also shows the limits of public health policies when they are at odds with individual rights. There has to be a balancing of both the individual and collective right to health whereby "limitations are legitimate

87 Compare Toebes, "Human rights and public health", above Fn. 3, 490 who argues that the ideas of the utilitarian philosopher Jeremy Bentham influenced the origins of public health in 19th century England.

88 Tomaeševski, "Health Rights", above Fn. 19, 125 et seqq.

89 Ibid., 137 et seqq.

90 Ibid., 139.

only when required on public health grounds, and compatible with the general human rights principles".[91]

Brigit Toebes also reflects on a clash of public health and the individual right to health.[92] She sees this tension especially when it comes to "health security threats" in the fields of infectious diseases, biomedical research with human beings, use of bio-banks, (forced) vaccinations as well as testing of medicines. With regard to the outbreak of Ebola she points to the "huge dilemmas under human rights law" and requests a careful balancing of a public health and an individual rights approach. Restrictions of the right of the individual should be "proportionate, pursue a legitimate aim and [...] taken solely for the interests of a democratic society".[93] According to *Toebes*, the right to health is in the first place a protection of individual health.[94] She states that "as a human right the right to health pertains to an individual rather than to a collective claim".[95] Therefore, she finds it problematic when the right to health is understood "as a norm that reflects the protection of 'public health'" as it would then amount to a "'collective' norm, protecting the health-related interests of a community or the population at large".[96] However, *Toebes* adds another dimension and also conceives the right to health as a "'bundle' of individual rights exercised by a collectivity".[97] In the latter function the right to health could potentially serve as a collective claim against actors who are a detriment to the health of the people (such as the tobacco industry or the polluting industry).

A rather critical view was put forward by *Laura Nieda-Avshalom*.[98] She examines the obligation of states to provide for medicines as part of the right to health under Article 12 ICESCR. As medicines can be costly and unaffordable, she asks how states should decide which medicine to provide and which legal, moral and political principles should guide the allocation

---

91 Ibid., 139.

92 Toebes, "Human rights and public health", above Fn. 3, 499; Toebes, "International health law", above Fn. 1, 311.

93 Toebes, "Human rights and public health", above Fn. 3, 500.

94 Toebes, "International health law", above Fn. 1, 308, 311.

95 Ibid., 311.

96 Ibid., 311.

97 Toebes, "Human rights and public health", above Fn. 3, 500; see also Toebes, "International health law", above Fn. 1, 311: "We could perceive the right as materially conferred on individual members of a group, but procedurally looked after by the collectivity. Hence this could potentially be overcome by perceiving the collective right to health as a bundle of individual rights."

98 Nieada-Avshalom, "Some skepticism", above Fn. 41, 527 et seqq.

and prioritization under the international right to health. Using the distribution of medicine as field of reference, *Nieda-Avshalom* argues that the right to health is still underdetermined and that the solution of allocation problems "entails legal, moral and political flaws".[99] She shows that the current interpretation of Article 12 ICESCR as provided by the CESCR is in line with a utilitarian view because it favors a distribution of resources which serves most people to the detriment of severely ill people with rare diseases who need expensive drugs. *Niedu-Avshalom* wonders why a rare and expensive illness would not fall under the right to health and asks: "Is this even a right?"[100] She stipulates that Article 12 ICESCR is primarily following a public health approach, pointing to the four dimensions of Article 12 (a-d):

> "Three out of four dimensions referred to by the ICESCR can be seen as public health interventions, namely, child health (article 12 (2)(a)), environmental and industrial hygiene (article 12 (2)(b)), and the management of epidemic, pandemic, occupational and other diseases (article 12 (2)(c))".[101]

She further argues that primary health care should not be viewed as public health policy, but as "*a* particular element of health assistance to be implemented in the context of health systems."[102] She concludes that "the ICESCR indicates several broad dimensions but overall it seems to have a penchant for a public health and primary health care that would improve the aggregate status of the population rather than specific individual curative needs."[103]

IV A Reflection on the Content of the Right to Health

So far we have seen that the normative content and structure of the right to health is still vague. This is due to a number of reasons, namely the fact that it is conceived in a broad manner as a "transversal right" embracing a set of different rights, and thus goes far beyond the right to medical treatment. Also, the ambiguous structure of an individual human right on the one hand and the obligation to promote public health on the other hand leads to confusion, especially when these concepts are in conflict with each other. Public health policies were pursued long before a "human right to health" was

99 Ibid., 527.
100 Ibid., 540.
101 Ibid., 531.
102 Ibid., 531.
103 Ibid., 539.

acknowledged. And even though a human right implies in the first instance an individual right, the human right to health has also been largely understood as public health strategy. In a way, two separate systems have become intertwined. But they can also be viewed as complementary because public health strategies, especially the control of contagious diseases, are having immediate effects on the individual's health. Therefore, it can make sense to see the right to health as an "umbrella" for both the individual's right to health and public health obligations.

1 Current Approaches

The problems associated with the wide scope of the right to health are obvious. *Heiner Bielefeldt*[104] differentiates between the state's responsibility of gradual development of the right to health, which includes health strategies, health planning, research funding, medical training, public health education as well as further infrastructure measures on the one hand, and the personal legal entitlement as to the right to health on the other hand. According to him, the first set of responsibilities is of a long-term character (successive development), while the right to health in terms of a legal entitlement should be effective immediately. He also refers to the idea of core obligations as justifiable rights.

The idea of core obligations[105] as a key concept of the CESCR to narrow the scope of the right to health in order to enlarge its effectiveness, has been largely accepted in the literature.[106] In its General Comment No. 14 on the Right to Health, the Committee defines the scope of core obligations as comprising non-discriminatory access to health facilities and equitable distribution of health facilities, access to minimum essential and safe food and water, access to basic shelter and sanitation, and essential drugs. The CESCR recognizes that State Parties have the obligation "to adopt and implement a national public health strategy and plan of action, on the basis of

104 Bielefeldt, "Menschenrechtsansatz", above Fn. 5, 48.

105 See above Fn. 39.

106 A. Müller, "Die Konkretisierung von Kernbereichen des Menschenrechts auf Gesundheit" in Frewer, A & Bielefeldt, H (eds.), *Das Menschenrecht auf Gesundheit*, 2016, 125 et seqq.; Riedel, "Human Right to Health", above Fn. 9, 32; Gostin, "Global Health", above Fn. 1, 1736.

epidemiological evidence, addressing the health concerns of the whole population".[107] Under the core obligations, the Committee identifies "obligations of comparable priority",[108] namely reproductive, maternal and child health care. It obliges states to provide "immunization against the major infectious diseases occurring in the community" as well as supplementary measures of epidemics control.[109] It also includes an obligation to provide for access to health education and to enable adequate training for health personnel. The designation of these core obligations is meant to help the states to prioritize within their duties of the right to health. At the same time, the idea is to support and enable the establishment of legal proceedings before national and international courts or quasi-judicial bodies.[110] Although the whole concept of core obligations is only persuasive if states cannot argue that they have insufficient resources to observe and fulfill these obligations,[111] it is nevertheless debated whether the core obligations form part of the body of duties which only needs to be progressively realized. The CESCR is not entirely clear on this point. In General Comment No. 14, it claims that "a state party cannot, under any circumstances whatsoever, justify its non-compliance with the core obligations".[112] The CESCR rejects the objection of *impossibilium nulla obligatio* by the argument that a state has the obligation to seek international help if the resources for the core obligations are missing.[113] This, however, presupposes that there is such an extraterritorial obligation of states, be it individually or collectively or via the support of the WHO or other international actors – a highly contested field.[114] Then again the practice of the CESCR within its concluding observations regarding the State reports under the ICESCR (Article 16 et seq.) is not clear in the same manner. Only very rarely did the CESCR criticize a state for its failure to provide access to basic medical care although this

---

107 CESCR, *General Comment 14*, above Fn. 8, para. 43.
108 CESCR, *General Comment 14*, above Fn. 8, para. 44.
109 CESCR, *General Comment 14*, above Fn. 8, para. 44.
110 Müller, "Die Konkretisierung von Kernbereichen", above Fn. 106, 130.
111 See only Riedel, *Right to Health*, above Fn. 6, para. 41.
112 CESCR, *General Comment 14*, above Fn. 8, para. 47-48.
113 Ibid., para. 45.
114 See the contribution of *Elif Askin*, "Extraterritorial Human Rights Obligations of States in the Event of Disease Outbreaks" in this volume; Müller, "Die Konkretisierung von Kernbereichen", above Fn. 106, 140 et seq., 150; Tobin, *Right to Health in International Law*, above Fn. 3, 369, visualizes international cooperation, at most, as a "soft" obligation.

obligation forms part of the core obligations.[115] This leads to an ongoing debate as to whether the core obligations are to be defined on a universal level or on a national level.[116] Writers in favor of a nationally defined core content[117] argue that it is delusive to assume that all states could provide the same core content for their inhabitants. While poor countries would not be able to reach the threshold, rich countries would become complacent and remain below their potential. Also, any universally defined core content would be too abstract and not flexible enough. Other writers oppose this view[118] and argue that any nationally defined core content would be about the same as the progressive realization because the latter depends on the capacity of the particular state. Thus the idea of a "core content" would lose its function. Furthermore, the core content embraces only very basic rights which should be realized by all states. As both views have deficits and approvable aspects, *Amrei Müller* combines elements of both.[119] According to her proposal, the universal core obligations which are necessarily broad and less concrete, need to be complemented by a further national definition and commitment. The universal core obligations would have to include access to medical care and could be formulated after utilitarian values. The national core obligations should focus for example on infectious diseases which are predominant in the respective country. With her approach, *Müller* aims at

115 Müller, "Die Konkretisierung von Kernbereichen", above Fn. 106, 133.

116 For an extensive overview of this debate compare Müller, ibid., 134 et seqq.

117 Craven, M, *The International Covenant on Economic, Social and Cultural Rights*, 1995, 141 et seq., 152 with further references (Craven speaks of lack of clarity "whether these standards are international or State-specific"; he sees the "current practice of the Committee" to suggest "that in the short term at least, State-specific minima are the only viable options"; however, he also sees evidence "that the Committee intends to establish international standards in future"); Scott, C & Alston, P, "Adjudicating Constitutional Priorities in a Transnational Context" (2000), 16 *South African Journal of Human Rights*, 206 (250).

118 Engbruch, K, *Das Menschenrecht auf einen angemessenen Lebensstandard*, 2007, 137 et seq.; Russel, S, "Minimum State Obligations" in Brand, D & Russell, S (eds.), *Exploring the Core Content of Socio-Economic Rights: South African and International Perspectives*, 2002, 11 (15); Economic and Social Council, ICESCR, *The Limburg Principles on the Implementation of the International Covenant on Economic, Social and Cultural Rights*, E/C.12/2000/13, para. 25; Bilchitz, D, *Poverty and Fundamental Rights*, 2007, 178 et seqq.; Ssenyonjo, M, *Economic, Social and Cultural Rights in International Law*, 2009, 66.

119 Müller, "Die Konkretisierung von Kernbereichen", above Fn. 106, 139 et seqq.; Her thesis is referring to the works of Bilchitz, *Poverty and Fundamental Rights*, above Fn. 118, 220-225.

defining "effective" core obligations whereby effectiveness is meant in the sense of the greatest possible range of rights which are as precise as possible. It seems that the view of *Müller* finds some support in recent general comments of the CESCR in which the Committee asked states to provide a benchmarking of indicators. However, the states have not shown much co-operation here.[120] *Müller*'s proposal would not only lead to different state obligations under the same treaty provision (which is already true within the conception of "progressive realization"), but would make these different obligations more obvious and the state's compliance verifiable. It is not very likely that states are willing to engage in this approach when their responsiveness to their own standards will be part of the states reporting procedure under the ICESCR.

2 Further Differentiated Approach

In the following, a further development of the current approaches shall be put forward. It combines the findings that the right to health according to Article 12 ICESCR has a subjective[121] (in the sense of an individual) rights component as well as an objective (in the sense of a public health) component (see above III.1) and furthermore differentiates between the different contents of the right to health.[122] International human rights law lacks clarity as to the question whether human rights necessarily imply subjective (= individual) international rights (which grant a claim) or whether they also include human rights which are framed as "standards" to be followed by the states ("objective" obligation of states) for the benefit and essential needs of human beings.[123] It is noted that "in its most basic form, a right is an

---

120 For more details see Riedel, "The Human Right to Health: Conceptual Foundations", above Fn. 8, 36.

121 Compare Peters, A, *Jenseits der Menschenrechte*, 2014, 469 et seqq.

122 The "group right" to health is not considered separately because it can partly be counted to the individual rights (individual having a right as part of the group). The genuine "group" as right-holder is underdeveloped in international law and it is argued here that in so far as there is no individual right, there is only an objective obligation of the states to grant certain rights to groups.

123 Compare Peters, *Menschenrechte*, above Fn. 121, 469 et seqq. She develops her position of the "subjective international law" as a legal position of human beings which is not merely derivative of the rights of states.

entitlement of X that gives rise to duties or obligations that can be claimed against Y".[124] Human rights law does not meet this threshold in different regards. The whole concept of a human "right" is under a broad discussion and the philosophical and legal reasoning behind the idea of human rights is facing many flaws.[125] The deficiencies of the theories behind are often superseded by the political will to promote the moral good.[126] *John Tobin* warns that an overly harsh critique of the deficient theories supporting human rights could eventually become "the enemy of the good".[127] He further argues for human rights "beyond individualism".[128] The right to health shall not simply "benefit individuals" but would also be "intended to bolster the interests of the broader community".[129] Under a social interest theory of rights "the justification in elevating an interest such as health to the status of a human right rests in the deliberative and collaborative process by which states (subject to lobbying and advocacy from civil society and institutional bodies) identify and elevate a particular interest to the status of a human right".[130]

Here it is argued that the international right to health has two dimensions, being of an individual (subjective) nature, as well as an objective nature (standard). One could argue that only the individual right to health is a true "human right" as a mere legal standard has no individualized, entitled party and that human rights are, by definition, rights of individuals.[131] However, the legal obligations acknowledged by states for the sake of serving basic needs of human beings, which ultimately go back to an understanding of a moral obligation towards human beings can also form part of the inter-

---

Compare also Beitz, C, *The Idea of Human Rights*, 2009, 137 (human rights as "urgent individual interests").

124 Tobin, *Right to Health in International Law*, above Fn. 3, 50.

125 Compare Bisaz, *The Concept of Group Rights*, above Fn. 11, 12 et seqq.

126 Compare Tobin, *Right to Health in International Law*, above Fn. 3, 50 et seqq.

127 Ibid., 53.

128 Ibid., 57 et seqq.

129 Ibid., 58.

130 Ibid., 59.

131 Riedel, *Right to Health*, above Fn. 6, para. 30 seems to require an individual right ("While policy programmes and practical guidelines play an essential role in the promotion of health care and protection for all, it is just as important that every human being is able to rely on a legal foundation which provides protection against intrusions upon one's personal health, and at the same time can serve as a tool to remind governments of their duties.").

national human rights body, as the concept of human social rights in international law is not exclusively linked to individual claims and recourse to legal action. Due to their different nature, the concept of human rights in international law and national law is not congruent. This view is strengthened by the finding that the human right to health first developed as an obligation of states to promote "public health"[132] and that – as shown above – even the CESCR is seeing public health as part of the human right to health. Therefore, the thesis put forward here aims at combining both aspects within the right to health, but at the same time differentiating them.

a Individual Right to Health

The first category is looking at the right to health from an individual's perspective and asking how it can become more effective for the single person. It is maintained that the individual's right to health should not be an "umbrella right" including all determinants for health, but rather focus more on a medical understanding of health. A multitude of factors can have a negative impact on a person's health – if all remedies are included in the individual's right to health, it would be more a "field of rights" and lose its power as a specific human right which can be claimed in a concrete situation. It seems to be persuasive to make the single human right more effective by being as precise as possible, as there is no need to cover "all with one" human right or to see a competitiveness between human rights.[133]

The right to "respect" health is clearly part of the individual right to health. The state must not infringe on a person's health. Also, the obligation of a state to protect a person's health from being hurt by third parties is part of the individual's right to health if there is a direct link (such as the duty to protect the individual from treatment without consent of the patient). With regard to the right to fulfill, the right to health should be understood to be basically a right to medical health care. Every person should have affordable access to basic medical care, including essential medicines.[134] This entails

132 Compare for a short historical overview Toebes, *The Right to Health as a Human Right*, above Fn. 15, 7 et seqq.

133 Some writers consider "health and human rights" as a new section of human rights law, compare Toebes, "International health law", above Fn. 1, 312.

134 As to the access to medicines, compare Marks, S P, "Access to Essential Medicines as a Component of the Right to Health" in Clapham, A & Robinson, M (eds.), *Realizing the Right to Health*, 2009, 80 et seqq.

that the state must provide for a health system which is available, accessible, acceptable and of proper quality (the so-called "AAAQs").[135] It does by no means imply that the state has to grant health care at no cost, but the state must establish a system (be it public or private) where it would be principally possible for everybody to participate. The WHO usually uses the classification of primary, secondary and tertiary health care whereby these three divisions display a different stage of specialization in health care.[136] Today the WHO is referring to "primary care" as a day-to-day health service. At least the access to basic medical care is a core obligation of the state. The boundary of self-responsibility and state's responsibility is fluent and to be decided in the particular country. The right to medical treatment should be guaranteed by each state including the possibility to take legal action. The quality of medical care should be as high as possible. As resources are always limited, the question of allocation needs to be decided by each state,[137] whereby the state needs to argue that it fulfilled its duty to take up measures to the maximum of its available resources (Article 2 para. 1 ICESCR).

b Obligation to Promote Public Health

The second category is looking at the right to health from the population's perspective. In fact, the right to health in international law is to a wide extent described to embrace those elements which usually go along with a public health approach. The focus lies on the objective obligation of states and possible other actors to promote public health. Looking at preventive measures in a narrower and broader sense, core obligations exist specifically with regard to infectious diseases. The control of infectious diseases is one of the basic ideas of public health.[138] The state bears the core duty to

135 For an elaboration on the right to health approach and health systems see Hunt & Backmann, "Health Systems and the Right", above Fn. 2, 40 et seqq.

136 For an overview Toebes, *The Right to Health as a Human Right*, above Fn. 15, 247. CESCR, *General Comment 14*, above Fn. 8, footnote 9.

137 Hunt & Backmann, "Health Systems and the Right", above Fn. 2, 49 argue that human rights have no "answer" to allocation questions, but "require that the questions be decided by way of a fair, transparent, participatory process, taking into account explicit criteria, such as the well-being of those living in poverty, and not just the claims of powerful interest groups". Compare also Weilert, A K & Pfitzner, J, "Konkurrenz im Gesundheitssystem" in Kirchhoff, T (ed.), *Konkurrenz. Historische, strukturelle und normative Perspektiven*, 2015, 313-340.

138 Fidler, D, *International Law and Public Health*, 2000, 3.

provide vaccination against diseases that occur regularly in a specific country. The states also need to ensure that the basic underlying determinants of health are met (such as clean water and safe food[139]). Those "preconditions" for health can be manifold, from obviously health-related conditions like access to clean water to broadly economic and social conditions. In order to avoid "public health" from becoming another term for socioeconomic policy, the underlying determinants for health should be closely connected to the condition of health. Furthermore, public health should not fully integrate all other health-related rights, but be defined as a separate field with overlapping edges.[140] Public health also includes access to basic health education and has a special focus on vulnerable groups (for example children, mothers, elderly people, and socially disadvantaged people). Main areas of the obligation to promote public health are the battle against infectious diseases, social medicine and the prevention of health threats including respective health research.

Within the endeavor to promote public health, the WHO plays a prominent role. In the founding document, the WHO's Constitution, the states transferred to it the task to enable and promote the highest possible level of health for all "peoples" (compare Article 1 WHO Constitution). It is noteworthy that the WHO's Constitution does not speak of "human beings", but in fact of "peoples". This goes along with the connotation of "public health" rather than an individual right to health. The term "human being" is only used once, namely in the preamble of the WHO Constitution where health is said to be a fundamental human right. It is significant that the operative part of the Constitution is not repeating health as a human right[141] and that Article 1 WHO Constitution, which sets out the objective of the WHO, speaks of the "attainment by all *peoples* of the highest possible level of health".[142]

---

139 Elements listed by Toebes, *The Right to Health as a Human Right*, above Fn. 15, 246.

140 Compare also Toebes, *The Right to Health as a Human Right*, above Fn. 15, 259 et seqq. and 272 who proposes a boundary between the right to health and other health-related rights such as life, physical integrity, privacy, education and information as well as housing, food and work. See also Giorgi, M, *The Human Right to Equal Access to Health Care*, 2012, 18 et seq.

141 Compare Hestermeyer, *Human Rights and the WTO*, above Fn. 2120, 114.

142 Compare also Murphy, *Health and Human Rights*, above Fn. 67, 28 (referring to the dispute whether the WHO's constitution is focusing on the "right to health of individuals" or rather the "security and well-being of states").

Also, the functions of the WHO as displayed in Article 2 WHO Constitution, clearly show the public health character (for example focus on epidemics control, nutrition, sanitation, environmental hygiene, and to promote health research). As public health has an international dimension (it becomes striking when it comes to epidemics control), the acknowledgement of a right to health automatically demands to provide for international structures. Besides the WHO there are many other actors, often of a private nature,[143] who promote health in the realm of "public health". Within the field of IHG, the relationships, obligations, and questions of authority of the different actors need to be further examined.[144]

c Enforcement Structures

The right to health, both in the sense of an individual right and in the meaning of an obligation to promote public health, needs enforcement structures in order to intensify its effectiveness, as well at the international as the national level. *Eibe Riedel* identifies five main types of accountability mechanisms, namely judicial, quasi-judicial, administrative, political and social.[145] Enforcement structures do not presuppose that the right to health is framed as an individual right. The review mechanism of the ICESCR via the assessment of States Parties' reports is independent of any individual claim and also works as a monitoring system towards the obligation of the states to promote public health. The Optional Protocol to the ICESCR (in force since May 5, 2013),[146] however, is building on the infringement of a person's right or a group right (Article 2 of the Optional Protocol). The international monitoring systems need to be accompanied by national enforcement structures.[147] The implementation of the right to health by the

143 See the contribution of *Mateja Steinbrück Platise*, "The Changing Structure of Global Health Governance" in this volume.

144 Compare also Toebes, "International health law", above Fn. 1, 321 et seqq.

145 Riedel, "Human Right to Health", above Fn. 9, 32 et seqq.; Riedel, "The Human Right to Health: Conceptual Foundations", above Fn. 8, 33.

146 Adopted by the United Nations General Assembly resolution on December 10, 2008 (A/RES/63/117).

147 Report of the Special Rapporteur on the right of everyone to the enjoyment of the highest attainable standard of physical and mental health, A/69/299 (August 11, 2014), para. 30 et seqq.; Flood, C & Gross, A, *The Right to Health at the Public/Private Divide. A Global Comparative Study*, 2014, provides insight into the enforcement structures of different countries.

particular states is so far not sufficiently monitored and enforced at the international level.

V Conclusion

The human right to health is a highly complex right. Already the definition of health is anything but obvious. If health is perceived not merely as the absence of disease, but as "a state of complete physical, mental and social well-being", the right to health loses its sharpness in the legal context. The main legal source of the international right to health is to be found in Article 12 ICESCR which was here referred to as main source for all further considerations. The structure of the right to health faces challenges in different dimensions: First, the right to health combines aspects from all three generations of human rights; second, the right to health often serves as an umbrella right and loses its specificity as virtually everything can have an impact on a person's health; and third, the right to health is a hybrid right combining elements of an individual's health approach and a public (in the sense of population's) health approach. In this contribution it is argued that as an individual human right, the right to health should be perceived in a narrower sense and be more closely linked to the right to medical treatment. As an obligation to promote public health, the human right to health can be seen in a broader context, embracing also the underlying determinants of health and therefore focusing more on the preventive dimension. The battle against epidemics falls into the public health approach. In the latter sense, its effectiveness should not be measured in terms of the possibility of individual legal actions, but seen more as a policy strategy, embracing national and international actors who need to be coordinated in terms of International Health Governance.

Extraterritorial Human Rights Obligations of States in the Event of Disease Outbreaks

Elif Askin[*]

Abstract

Within the scholarly discourse on international health governance, the regulation of global health crises has predominantly been discussed within the international legal regime of the World Health Organization. Beyond that, the present contribution demonstrates that insufficient reflection has been given to the extraterritorial applicability of human rights obligations of states arising from international human rights treaties that aim to protect individuals situated in foreign states when disease outbreaks occur. Against this backdrop, the article focuses on the obligations of states with respect to the right to health and seeks to explore whether, in the context of disease outbreaks, states other than the territorial state of the right-holders bear legal duties towards individuals living in the afflicted state. While a state's human rights obligations under international law primarily apply within its territory, this article fosters the understanding that under contemporary international human rights law, states not only have commitments caused by political virtues or moral considerations towards victims of disease, but also under certain conditions bear legally-binding extraterritorial obligations, including positive obligations, to secure the realization of the right to health of the affected individuals in foreign states, particularly in developing countries.

* Research Fellow at the Max Planck Institute for Comparative Public Law and International Law in Heidelberg, Germany (askin@mpil.de). Her current research relates to public international law, international human rights law with a particular focus on the extraterritorial applicability of socio-economic rights, the law on state responsibility and global governance. All websites last accessed January 23, 2017.

I Introduction

In the age of globalization, actors and processes that have an impact on the right to health are increasingly internationalized.[1] Governmental action as well as inaction may therefore have detrimental effects anywhere on the globe. In this respect, already at the beginning of the 21st century the outbreak of the Severe Acute Respiratory Syndrome (SARS) disease[2] and its unprecedented worldwide spread in a short period of time prompted attention to *global health crises* that, as explained by the Committee on Economic, Social and Cultural Rights (CESCR), is due to "the formidable structural and other obstacles resulting from international and other factors beyond the control of States that impede the full realization of Article 12 [ICESCR] in many States parties".[3] This might be conceived to be most relevant in economically disadvantaged states where national health policies are considerably impacted by the policies of (affluent) states, for instance, when the latter require unaffordable fees to be imposed for primary health care as a conditionality for development cooperation and international aid programs.[4]

In the most recent example of a global health crisis, West Africa has been confronted with the largest outbreak of the Ebola[5] disease ever seen in history.[6] In August 2014, the World Health Organization (WHO) declared Ebola a Public Health Emergency of International Concern (PHEIC), stressing that a coordinated international response was essential to halt the cross-

---

1 Bueno de Mesquita, J, Hunt, P & Khosla, R, "The Human Rights Responsibility of International Assistance and Cooperation in Health" in Gibney, M & Skogly, S (eds.), *Universal Human Rights and Extraterritorial Obligations*, 2010, 104.

2 WHO, *Severe Acute Respiratory Syndrome (SARS)*, available at http://www.who.int/csr/sars/en/. According to the WHO SARS affected 26 countries.

3 CESCR, General *Comment No. 14, The right to the highest attainable standard of health*, Article 12 of the ICESCR, August 11, 2000 (UN Doc. E/C.12/2000.4), para. 5.

4 Bueno de Mesquita, Hunt & Khosla, "The Human Rights Responsibility of International Assistance and Cooperation in Health", above Fn. 1, 804.

5 See for more information on Ebola the contributions of *Michael Marx*, "Ebola Epidemic 2014-2015: Taking Control or Being Trapped in the Logic of Failure – What Lessons Can Be Learned?" and *Wolfgang Hein*, "The Response to the West African Ebola Outbreak (2014-2016): A Failure of Global Health Governance?" in this volume.

6 WHO, *Ethical considerations for use of unregistered interventions for Ebola viral disease, Report of an advisory panel to WHO*, 2014 (WHO/HIS/KER/GHE/14.1), 3.

border spread of the disease.[7] The disastrous impact of the virus within the affected states and its spread beyond national boundaries have obviously demonstrated the ineffectiveness and insufficiency of national measures taken by the post-conflict countries affected by Ebola – Guinea, Liberia and Sierra Leone – to tackle the disease, in large part due to domestic factors, such as weak health systems and a lack of resources, but also due to rampant fear and mistrust among the affected population.[8]

Concomitantly, the Ebola crisis has also highlighted the reluctance of many non-affected states to respond to the Ebola crisis in the afflicted countries, although, in most instances, these states would have been able to do so.[9] In the first months after the outbreak, only a few states offered assistance to countries where Ebola had occurred.[10] It was mainly neighboring African states, such as Cape Verde, Cote d'Ivoire, Ghana, Mali and Senegal, that offered aid to Guinea, Liberia and Sierra Leone.[11] According to the WHO, by June 2012, only 42 (21 %) of the 193 States Parties met their core capacity requirements imposed by the WHO's International Health Regulations (IHR).[12] Two years later, former US President *Obama*

---

7 Article 1 of the International Health Regulations (IHR) of the WHO defines Public Health Emergency of International Concern (PHEIC) as follows: "an extraordinary event which is determined […] to constitute a public health risk to other States through the international spread of disease and to potentially require a coordinated international response". See also BBC, "Ebola: Mapping the outbreak" (January 14, 2016), available at http://www.bbc.com/news/world-africa-2875 5033.

8 Largent, E, "EBOLA and FDA: reviewing the response to the 2014 outbreak, to find lessons for the future" (2016), 3 *Journal of Law and the Biosciences*, 489 (490); see on the outbreak of SARS WHO, *SARS: How a Global Epidemic Was Stopped*, 2006; Fidler, D, *SARS, Governance and the Globalization of Diseases*, 2004. See also WHO, *Factsheet No. 103 on Ebola virus disease*, January 2016, available at http://www.who.int/mediacentre/factsheets/fs103/en/.

9 Kian, T & Lateef, F, "Infectious Diseases Law and Severe Acute Respiratory Syndrome – Medical and Legal Responses and Implications: The Singapore Experience" (2004), 7 *APLAR Journal of Rheumatology*, 123 (129).

10 See for an overview of Ebola The Guardian, "Ebola outbreak response: a breakdown of the key funding pledges" (October 9, 2014), available at http://bit.ly/2lun-Wxy.

11 See United Nations (UN) Security Council Resolution 2177 (December 18, 2014), preambular para. 10.

12 The WHO obliges all States Parties in its IHR to establish and maintain core capacities for surveillance, risk assessment, reporting and response to public health risks and emergencies. These capacities need to be operational at national and

called on states to accelerate the global response to the Ebola crisis in stating that the world "has the responsibility to act, to step up and to do more. The United States intends to do more."[13] The delay of a coordinated and effective international response led to Resolution 2177 (2014) by the United Nations (UN) Security Council,[14] declaring for the very first time a disease outbreak as a threat to international peace and security, and to the establishment of the first UN health emergency mission.[15]

What might be the added value of applying international human rights law to global health crises, as far as the human rights obligations of states outside their territories are concerned? International human rights law is struggling with the phenomenon that states often escape accountability when it comes to actions and omissions beyond their national borders.[16] Traditionally, states bear human rights obligations only within their jurisdiction, based on territorial control.[17] However, the Westphalian territorial

international levels, WHO, *Implementation of the International Health Regulations (2005), Report of the Review Committee on the Role of the International Health Regulations in the Ebola Outbreak and Response, Report by the Director-General*, May 13, 2016 (A69/21), para. 19-20. See for more information on the core capacity requirements within the framework of the WHO's regulations the contributions of *Michael Marx*, "Ebola Epidemic 2014-2015: Taking Control or Being Trapped in the Logic of Failure – What Lessons Can Be Learned?" and *Wolfgang Hein*, "The Response to the West African Ebola Outbreak (2014-2016): A Failure of Global Health Governance?" in this volume.

13 Cooper, H & Fink, S, "Obama Presses Leaders to Speed Ebola Response" (September 16, 2014), *New York Times*, available at http://nyti.ms/2lJf1Zs.

14 See for further information on UN Security Council Resolution 2177 (2014) the contribution of *Robert Frau*, "Combining the WHO's International Health Regulations (2005) with the UN Security Council's Powers: Does it Make Sense for Health Governance?" in this volume.

15 BBC News, "Ebola global response was 'too slow', say health experts" (November 23, 2015), available at http://www.bbc.com/news/health-34877787. The UN Mission for Ebola Emergency Response (UNMEER) was established on September 19, 2014 and finished by July 31, 2015, available at http://ebolaresponse.un.org/un-mission-ebola-emergency-response-unmeer.

16 See Coomans, F, "Situating the Maastricht Principles on Extraterritorial Obligations of States in the Area of Economic, Social and Cultural Rights" (April 26, 2013), Maastricht University, available at https://papers.ssrn.com/sol3/papers.cfm?abstract_id=2256836.

17 ICJ, *Legal Consequences for States of the Continued Presence of South Africa un Namibia*, Advisory Opinion of 21 June 1921, ICJ Reports 1971, 16, para. 131; see also Skogly, S, "The obligation of international assistance and cooperation in the International Covenant on Economic, Social and Cultural Rights" in Bergsmo, M

framing of human rights, that might be the corrective to the domestic failure of a state, has been at the same time shaped by the rise of (economic) globalization, and has been challenged in situations where, in particular, socio-economic rights are negatively impacted by the policies of foreign states.[18] As has been argued by a growing number of scholars:

> "ETOs [extraterritorial obligations] are a missing link: Without ETOs, human rights could not assume their proper role as the legal bases for regulating globalization. With ETOs, an enabling environment for ESCRs [economic, social and cultural rights] can be generated, the primacy of human rights can be implemented, climate and eco-destruction can be stopped, the dominance of big money broken, TNCs regulated, and IGOs made accountable [...]. This reductionism to territorial obligations has led to a vacuum of human rights protection in a number of international political processes and a paucity of regulations for the protection of human rights. The situation is particularly challenging in the field of economic, social and cultural rights [...]."[19]

The present contribution examines the following question: Do non-affected states have *legal* obligations, here defined as *extraterritorial obligations*, in cases where the territorial state of the rights-holder fails to guarantee the right to health of its own population?

From a methodological perspective, this article takes a legalistic approach (leaving aside the various political, economic and philosophical intellectual strands and theories that arise when discussing human rights obligations of foreign states), and focuses on *states* in particular. As a rule,

---

(ed.), *Human Rights and Criminal Justice for the Downtrodden: Essays in Honour of Asbjørn Eide*, 2003, 403 (403).

18 Vandenhole, W, "Extraterritorial Human Rights Obligations: Taking Stock, Looking Forward" (2013), 5 *European Journal of Human Rights*, 804 (808). See also for example Coomans, F & Künnemann, R, *Cases and Concepts on Extraterritorial Obligations in the Area of Economic, Social and Cultural Rights*, 2012; Langford, M, Vandenhole, W & Scheinin, M et al. (eds.), *Global Justice, State Duties: The Extraterritorial Scope of Economic, Social and Cultural Rights in International Law*, 2013; Vandenhole, W, "Beyond Territoriality: The Maastricht Principles on Extra-Territorial Obligations in the Area of Economic, Social and Cultural Rights" (2011), 29 *Netherlands Quarterly of Human Rights*, 429; Salomon, M & Seiderman, I, "Human Rights Norms for a Globalized World: The Maastricht Principles on the Extraterritorial Obligations of States in the Area of Economic, Social and Cultural Rights" (2012), 3 *Global Policy*, 458.

19 See website of the Extraterritorial Obligations Consortium, a network of experts and Non-Governmental Organizations (NGOs) in the field of human rights, available at http://www.etoconsortium.org/en/main-navigation/our-work/. See also Wilde, R, "Dilemmas in Promoting Global Economic Justice through Human Rights Law" in Bhutal, N, *The Frontiers of Human Rights. Extraterritoriality and its Challenges*, 2016, 127 (134).

international human rights law primarily imposes obligations on states. Therefore, the enquiry of the expansion of the territorial scope of international human rights treaties in the area of socio-economic rights, especially the International Covenant on Economic, Social and Cultural Rights[20] (ICESCR), via states' obligations may help to consider how international human rights obligations of International Organizations and non-state actors can be further developed. Notably, the reference to the obligation of international cooperation in the Charter of the United Nations[21] (UN Charter) and in various international human rights instruments, such as in the Universal Declaration of Human Rights[22] (UDHR) entitling individuals to "a social and international order",[23] reflect, as described by *Simma*, "the maturing of international law into a much more *socially conscious legal order*, [...], a rising awareness of the common interests of the international community, a community that comprises not only States, but in the last instance all human beings [...]."[24] The debate about extraterritorial obligations of states, including the obligation of international cooperation, therefore plays a crucial role in certain areas of international law, at least as a guideline for the interpretation of human rights treaties and as a source of new obligations.[25] By zooming in on the law as it stands, this article intends

---

20 International Covenant on Economic, Social and Cultural Rights (ICESCR) of December 16, 1966 (993 UNTS 3).

21 Article 55 and 56 of the Charter of the United Nations (UN Charter) of October 24, 1945 (1 UNTS XVI).

22 Universal Declaration of Human Rights (UDHR) of December 10, 1948 (A/RES/3/217 A).

23 Article 28 of the UDHR.

24 Simma, B, "From Bilateralism to Community Interest in International Law" (1994), 250 *Recueil des Cours de l'Académie de Droit International*, 217 (234) (emphasis added).

25 Vandenhole, "Extraterritorial Human Rights Obligations: Taking Stock, Looking Forward", above Fn. 18, 807. See also on that De Schutter, O, "Foreword" in Coomans, F & Künnemann, R (eds.), *Cases and Concepts on Extraterritorial Obligations in the Area of Economic, Social and Cultural Rights*, above Fn. 18, at viii: "The Maastricht Principles [...] contribute to [...] renewal of human rights: they invite us to see human rights as global public goods, a guide for the reshaping of the international legal order. As these norms and procedures develop, human rights gradually can turn into [...] a 'global public standard' to assess the normative legitimacy of global governance institutions – i.e., the 'right to rule' of these institutions, which cannot ensure compliance with their decisions unless they are perceived as legitimate by those, including States, whom such decisions are addressed to."

to address some of the complex issues arising within the context of extraterritorial obligations of states; to that end this contribution provides an overview of the topic of extraterritorial obligations rather than an in-depth analysis of specific questions.

The present piece introduces the obligations of the affected states in the event of disease outbreaks that arise from Article 12 of the ICESCR (II). The following section establishes the context for this article and analyzes the legal basis and status of extraterritorial obligations, with a special focus on positive obligations to fulfill of states (III). It then sheds light on the jurisdiction threshold and on potential parameters that might trigger extraterritorial obligations of non-affected states (IV). The concluding section sums up the outcomes of the article (V).

II An Overview of the Affected State's Domestic Obligations

1 Obligations Imposed by the Right to Health

On the analytical plane, it is necessary to briefly revise the obligations of states arising from the right to health. In this vein, as stated above, these obligations are primarily directed towards affected states (in the case of Ebola, Guinea, Liberia and Sierra Leone), on the basis that they are the primary duty-bearers under international human rights law and have the primary duty to respond to the Ebola outbreak.[26] In a next step, the question whether these duties can form the basis for extraterritorial obligations will be analyzed. The core question is a two-pronged one: When (beyond which threshold) does an extraterritorial obligation of a state arise under international human rights law (here under the ICESCR), and how should these obligations be allocated among various obligated states?

At the international level, the right to health is enshrined in Article 12 of the ICESCR, which contains the most complete guarantee of that right.[27] In

---

26 See Toebes, B, "The Ebola crisis: challenges for Global Health Law" (February 4, 2015), available at http://www.sharesproject.nl/the-ebola-crisis-challenges-for-global-health-law/; see also Langford, M, Vandenhole, W & Scheinin, M et al., "Introduction. An Emerging Field" in Langford, Vandenhole & Scheinin et al. (eds.), *Global Justice, State Duties*, above Fn. 18, 3.

27 See for more details on the content of the right to health, see the contribution of *A. Katarina Weilert*, "The Right to Health in International Law – Normative Foundations and Doctrinal Flaws" in this volume.

being an "inclusive"[28] right, the normative content of the right to health encompasses the right to enjoy appropriate health care, including access to medicines,[29] on the one hand, and on the other embraces a range of factors that promote the underlying components of health,[30] such as safe water, food and housing, as well as a healthy environment that guarantees that individuals enjoy the highest attainable level of health.[31] The right to health also includes access to health-related education and information.[32]

Moreover, social determinants of health, such as social, political, economic and cultural factors (such as poverty) are equally significant to the realization of the right to health.[33] In this respect, the underlying social determinants of the right to health illustrate the crucial role that these "global" factors can play in the interlinkage between territorial and extraterritorial obligations of states, including issues of the global institutional structure that are beyond the reach of any single state.[34] This is in line with Article 28 of the Universal Declaration of Human Rights (UDHR), which entitles individuals to *a social and international order* in which human rights can be fully realized.[35]

Turning to the obligations of states, Article 12 (1) of the ICESCR stipulates that States Parties "recognize" the right to health, whereas other rights

---

28 Economic and Social Council, *The right of everyone to the enjoyment of the highest attainable standard of physical and mental health*, Report of the Special Rapporteur, Paul Hunt, Addendum, Mission to the World Trade Organization, 1 March 2004 (UN Doc. E/CN.4/2004/49/Add.1), para. 18.

29 Ibid., para. 19.

30 CESCR, *General Comment No. 14*, above Fn. 3, para. 11.

31 Ibid., para. 8, 11; see also Saul, B, Kinley, D & Mowbray, J, *The International Covenant on Economic, Social and Cultural Rights. Commentary, Cases, and Materials*, 2014, 984.

32 CESCR, *General Comment No. 14*, above Fn. 3, para. 11.

33 UN GA, *Report of the Special Rapporteur on the right of everyone to the enjoyment of the highest attainable standard of physical and mental health*, August 8, 2007 (UN Doc. A/62/214), para. 45. See also WHO, *Social determinants of health*, available at http://www.who.int/social_determinants/en/.

34 See on the issue of the right to health and global institutional reform Tobin, J, *The Right to Health in International Law*, 2012, 344.

35 Article 28 of the UDHR.

in the Covenant need to be "respected"[36], "ensured"[37] or even "guaranteed"[38]:

> "1. The States Parties to the present Covenant *recognize* the right of everyone to the enjoyment of the *highest attainable standard of physical and mental health.*
> 2. The *steps to be taken* by the States Parties to the present Covenant to achieve the full realization of this right shall include those necessary for:
> [...]
> (c) The *prevention, treatment and control* of epidemic, endemic, occupational and other *diseases*; [...]."[39]

It has been argued that the obligations of states arising from the right to health rank lower or are less legally binding ("soft legal obligations").[40] It is important to keep in mind that the provision reflects the reluctance towards socio-economic rights in general, notably with respect to their implementation.[41] As pointed out by *Tobin,* the wording of the provision does not offer a precise meaning of the actual obligations of states under the right to health.[42] However, according to the drafting history of the ICESCR, the term "recognized" gives the provision less operative force in order for states to "construe the meaning more or less liberally",[43] as the realization of the right to health depends on resources and social conditions within a state, which in turn "would assist in securing its general acceptance by the States".[44]

While Article 12 of the ICESCR grants states a wide margin of appreciation for the realization of the right concerned, it must be read in conjunction with Article 2 (1) of the ICESCR, the umbrella clause of the Covenant:

> "Each State Party to the present Covenant undertakes *to take steps*, *individually* and through *international assistance and co-operation*, especially economic and technical, to the *maximum of its available resources*, with a view to achieving *progressively* the full realization of the rights recognized in the present Covenant *by all appropriate means*, including particularly the adoption of legislative measures."[45]

---

36 See for example Article 13 (3) and Article 15 (3) of the International Covenant on Economic, Social and Cultural Rights (ICESCR).
37 See for example Article 3 and Article 8 of the ICESCR.
38 See for example Article 2 (2) and Article 7 (a) (1) of the ICESCR.
39 Article 12 of the ICESCR (emphasis added).
40 Toebes, B, *The Right to Health as a Human Right in International Law*, 1999, 293.
41 See Tobin, *The Right to Health,* above Fn. 34, 176.
42 Ibid., 175.
43 UN, General Assembly, 9th meeting, Third Committee, 566th meeting, October 28, 1954 (UN Doc. A/C.3/SR.566), para. 11.
44 Ibid.
45 Article 2 (1) of the ICESCR.

According to Article 2 (1) of the ICESCR, the realization of the right to health depends on the *resources that are available* to the state.[46] In consequence, "the right to health must be understood as a right to the enjoyment of a variety of facilities, goods, services and conditions"[47] that are essential for the realization of that right.[48] In concrete terms, this is not merely directed towards the availability of financial resources, but also includes, for instance, human, technological, organizational, natural and informational resources.[49] It is because of this that states, *inter alia*, have to "increase public spending on health",[50] "train and recruit [...] medical staff"[51] and "increase expenditure for health care and to take all appropriate measures to ensure universal access to health care at prices affordable to everyone".[52] States are obliged to ensure that the allocation of resources is adequate and appropriate as well as effective and sustainable.[53] This also includes resources available from the *international community*.[54]

While resource constraints might derive from structural deficits that have built up in a short period of time, making them difficult to correct immediately, Article 2 (1) of the ICESCR allows for the *progressive realization* of the right to health. States have a specific and continuing obligation to move as expeditiously and effectively as possible towards the full realization of the right to health.[55] But, at the same time, they also have *immediate obligations* that include the guarantees of non-discrimination and equal treatment,[56] as well as the *obligation to take steps* towards the full realization of

---

46 CESCR, General *Comment No. 14*, above Fn. 3, para. 9. See also Tobin, *The Right to Health*, above Fn. 34, 175, 252.

47 CESCR, *General Comment No. 14*, above Fn. 3, para. 9.

48 Ibid., para. 9.

49 CRC Committee, *Report on the Forty-Sixth Session*, April 22, 2008 (UN Doc. CRC/C/46/3), chapter VII, para. 65; see also Tobin, *The Right to Health*, above Fn. 34, 226 et seq.

50 CESCR, *Concluding Observations on Kazakhstan*, June 7, 2010 (UN Doc. E/C.12/KAZ/CO/1), para. 40.

51 Ibid.

52 CESCR, *Concluding Observations on the Republic of Korea*, December 17, 2009 (UN Doc. E/C.12/KOR/CO/3), para. 30.

53 Tobin, *The Right to Health*, above Fn. 34, 228.

54 CESCR, *General Comment No. 3, The Nature of States Parties' Obligations*, Article 2 (1) of the ICESCR, December 14, 1990 (UN Doc. E/1991/23), para. 13.

55 CESCR, *General Comment No. 14*, above Fn. 3, para. 31.

56 Article 2 (2) of the ICESCR: "The States Parties to the present Covenant undertake to guarantee that the rights enunciated in the present Covenant will be exercised

the right to health that need to be "deliberate, concrete and targeted"[57], such as the introduction of a national public health strategy or a plan of action.[58] *Alston* and *Quinn* explain that these obligations are "hybrids between obligations of conduct and obligations of result".[59] On the one hand, states must match their performance with their objective capabilities, which are obligations of result; on the other hand, they are obliged to take active – but unspecified – steps towards the realization of the relevant right that are obligations of conduct.[60]

Furthermore, the CESCR emphasizes a series of concepts and principles that have to be met by states, notably the *minimum core obligations* and the *principle of non-retrogression,* i.e. that the state should not take steps backwards in its realization of the right concerned.[61] Apart from the essential primary health care that is read into the core of the right and that has to be guaranteed by every state, the CESCR establishes "obligations of comparable priority".[62] These encompass, among others, the *prevention, treatment and control of epidemic and endemic diseases,* as well as education and access to information concerning the main health problems in the community, including methods of prevention and control.[63] In any event, these minimum core obligations must be met by states. In order to justify the failure to meet at least the minimum core obligations due to a lack of available resources, the state is obliged to prove that every effort has been made to use all resources that are at its disposal.[64] The CESCR stressed that "a State claiming that it is unable to carry out its obligation for reasons beyond its control therefore has the burden of proving that this is the case and that it

without discrimination of any kind as to race, colour, sex, language, religion, political or other opinion, national or social origin, property, birth or other status."

57 CESCR, *General Comment No. 14*, above Fn. 3, para. 30.

58 Economic and Social Council, *The right of everyone to the enjoyment of the highest attainable standard of physical and mental health*, above Fn. 28, para. 22.

59 Alston, P & Quinn, G, "The Nature and Scope of States Parties' Obligations under the Covenant on Economic, Social and Cultural Rights" (1987), 9 *Human Rights Quarterly*, 159 (185).

60 Ibid.

61 CESCR, General *Comment No. 3,* above Fn. 54, para. 9-10.

62 CESCR, *General Comment No. 14*, above Fn. 3, para. 43.

63 Ibid., para. 44 (c) and (d).

64 See also CESCR, *General Comment No. 3*, above Fn. 54, para. 10. See also Forman, L, "Can Core Obligations under the Right to Health Achieve their Ambitions" (2015), 9 *Zeitschrift für Menschenrechte*, 36 (38).

has unsuccessfully sought to obtain *international support*".[65] Concomitantly, the Committee emphasized "that it is particulary incumbent on States parties and other actors in a position to assist, to provide 'international assistance and cooperation, especially economic and technical' which enable developing countries to fulfil their core and other obligations".[66]

Consequently, the territorial state will be in breach of international law if it cannot meet the minimum core obligations arising from the right to health, regardless of whether the state is unwilling or unable to abidc by that obligation. Nevertheless, a possible exculpation from the violation in question might exclude wrongfulness at the secondary level of international responsibility.

2 The Obligation to Prevent, Treat and Control Diseases

The fact, however, that a number of non-limitative steps are mentioned in Article 12 (2) of the ICESCR implies that the right to health is more concrete than similar provisions, which do not enumerate concrete steps.[67] As articulated by the CESCR:

> "'The prevention, treatment and control of epidemic, endemic, occupational and other diseases' […] requires […] the promotion of social determinants of good health, such as environmental safety, education, economic development and gender equity. The right to treatment includes the creation of a system of urgent medical care in cases of accidents, epidemics and similar health hazards, and the *provision of disaster relief and humanitarian assistance in emergency situations*. The control of diseases refers to *States' individual and joint efforts* to, inter alia, make available relevant technologies, using and improving epidemiological surveillance and data collection on a disaggregated basis, the implementation or enhancement of immunization programmes and other strategies of infectious disease control."[68]

The right to health imposes on states the tripartite typology of duties: the obligation to respect, protect and fulfill.[69] Accordingly, the obligation to

65 CESCR, *General Comment No. 12, The right to adequate food*, Article 11 of the ICESCR, May 12, 1999 (UN Doc. E/C.12/1999/5), para. 17 (emphasis added).

66 CESCR, *General Comment No. 14*, above Fn. 3, para. 45.

67 Article 12 (2) (c) of the ICESCR. Article 24 (2) (c) of the Convention of the Rights of the Child (CRC) of November 20, 1989 (adopted by UN GA Resolution 44/25) also refers to the obligation to combat diseases.

68 CESCR, *General Comment No. 14*, above Fn. 3, para. 16 (emphasis added).

69 Ibid., para. 33; Eide, A, Giacca, G & Golay, C, "Economic, Social and Cultural Rights as Human Rights" in Eide, A, Krause, C & Rosas, A (eds.), *Economic,*

respect, as a negative obligation, requires states to refrain from interfering directly or indirectly with the enjoyment of the right to health.[70] This, among others, entails the obligation to refrain from "denying or limiting equal access for all persons [...] to preventive, curative and palliative health services [and] abstaining from enforcing discriminatory practices as a state policy".[71]

On the other hand, the obligation to *protect* refers to the states' positive obligation to take preventive measures to reduce or eliminate human rights violations by non-state actors.[72] The obligation to protect contains a number of elements, some of which are obligations of *due diligence*. For instance, states should have a preventive apparatus to ensure the protection of the right to health, in order to prevent or mitigate the outbreak of a disease.[73] It is a matter of due diligence how these institutions function.[74] Furthermore, the obligation to protect requires states to adopt legislation or other measures ensuring equal access to health care and health-related services provided by third parties, as well as to ensure that privatization of the health sector does not constitute a threat to the availability, accessibility, acceptability and quality of health facilities.[75] For example, an intellectual property framework should encourage research and development activities, but should not deny or restrict individuals' access to medicine.[76]

Finally, the positive obligation to *fulfill* requires states to adopt appropriate legislative, administrative, budgetary and judicial as well as other measures.[77] At the national level, the obligation to fulfill imposes on states a need, for instance, to give sufficient recognition to the right to health in

---

Social and Cultural Rights: A Text Book, 2014, 18 et seqq. See also the Maastricht Guidelines on Violations of Economic, Social and Cultural Rights, 1997, para. 6.

70 CESCR, *General Comment No. 14*, above Fn. 3, para. 33.

71 Ibid., para. 34.

72 ILA Study Group on Due Diligence in International Law, *First Report*, Duncan French (Chair) and Tim Stephans (Rapporteur), March 7, 2014, 16.

73 Pisillo-Mazzeschi, R, *Responsabilité de l'état pour violations des obligations positives relatives aux droits de l'homme. Collected Courses of the Hague Academy of International Law 2008*, vol. 333, chapter III, 2009, 334 et seq.

74 Ibid. See also for example ECtHR, *Kelly and Others v UK*, Judgment of May 4, 2001 (App. No. 30054/96), para. 96.

75 CESCR, *General Comment No. 14*, above Fn. 3, para. 35.

76 CESCR, *General Comment on States Obligations under the International Covenant on Exonomic, Social and Cultural Rights in the context of Business Activities*, Draft prepared by Olivier De Schutter and Zdzislaw Kedzia, Rapporteurs, October 17, 2016 (E/C.12/60/R.1), para. 20.

77 CESCR, *General Comment No. 14*, above Fn. 3, para. 33.

national political and legal systems, preferably by way of legislative implementation, and to adopt national health policies for realizing that right. States have to ensure the provision of health care, including immunization programs and the guarantee of equal access for all to the underlying (social) determinants of health.[78]

3 The Affected States: "Unwilling or Unable"?

Based on the above, the question arises whether the Ebola-affected states, which have the primary obligation to ensure the right to health of their own population, have taken sufficient measures to ensure the right to health of the victims of disease. From a preventive perspective, this also includes functioning health systems as well as good infrastructure able to respond to foreseeable threats, such as disease outbreaks.[79]

In practice, reports on the Ebola crisis have shown that the health systems in Sierra Leone, Guinea and Liberia have been considerably weakened by armed conflict, lacking the necessary resources for the realization of the right to health. *Toebes* has demonstrated that the affected countries have asserted that they have investet the "maximum of their available resources" in the Ebola crisis.[80] However, states are required to guarantee the minimum core of the right by not falling below the minimum threshold.[81] To illustrate, according to the World Bank, in 2014 Guinea spent only 5.6 % of the GDP on public health, whereas in the case of Liberia this was 10 % and Sierra Leone 11.1 %, similar to Germany with 11.3 %.[82] The question that arises here is whether Guinea has violated the minimum core of the right to health because it failed to invest in public health in order to protect the right to

78 Ibid., para. 36.
79 Toėbes, "The Ebola crisis", above Fn. 26.
80 Ibid.
81 Ibid.
82 The World Bank, *Database on health expenditure, total (% of GDP)*, available at http://data.worldbank.org/indicator/SH.XPD.TOTL.ZS?locations=GN-LR-SL. See also Toebes, "The Ebola crisis", above Fn. 26.

health of its own population. In principle, the fundamental problem is attached to the inefficiency of the money spent, as well as corruption.[83] Transparency International stated in its report of 2006 that the health sector is among the most corrupt state sectors.[84]

The question arises whether states other than the territorial state – in a subsidiary or even complementary way – have obligations to assist the affected states in cases of a disease outbreak, where the territorial state is unwilling or unable to deal with a health crisis.

III Assessment of Non-Affected States' Obligations Concerning Disease Outbreaks

1 Extraterritorial Obligations

The term *extraterritorial obligations* (also referred to as international or transnational obligations, third states obligations or global obligations[85]) is one of the notions that has emerged in the recent debate on the "paradigmatic shift of mainstream human rights law"[86] as it adjusts to new realities where states other than the territorial (or jurisdictional) state are considered to be the bearers of human rights obligations. Extraterritorial obligations here mean obligations of non-affected states towards individuals that are situated in other countries.

The idea of invoking obligations against states other than the territorial (or jurisdictional) state, as far as socio-economic rights are concerned, can be found in the *Maastricht Principles on Extraterritorial Obligations of States in the area of Economic, Social and Cultural Rights* (Maastricht Principles).[87] This set of non-legally binding principles was adopted in 2011

---

83 Toebes, "The Ebola crisis", above Fn. 26.

84 Transparency International, *Global Corruption Report 2006: Corruption and Health*, available at http://bit.ly/2lJkiQP; see also Toebes, "The Ebola crisis", above Fn. 26.

85 See on terminology Gibney, M, "On Terminology. Extraterritorial Obligations" in Langford, Vandenhole & Scheinin et al. (eds.), *Global Justice, State Duties*, above Fn. 18, 32 et seqq.

86 Vandenhole, "Extraterritorial Human Rights Obligations: Taking Stock, Looking Forward", above Fn. 18, 805.

87 *Maastricht Principles on Extraterritorial Obligations of States in the area of Economic, Social and Cultural Rights*, adopted in September 2011 by leading human rights experts and NGOs, is available at http://bit.ly/2mbsSsx.

by a group of international human rights experts and reflects a "landmark development in international law".[88]

Against this backdrop, international legal relationships which might trigger extraterritorial obligations in particular unfold in a triangle of actors: a potentially obliged state, a potential recipient state, and affected individuals. Potential obligations to act will therefore typically have an extraterritorial dimension that involves action outside the acting state's territorial boundaries. This is the case concerning acts or omissions[89] of a state outside its national borders or when its domestic policies have extraterritorial effects outside its territory (for example based on policy measures that have been taken inside that state).[90] Extraterritorial obligations might therefore not only be relevant and effective in the area of international assistance but also, as in the field of intellectual property for medicines and other key goods, international trade and investment protection law.[91]

The following analysis on extraterritorial obligations is twofold. First, it will be scrutinized whether the ICESCR enshrines extraterritorial obligations on states and as regards the right to health, whether these obligations are legally binding. The second step considers the question when and beyond which threshold extraterritorial obligations of states arise in practice.

Any attempt to analyze extraterritorial obligations from a legal perspective is inevitably confronted with the strong politicization of the issue at hand. Different regional blocs (for example Global North vs. Global South) have taken different positions.[92] For instance, the African group of states has emphasized that international assistance is a legally binding obligation, whereas states from the Global North, such as the UK, Canada and France,

---

88 Wilde, "Dilemmas in Promoting Global Economic Justice through Human Rights Law", above Fn. 19, 132.

89 See ILC Draft Articles on Responsibility of States for Internationally Wrongful Acts of 2001 (UN Doc. A/56/10 (2001)). According to Article 2 of the ILC Draft Articles the international responsibility of a state can be also triggered by an omission.

90 Bartels, L, "The EU's Human Rights Obligations in Relation to Policies with Extraterritorial Effects" (2014), 25 *European Journal of International Law*, 1071 (1071).

91 Vandenhole, "Extraterritorial Human Rights Obligations: Taking Stock, Looking Forward", above Fn. 18, 806.

92 Ibid., 811 et seq.

have pointed out that international cooperation and assistance is a moral obligation but not a legal entitlement.[93]

Nevertheless, a growing body of scholarship argues that extraterritorial obligations do exist under the ICESCR.[94] Crucially, unlike the International Covenant on Civil and Political Rights (ICCPR) that obliges states to respect and to ensure the rights of the individuals "within its territory and subject to its jurisdiction"[95] and the European Convention on Human Rights[96] (ECHR), the ICESCR does not contain a general jurisdictional clause (Article 2 para. 1), but it does makes several references to international cooperation and assistance.[97] However, international courts and human rights bodies have previously dealt with and clarified the meaning of the absence of a jurisdictional clause in treaty law (for example with respect to the ICESCR, the Genocide Convention and the Geneva Conventions). The International Court of Justice (ICJ) held in its advisory opinion on the *Legal Consequences of the Construction of a Wall in the Occupied Palestinian Territory*, considering whether Israel had obligations under the ICESCR to individuals in the Occupied Territories, that

---

93 Ibid., 811. Report of the Open-Ended Working Group on an Optional Protocol to the Covenant on Economic, Social and Cultural Rights on its fourth session (Geneva July 16-27, 2007), August 30, 2007 (A/HRC/6/8), para. 164; Report on the Open-Ended Working Group to Consider Options Regarding the Elaboration of an Optional Protocol to the International Covenant on Economic, Social and Cultural Rights on its second session, February 10, 2005 (E/CN.4/2005/52), para. 76.

94 Langford, M, Coomans, F & Gómez Isa, F, "Extraterritorial Duties in International Law" in Langford, Vandenhole & Scheinin et al. (eds.), *Global Justice, State Duties*, above Fn. 18, 51; Coomans, F, "Some remarks on the Extraterritorial Application of the International Covenant on Economic, Social and Cultural Rights" in Coomans, F & Kamminga, M (eds.), *Extraterritorial Application of Human Rights Treaties*, 2004, 183.

95 Article 2 (1) of the ICCPR (emphasis added).

96 European Convention on Human Rights (ECHR) of November 4, 1950 (ETS No. 005), Article 1: "The High Contracting Parties shall secure to everyone *within their jurisdiction* the rights and freedoms defined in Section I of this Convention." (emphasis added).

97 See for the wording of Article 2 (1) of the ICESCR above II.1. The only exception is Article 14 of the ICESCR as well as Article 2 of the Optional Protocol to the ICESCR of December 10, 2008 (adopted in General Assembly Resolution A/RES/63/117) that contains references to jurisdiction. See also Milanovic, M, *Extraterritorial Application of Human Rights Treaties. Law, Principles, and Policy*, 2011, 11 et seqq.

> "[t]he International Covenant on Economic, Social and Cultural *Rights contains no provision on its scope of application.* This may be explicable by the fact that the Covenant guarantees rights *which are essentially territorial.* However, it is not to be excluded that it applies both to territories over which a State party has sovereignty and to those over which that State *exercises territorial jurisdiction.*"[98]

In *Georgia v. Russian Federation*, the ICJ found that the

> "provisions of CERD [Convention on the Elimination of All Forms of Racial Discrimination] generally appear to apply, like other provisions of instruments of that nature, to the actions of a State party *when it acts beyond its territory.*"[99]

With respect to the Geneva Conventions, the ICJ has clarified that negative and positive extraterritorial obligations do exist under common Article 1 of the Geneva Conventions.[100] Furthermore, in the *Application of the Convention on the Prevention and Punishment of the Crime of Genocide (Genocide Case)*, the court stated that the obligations of states as contained in the Genocide Convention are obligations *erga omnes* and that the obligation to prevent genocide is not territorially limited.[101]

In a number of judgments, the European Court of Human Rights (ECtHR) has argued that jurisdiction is primarily territorial and only in exceptional circumstances extraterritorial.[102] Furthermore, in *Franklin Guillermo Aisalla Molina (Ecuador/Colombia)* the Inter-American Commission on Human Rights (IACHR) held

> "that it has competence *ratione loci* with respect to a State for acts occurring on the territory of another State, when the alleged victims were subjected to the authority and control of its agents."[103]

---

98 ICJ, Legal *Consequences of the Construction of a Wall in the Occupied Palestinian Territory,* Advisory Opinion of July 9, 2004, ICJ Reports 2004, 136, para. 112 (emphasis added).

99 ICJ, Case Concerning Application of the International Convention on the Elimination of all Forms of Racial Discrimination (Georgia v. Russian Federation), provisional measures, order of October 15, 2008, ICJ Reports 2008, 353, para. 109.

100 ICJ, Legal Consequences of the Construction of a Wall in the Occupied Palestinian Territory, above Fn. 98, para. 158 (positive duty); ICJ, Military and Paramilitary Activities in and against Nicaragua (Nicaragua v. United States of America), Judgment of June 27, 1986, ICJ Reports 1986, 114, para. 220.

101 ICJ, Application of the Convention on the Prevention and Punishment of the Crime of Genocide (Bosnia and Herzegovina v. Serbia and Montenegro), Preliminary Objections of July 11, 1996, ICJ Reports 1996, 595, para. 31.

102 See for example ECtHR, *Case of Ilascu and Others v. Moldova and Russia*, Judgment of July 8, 2004 (App. No. 48787/99), para. 312; *Al-Skeini and others v. UK,* Grand Chamber Judgment of July 7, 2011 (App. No. 55721/07), para. 131.

103 IACHR, *Franklin Guillermo Aisalla Molina (Ecuador/Colombia)*, Admissibility Decision of October 21, 2010, Report No. 112/10 (OEA/Ser.L/V/II.140), para. 98.

Otherwise, it is asserted, there would be a legal lacuna in the protection of the individuals' human rights, which would be contrary to the object and purpose of the American Convention of Human Rights.[104] Consequently, the absence of a jurisdictional clause has not been considered a barrier against extraterritorial application of the abovementioned treaties.[105]

The CESCR has also explicitly confirmed the existence of extraterritorial obligations on a number of occasions,[106] in particular with respect to the obligations arising from the right to health as discussed above:

> "To comply with their international obligations in relation to article 12, States parties *have to* respect the enjoyment of the right to health *in other countries*, and to prevent third parties from violating the right *in other countries*, if *they are able to influence* these third parties by way of legal or political means, in accordance with the Charter of the United Nations and applicable international law. *Depending on the availability of resources*, States *should facilitate* access to essential health facilities, goods and services *in other countries*, wherever possible and provide the necessary aid when required. States parties *should* ensure that the right to health is *given due attention in international agreements* and, to that end, should consider the development of further legal instruments. In relation to the conclusion of other international agreements, States parties *should* take steps to ensure that these instruments do not adversely impact upon the right to health. Similarly, States parties have an obligation to ensure that *their actions as members of international organizations* take *due account* of the right to health. Accordingly, States parties which are members of international financial institutions, notably the International Monetary Fund, the World Bank, and regional development banks, *should* pay greater attention to the protection of the right to health in *influencing the lending policies, credit agreements and international measures of these institutions*."[107]

As in the domestic context, the CESCR uses the tripartite typology of duties with regard to extraterritorial obligations. Although the General Comments of the CESCR are not legally binding, it should be noted that the Committee

104 Ibid., para. 98.

105 See also Bartels, "The EU's Human Rights Obligations in Relation to Policies with Extraterritorial Effects", above Fn. 90, 1084. See also ICJ, *Armed Activities on the Territory of the Congo (Democratic Republic of the Congo v. Uganda)*, December 19, 2005, ICJ Reports 2005, 168, para. 216.

106 See for example CESCR, *General Comment No. 15, The right to water*, Article 11 and 12 of the ICESCR, January 20, 2003 (UN Doc. E/C.12/2002/11, para. 31; on the right to food see *General Comment No. 12*, above Fn. 65, para. 36.

107 CESCR, *General Comment No. 14*, above Fn. 3, para. 39. (emphasis added). See also Milanovic, *Extraterritorial Application of Human Rights Treaties*, above Fn. 97, 228.

uses stronger ("have to") in respect of negative obligations.[108] The negative obligation to respect entails refraining from actions that interfere, directly or indirectly, with the enjoyment of the right to health.[109] For instance, states should refrain at all times from imposing *embargoes or similar measures* restricting the supply of medicines and medical equipment to another state.[110] Sanctions should never be used as an instrument of political and economic pressure.[111] Negative obligations are, in the work of the CESCR, but also politically, the least controversial.[112] Therefore, according to *Milanovic*, negative obligations have no territorial limitation.[113]

As regards the positive obligation to protect, states as members of international financial institutions, such as the International Monetary Fund (IMF) or the World Bank, should take into account their obligations arising from the right to health and ensure that the policies and decisions of these institutions are in conformity with their obligations under the ICESCR.[114] This does not concern the direct obligations of these institutions, but rather the conduct of states, which have the capacity to *influence* the behavior of such institutions. A state should demonstrate that it has taken all reasonable measures, for example in the decision-making processes, to prevent institutional activities from harming the right to health of the individuals concerned.[115] Furthermore, the obligation to protect extends to business entities, such as multinational corporations, whose activities have an impact on the right to health of individuals in other territories.[116] In that context, the

---

108 Bartels, "The EU's Human Rights Obligations in Relation to Policies with Extraterritorial Effects", above Fn. 90, 1085, 1087.

109 Tobin, *The Right to Health*, above Fn. 34, 332.

110 CESCR, *General Comment No. 14*, above Fn. 3, para. 41.

111 Ibid., para. 41.

112 Salomon, M, *Global Responsibility for Human Rights: World Poverty and the Development of International Law*, 2007, 189.

113 Milanovic argues that negative obligations to respect are territorially unlimited, while the positive obligations arising from such treaties would generally require the exercise of territorial jurisdiction, Milanovic, *Extraterritorial Application of Human Rights Treaties*, above Fn. 97, 228.

114 See for example CESCR, Concluding Observations on United Kingdom, June 5, 2002 (UN Doc. E/C.12/1/Add.79), para. 26. See also Tobin, *The Right to Health,* above Fn. 34, 333 et seq.

115 Tobin, ibid., 338.

116 Tobin, ibid., 339.

CESCR uses language that is non-obligatory ("should"),[117] presumably due to the controversial nature of positive obligations.

In the same line, the CESCR remains quite reluctant as regards the obligation to fulfill that requires states to provide aid to other countries.[118] The obligation of international assistance and cooperation thereby provides the basis for the obligation to fulfill.[119]

2 The Obligation of International Cooperation and Assistance

Article 2 (1) of the ICESCR explicitly anchors a general "obligation of international assistance and cooperation" among states.[120] Article 56 of the UN Charter, with reference to Article 55, also contains a duty to cooperate: "All Members pledge themselves to take joint and separate action in cooperation with the Organization for the achievement of the purposes set forth in Article 55."[121] Moreover, the CESCR articulates with regard to the right to health that

> "the existing gross inequality in the health status of the people, *particularly between developed and developing countries*, as well as within countries, is politically, socially and economically unacceptable and is, therefore, of *common concern to all countries*".[122]

---

117 Bartels, "The EU's Human Rights Obligations in Relation to Policies with Extraterritorial Effects", above Fn. 90, 1085 et seq.

118 Ibid., 1086.

119 CESCR, *General Comment No. 3*, above Fn. 54, para. 14; Salomon, *Global Responsibility for Human Rights,* above Fn. 112, 189 et seq.

120 Article 2 (1) of the ICESCR.

121 Article 55 of the UN Charter reads: "With a view to the creation of conditions of stability and well-being which are necessary for peaceful and friendly relations among nations based on respect for the principle of equal rights and self-determination of peoples, the United Nations shall promote:
a. higher standards of living, full employment, and conditions of economic and social progress and development;
b. solutions of international economic, social, health, and related problems; and international cultural and educational cooperation; and
c. universal respect for, and observance of, human rights and fundamental freedoms for all without distinction as to race, sex, language, or religion."

122 See CESCR, *General Comment No. 14*, above Fn. 3, para. 38 (emphasis added).

Against this backdrop, it is not surprising that the CESCR has taken a clear stance, affirming that the obligation of international cooperation and assistance is an obligation on *all* states.[123]

The obligation to cooperate operates generally, as it requires that states work together internationally in order to realize the right to health everywhere.[124] International cooperation includes the development of international rules to establish an enabling environment for the realization of socio-economic rights, but also financial and technical assistance.[125] Furthermore, states should refrain from nullifying or impairing human rights in other countries.[126] However, the scope of the obligation remains vague, and it is not clear what it might *concretely* entail.[127] As regards the Ebola outbreak, for instance, UN Security Council Resolution 2177 (2014) states that

> "the control of outbreaks of major infectious diseases requires urgent action and greater national, regional and international collaboration [...] stressing the crucial and immediate need for a *coordinated international response*."[128]

Here, General Comment No. 14 on the right to health seems to be of importance with respect to disaster relief and emergency situations. It provides:

> "States parties have a joint and individual responsibility, in accordance with the Charter of the United Nations and relevant resolutions [...] *to cooperate in providing disaster relief and humanitarian assistance in times of emergency* [...]. Each State should contribute to this task *to the maximum of its capacities* [...]. Moreover, given that some diseases are easily transmissible beyond the frontiers of a State, the international community has a *collective responsibility* to address this problem. The economically *developed States* parties have a *special responsibility* and interest to assist the poorer *developing States* in this regard."[129]

The potential duty to cooperate as enshrined under Article 2 (1) of the ICESCR asks first whether the affected state has an obligation to seek assistance from other states where that state is unable or unwilling to protect its population in acute health emergencies (a) and, second, whether non-

123 CESCR, *General Comment No. 3*, above Fn. 54, para. 14.

124 Peters, A, *Beyond Human Rights. The Legal Status of the Individual under International Law*, 2016, 245.

125 De Schutter, O, Eide, A & Khalfan, A et. al., "Commentary to the Maastricht Principles on Extraterritorial Obligations of States in the area of Economic, Social and Cultural Rights" (2012), 34 *Human Rights Quarterly,* 1084 (1104).

126 Ibid.

127 Tobin, *The Right to Health,* above Fn. 34, 340, 342.

128 Preamble of the UN Security Council Resolution 2177 (2014), above Fn. 11.

129 CESCR, *General Comment No. 14*, above Fn. 3, para. 40 (emphasis added).

affected states, essentially developed ones, bear an obligation to provide assistance and cooperation to the individuals concerned (b).

a The Obligation to Seek International Assistance and Cooperation

The affected (or territorial) state's obligation to seek international assistance and cooperation is derived from that state's positive obligations to take action towards the realization of the right to health as required by Article 2 (1) of the ICESCR, which also requires states to work together through international assistance and cooperation.[130] As alluded to above, the territorial state's obligation "to take steps [...] to the maximum of its available resources"[131] not only refers to that state's own resources, but also includes resources that are available from the international community through international assistance and cooperation.[132] Hence, the territorial state is obliged to seek assistance in cases where its capacity is exhausted.[133] Concurringly, Principle 34 of the Maastricht Principles also confirms that a state has an obligation to seek international assistance and cooperation on mutually agreed terms when that state is unable to guarantee socio-economic rights within its territory.[134]

In this regard, Article 10 of the *ILC Draft Articles on the Protection of Persons in the Event of Disasters* (ILC Articles on Disaster Protection of 2016), although not legally binding, stresses that the affected state has the primary duty to ensure the protection of the individuals' rights in its territory or under its jurisdiction.[135] Article 11 of the ILC Articles on Disaster Protection of 2016 *transforms* this primary duty of the territorial state into a secondary one in stating that the territorial state has the duty to *seek* assistance from other states where its national response capacity is exceeded by the disaster in question.[136]

---

130 Article 2 (1) of the ICESCR. See above II.

131 Article 2 (1) of the ICESCR.

132 CESCR, *General Comment No. 3*, above Fn. 54, para. 14.

133 ILC, *Fourth report of the Special Rapporteur Eduardo Valencia-Ospina, on the Protection of Persons in the Event of Disasters*, May 11, 2011 (UN Doc. A/CN.4/643), para. 60.

134 Principle 34 of the Maastricht Principles, above Fn. 87.

135 Article 10 of the ILC Draft Articles on the Protection of Persons in the Event of Disasters, May 27, 2016 (A/CN.4/L.871).

136 Ibid., Article 11.

The principle of sovereignty requires that external assistance must be provided with the affected state's consent.[137] However, the affected state does not have an unlimited right to refuse assistance.[138] Consent to external assistance should not be withheld *arbitrarily*.[139]

b The Obligation to Provide International Assistance and Cooperation

Alston and *Quinn* argue that "on the basis of the preparatory work it is difficult, if not impossible, to sustain the argument that the commitment to international cooperation contained in the Covenant can accurately be characterized as a legally binding obligation upon any particular state to *provide* any particular form of assistance."[140] Under contemporary circumstances, too, it is disputed whether developed states have a duty to provide assistance to developing countries.[141] Article 12 of the ILC Articles on Disaster Protection of 2016 includes a right to *offer* assistance to the affected state.[142] However, controversially, states are only obliged to give due consideration to a request for assistance.[143]

In contrast to this, it is increasingly argued that non-affected states should be obliged to provide assistance where it is required.[144] Principle 33 of the

---

137 Sivakumaran, S, "Arbitrary Withholding of Consent to Humanitarian Assistance in Situations of Disaster" (2015), 64 *International and Comparative Law Quarterly* 501 (505 et seq.).

138 Peters, *Beyond Human Rights*, above Fn. 124, 243. See also Akande, D & Gillard, E-C, "Arbitrary Withholding of Consent to Humanitarian Relief Operations in Armed Conflict" (2016), 92 *International Law Studies*, 483 (510).

139 Article 13 (2) of the ILC *Draft Articles on the Protection of Persons in the Event of Disasters*, above Fn. 135. See for the meaning of "arbitrary" in this context Akande, D & Gillard, E-C, "Arbitrary Withholding of Consent to Humanitarian Relief Operations in Armed Conflict", above Fn. 138, 492 et seqq.; Peters, *Beyond Human Rights*, above Fn. 124, 243.

140 Alston & Quinn, "The Nature and Scope of States Parties' Obligations", above Fn. 59, 191 (emphasis added).

141 Bartels, "The EU's Human Rights Obligations in Relation to Policies with Extraterritorial Effects", above Fn. 90, 1086.

142 Article 12 of the ILC *Draft Articles on the Protection of Persons in the Event of Disasters*, above Fn. 135.

143 Ibid.

144 Peters, *Beyond Human Rights*, above Fn. 124, 245.

Maastricht Principles obliges states to provide international assistance to affected states when they are in a position to do so.[145]

Essentially, a legal obligation on states to provide assistance can be based on Article 2 (1) of the ICESCR because international cooperation as such requires that states work together, and international assistance is a component of international cooperation.[146] The duty to cooperate is therefore a mutual obligation that is directed to the affected state as well as to non-affected states. This is also in line with the purpose of such an obligation, namely the action or process of working together to the same end.[147] The obligation to provide assistance and cooperate therefore remains a legal obligation, although only a "weak conduct obligation".[148]

As alluded to above, this section has argued that the field of extraterritorial obligations is in an evolutionary phase and that there are considerable legal foundations in international human rights confirming the existence of extraterritorial obligations of states under the law as it stands.[149] However, it has not been sufficiently elaborated what the applicable benchmarks would be in an extraterritorial context, that would justify assigning these obligations to a particular state or states.[150]

VI Assigning Extraterritorial Obligations to Non-Affected States

1 The Scope of Jurisdiction

Principle 8 of the Maastricht Principles differentiates between two dimensions of extraterritorial obligation, and define them as follows:

> "a) obligations relating to the *acts and omissions of a State*, within or beyond its territory, that *have effects* on the enjoyment of human rights *outside of that State's territory*; and

145 Principle 33 of the Maastricht Principles, above Fn. 87.

146 De Schutter, Eide & Khalfan et al., "Commentary to the Maastricht Principles", above Fn. 125, 1157.

147 See for the definition of cooperation English Oxford Living Dictionaries, available at https://en.oxforddictionaries.com/definition/cooperation.

148 Tobin, *The Right to Health,* above Fn. 34, 342.

149 Vandenhole, "Extraterritorial Human Rights Obligations: Taking Stock, Looking Forward", above Fn. 18, 817.

150 Salomon, *Global Responsibility for Human Rights,* above Fn. 112, 190.

> b) obligations of a *global character* that are set out in the Charter of the United Nations and human rights instruments to take action, *separately, and jointly through international cooperation*, to realize human rights universally."[151]

Under the first paragraph, extraterritorial obligations might be triggered by domestic measures of a state, which have extraterritorial effects on socio-economic rights of individuals outside of its territory.[152] With respect to the right to health, States Parties to the ICESCR have to respect the right to health in other countries and to prevent third parties form violating the right in other countries, if they are able to influence these third parties by way of legal or political means.[153] This implies a form of specific relationship or link that has to be present between the state and individuals situated outside that state's territory.[154]

Second, global obligations, *such as the obligation of international cooperation, in turn* operate generally and do not require any link between the state concerned and individuals residing in other countries in order to be triggered.[155] With respect to the obligation to cooperate, notably the obligation to *provide* assistance, the Commentary to the Maastricht Principles stipulates that:[156]

> "[…] the obligation to provide assistance to other states in order to strengthen respect for human rights in those states, *in the absence of any particular link* between a state and the denial of human rights in those states, arises only by virtue of the obligation of a global character as described in Principle 8 (b)."[157]

The extraterritorial applicability of obligations in the area of socio-economic rights has been increasingly scrutinized within the context of an extended scope of *jurisdiction*. Jurisdiction refers to "the relationship between the individual and the state in connection with a violation of human rights, wherever it occurred, so that acts of states that take place or produce effects outside their territories may be deemed to fall under the jurisdiction of the

---

151 Principle 8 of the Maastricht Principles, above Fn. 87 (emphasis added).

152 Bartels, "The EU's Human Rights Obligations in Relation to Policies with Extraterritorial Effects", above Fn. 90, 1071.

153 CESCR, *General Comment No. 14*, above Fn. 3, para. 39.

154 De Schutter, Eide & Khalfan et al., "Commentary to the Maastricht Principles", above Fn. 125, 1102; see also Wilde, "Dilemmas in Promoting Global Economic Justice through Human Rights Law", above Fn. 19, 156.

155 Wilde, ibid., 160.

156 Ibid. See also section III.2.b.

157 De Schutter, Eide & Khalfan et al., "Commentary to the Maastricht Principles", above Fn. 125, 1101 et seq.

state concerned."[158] Under international human rights law, the notion of jurisdiction functions as a restraint of state power.[159] However, it remains disputed what role jurisdiction plays with respect to socio-economic rights (as opposed to civil and political rights) and how it is defined.[160] The Maastricht Principles define the concept of jurisdiction as follows:

> Principle 9:
> "A State has obligations to respect, protect and fulfil economic, social and cultural rights in any of the following:
> a) situations over which it exercises *authority or effective control* [...];
> b) situations over which State acts or omissions bring about *foreseeable effects* on the enjoyment of economic, social and cultural rights, whether within or outside its territory;
> c) situations in which the State [...] is *in a position to exercise decisive influence or to take measures* to realize economic, social and cultural rights extraterritorially."[161]

Principle 9 of the Maastricht Principles refer to a broad notion of jurisdiction that goes further than the existing law: it not only covers situations over which a state exercises authority or effective control but also acts or omissions by a state which bring about *foreseeable effects* outside its territory or where states are even in a position to exercise *decisive influence* or *to take measures* extraterritorially.[162]

First, extraterritorial obligations may be present in cases of *factual power*, where effective control is exercised over a territory, such as in cases of military occupation,[163] or over persons, for instance in cases of detention

158 Ibid., 1106.
159 Vandenhole, "Extraterritorial Human Rights Obligations: Taking Stock, Looking Forward", above Fn. 18, 818.
160 Ibid., 818. See on human rights jurisdiction Besson, S, "The Extraterritoriality of the European Convention on Human Rights: Why Human Rights Depend on Jurisdiction and What Jurisdiction Amounts to" (2012), 25 *Leiden Journal of International Law*, 857.
161 Principle 9 of the Maastricht Principles, above Fn. 87 (emphasis added).
162 See also Wilde, "Dilemmas in Promoting Global Economic Justice through Human Rights Law", above Fn. 19, 158; Principle 25 of the Maastricht Principles that contains a very broad notion of jurisdiction over companies, above Fn. 86.
163 See for example ECtHR, *Case of Cyprus v. Turkey*, Grand Chamber Judgment of May 10, 2001 (App. No. 25781/94), para. 77.

in foreign countries.[164] The ECtHR has developed the effective control doctrine with respect to civil and political rights.[165] But the situation is different in regard to deprivations of socio-economic rights as these will mainly occur in situations where a state does not exercise factual power, but where its domestic measures produce negative repercussions outside its territory.[166]

Second, extraterritorial obligations are triggered when a state knows or should have known that its policy measures would have extraterritorial effects – directly or indirectly – in another country (*normative power*). Direct extraterritorial effects cover domestic actions such as the imposition of embargoes on medicines that will have negative impact on the right to health of the individuals concerned.[167] In the case of indirect effects of a state's conduct that are based on a chain of events occurring outside the relevant state's control – and that are most likely not identifiable and foreseeable – it will be much more difficult to attribute human rights violations to the state in question.[168] Therefore, the state will not necessarily be held responsible for the negative impacts of its conduct.[169] While the ECtHR clearly articulates that jurisdiction may extend to the conduct of a state that produces effects outside its territory, it is not clear whether the ICESCR is applicable to domestic measures that (merely) have effects abroad.[170]

Third, the inclusion of situations where a state is in a position to take measures to realize socio-economic rights, regardless of any notion of effect or causation, seems to go beyond any doctrinal consensus, and may have

---

164 See for example *Öcalan v. Turkey*, Judgment of March 12, 2003 (App. No. 46221/99), para. 93.

165 See ECtHR, *Case of Al-Skeini and Others v. UK*, above Fn. 102, para. 138-140; see also Langford, Vandenhole & Scheinin et al., "Introduction. An Emerging Field", above Fn. 26, 9.

166 Langford, Vandenhole & Scheinin et al., "Introduction. An Emerging Field", above Fn. 26, 9; Vandenhole, "Extraterritorial Human Rights Obligations: Taking Stock, Looking Forward", above Fn. 18, 820.

167 Canizzaro, E, "The EU's Human Rights Obligations in Relation to Policies with Extraterritorial Effects: A Reply to Lorand Bartels" (2015), 25 *European Journal of International Law*, 1093 (1096).

168 Ibid., 1097.

169 De Schutter, Eide & Khalfan et al., "Commentary to the Maastricht Principles", above Fn. 125, 1109.

170 ECtHR, *Case of Al-Skeini and Others v. UK*, above Fn. 102, para. 133; *Case of Ilascu and Others v. Moldova and Russia*, above Fn. 102, para. 317. See also Bartels, "The EU's Human Rights Obligations in Relation to Policies with Extraterritorial Effects", above Fn. 90, 1084 et seq.

far-reaching implications.[171] This is the case with positive obligations, namely the obligation to protect and fulfill. The latter requires positive measures by a state, which is usually cost-dependent and assumes the redistribution of resources that (in principle) falls into the domestic realm of states.[172]

2 The Threshold for Positive Obligations

As a first point of critique, the most controversial aspect of extraterritorial obligations under the ICESCR relates to the positive obligations to protect and fulfill. The obligation to fulfill is divided into three categories. The duty to *facilitate* does not necessarily require resources in the form of international aid, but rather that states cooperate with each other to provide an enabling environment for the fulfillment of ICESCR rights.[173] The duty to *promote* requires, for example, the dissemination of information and the raising of awareness of the right. The duty to *provide* demands that states deliver assistance according to their available resources to the individuals in need.[174] The latter also concerns emergency aid in the context of disaster relief and humanitarian assistance.[175]

The core question is when and beyond which jurisdictional threshold a positive extraterritorial obligation under the ICESCR arises. Against this backdrop, *Milanovic* differentiates between negative and positive obligations, arguing that negative obligations to respect are territorially unlimited, while positive obligations to protect and fulfill require the exercise of *effective control* over an area.[176] This would notably imply that non-affected states are obliged to provide assistance to the affected states merely on the basis that these states exercise effective control over the territory or persons concerned. According to *Milanovic*, the exercise of *legal power* or *authority*

---

171 Bartels, "The EU's Human Rights Obligations in Relation to Policies with Extraterritorial Effects", above Fn. 90, 1084 et seq.

172 Wilde, "Dilemmas in Promoting Global Economic Justice through Human Rights Law", above Fn. 19, 162.

173 Commission on Human Rights, *Report of the Special Rapporteur on the right to food, Jean Ziegler*, January 24, 2005 (UN Doc. E/CN.4/2005/47), para 57.

174 Ibid., para. 58.

175 Ibid.

176 Milanovic, *Extraterritorial Application of Human Rights Treaties*, above Fn. 97, 228.

by a state over individuals outside of its territory would suffice to satisfy the jurisdiction threshold; however, "it would open the door to abuse creating an incentive for states to potentially violate the human rights of individuals abroad.[177] On the other hand, it has been argued that extraterritorial obligations might be triggered where purely legal effects have been created, namely through authority over persons, rather than factual power over territory.[178] Furthermore, it has been argued by *Besson* that the exercise of authority must be combined with effective power and overall control.[179]

Importantly, as regards socio-economic rights, a distinction between the extraterritorial applicability of negative and positive obligations must be assumed: first, because of the CESCR's statements, where the Committee has used different language ("must" versus "should")[180] to distinguish between the two sets of obligations; and second, because positive obligations, notably the obligation to fulfill, requires the redistribution of resources at the international level, requiring a higher threshold to be triggered. In this regard, the effective control doctrine developed in the area of civil and political rights is too restrictive.[181] As has been mentioned above, deprivations of socio-economic rights are mainly committed outside of limited situations such as occupation or control over armed forces.[182] Moreover, such deprivations may occur because of structural obstacles that result in gross violations of socio-economic rights.[183] In that sense, the question arises whether even a positive obligation to promote a *global institutional order* exists, that could contribute to the realization of the right to health.[184] It is important that states take the right to health into consideration in their international relations making that right visible in contexts where it may previously have been marginalized or devalued.[185]

---

177 Ibid., 207; see also Ganesh, A, "The European Union's Human Rights Obligations Towards Distant Strangers (2016), 37 *Michigan Journal of International Law*, 475 (519).

178 Ganesh, ibid., 523.

179 Besson, "The Extraterritoriality of the European Convention on Human Rights", above Fn. 160, 873.

180 See above III.1.

181 Narula, S, "International Financial Institutions, Transnational Corporations and Duties of States" in Langford, Vandenhole & Scheinin et al. (eds.), *Global Justice, State Duties*, above Fn. 18, 124.

182 Ibid., 125.

183 Salomon, *Global Responsibility for Human Rights,* above Fn. 112, 191.

184 Tobin, *The Right to Health,* above Fn. 34, 344 et seqq.

185 Ibid.

At the international level, negative obligations to respect and positive obligations to protect and fulfill are therefore not subject to the same jurisdictional rules.[186] Concomitantly, the disparity in power and influence among states also presupposes that they cannot be the duty-bearers of the same "extraterritorial" obligations.[187]

3 The Capacity of the Non-Affected State

Where the jurisdiction that activates extraterritorial obligations in general is established, a second essential prerequisite has to be extended in terms of *positive* extraterritorial obligations: A state must be "in a position to assist".[188] It must have the *capacity* to act, otherwise no extraterritorial obligation can arise. Consequently, a lesser capacity might give rise to less demanding obligations as capacity is a flexible criterion that depends on the action required and the resources available to the state. In a second step, (additional) normative requirements may come into play that limit the (general) obligations of *all* capable states, for example obligations that might be derived from a former historical link, such as the prior status of a state as a colonial power.

a Being "in a Position to Assist"

Positive extraterritorial obligations depend on the capacity of the state to act.[189] The CESCR has confirmed that states have extraterritorial obligations when they are "in a position to assist".[190] International human rights law, however, does not determine a system of international coordination and allocation.[191] The redistribution of resources is challenging even within

186 Contrast Ganesh, "The European Union's Human Rights Obligations Towards Distant Strangers", above Fn. 177, 524.
187 Salomon, *Global Responsibility for Human Rights*, above Fn. 112, 56.
188 CESCR, *General Comment No. 14*, above Fn. 3, para. 45.
189 See also Langford & Darrow, "Moral Theory, International Law and Global Justice", above Fn. 18, 441.
190 CESCR, *General Comment No. 14*, above Fn. 3, para. 45; see also *General Comment No. 3,* above Fn. 54, para. 14; *General Comment No. 12,* above Fn. 65, para. 35; *General Comment No. 15,* above Fn. 106, para. 38.
191 De Schutter, Eide & Khalfan et al., "Commentary to the Maastricht Principles", above Fn. 125, 1149.

a state, not least because of different political systems, but face particular difficulties in an extraterritorial context, where resources must be allocated to individuals of other countries.[192]

The obligation of international assistance and cooperation is not limited to the transfer of financial resources, but also includes material assistance.[193] With respect to the right to health, this would include, for instance, not only direct distribution of economic and technical resources, but also the influence of powerful states on pharmaceutical companies to deliver vaccines to affected countries, or on the decision-making processes of international organizations (such as the WHO) to ensure that measures be taken to respect the right to health of the affected individuals. Moreover, this would require that states engage in a discussion that not simply pursues the interests of (pharmaceutical) companies, but also takes into account strategies and action plans to provide access to medicines for the affected individuals.[194]

Arguably, capacity is therefore an indispensable and primary basis for assigning extraterritorial obligations to non-affected states.[195] A capacity requirement would essentially impose extraterritorial obligations on developed states. In principle, however, the obligation of cooperation is not limited to developed states but to all those with capacity and resources. Any state with the capacity and resources – be they economic, technical, technological, or the ability to influence the decision-making in an International Organization (such as the WHO) – might be obliged to also provide them to victims of disease in other countries.[196] There might even be important procedural components of a state's obligation to cooperate in devising a suitable international division of responsibilities necessary to give effect to the obligation to cooperate.[197] A state is not relieved of its obligation in this area because it lacks resources. It could still be held internationally responsible for not having worked towards the creation of an international system

192 See also Wilde, "Dilemmas in Promoting Global Economic Justice through Human Rights Law", above Fn. 19, 162.

193 Tobin, *The Right to Health,* above Fn. 34, 343.

194 Ibid., 367.

195 However, there are additional requirements that must be fulfilled, see section IV.3.b.

196 See principle 31 of the Maastricht Principles, above Fn. 87.

197 De Schutter, Eide & Khalfan et al., "Commentary to the Maastricht Principles", above Fn. 125, 1150.

of cooperation and for failing to have sought to mobilize the necessary resources *globally*.[198]

The dilemma of choosing amongst a multiplicity of possible duty-bearers possessing the needed resources is resolved by the CESCR in a way that the degree to which each state should assist depends on its individual capacity.[199] This can be assessed through an "adequate and reasonable" test developed by the CESCR to determine whether a state has met its extraterritorial obligations according to its available resources.[200]

Furthermore, the redistribution of resources also touches upon the question whether the obligation of states, for instance, to contribute to the realization of the right to health in the affected states is framed as a subsidiary obligation triggered only when the rights-holders' own state is *unable or unwilling* to fulfill it.[201] It is generally acknowledged that the obligation to fulfill socio-economic rights rests with the territorial state.[202] The obligation to fulfill socio-economic rights by states other than the rights-holders' own is argued to be based on a secondary or subsidiary obligation in circumstances where the affected state is unable or unwilling to accomplish them.[203] However, in the majority of cases, an outbreak of a disease will not be contained in the affected state(s) and will be transmitted to other countries, as was the case with Ebola. Therefore, one might argue that where the cross-border effects of the disease exceed a certain benchmark, positive measures are required by states in *complement* to the primary duty-bearer's obligations to protect their own population, at least with respect to the minimum core of the relevant right.[204]

In the *Genocide Case*, the ICJ further elaborated on various criteria concerning the allocation of extraterritorial obligations, including "the capacity

---

198 CESCR, *General Comment No. 3,* above Fn. 54, para. 13.

199 CESCR, *General Comment No. 14*, above Fn. 3, para. 40.

200 De Schutter, Eide & Khalfan et al., "Commentary to the Maastricht Principles", above Fn. 125, 1151.

201 Wernar, L, "Responsibility and Severe Poverty" in Pogge, T (ed.), *Freedom from Poverty as a Human Right: Who Owes What to the Very Poor?*, 2007, 255 (265).

202 See for a philosophical discussion on that Miller, D, *National Responsibilty and Global Justice*, 2012.

203 Salomon, M, "How to keep promises: making sense of the duty among multiple states to fulfil socio-economic rights in the world" (2014), 53 *SHARES Research Paper*, 1 (5). See also 2005 World Summit Outcome, October 24, 2005 (UN Doc. A/RES/60/1), para. 139.

204 See also 2005 World Summit Outcome, ibid.

to influence effectively".[205] Since the obligation to prevent genocide rises to the level of *ius cogens*, such an obligation might arguably impose on states a higher threshold when it comes to the allocation of their resources. However, one might consider that in health emergencies the right to health is directly related to the right to life and therefore crucial for an individual's life. A state that is in a position to assist should use its available resources, or at least meet its core obligations towards individuals living in foreign states. The concept of minimum core obligations, however, has been criticized with respect to whether a universal minimum core obligation or a country-based minimum core obligation should be established, according to the variety of levels of development of the recipient state, on the one hand, or, on the other hand, according to the available resources of the state in action.[206] Country-specific thresholds could be developed by indicators that, for example, measure nutrition, disease frequency, life expectancy and adequate food consumption.[207] Different core contents according to the level of development could also be formulated, for instance, with respect to the classification of countries by the World Bank according to their GNI (gross national income) per capita.[208] Nevertheless, a relative standard concerning the core minimum obligations seems to be almost impossible to enforce and is refused here, especially due to the difficulties that arise in assessing such benchmarks.[209] This is also in line with the findings of the CESCR that enumerate the core obligations that every state has to realize, regardless of the different health levels in the world.[210]

Additionally, the ICJ has required a causal link, such as geographical distance, between non-affected states and individuals concerned.[211] In health emergencies, the geographical distance from the events in question

205 ICJ, Application of the Convention on the Prevention and Punishment of the Crime of Genocide, above Fn. 101, para. 430.

206 Toebes, *The Right to Health as a Human Right*, above Fn. 40, 278.

207 Andreassen, B A, Skålnes, T & Smith, A G et al., "Assessing Human Rights Performance in Developing Countries: The Case for a Minimum Threshold Approach" in Andreassen, B A & Eide, A, *Human Rights in Developing Countries 1987/1988*, 1988, 333 (341).

208 Toebes, *The Right to Health as a Human Right*, above Fn. 40, 279 et seq. See also World Bank, *How does the World Bank classify countries?*, available at http://bit.ly/2luxClo

209 Toebes, *The Right to Health as a Human Right*, above Fn. 40, 279.

210 Ibid., 280; see also CESCR, *General Comment No. 14*, above Fn. 3, para. 43.

211 ICJ, Application of the Convention on the Prevention and Punishment of the Crime of Genocide, above Fn. 101, para. 430.

would indicate that neighboring states bear a "stronger" obligation to assist the affected states – on the premise that they are in position to do so.

Furthermore, the principle of "Common but Differentiated Responsibilities",[212] which stems from international environmental law, is based on the reality of historical differences in the contributions made by both developed and developing states to global issues. While this principle does not provide a basis for assigning obligations to non-affected states, it recognizes that states should possess different and specific duties relative to the different categorizations of states.[213] The principle of "*common but differentiated responsibility*" can be seen as a normative development in international law that requires action on the part of those who are in a position to assist. Furthermore, it also points to an emerging procedural requirement for states to coordinate with each other in the allocation of particular obligations.[214]

b Historical Relationship Between a State and Individuals in other Countries

A special relationship that might operate as a trigger for extraterritorial obligations concerns a former *historical link* between the right-holders and the relevant state that has previously contributed to the harm, for example as a prior colonial power. Extraterritorial obligations would thus be attributed on the basis of historical responsibility for past exploitation.[215] Current deprivations of socio-economic rights might then be traceable to the harmful effects of past actions. This notion is also inherent in the concept of "Common but Differentiated Responsibilities".

---

212 Common but Differentiated Responsibilities is a principle of international environmental law that recognizes historical differences in the contributions of developed and developing countries and differences in their respective economic and technical capacity to tackle environmental problems.

213 Salomon, "How to keep promises: making sense of the duty among multiple states to fulfil socio-economic rights in the world", above Fn. 203, 11.

214 See Principle 30 of the Maastricht Principles on Extraterritorial Obligations, above Fn. 87; Khalfan, A, "Division of Responsibility between States" in Langford, Vandenhole & Scheinin et al. (eds.), *Global Justice, State Duties*, above Fn. 18, 299.

215 Salomon, "How to keep promises: making sense of the duty among multiple states to fulfil socio-economic rights in the world", above Fn. 203, 8 et seq.

The claim that prior colonial powers bear specific extraterritorial obligations is traditionally advanced by developing countries.[216] According to an article in the *New York Times*, for instance, US administration officials urged the UK and France, which both have colonial ties to the Ebola-affected states, to come up with stronger responses.[217] In practice, former colonial powers do tend to direct international assistance to their former colonies, based on a *moral* sense of historical responsibility.[218]

The practice of former colonial powers supporting their "own" former colonies points towards historical responsibility forming a legitimate criterion for assigning extraterritorial obligations to non-affected states, under the promise that capacity would still be a necessary element.[219]

V Conclusion

The answer to the question raised in this article is that under the paradigmatic shift of international human rights law, extraterritorial obligations of non-affected states are increasingly considered to be acknowledged under the law as it stands. Extraterritorial obligations are derived from Article 2 (1) of the ICESCR, which does not contain a jurisdictional clause. On the one hand, these are extraterritorial obligations of particular states, and, on the other hand, a general "global" obligation to cooperate. International courts, the CESCR as well as other human rights bodies have also recognized the existence of extraterritorial obligations of states, but to a limited extent.

The ICESCR does not mention whether all States Parties to the ICESCR are the duty-bearers of extraterritorial obligations. Therefore, the core question is when and beyond which jurisdictional threshold extraterritorial obligations under the ICESCR might arise. In that respect, it is necessary to differentiate between negative obligations to respect and positive obligations to protect and fulfill that are not subject to the same jurisdictional rules. The latter is more controversial as positive obligations depend on the capacity of the state in question and require emergency aid in the form of the allocation of resources during health crises.

216 Ibid., 9.

217 Cooper & Fink, "Obama Presses Leaders to Speed Ebola Response", above Fn. 13.

218 Ibid.

219 Salomon, "How to keep promises: making sense of the duty among multiple states to fulfil socio-economic rights in the world", above Fn. 204, 8 et seq.

Therefore, the availability of resources is the key criterion for assigning extraterritorial obligations to non-affected states. Another special relationship between non-affected states and individuals in other countries might be derived from a former historical link (colonization) between the relevant actors. Besides states having historical or colonial ties with an affected state, it is argued that neighboring states, in particular, would also bear extraterritorial obligations towards victims of disease. Such a reading would be consistent with the ICJ's view in the *Genocide case*, where the Court affirmed that states have the duty to prevent genocide in cases where there is a geographic proximity to the occurrence of the events. African states have also been called on by the UN Security Council Resolution 2177 (2014) to "facilitate the delivery of assistance, including qualified, specialized and trained personnel and supplies".[220]

In practice, however, states such as Brazil, Canada and India have shown their (moral) solidarity by donating money or sending medical staff, medicine and equipment to Ebola-affected states.[221] While the decision to support the countries in need was based on moral considerations, it confirms a shift towards the acceptance of the applicability of extraterritorial human rights obligations beyond a state's territorial boundaries. Finally, it remains an open question whether this paradigmatic shift might be able to transform extraterritorial obligations into solid legal obligations complied with by all states, including developed countries.

220 UN Security Council Resolution 2177 (2014), above Fn. 11, para. 5.
221 Cooper & Fink, "Obama Presses Leaders to Speed Ebola Response", above Fn. 13.

The Real Versus the Ideal in NGO Governance: Enacting the Right to Mental Healthcare in Liberia During the 2014-2016 Ebola Epidemic

*Hunter Keys, Bonnie Kaiser, André den Exter**

Abstract

Increasingly, transnational Non-Governmental Organizations (NGOs) figure heavily among the institutions and actors that constitute humanitarian governance during disease outbreaks. However, while NGOs may "self-task" in their work to provide healthcare, they are not the original subjects of international legal frameworks on the right to health. One argument to strengthen accountability of NGOs is to evaluate their operational activities against the rubric of consensus guidelines for humanitarian non-state actors. Examining on-the-ground, contextual pressures felt by NGOs alongside principles charted out in guidelines exposes unresolved challenges in relying on an "ideal" framework to evaluate "real-world" dilemmas. This contribution begins by discussing the Inter-Agency Standing Committee (IASC) Guidelines on Mental Health and Psychosocial Support in Humanitarian Settings, which contain core principles for NGOs and others to follow. After tracing the development of the IASC Guidelines back to right-to-health norms found in international legal instruments, the discussion considers the Liberian context by reviewing the country's history and health policies, with attention focused on the National Mental Health Policy. This section draws on findings from interviews with key informants at an NGO that assisted the Liberian Ministry of Health to develop and implement the policy. This is followed by a case study of the contextual challenges faced

* *Hunter Keys* is a PhD candidate in anthropology at the University of Amsterdam, the Netherlands and is supported by the Netherlands Organization for Scientific Research. *Bonnie Kaiser* is a postdoctoral researcher at Duke University, Durham, USA. *André den Exter* is lecturer in health law at Erasmus University, Rotterdam, the Netherlands. The authors thank the key informants for their time in granting interviews to share their experiences and perspectives on mental health in Liberia as well as offer feedback on earlier versions of this contribution. The authors also thank the editors for their time in reviewing this contribution as well. All websites last accessed January 14, 2017.

by an NGO in Liberia during the 2014-2016 West Africa Ebola epidemic. This vignette provides a springboard for arguing that the IASC Guidelines, while extremely useful in their operationalization of ideals and rights norms, only go so far when applied in practice. Given that NGOs must bend and adapt to contextual pressures, accountability approaches must recognize the need for flexibility in addition to a grounding in rights norms.

I Introduction

Governance, the traditional province of states, has been partly reconfigured by non-states, the NGOs whom nobody elects but through whom lives are saved.[1] The entry of NGOs into the "humanitarian space" has sharpened the moral and political contours of providing aid and to whom: moral in the sense of "doing good" and political by way of delivering care to a hierarchy of victims.[2] Even as NGOs have helped carve out the moral and political dimensions of humanitarian governance, their relationship – as non-state actors – to legal frameworks on the right to health has remained largely undefined.

In fact, this murky relationship between humanitarian NGOs and international legal frameworks points to a core dilemma within the legal analysis of global authority structures and their publics: within the realm of global

---

1 Barnett, M, "Humanitarian governance" (2013), 16 *Annual Review of Political Science*, 379 (379). In reference to the term "global governance", this contribution draws chiefly on the ideas proposed by *Barnett*, in that the "international humanitarian order, [or] the self-conscious effort by the global community to relieve the suffering of distant strangers" (380) has to a large degree become "legitimated and organized in and around international institutions, norms, and laws, and undertaken in the name of compassion, care, and responsibility" (380). In this contribution, this conceptual framing of governance is limited to the interactions of NGOs (non-state actors), state institutions such as Ministries of Health, and individuals, including expatriate humanitarian aid workers and local community members on-the-ground during both an "inter-crisis" or rehabilitation period, as well as amidst the Ebola outbreak. Of interest in this contribution are the power dynamics among these various actors and the discrepancies that arise between ideal norms as envisaged by guidelines or rights frameworks and complex real-world dilemmas that embroil and implicate such a governance structure.

2 Fassin, D, *Humanitarian Reason: a Moral History of the Present*, 2012; see also Ticktin, M, "Transnational humanitarianism" (2014), 43 *Annual Review of Anthropology*, 273.

governance, what acts, and by whom, should be the focus of *legal* discourse? How may such acts acquire legitimacy? Global health governance in particular involves complex linkages among states, the private sector, and hybrid bodies such as International Organizations like the World Bank[3] – in sum, a constellation of actors and institutions that "escape the grasp of established legal concepts".[4] Legal scholars have recently developed the analytical concept of *the exercise of international public authority* to circumscribe the activities of any institution, administration, state, or non-state actor that *determines* others, that "unilaterally shape[s] their legal or factual situation"[5] in regards to a *public interest.*[6] In this vein, humanitarian NGOs qualify as international public authorities through, first, their engagement in civil society writ large,[7] but also through such programmatic activities as generating and disseminating information about a given crisis through reports, media profiles, and statistics; fundraising and delivery of material goods and human resources; or producing standardized guidelines and instruments for decision-making – all in the public interest of curbing the toll of disease, delivering aid, or promoting human rights.

Qualified as international public authorities, NGOs serve the interests of broad publics: "on-the-ground" beneficiaries as well as donors, political stakeholders, and policymakers. The expertise that underlies these activities further bolsters their "self-legitimacy"[8] on the international scene, yet no international legal framework formally contains them.[9] Indeed, international legal instruments[10] and dozens of national constitutional

---

3 Hein, W & Kohlmorgen, L, "Global health governance" (2008), 8 *Global Social Policy*, 80.

4 Bogdandy, A von, Dann, P & Goldmann, M, "Developing the Publicness of Public International Law: Towards a Legal Framework for Global Governance Activities" in Bogdandy, A von, Wolfrum, R & Bernstorff, J von et al. (eds.), *The Exercise of Public Authority by International Institutions*, 2010, 7.

5 Ibid., 11.

6 Bogdandy, A von, Goldmann, M & Venzke, I, "From Public International to International Public Law: Translating World Public Opinion into International Public Authority", *European Journal of International Law* (in press).

7 Ryfman, P, "Non-governmental organizations: an indispensable player of humanitarian aid" (2007), 89 *International Review of the Red Cross*, 21.

8 Ibid., 34.

9 Ibid.

10 International Covenant on Economic, Social, and Cultural Rights (ICESCR), 1976, available at http://bit.ly/J1E1V3. This article is devoted almost exclusively on a specific set of guidelines intended for humanitarian NGOs and foregoes in-depth discussion of the legal basis for the right to health. For further reading on

measures[11] stipulating the right to health all pertain to responsibilities of states – and even then, the "soft law" of these legal instruments is essentially unenforceable through any institutionalized process.[12]

Nonetheless, despite the lack of specific international legal frameworks to address the role of NGOs in emergencies, what have emerged in recent decades are consensus guidelines, which are often rooted in right-to-health norms that arose in response to health disparities and unequal access to care. In effect, non-binding standards[13] like operational guidelines can further buttress the exercise of international public authorities like NGOs, since "the benefits of observing them outweighs the disadvantages of ignoring them".[14] In the absence of formal legal frameworks, consensus guidelines for NGOs may serve as a critical link between ideal principles and real-world contexts, perhaps going further to function as an accountability mechanism.

This contribution uses the example of the 2014-2016 West Africa Ebola epidemic to contrast ideal principles enumerated in NGO guidelines with the real-world contexts in which they are implemented. Section II provides a concrete example of ideal principles by reviewing the Inter-Agency Standing Committee (IASC) Guidelines for Mental Health and Psychosocial Support in Humanitarian Settings (hereafter, "the IASC Guidelines").[15] The IASC Guidelines (2007) were developed within the UN system by partnering NGOs and research institutions. On the one hand, they represent a tremendous political feat in outlining agreed-upon principles; on the other, they emanate from spheres of power and influence that can be far removed from the humanitarian contexts in which they are intended, leading to operational challenges and ethical tensions.

To illustrate these points, Section III reviews the historical context of Liberia, with attention on the role of both state and non-state actors working on the right to mental healthcare in the years before the epidemic. Drawing

---

the international legal basis for the right to health, see the contribution of *A. Katarina Weilert*, "The Right to Health in International Law – Normative Foundations and Doctrinal Flaws" in this volume.

11 Backman, G, Hunt, P & Khosla, R et al., "Health systems and the right to health: an assessment of 194 countries" (2008), 372 *Lancet*, 2047.

12 Hein & Kohlmorgen, "Global health governance", above Fn. 3.

13 Bogdandy, Dann & Goldmann, "Developing the Publicness of Public International Law", above Fn. 4, 12.

14 Ibid.

15 Inter-Agency Standing Committee (IASC), *IASC Guidelines on Mental Health and Psychosocial Support in Emergency Settings*, 2007.

on interview data obtained from two key informants at an NGO that assisted the Liberian Ministry of Health,[16] Section III recalls important Liberian health policy achievements, notably the National Mental Health Policy, and then moves into a case study of *Global Care* (pseudonym), an NGO that recruited and sent expatriate clinicians to Liberia during the Ebola response. The case study of Global Care is based on the experiences and observations of the lead author, a clinician who worked for Global Care in early 2015 to help strengthen mental health and psychosocial care services in a remote area of Liberia.[17] The case study provides a snapshot of challenges in applying ideal principles in a given context.

Bearing the case study in mind, Section IV reconsiders ideal principles as an accountability mechanism for real-world dilemmas. While guidelines can provide useful evaluative criteria for NGOs, the more fundamental question rests on whether such guidelines are even appropriate as an accountability mechanism, given the challenging and conflicting circumstances encountered on the ground. Section IV returns to the concept of NGOs as international public authorities, serving the health interests of a population but acting outside traditional right-to-health legal frameworks. While it is tempting to substitute guidelines in the place of those frameworks, it must be recalled that guidelines do not (or cannot) account for the dynamic, day-to-day realities of a given crisis, its geopolitical and cultural setting, and the constraints faced by NGOs and their publics. While praiseworthy for their efforts to steer NGOs towards an ethical praxis of the right

16 In 2016, the lead author conducted three semi-structured interviews by telephone, each lasting approximately one hour, with two key informants at a well-known NGO that assisted the Liberian Ministry of Health to develop and implement the National Mental Health Policy before and during the Ebola outbreak. In their various roles, these informants worked closely with high-level executives within the Liberian Ministry, served in country-level leadership positions, undertook community-level research and anti-stigma campaigns, and/or worked with community leaders, clinicians, and practitioners as they developed the policy and responded to the outbreak. Hereafter, citations from these interviews will reference each informant sequentially as "Key informant 1 [or 2], NGO, 2016."

17 There is a debate in the global mental health discipline concerning appropriate terminology. It is beyond the scope of this article to address these issues, but for this discussion, the general phrase "mental health and psychosocial care" will be used to reference the broad realm of human experience that considers mental health, interpersonal relationships, human functioning, and ability to cope with stress in a given social and cultural context. For further reading, see Patel, V, Minas, H & Cohen, A et al. (eds.), *Global Mental Health: Principles and Practice*, 2014.

to health, operational guidelines should not be held as a gold standard. In Section V, we describe how modes of accountability for NGOs must leave enough space for contextual bending but keep a firm grounding on right-to-health norms.

II IASC Guidelines and Mental Health in Humanitarian Emergencies

A useful starting point is to review how the humanitarian sector took up the goal of standardizing the psychosocial response to emergencies. Mental health effects of war and disasters had long been acknowledged among public health practitioners.[18] Interventions followed the premise that repairs to the "social fabric" were necessary for collective healing in the aftermath of disasters.[19] This trend reflects how human rights and mental health became increasingly inter-connected in spheres of NGO policy and practice. For example, in the aftermath of Liberia's devastating civil wars, the Carter Center, a non-profit NGO, partnered with the Liberian government to implement an access-to-justice program for war-affected communities and victims of atrocities.[20] The networks and institutional trust that emerged from this program contributed to the country's National Mental Health Policy. Additionally, the policy includes a sub-section on the rights of persons with mental illness and the need for consistency with international human rights norms.[21] Thus, the push for psychosocial and mental health care in contexts of widespread human rights violations became a means of restoring and strengthening a human rights platform in affected communities. Human rights and mental health became understood as fundamentally inextricable from each other: rights violations harm mental health, and mental health is requisite to enjoy other human rights.[22]

---

18 Mollica, R, Lopes Cardozo, B & Osofsky, H J et al., "Mental health in complex emergencies" (2004), 364 *Lancet*, 2058.

19 Abramowitz, S & Kleinman, A, "Humanitarian intervention and cultural translation: a review of the IASC guidelines on Mental Health and Psychosocial Support in Emergency Settings" (2008), 6 *Intervention*, 219 (220).

20 The Carter Center, *Where We Work: Liberia*, available at https://www.cartercenter.org/countries/liberia.html.

21 Republic of Liberia, *National Mental Health Policy*, 2009.

22 Gostin, L & Gable, L, "The human rights of persons with mental disabilities: a global perspective on the application of human rights principles to mental health" (2004), 63 *Maryland Law Review*, 20.

At the same time, while NGOs increasingly incorporated mental health and psychosocial care into their practices, often predicated on a rights framework, there had been no formal effort to standardize the response.[23] Such diversity among psychosocial actors reflected "fundamentally different theoretical perspectives on the nature of psychosocial issues and the causes of problems".[24] In the absence of consensus guidelines regarding humanitarian psychosocial response, there remained a greater risk of uncoordinated activities, duplicated efforts, and unintentional harm. The existence of competing "camps" – such as those taking a biomedical, trauma-focused approach and those taking a public health approach – led to fierce debate, competition for funding, and rarely cooperation.[25]

Efforts to develop a standardized framework for mental health and psychosocial support coincided with broader movements within the humanitarian system. Despite their occurrence in diverse geopolitical and historical contexts, humanitarian emergencies were eventually understood to share a set of universal characteristics, including complex political antecedents; massive population displacement and disruption of political, economic, sociocultural, and healthcare infrastructures beyond their capacity to cope; in settings of armed conflict, insecurity affecting those not engaged in fighting; and the emergence of "predatory social formations"[26] that threaten livelihoods.[27]

This macro-perspective in conceptualizing humanitarian emergencies helped prompt the standardization of certain "clusters", or sub-specialties within the humanitarian system itself, such as water and sanitation, health, and logistics. UN Resolution 46/182 (1991) provided a framework for

23 Wessells, M & Ommeren, M van, "Developing inter-agency guidelines on mental health and psychosocial support in emergency settings" (2008), 6 *Intervention*, 199.

24 Strang, A & Ager, A, "Psychosocial interventions: some key issues facing practitioners" (2003), 1 *Intervention*, 2 (2).

25 Ventevogel, P, "From the editor: the IASC Guidelines on Mental Health and Psychosocial Support in Emergency Settings, from discussion to implementation" (2008), 6 *Intervention*, 193; see also Wessells & Ommeren, "Developing inter-agency guidelines", above Fn. 23.

26 Ventevogel, P, *Borderlands of Mental Health*, 2016, 21.

27 Toole, M & Waldman, R, "The public health aspects of complex emergencies and refugee situations" (1997), 18 *Ann Rev Public Health*, 283.

Member States and relevant organizations and agencies to coordinate humanitarian assistance.[28] The resolution also authorized the IASC to issue guidelines on humanitarian practice as well as improve coordination, knowledge-sharing, and delegation of responsibilities among humanitarian actors. The IASC Guidelines are therefore part of international administrative law and aim to coordinate humanitarian assistance among the UN, other multilaterals, and NGOs. Meanwhile, outside the UN system, the Sphere Project assembled an array of International Organizations and NGOs to publish the Humanitarian Charter and Handbook in 1997, detailing minimum standards for affected populations based on the core principles that people affected by disasters have a right to life with dignity and that all steps be taken to alleviate suffering.[29] The Sphere Project epitomizes the operationalization of human rights norms into humanitarian practice.[30]

Thus, IASC and the Sphere Project both grew out of this movement towards developing criteria for minimum response and improved coordination.[31] The approach taken by IASC is to include all stakeholders involved in humanitarian assistance, including both UN and other multilateral organizations, such as the World Health Organization (WHO), the United Nations International Children's Emergency Fund (UNICEF), the International Committee of the Red Cross, and the International Federation of Red Cross and Red Crescent Societies. Relevant NGOs can be invited to participate on an ad-hoc basis.[32] Various subsidiary bodies break off into different reference groups to support implementation of practice guidelines, among them early warning and preparedness, financing, protracted displacements, and – relevant here – mental health and psychosocial support.

Encouraged by the success of IASC HIV/AIDS guidelines and buoyed by the political support of the top-ranked WHO emergency official, a task

---

28 UN General Assembly Resolution 46/182, *Strengthening of the coordination of humanitarian assistance of the United Nations*, 1991; see also Office for the Coordination of Humanitarian Affairs, *What is General Assembly Resolution 46/182?*, available at https://docs.unocha.org/sites/dms/documents/120402_oom-46182_eng.pdf.

29 The Sphere Handbook, *Humanitarian Charter and Minimum Standards in Humanitarian Response*, 2011, available at http://www.sphereproject.org/handbook/.

30 Hilhorst, D, "Being good at doing good? Quality and accountability of humanitarian NGOs" (2002), 26 *Disasters*, 193.

31 UN General Assembly Resolution 46/182, *Strengthening of the coordination*, above Fn. 28.

32 IASC, *IASC Membership*, 2016, available at https://interagencystandingcommittee.org/iasc/membership-and-structure.

force was formed to develop the IASC Guidelines on Mental Health and Psychosocial Support in Emergency Settings.[33] The Guidelines were released in 2007 following a lengthy consultative and participatory process among various NGOs and UN bodies,[34] with input from academic researchers. Despite some critiques that they fail to prioritize data-driven response efforts[35] or that the context in which they were developed (within the politically charged UN system) may compromise independent humanitarian action,[36] the Guidelines have been praised for being "field driven"[37] and are a major stride in responding to lack of consensus among aid agencies in providing psychosocial services in disaster settings.[38]

Referring directly to International Organizations, NGOs, donor agencies, and national governments, the Guidelines are intended for "all humanitarian actors [...] operating in emergency settings at local, national, and international levels".[39] In the words of one figure instrumental in their development, the Guidelines have

> "contributed tremendously to the unity and spirit among policy makers, researchers, and practitioners alike [...]. Moreover, the guidelines provide a framework, not only for action, but also for the systematic collection of empirical data on what works and what does not."[40]

They "are not just any guidelines"[41] but rather an authoritative document, a "political achievement".[42]

There are six core principles that underlie the IASC Guidelines: to (1) promote human rights of all affected persons and protect those at risk of

33 Wessells & Ommeren, "Developing inter-agency guidelines", above Fn. 23.

34 Ventevogel, "From the editor", above Fn. 25.

35 Lopes Cardozo, B, "Guidelines need a more evidence based approach: a commentary on the IASC guidelines on Mental Health and Psychosocial Support in Emergency Settings" (2008), 6 *Intervention*, 252; see also Miller, K & Fernando, G, "Epidemiological assessment in emergency settings: recommendations for enhancing a potentially useful tool" (2008), 6 *Intervention*, 255.

36 Jong, K de, Mills, C & Mackintosh, K, "Humanitarian issues beyond the technical tools: the *IASC Guidelines on Mental Health and Psychosocial Support in Emergency Settings*" (2008), 6 *Intervention*, 334.

37 Ibid.

38 Wessells & Ommeren, "Developing inter-agency guidelines", above Fn. 23.

39 IASC, *IASC Guidelines on Mental Health*, above Fn. 15.

40 Ventevogel, "From the editor", above Fn. 25.

41 Ibid.

42 Ager, A, "Consensus and professional practice in psychosocial intervention: political achievement, core knowledge-base, and prompt for further enquiry" (2008), 6 *Intervention*, 261 (261).

rights violations; (2) maximize the participation of populations affected by an emergency; (3) do no harm; (4) build on available resources and capacities; (5) avoid stand-alone services and instead build integrated support systems; and (6) provide multi-layered supports, which take into account the different priorities of need (food, water, shelter). The Guidelines include "action sheets" for completing needs assessments, mobilizing communities, and linking psychosocial services to general healthcare structures. In the time since their development, the IASC Guidelines have had considerable impact on the delivery of psychosocial aid in humanitarian settings, serving as the key document for guiding minimum responses (as distinct from professional *standards*) in psychosocial aid.[43]

Indeed, the primary purpose of the Guidelines "is to enable humanitarian actors and communities to plan, establish and coordinate a set of *minimum* multi-sectoral responses to protect and improve people's mental health and well-being in the midst of an emergency"[44] (emphasis by authors). These minimum responses "are the first things that ought to be done", or in other words, the essential services done amid an emergency (acute, or relief phase) that lay the groundwork for comprehensive efforts undertaken in the (stable) rehabilitation phase.

Conceptually and practically, there is an enormous gap between minimum response, as envisaged by the IASC Guidelines, and the highest attainable standard of health, as promoted by key international legal frameworks. Nonetheless, a common thread still connects the IASC Guidelines to normative ideas found in the International Covenant on Economic, Social, and Cultural Rights (ICESCR) as well as General Comment 14 (GC 14) (the formal legal interpretation of Article 12, ICESCR, which articulates the right to health)[45]: both stipulate responsibilities of actors responding to health disparities, or the disproportionate suffering borne by some more than others. Unfair social, political, and economic arrangements are increasingly implicated in contributing to poor health.[46] This understanding was

---

43 Meyer, S & Loughry, M, *Review of the Implementation of the IASC guidelines on Mental Health and Psychosocial Support in Emergency Settings: How Are We Doing?*, 2014; see also IASC, *IASC Guidelines on Mental Health*, above Fn. 15, 5.

44 IASC, ibid., 5.

45 Again, the reader is directed to the contribution of *A. Katarina Weilert*, "The Right to Health in International Law – Normative Foundations and Doctrinal Flaws" in this volume, for in-depth discussion of the ICESCR and GC 14.

46 Marmot, M, "Social determinants of health" (2005), 365 *Lancet*, 1099.

even explicit in GC 14, which affirmed that the right to health was a right "closely related to and dependent upon the realization of other human rights".[47] The right to health went beyond access to health*care* to include rights to specific conditions that underlie health, such as food, housing, human dignity, non-discrimination, and freedoms of association and movement, among many others.[48] This broader conceptualization of health as envisaged by the ICESCR and GC 14 is especially relevant to international humanitarian law (IHL), which legally obligates state and non-state actors to deliver the so-called "second-generation rights" of the ICESCR (food, clothing, housing, water) during emergencies.[49] In essence, the approach to harmonize the delivery of mental health and psychosocial care during emergencies is integral to a broader conceptualization of health, understood as interdependent on many other rights, and essential to a life with dignity.

The ideals of "minimum response" and "highest attainable standard" thus represent poles on a spectrum of progressive realization: both state and non-state actors, whether implementing minimum response during an emergency or strengthening health systems per the ideals of the ICESCR and GC 14, must fulfill their obligations in an ethical and consistent way.

III Liberia: Historical Overview, Healthcare Structure, and Mental Health Policy

In the early 19th century, the American Colonization Society, an organization seeking to resolve the growing political tension posed by increasing numbers of free blacks in the United States, launched a policy of repatriation to Africa. Liberia's subsequent founding was, in a way, a premonition of the over-sized role that external, civil society organizations would have in its governance. The "Americo-Liberians" understood little of the sixteen different indigenous ethnic groups already living in the territory of what would become Liberia. The small, American-descended elite held the levers of political power until 1980, when *Samuel Doe*, a member of the Krahn

47 Committee on Economic, Social, and Cultural Rights (CESCR), *General Comment 14: the Right to the Highest Attainable Standard of Health*, 2000, para. 3.

48 Toebes, B, "Health and humanitarian assistance: towards an integrated norm under international law" (2013), 18 *Tilburg Law Review*, 133.

49 Ibid.

ethnic group, overthrew President *Tolbert, Jr* in a military coup, unleashing decades of domestic strife and back-and-forth attempts to assert authority.

The Liberian civil wars began in 1989, when *Charles Taylor* led an insurrection against *Doe*. After gaining victory, *Taylor*'s rebel force split off into factions, leading to a period of horrific violence. Lacking any ideological foundation, the conflict became notorious for war crimes.[50] Over 14 years of conflict, nearly 10 % of the population was killed and nearly everyone at one point displaced.[51] A fragile peace was brokered in 2003, overseen by the United Nations Mission in Liberia.[52] A long process of reconstruction began, including processing and dealing with the widespread psychosocial consequences of the wars.[53]

This backdrop provides perspective on the state of mental health in post-conflict Liberia. Liberia ranks 177th of 188 countries on the United Nations Human Development Index.[54] 64 % of the population lives below the poverty line. After the wars, healthcare infrastructure was almost non-existent, while what remains is overwhelmingly dependent on donor assistance,[55] a lingering consequence of not only civil war but externally imposed macroeconomic policies that restructured public sector spending.[56] The state of Liberia's public health sector is evident in a staggering statistic: before Ebola, around 50 doctors were available for a population of 4 million; the

---

50 Abramowitz, S, "Trauma and humanitarian translation in Liberia: the tale of Open Mole" (2010), 34 *Culture, Medicine, and Psychiatry*, 353.

51 Ibid.

52 United Nations Mission in Liberia, *UNMIL Background*, available at http://www.un.org/en/peacekeeping/missions/unmil/background.shtml.

53 Abramowitz, "Trauma and humanitarian translation", above Fn. 50.

54 United Nations Development Program (UNDP), *Human development reports*, 2014, available at http://bit.ly/1wPFLUk.

55 Kruk, M, Rockers, P C & Williams, E H et al., "Availability of essential health services in post-conflict Liberia" (2010), 88 *Bulletin of the World Health Organization*, 527.

56 Kieh, Jr. G, *The First Liberian Civil War: the Crises of Underdevelopment*, 2008; for more description of the impact of international financial institutions and structural adjustment programs (SAPs) on the health sector in this region, see the contribution of *Susan L. Erikson*, "The Limits of the International Health Regulations: Ebola Governance, Regulatory Breach, and the Non-Negotiable Necessity of National Healthcare" in this volume.

virus eventually claimed the lives of 8 % of the country's healthcare workforce.[57]

During and immediately after the civil wars, biomedical[58] healthcare remained largely under the purview of humanitarian governance, provided almost exclusively by international NGOs. The proliferation of NGOs across the landscape of post-conflict Liberia led to a formal National Policy on NGOs (2008), which, in a moving passage, remarks on the phenomenon of non-state NGOs "filling in" for weak states like Liberia:

> "The war years (1989-2003) shattered the governance structure and systems, the rule of law disappeared and a humanitarian crisis arose that needed immediate attention which no national authority could address. The international community had to take the lead in ensuring not only the provision of humanitarian assistance, but also the protection of life and property and eventual return to peace. Non-Governmental Organizations (NGOs) became the main instrument through which such support could be provided."[59]

In effect, the policy conferred ultimate authority to the Liberian State regarding regulation and accountability of NGOs.[60] For example, health-related NGOs must agree to oversight by the Ministry of Health and Social Welfare (MOHSW) to ensure that their activities are in line with national priorities.[61]

Despite the near-total destruction of its civil infrastructure and limited health budget, Liberia ratified the ICESCR,[62] in 2004. The Covenant's right to health was implicitly accepted in the 1984 national Constitution under "the right of enjoying and defending life".[63] As good health is inherent to

---

57 Evans, D, Goldstein, M & Popova, A, "Healthcare worker mortality and the legacy of the Ebola epidemic" (2015), 3 *Lancet Global Health*, e439; WHO, *World health statistics 2011*, 2011, available at http://www.who.int/whosis/whostat/2011/en/.

58 The authors acknowledge that healthcare is provided by a variety of figures and institutions (including neighbors, so-called "traditional" healers, religious leaders and congregations, etc.) and admit this discussion does not elaborate on their place in Liberian society. This is due to limited published data on these "informal" care providers, but their contribution deserves recognition and more scholarly attention.

59 Republic of Liberia, *National Policy on Non-Governmental Organizations in Liberia*, 2008, 5.

60 Griffiths, C, "Liberia" (2010), 12 *International Journal of Not-for-Profit Law*, 39.

61 Ibid.

62 ICESCR, see above Fn. 10.

63 Republic of Liberia, *Constitution of the Republic of Liberia, Article 11(a)*, 1984, available at http://onliberia.org/con_1984_1.htm.

"enjoying and defending life", Article 11 of the Liberian Constitution creates health obligations on the part of the State.

Developed under the leadership of President *Ellen Johnson-Sirleaf* and then-Minister of Health Dr. *Walter Gwenigale*, the National Health Plan (2007) contains statutory obligations by establishing public health infrastructure and formulating major public health responsibilities. Wishing "to serve as a model of post-conflict recovery"[64] and "committed to efficient use of its resources in order to achieve maximal health outcomes at the lowest possible cost",[65] the Plan explicitly sought to decentralize health services by outlining the Basic Package of Health Services, provided free of charge at the community and county levels, where "primary health care shall be the foundation of the health system".[66]

In 2009, Liberian health policy planners observed that "[m]ental health care is virtually non-existent in the country".[67] The only psychiatric hospital in the country, the Catherine Mills Rehabilitation Center outside Monrovia, was completely destroyed during the civil wars, while the one built in its place, the 75-bed Grant Hospital in Monrovia, was finally turned over from an international NGO to the Liberian Ministry of Health in 2010.[68] Prior to the 2009 National Mental Health Policy (discussed in detail below), only one NGO had an established network of mental health and psychosocial care services outside the capital; traditional healers, family members, and religious leaders were thought to provide most care.[69] The few psychiatric medicines on the Ministry's Essential List of Drugs were unavailable or too costly for most.[70] There were scarce opportunities for clinical training in psychiatry for both nurses and physicians or any standard curriculum or accreditation process.[71] Epidemiologic studies suggested a staggering burden of unmet mental health needs. For example, in 2008, a survey indicated nearly 40 % of the population lived with symptoms indicative of depression

64 Ministry of Health and Social Welfare (MOHSW), *National Health Plan: 2007-2011*, 2007, available at http://apps.who.int/medicinedocs/documents/s18363en/s18363en.pdf, 5.
65 Ibid.
66 Ibid., 10.
67 Republic of Liberia, *National Mental Health Policy*, above Fn. 21, 16.
68 Ibid.
69 Abramowitz, "Trauma and humanitarian translation", above Fn. 50.
70 Republic of Liberia, *National Mental Health Policy*, above Fn. 21.
71 Ibid.

and 44 % with some degree of post-traumatic stress disorder.[72] Admittedly, statistics such as these rely on preconceived notions of how mental disorders and forms of care should be measured[73] and likely miss informal systems of care,[74] such as among family members, community leaders, and healers. Nonetheless, as Liberia began taking steps to rebuild its health system, there was widespread agreement among government planners and external actors alike that the country needed to take an institutional-level response to mental health and psychosocial needs.[75]

1 Liberia's National Mental Health Policy

Liberia's response to mental health needs reflected broader trends in research, policy, and funding. Recognition of the toll of mental, neurological, and substance use disorders, especially in low-income countries, combined with publications like a special issue of the *Lancet,* led to the launch of a Movement for Global Mental Health[76] and the WHO-released Mental Health Gap Action Program (*mhGAP*), which provides health planners, policymakers, and donors with a set of clear and coherent recommendations and programs for scaling up care.[77]

These important frameworks helped to guide policymakers to include mental healthcare services within Liberia's nascent primary healthcare system. Both state and non-state actors, including the Liberian Ministry of Health and a variety of outside experts and funders[78] worked on developing a policy consistent with the premise of decentralized care articulated in the

---

72 Johnson, K, Asher, J & Rosborough, S et al., "Association of combatant status and sexual violence with health and mental health outcomes in postconflict Liberia" (2008), 300 *Journal of the American Medical Association*, 676.

73 Bass, J, Bolton, P A & Murray, L K et al., "Do not forget culture when studying mental health" (2007), 370 *Lancet*, 918.

74 Key informant 2, NGO, 2016; for explanation behind the interview data, see above Fn. 16.

75 Ibid.

76 Lancet Global Mental Health Group (LGMHG), "Scale up services for mental disorders: a call for action" (2007), 370 *Lancet*, 1241; see also Prince, M, Patel, V & Saxena, S et al., "No health without mental health" (2007), 370 *Lancet*, 859.

77 WHO, *mhGAP Intervention Guide for Mental, Neurological and Substance Use Disorders in Non-Specialized Health Settings*, 2010, available at http://bit.ly/2a2IuoO.

78 Republic of Liberia, *National Mental Health Policy*, above Fn. 21.

National Health Policy.[79] The task was not to build a parallel system, but to integrate mental health services into the primary healthcare model, notably through County Mental Health teams and Wellness Units.[80] One leading global mental health scholar, who was heavily involved in assisting the Liberian Ministry of Health and an NGO on the ground in Liberia at the time, echoed the importance of building into the primary healthcare system:

> "In health systems throughout the world, the referral between primary care and mental health services is a chasm. A referral means that the patient and his/her family need to make a second visit to a healthcare provider. That involves much more transportation costs and time. Specialists are typically much further away – if you are in rural Liberia, a mental health specialist can mean 2-3 days' travel. [...] In contrast, through primary care integration, there is no extra step [...]. If you want to do successful mental illness prevention, by nature it must be a primary care and community-based process."[81]

Crucial to the success of a decentralized model was fostering a sense of trust between official institutions, tasked with implementing the policy, and local communities, where most care would be provided.[82]

While integration into the primary healthcare system was a defining aspect of the policy, a potential consequence was the demoralization of already over-burdened care providers. In places like rural Liberia, providers can feel incapable of addressing all of a patient's needs.[83] For these providers, the impetus to change may be perceived as top-down, whereby frameworks for developing mental healthcare services such as WHO's *mhGAP* originate in high-resource countries and amid powerful institutions, with the expectation that they be implemented in low-resource settings.[84] Such critiques of global health as a postcolonial project[85] bear relevance in Liberia, not only due to its own history as a state founded by colonizers but in light

---

79 Ibid.

80 Ibid.

81 The lead author communicated by email with a global mental health specialist who had first-hand experience consulting for an NGO in Liberia. Hereafter, citation provided as: Global mental health specialist, personal communication, 2016.

82 Key informant 1, NGO, 2016.

83 Merlin, *Mental Health in Liberia: Mapping, Overview, and Recommendations*, 2010, internal report obtained by authors.

84 Kohrt, B & Griffith, J, "Global mental health: perspectives from cultural psychiatry on research and intervention" in Kirmayer, L, Lemelson, R & Cummings, C A (eds.), *Re-Visioning Psychiatry: Cultural Phenomenology, Critical Neuroscience, and Global Mental Health*, 2015.

85 Anderson, W, "Making global health history: the postcolonial worldliness of biomedicine" (2014), 27 *Social History of Medicine*, 372.

of a startling discovery made during the epidemic itself. A scientific article published in 1982 was unearthed in April 2015, detailing how some blood samples taken in the late 1970s from a sample of Liberians working on a corporate rubber plantation had in fact tested positive for Ebola antibodies, indicating a potentially longstanding, latent presence of the virus in the region.[86] The fact that this alarming finding was never shared with Liberian healthcare workers or policymakers only underscored the political-economic arrangements that structure not only heightened disease risk but the lopsided allocations of knowledge-sharing, resources, and technologies.[87]

Ebola was first confirmed in Liberia on March 30, 2014.[88] As described by key informants at an NGO that worked closely with the Liberian Ministry of Health, an emergency policy issued by the Liberian government effectively closed all non-essential operations, affecting some core programs of the National Mental Health Policy.[89] And yet, as the outbreak unfolded, much of the work that the policy had already put in place proved crucial to the response, especially in terms of a human network between communities and health institutions. For example, there was an urgent need to address fear-based behavior, such as when family members hid sick relatives from health teams, patients escaped from Ebola Treatment Units (ETUs), or people spread false rumors about the disease, which all contributed to Ebola's spread.[90] Misunderstandings only deepened as outside actors, rather than trying to contextualize such behavior as part of a legacy of deep suspicion and mistrust towards authorities, began casting Liberians as ignorant or superstitious.[91]

As a counterweight, existing networks among county-level health teams and local healers and figureheads, which had grown in the years up to and since the adoption of the Mental Health Policy, facilitated clear and effective health messages.[92] Finally, in the years preceding the epidemic, the National Mental Health Policy's focus on graduating trained mental health

---

86 Dahn, B, Mussah, V & Nutt, C, "Yes, We Warned About Ebola" (April 7, 2015), *New York Times Opinion Pages*, available at http://www.nytimes.com/2015/04/08/opinion/yes-we-were-warned-about-ebola.html.

87 Biehl, J, "Theorizing global health" (2016), 3 *Medicine Anthropology Theory*, 127.

88 WHO, *Liberia: a country – and its capital – are overwhelmed with Ebola cases*, 2015, available at http://bit.ly/2mgGlw3.

89 Key informant 1, NGO, 2016.

90 Key informant 2, NGO, 2016.

91 Ibid.

92 Ibid.

clinicians helped provide manpower to not only staff ETUs as psychosocial care providers but to assist survivors to reintegrate into their communities and care for fellow healthcare workers and others exposed to high levels of traumatizing experiences, such as burial teams.[93]

In sum, the National Mental Health Policy incorporates guiding principles for scaling up mental health services in low-resource, post-conflict settings. The policy itself emerged out of a governance structure composed of various state and non-state actors, including government ministries and policy advocates as well as research centers, funders, and NGOs primarily based in the Global North. Still, as one key informant explained, it was ultimately a collective effort on the ground that led to the policy's realization.[94] This informant's perspective is insightful because it speaks to the commitment of Liberian State institutions in taking a leading role in developing the National Mental Health Policy and National Health Plan. The implementation of rights norms (including the right to health) often occurs "in societies where the legitimacy of the state is low or even completely lacking, at least in the eyes of some groups in the society";[95] such contexts can fuel the "self-legitimacy" that NGOs may assume for themselves as they go about their work. The following case study scrutinizes in further detail the role of NGOs working within and alongside Liberian institutions by recalling the experiences and observations of the lead author, who worked in Liberia during the outbreak with an NGO.

2 Where the Ideal Meets the Real: The Case of Global Care

In late 2014, as the Ebola epidemic spiraled out of control, more NGOs, many never having worked in West Africa, poured into the region to provide aid. One was Global Care (pseudonym), an international health and human rights NGO committed to provision of equitable healthcare and invested in rebuilding Liberia's healthcare infrastructure. Global Care's entry into the Ebola response came after invitation by the Liberian Ministry of Health, a point that underscores Global Care's operating ethos of working within existing health systems, rather than parallel to them. As a short-term clinical volunteer, the lead author gained first-hand experience with Global

93 Ibid.
94 Key informant 1, NGO, 2016.
95 Hilhorst, "Being good at doing good?", above Fn. 30, 195.

Care in Liberia; as such, the findings below derive from the ethnographic process of *participant observation*,[96] wherein the line between observer and active participant is intentionally blurred to facilitate more reflexivity and understanding of on-the-ground realities. To enrich the discussion of NGO governance and accountability, the case study is shared to reveal ethical conflicts and "micro-challenges" that arose in a specific context where Global Care staff tried bridging the figurative space between ideals and local realities.

The strain on healthcare workforces across the three Ebola-affected countries led to a worldwide call among many international NGOs for expatriate clinicians to help provide care in Ebola Treatment Units (ETUs). Global Care was one such NGO that began dispatching expatriate clinicians to work in public health facilities throughout the country. For these clinicians, the focus was not to staff ETUs but to work alongside Liberian clinicians in existing health facilities, with the well-intentioned but vague mission of "health systems strengthening". In early 2015, the lead author, a clinically licensed healthcare provider, joined these efforts.

Given a short, six-week assignment, the small cadre of expatriate doctors and nurses arrived by UN helicopter to one of Liberia's remote counties, where Global Care had begun its work. Throughout the entirety of the epidemic, the county had only one case: a man who had been infected in Monrovia and who voluntarily admitted himself to an ETU before he could infect anyone. The region's remoteness, combined with the deplorable state of Liberia's roads, had limited transmission. In humanitarian parlance, the focus would be on health systems strengthening. But what exactly did that look like in practice? Without clear direction from Global Care's country-level leadership, the expatriate team took it upon themselves to flesh out its operational activities, first by meeting Liberian clinicians at the nearby public hospital, a facility that lacked electricity most hours of the day, had no running water, and went without the most basic supplies.

It is crucial to underscore that Global Care did not delegate specific operational objectives or responsibilities to its expatriate team once in-country, nor was it clear how and under what circumstances Global Care had already contacted local Liberian clinical and public health figures there. In retrospect, the shifting political (and financial) currents of the Ebola response at the time likely contributed to an "adhocracy" within Global Care

96 DeWalt, K & DeWalt, B, *Participant Observation: A Guide for Fieldworkers*, 2011.

and its frenetic relationship towards its expatriate staff.[97] This was compounded by the fact that this was Global Care's first venture into West Africa, let alone during the worst Ebola outbreak on record. These conflicts point to a deeper distinction as well: by all measures, Global Care operates and prides itself as a *development* organization, one committed to long-term engagement with communities. But if the goal was not to staff ETUs anyway, was not Global Care well positioned to assist with rebuilding Liberia's health system?

Ultimately acting under a short timeframe and without clear objectives, the expatriate team members worked closely with a Liberian clinician to contact the County Mental Health Team and other psychosocial staff at the nearby public hospital. These meetings eventually led to a training workshop for care providers throughout the area who sought improved communication strategies among clinical, community, and administrative health staff. The workshop was animated, beginning with participants citing core communication barriers with other providers outside their respective disciplines. The second half of the workshop was devoted to formulating strategies for overcoming those challenges. Afterwards, participants expressed their interest in additional collaborative sessions.

Towards the end of the team's assignment, Global Care's country-level leadership informed the team that the only two psychosocial workers at the hospital would be diverted to a larger project run by a different NGO for an unknown amount of time. At a later site visit, the country director, an expatriate, extolled the important work Global Care was doing in Liberia, from building a new teaching hospital, to developing medical school curricula, to what was envisioned for the county where the team was sent: a staff of more than 60 people; a team of building experts to "re-vamp" the hospital; and ranking needs by priority, divided between short- and long-term.

However, at the in-person meeting, the official alluded to the bind in which Global Care found itself. Through different channels, the team became aware that much of the money supporting Global Care's activities was strictly ear-marked for Ebola-related programs, such as ETU management and Ebola surveillance. A Global Care official later explained that the nature of Global Care's funding, which had been granted through the US

97 Dunn, E, "The chaos of humanitarian aid: adhocracy in the Republic of Georgia" (2012), 3 *Humanity: An International Journal of Human Rights, Humanitarianism, and Development*, 1.

Office of Foreign Disaster Assistance, constrained its long-term interest in health systems strengthening.[98] If, for example, the team wanted to train Liberian staff to provide psychosocial services *at an ETU*, or focus exclusively on Ebola-related stigma, higher-level approval and funding would have been expedited. But challenges such as scaling up psychosocial services throughout the county or supporting providers struggling to respond to chronic psychosocial issues in the community could not easily be justified at that point in time. The expatriate team left Liberia without any clear indication that their work would be carried forward. Later, some caught word that Global Care's presence had been drastically scaled back in the remote county to focus on needs elsewhere in Liberia.

IV IASC Guidelines: Reconsidering Global Care

The case study of Global Care provides an example of the way principles and normative guidelines encounter serious challenges by way of shifting political winds, unclear objectives, and communication breakdowns, and the tensions that arise when sending short-term clinicians to initiate long-term work. A case in point is the emphasis on power relations between outside agencies and emergency-affected people under the core principle of *do no harm* (IASC principle #3). "During emergencies", read the Guidelines,

> "large numbers of people rely on humanitarian actors to meet basic needs. This reliance, together with disrupted or destroyed protection systems (e.g. family networks), contributes to inherently unequal power relationships between those delivering services and those receiving them."[99]

How did power relations shape up in practice? First, the deployment of a small group of expatriate clinicians to a remote corner of the country – and their quick exit – recalls what anthropologist *Peter Redfield* has termed "the easy passage of the privileged",[100] or the ease with which expatriate aid workers come in and out of crisis zones. The power to be present (and leave) figured heavily into how the expatriate team interacted with Liberian colleagues and surrounding community. Foremost, the decision to devote time and human resources to an exploratory study of psychosocial care in the area was made at the field level, between a few expatriate staff and local

98 Country-level official of Global Care, personal communication, 2015.

99 IASC, *IASC Guidelines on Mental Health*, above Fn. 15, 76.

100 Redfield, P, "The unbearable lightness of ex-pats: double binds of humanitarian mobility" (2012), 27 *Cultural Anthropology*, 358 (358).

contacts with professional training. This course of action illustrates how "every organization has to find a justification for being there"[101] and more fundamentally the "self-legitimacy" a NGO can grant itself at even the local level. As representatives of a well-known NGO with mixed degrees of experience and little oversight, the expatriate team had the power to interpret health systems strengthening for themselves and how to go about it. While reaching out and involving Liberian psychosocial workers at the nearby hospital and from the community was in keeping with the principle of building on available resources and integrating support systems (IASC principle #4), what to make of the way in which the team left, with little hand-off or continuity? Was this not an "unintended consequence" that the guidelines warn can result from a lack of understanding power relations?[102]

A more helpful approach to these questions comes from extending the analysis of power relations to the country-level leadership of Global Care and the pressures placed on it by the various publics to whom the NGO was held. By outward appearances, the recruitment, deployment, and extrication of field staff presents Global Care as an unfettered "do-gooder" that effortlessly moves from scene to scene based on need. Yet based on the experiences recounted here, such a (mis)characterization would incorrectly project too much agency onto Global Care and its decision-making capacity. For example, the decision to reassign psychosocial workers undergoing training came at the behest of a much more established, politically connected NGO; while frustrating to those on the ground, the need to re-allocate limited resources sprang from relationships between Global Care and other NGOs at the national level.

Furthermore, it is unsurprising that the needs of the psychosocial team were not prioritized considering that Global Care had not explicitly prioritized psychosocial care at the outset. Despite encouraging messages regarding the team's initial work, other needs forced Global Care to refocus elsewhere. Global Care seemed caught in that gray zone of transition between a humanitarian mode of governance and a vague, "development-oriented" phase that sought to work within the remaining Liberian infrastructure left in Ebola's wake – as though Global Care was trapped between the ideal of "minimum response" and its desire to work towards "the highest attainable standard" via health systems strengthening. In this regard, power relations between expatriate staff and local partners, as well as between field staff

101 Fritsche, G, "Controlling humanitarian aid cowboys in Afghanistan" (2001), 358 *Lancet* 2002.

102 IASC, *IASC Guidelines on Mental Health*, above Fn. 15, 76.

and executive-level leadership, reflect deeper tensions and conflicts at play, challenging the implementation of such a bedrock principle as *do no harm*.

V Conclusion: Principles, Practice, Accountability

Accountability is rooted in the principles of good governance and the fundamental values of a democratic society, including transparency, access to information, the use of explicit standards for the delivery of mental health services and their quality ensured through regular scrutiny, inspection and accreditation,[103] as well as public participation, civil society engagement, and corporate compliance. For non-state actors such as NGOs, which were not the original subjects of international legal instruments on the right to health, can consensus guidelines serve as an effective accountability mechanism for these international public authorities that "escape the grasp of established legal concepts?"[104]

Consider the IASC Guidelines, part of the broader human rights tradition, as a potential accountability mechanism for NGOs like Global Care. In practical terms, this could rely on indicator surveys, health benchmarks, and human rights assessments that glean quantitative information on the impact of an NGO's activities. As one informant explained:

> "One of the challenges has been clearly documenting how much mental health work is done when you use an integrated framework. How do we best count how much time a primary care provider spends on mental health after they get training? [...] Then there is the impact on the community through religious leaders, pharmacists, police, and other stakeholders training in mental health now. Although there is very likely widespread impact through the health system and community, it can be challenging to capture that in numbers salient to domestic and international policymakers."[105]

Tracking practices among both international NGOs and state infrastructures like the public health system can be useful for assessing compliance with norms and standards and informing policy development for the future. Such

103 Chichevalieva, S, *Developing a framework for public health law in Europe*, WHO Regional Office for Europe, 2011, 32 et seq.

104 Bogdandy, Dann & Goldmann, "Developing the Publicness of Public International Law", above Fn. 4, 7.

105 Global mental health specialist, personal communication, 2016.

an "audit culture"[106] has also been met with its fair share of critique, however. For example, overreliance on numerical data can obscure local complexities, or worse, slip into a regressive pattern of counting and itemizing reminiscent of a colonial era, when counting was done to control.[107]

It must be recalled, of course, that accountability for compliance with the right to health, as stipulated in legal frameworks like the ICESCR and constitutional measures such as those in Liberia, lies squarely with states. The example of Liberia's mental health policy, before and during Ebola, demonstrates how states may adapt and bend along the continuum from "minimum response" to "highest attainable standard". First, in the aftermath of civil wars, Liberia's National Mental Health Policy corresponds to the "comprehensive responses" that the IASC Guidelines suggest should be undertaken in the post-emergency or "stabilized phase". These comprehensive responses include integrating psychosocial and mental healthcare into national policy; ensuring monitoring and evaluation mechanisms; strengthening human rights monitoring and accountability; and scaling up training of psychosocial care providers and clinicians.[108] At the same time, the way in which the policy adapted to the Ebola outbreak demonstrates how priorities shift in times of emergency. Rapid transitioning of resources away from "routine activities" such as general training to Ebola-specific needs (for example ETU staffing, collaborating with local healers, and developing appropriate Ebola-related health messages) are all examples of how the policy adapted to meet "minimum responses" as laid out in the IASC Guidelines.[109] Still, even four years *before* the epidemic, an exploratory mission report on the state of Liberian mental healthcare services concluded bleakly that the National Mental Health Policy "describes an 'ideal world' which will never be achieved in any African country and certainly not Liberia",[110] a dire assessment based on the dearth of available resources at the community/primary healthcare level, poor coordination between NGOs and the Ministry of Health, and lack of professional staff. Nonetheless, for

106 Strathern, M (ed.), *Audit Cultures: Anthropological Studies in Accountability, Ethics, and the Academy*, 2000.

107 Adams, V (ed.), *Metrics: What Counts in Global Health*, 2016.

108 IASC, *IASC Guidelines on Mental Health*, above Fn. 15, 21-29.

109 Ibid., 21.

110 Dealing with Disasters Conference, *From Mental Health Policy to the Provision of Care: Challenges for INGOs in Liberia*, 2010.

a country wracked by civil conflict, entrenched poverty, and Ebola, the policy is a laudable achievement incorporating right-to-health norms from various legal (ICESCR, GC 14) and guiding (IASC, *mhGAP*) frameworks.

While Liberian institutions have come far by way of policy development, many chief implementers remain non-state NGOs. Administrative and judicial capacity are therefore essential for states to regulate the activities of NGOs and ensure that their practices comply with rights norms. Liberia's official NGO policy delegates specific oversight roles to certain Ministries, implicating the responsibility of the state to monitor NGOs in the country.[111] In post-conflict states, where stability and institutional capacity may be present, mechanisms could be developed that are transparent, participatory, and independent to review progress, measure core indicators, and recommend corrective measures to realize the right to health.[112] These governmental and administrative accountability mechanisms function in addition to judicial means of accountability, referring to the ability to claim a remedy before an independent and impartial body when a violation of a (human) right has occurred ("justiciability"). On several occasions, domestic and regional courts held claims on healthcare access justiciable, providing an effective remedy to enforce its realization.[113]

Of course, what NGOs have once "in the field" are guidelines, which may share common norms with legal instruments but are not in themselves enforceable. But perhaps they should not be. Guidelines are intended to do exactly that: to guide the operational role of NGOs and other agencies. Although guidelines reflect best practices on paper, they are not magic bullets in practice; indeed, a major critique of the IASC Guidelines is a lack of evidence base or strong call for collecting evidence at local levels (although they do emphasize the importance of culture and local adaptation of interventions). As the West Africa Ebola outbreak attests, each humanitarian emergency occurs in context, in a specific historical and geopolitical time and place and among socially differentiated groups of people. Not only that,

111 Republic of Liberia, *National policy*, above Fn. 59.

112 Friedman, E A, "An Independent Review and Accountability Mechanism for the Sustainable Development Goals: The Possibilities of a Framework Convention on Global Health" (2016), 18 *Health and Human Rights Journal*, 1

113 For an interesting overview see Flood, C & Gross, A (eds.), *The Right to Health at the Public/Private Divide: A Global Comparative Study*, 2014, describing national experiences on litigating healthcare access such as: *Minister of Health v. Treatment Action Campaign* (TAC) 2002 5 SA 721 (CC) South Africa; Colombian Constitutional Court ruling T-760/08, July 31, 2008, etc.

guidelines themselves may be taken as "cultural artifacts" produced in a specific culture of moral humanitarianism, where the power to produce and disseminate knowledge can be too easily taken for granted.[114] Finally, an NGO itself has its own ethos, operating culture, levels of expertise, and relationships with the communities they try to serve.

Clearly, in times of emergency, many other competing forces besides medical needs push and prod along the track hollowed out by guidelines like IASC. In front of such a broad array of contingencies, surely some "room to maneuver" must be left open based on the intricacies of context and the micro-scaled setting where highly mobile expatriate (and sometimes inexperienced) staff bump up against local realities.[115]

In the end, the point resurfaces: as an international public authority, the NGO is accountable to multiple publics, from donors and executive boards, to most importantly, their supposed beneficiaries. The Liberian people whom Global Care's staff encountered and worked with, for example, did not have a say in how and in what form aid would come to them, nor were their voices heard when Global Care left. Nor could Global Care, supported financially by ear-marked money, justify its deployment of resources, however short-term, to a remote corner of Liberia left relatively unscathed by Ebola but still in dire need of health systems strengthening. Core principles of IASC, especially that of *do no harm*, can be insightful for NGO representatives as they try to go about implementing the right to health on the ground. Arguably, by this measure, Global Care's work in this corner of Liberia was left unfinished and only exposed the fault lines of power coursing through regimes of global health governance.

At the same time, working relationships among local clinical staff were indeed fostered in this area of Liberia, however short-lived, and Global Care has maintained a fruitful relationship with the Liberian Ministry of Health while re-focusing its attention to other areas of the country thought to be in higher need and where its impact might be stronger. These realities point to ways in which hierarchies of need materialize along the course of the humanitarian timeline, marked by phases such as emergency, post-emergency, or rehabilitation, with each demanding different operational paradigms among NGOs and states as well as different guidelines to follow. Once on the ground, these conceptual phases become even harder to differentiate.

114 Kohrt, B & Jallah, B, "People, praxis, and power in global mental health: anthropology and the experience gap" in Kohrt, B & Mendenhall, E (eds.), *Global Mental Health: Anthropological Perspectives*, 2015.

115 Hilhorst, "Being good at doing good?", above Fn. 30.

A lesson of the Global Care experience is that context can be a powerful determinant of whether certain ideals get translated into practice. Context in this sense refers to the historical legacy of external, non-state actors "filling in" for a weak, war-torn, and ultimately post-conflict state, but one that has also honored deep commitments to realizing the right to health through policy achievements and was, to some degree, equipped to mount a psychosocial response to the Ebola outbreak through its existing health system.

However, context also refers to upstream actors and institutional sites of power, such as host country Ministries of Health, the WHO, the US Office of Foreign Disaster Assistance, and the IASC itself, whose decisions bear consequences in the smaller-scaled, local settings where they are intended to have a positive effect. Simply consider how the International Health Regulations (2005), which enabled the WHO to declare the outbreak a "public health emergency of international concern" and thereby set in motion the large-scale international response,[116] only revealed the fundamentally *reactive* nature of the humanitarian system: "The world sought to 'respond' to Ebola – when it should have responded to deep-seated problems that gave rise to it."[117] Perhaps one of the greatest sources of power within this governance structure is the way in which international legal frameworks, regulations, and NGO guidelines "are so obviously rationally and inclusively framed, [that] their users are assumed also to act rationally and inclusively",[118] an assumption called into question by the case study above.

The activities of NGOs like Global Care should not be separated from this larger web of relations, and as such accountability mechanisms cannot rely exclusively on "ideal principles" that pertain mostly to the interactions between an NGO and the local population. Such principles serve their purpose, but only to a point. Humanitarian NGOs often find themselves in a bind; accountability approaches must remain flexible to this reality while also tending to macro-level political decisions made in distant sites of power. A helpful way forward may be found by strengthening the normative links between operational guidelines like those of IASC and the primary legal frameworks on the right to health, the ICESCR and GC 14. Clarifying

---

116 WHO, *International Health Regulations*, 2007, available at http://www.who.int/topics/international_health_regulations/en/.

117 Nunes, J, "Doctors Against Borders: Médecins sans Frontières and Global Health Security" in Hofman, M & Au, S (eds.), *The Politics of Fear: Médecins sans Frontières and the West Africa Ebola Epidemic*, 2017, 8.

118 Martínez, S & Kiper, J, "Perpetrators, responders, and the construction of moral distance in human rights", forthcoming, 31.

these links in turn enriches the perspectives at both standpoints: it encourages NGOs to remind themselves of rights principles that form the basis for much of their work in fragile or weak states, while for policy, legal, and academic circles, case studies from the field can reveal points of tension and breakdown in applying those principles, and as such suggest areas for improvement. Scholarship that untangles the convergence of principles, policy, and practice can shed additional light on the gap between the ideal and the real.

International and Regional Organizations and the Securitization of Health

The World Health Organization's Governance Framework in Disease Outbreaks: A Legal Perspective

*Pedro A. Villarreal**

Abstract

The 2014-2016 West African Ebola outbreak displayed a plethora of shortcomings within the governance for disease outbreak alert and response, with the World Health Organization (WHO) at the epicenter. Although part of the possible explanation for these failures may be grounded on the technical complexities inherent when assessing the magnitude of this public health event, governance-related problems due either to the institutional background or to the exercise of authority through administrative discretion cannot be overlooked. This article employs an understanding of a governance framework that includes not only norms such as the International Health Regulations, but also the ways in which organs such as WHO's Director-General and its Emergency Committee exercise the discretion granted by such norms. For this goal, a presumption of the idea of International Organizations as bureaucracies largely based on rational authorities will be used. Lastly, the article argues that this prima facie descriptive endeavor can serve as a basis for future normative proposals aimed at addressing governance deficiencies, whether through legal reforms, or even by focusing on the way in which officials themselves exercise authority on a case-by-case basis.

---

* Research Fellow, Max Planck Institute for Comparative Public Law and International Law, Heidelberg, Germany. Special thanks to *Armin von Bogdandy*, *Leonie Vierck*, *A. Katarina Weilert*, *Matthias Goldmann*, *Michael Ioannidis*, *Michael Marx*, *Edefe Ojomo*, *Simon Hentrei*, *Mateja Steinbrück Platise*, *Joel Maupin* and *Simeon Prechtel*, as well as attendants to the Tuesday Meetings (Dienstagsrunde) at the aforementioned Institute, for their input. I also extend my gratefulness to the participants of the workshop which took place March 3-4, 2016, at the Max Planck Institute for Comparative Public Law and International Law, for multiple exchanges on this subject matter. All websites last accessed January 5, 2017.

I Introduction

On March 29, 2016, the WHO issued a statement declaring that the West African Ebola outbreak was no longer a Public Health Emergency of International Concern (PHEIC),[1] thus marking a conclusion to the initial declaration of August 8, 2014.[2] A mere three days later, there was yet another WHO statement reporting a new fatality in Liberia due to the Ebola virus.[3] However, this fact did not lead to another declaration of a PHEIC by the WHO's Director-General. Concurrently, on February 1, 2016, another PHEIC had already been declared, this time due to the explosive spread of Zika virus throughout the Americas, and mainly in light of a suspected link between the virus and microcephaly in newborns.[4] Moreover, another statement by the WHO on November 18, 2016, declared that the Zika epidemic no longer constituted a PHEIC, thus limiting its formal duration to less than ten months.[5] By contrast, a new coronavirus later named as Middle East respiratory syndrome emerged in 2012 in Saudi Arabia, also causing an outbreak in South Korea in 2015.[6] Even though by December 2016 the virus had infected more than 1840 persons, killing more than 650 in the process,[7]

---

1 WHO, *Statement on the 9th meeting of the IHR Emergency Committee regarding the Ebola outbreak in West Africa*, available at http://www.who.int/mediacentre/news/statements/2016/end-of-ebola-pheic/en/.

2 WHO, *Statement on the 1st meeting of the IHR Emergency Committee on the 2014 Ebola outbreak in West Africa*, available at http://www.who.int/mediacentre/news/statements/2014/ebola-20140808/en/.

3 Resurgences of the Ebola virus across zones which had been previously deemed Ebola-free are referred to as "flare-ups". See the WHO's Statement, *New positive case of Ebola virus disease confirmed in Liberia*, available at http://www.who.int/mediacentre/news/statements/2016/liberia-ebola/en/.

4 Heymann, D L, Hodgson, A & Sall, A A et al., "Zika virus and microcephaly: why is this situation a PHEIC?" (2016), 387 *The Lancet*, 719 (719-720).

5 See WHO, *Fifth meeting of the Emergency Committee under the International Health Regulations (2005) regarding microcephaly, other neurological disorders and Zika virus*, available at http://www.who.int/mediacentre/news/statements/2016/zika-fifth-ec/en/.

6 Butler, D, "South Korean MERS outbreak is not a global threat" (June 5, 2015), *Nature News*, available at http://go.nature.com/1FSEdvy.

7 See the WHO's situation report on Middle East respiratory syndrome, December 5, 2016, available at http://www.who.int/emergencies/mers-cov/en/.

after several discussions the WHO's Director-General has explicitly decided not to declare outbreaks of Middle East respiratory syndrome as a PHEIC.[8]

These parallel outbreaks of diverging diseases showcase how variable the application of the legal definition of a PHEIC can be. Enshrined in the International Health Regulations (IHR), the main authorities in charge of interpreting its scope are the WHO's Director-General and the corresponding Emergency Committee.[9] As the use of PHEIC Declarations referred to in the previous paragraph illustrates, the criteria used for the application of the IHR to specific facts are not manifestly straightforward. To the contrary, it can be argued that WHO officials exercise a visible amount of discretion in their use of the legal mandate provided by the IHR.

In this sense, the delay of the PHEIC Declaration at the beginning of the 2014-2016 West African Ebola outbreak is a dramatic case in point. The catastrophic consequences of the belated response to the crisis displays how the international community, as a whole, is simply unable to meet the minimum requirements for effective disease outbreak preparedness and response. Arguably, this goal has been the driving motif of international cooperation in health ever since the first International Sanitary Conference took place in 1851.[10] Yet, even with the long-standing tradition of international coordination in communicable disease control, and despite the advances in medical science and technology ever since, the claim that the world is insufficiently prepared for public health emergencies still stands.

Given that the WHO is the International Organization with the specific mandate to act as the "directing and co-ordinating authority on international health work",[11] its legal powers merit particular scrutiny when revisiting recent events such as the West African Ebola crisis and the Zika outbreak in the Americas. For this goal, governance is understood in this contribution as encompassing both formal and informal instruments aimed at decision-

---

8 By January, 2017, an Emergency Committee had met ten times, the last of which occurred in September 2015. See WHO, *Statement on the tenth meeting of the IHR Emergency Committee regarding MERS*, September 3, 2015, available at http://bit.ly/2mXVshE.

9 Articles 12, 48 and 49, IHR.

10 Goodman, N, *International Health Organizations and their Work*, 1971, 247; Fidler, D, *International Law and Infectious Diseases*, 1999, 7; Burci, G, "Health and Infectious Disease" in Weiss, T & Daws, S (eds.), *The Oxford Handbook on the United Nations*, 2007, 583.

11 Article 2(a), Constitution of the WHO.

making.[12] The fact that the current analysis is limited to an International Organization does not imply disregarding the relevance of other institutions and actors as part of the broader governance framework of disease outbreaks. Such an understanding of governance includes norms, regulations and internal resolutions, regardless of whether they are legally binding for States or not.

This article deals with the governance framework designed within the WHO *qua* specialized agency of the United Nations (UN), aimed at infectious disease outbreak preparedness and response.[13] As for legal sources, the central focus will be the International Health Regulations (IHR) of 2005, considered as the core instrument designed at the international level for dealing with public health emergencies such as epidemics and pandemics. These Regulations will be addressed jointly with resolutions, and also by the institutional practice of WHO, deriving mainly from the World Health Assembly and the Secretariat.[14] Such institutional practice becomes all the more relevant, particularly since dispute settlement case law within the WHO is scarce.[15]

Furthermore, although this article focuses on a legal analysis of the governance structure of the WHO, a broader vision on how administrative-based discretion is exercised by International Organizations will be adopted, which includes issues located beyond the limits of positive law. The idea of authority is useful for this goal, given how it can operate as a

12 See the seminal work of Rosenau, J & Czempiel, E (eds.), *Governance without government: Order and change in world politics*, 1992, 4; likewise, Levi-Faur, D, "From 'Big Government' to 'Big Governance'?" in Levi-Faur, D (ed.), *Oxford Handbook of Governance*, 2013, 3 et seq. From a legal standpoint, see also Bogdandy, A von, Goldmann, M & Dann, P, "Developing the Publicness of Public International Law: Towards a Legal Framework for Global Governance Activities" in Bogdandy, A von, Wolfrum, R & Bernstorff, J von et al. (eds.), *The Exercise of Public Authority by International Institutions: Advancing International Institutional Law*, 2010, 10-12; Kingsbury, B, Krisch, N & Stewart, R, "The Emergence of Global Administrative Law" (2005), 68 *Law and Contemporary Problems,* 15 (17 et seq.).

13 Other UN agencies also have a direct role in combatting infectious diseases. For instance, UNICEF has actively participated in disease-eradication campaigns alongside the WHO. See Burci, "Health and Infectious Disease", above Fn. 10.

14 For a legal framing of the institutional practice of International Organizations when interpreting norms, see Alvarez, J, *International Organizations as Law-makers*, 2005, 87-92.

15 See the contribution of *Leonie Vierck*, "The Case Law of International Public Health and Why its Scarcity is a Problem" in this volume.

conceptual bridge between legal and political theory.[16] Authority by International Organizations in general, and by the WHO in particular, is addressed here in its "legal-rational" model rooted in the Weberian tradition.[17] In general terms, the WHO can be viewed as a technocratic[18] institution in which the expertise of its members is seen as enhancing its legitimacy *vis-à-vis* Member States, and perhaps even the public at large.[19] Consequently, the theoretical background of this article rests upon the concept of authority as understood within the project of International Public Authority (IPA), which visualizes authority as the possibility to shape a legal or factual situation.[20]

Although States have a primary role in confronting disease outbreaks, particularly in terms of the IHR, this article will be limited to the governance structure within the WHO. However, as mentioned below, it should be noted that a major part of WHO governance is based upon the direct link to Member States' authorities, and in the case of events like outbreaks, it occurs mainly through IHR National Focal Points. Besides, ultimately the IHR are the product of State consent, albeit a peculiar form of it with regard to standard treaty-making in the sense of the 1969 Vienna Convention on the Law of Treaties. In the facts, the framework designed for disease outbreak alert and response displays an inseparable link between the WHO's organs and Member States.

---

16 For a general understanding of the authority exercised by International Organizations see Barnett, M & Finnemore, M, *Rules for the World. International Organizations in Global Politics*, 2004, 29-31.

17 See this influential distinction in Weber, M, Mommsen, W (ed.) & Schluchter, W (ed.), *Wissenschaft als Beruf 1917/1919 - Politik als Beruf, 1919*, 1992, 160-161.

18 Here, "technocracy" is understood as decision-making by a body of experts which do not necessarily rely on democratic credentials in their authority. It is not used in a pejorative sense whatsoever. See Barnett & Finnemore, *Rules for the World*, above Fn. 16, 24-25; Delbrück, J, "Exercising Public Authority Beyond the State: Transnational Democracy and/or Alternative Legitimation Strategies" (2003), 10 *Indiana Journal of Global Legal Studies*, 29 (34); Venzke, I, "International Bureaucracies from a Political Science Perspective. Agency, Authority and International Institutional Law" in Bogdandy, Wolfrum & Bernstorff et al. (eds.), *The Exercise of Public Authority*, above Fn. 12, 83-85.

19 However, the idea of how this international community is to be framed *vis-à-vis* states and peoples, is a matter of further debate. For a proposal on this matter with regard to international courts, see Bogdandy, A von & Venzke, I, *In Whose Name? A Public Law Theory of International Adjudication*, 2014, 207-216.

20 Bogdandy, Dann & Goldmann, "Developing the Publicness", above Fn. 12, 11.

With this introductory input in mind, the article is structured as follows: The following section (II) will briefly relate the most visible transborder disease outbreaks since the turn of the 21st Century. It shows how the legal interpretation of the IHR was, and continues to be shaped as a response to diverging facts which are difficult to pinpoint under concise, pre-established rules. Next (III), two of the international legal instruments related to the containment of the spread of disease throughout countries are addressed, namely the Constitution of the WHO and the IHR. Certain salient features are underscored for understanding some of the current debates about their potential as well as their possible pitfalls. Later (IV) and in a similar vein, an overview of the legal role of bodies within the WHO intervening in disease outbreaks, namely the World Health Assembly, the Secretariat and the Regional Organizations,[21] is developed. Afterwards (V), a descriptive outline of the existing "bad" governance arrangements within the WHO is followed by some normative considerations. The closing section (VI) presents conclusions deriving from the arguments formulated throughout the article.

II Transborder Disease Outbreaks on the 21st Century

A brief account of recent transborder disease outbreaks can set the stage for the following sections and arguments. The aim is to provide a factual background with which the legal reasoning will be contrasted. The current shape of the governance framework for epidemics and pandemics within the WHO can be understood as an adaptive process, insofar as it resulted from reactions to various public health events transcending geographical borders. In turn, this reaffirms the notion that leeway granted to officials is based mostly on technical grounds, in order to accommodate the heterogeneous nature of events which may fall under general legal hypotheses.

In order to further grasp this leeway, a brief overview of recent disease outbreaks of international reach can be useful for understanding some elements that might be shared, and others that are contrasted between them. The following paragraphs address the different responses in the cases of

21 While the Executive Board also has a role to play in light of the extraordinary powers it can expressly confer to Director-General according to Article 28(i) of the Constitution of the WHO, it is thus far merely a theoretical possibility, as it has never been exercised in practice. Therefore, this legal power will not be developed in further detail in this contribution. For more on this issue, see Kamradt-Scott, A, *Managing Global Health Security. The World Health Organization and Disease Outbreak Control*, 2015, 33-38.

SARS, A(H1N1) Influenza, Poliomyelitis, Ebola and Zika. These events are divergent in many ways, including the epidemiological features of each virus and the geographical context in which they took place. Therefore, they may not be comparable for extrapolating general statements or conclusions. Although distinct from one another, an overview can also help to retrospectively identify common threads, such as a consistency, or lack thereof, in decision-making.

1 The 2002-2003 SARS Outbreak

During November 2002, an outbreak of a previously unknown virus, later named Severe Acute Respiratory Syndrome (SARS), began in China. But officials from the Chinese government failed to formally notify the WHO at the initial stage of its emergence.[22] As the international community at large was not aware of its presence, other countries did not implement screening processes accordingly.[23] The virus eventually spread to other regions,[24] whereby authorities only identified the pathogen after it was already inside their borders.

After the 2002-2003 SARS crisis and the subsequent response by the WHO, there was political momentum within the international community for an overarching reform of the then-existing legal framework of disease outbreak alert and response.[25] Some of the salient legal problems around the SARS crisis were focused, on the responsibility of States in the absence of explicit legal obligations to notify the WHO of the emergence of new

22 The Chinese government notified the presence of SARS to the WHO on February 2003, several months after the outbreak had been detected. Heymann, D & Rodier, G, "SARS: A global response to an international threat" (2004), 10 *Brown Journal of World Affairs*, 185 (189-190).

23 Awareness of the presence of a virus directly affects surveillance, insofar as individual medics resort to known pathogens for reaching a diagnosis. This is more acute in the case of emergencies, as contact-tracing is essential for curtailing the spread of a pathogen. See Cookson, S & Buehler, J, "Emergency and Disaster Health Surveillance" in Ahrens, W & Pigeot, I (eds.), *Handbook of Epidemiology*, 2nd edition, 2014, 732-738.

24 Heymann & Rodier, "SARS: A global response", above Fn. 22, 190.

25 Fidler, D, "From International Sanitary Conventions to Global Health Security: The New International Health Regulations" (2005), 4 *Chinese Journal of International Law*, 325 (354-355).

diseases within their territory.[26] The failure to do so in the case of SARS raised questions about the applicability of the legal instrument originally designed for such situations, the 1969 version of the IHR.[27] Then in force, the 1969 IHR played at most a marginal role, if any at all. Its obsolescence was mostly due to its scope: It was only applicable on a casuistic model towards diseases that, by 2002-2003, only established cholera, plague and yellow fever as falling under its purview.[28]

The WHO took center stage in the international response to the outbreak during the SARS crisis. Concerns about the possible outreach of the WHO's powers were raised, given that it had no explicit mandate for dealing with SARS – or other novel pathogens – according to the 1969 IHR.[29] By following the doctrine of implied powers,[30] the WHO would not be acting *ultra vires*, as all matters of international health, and communicable diseases in particular, would fall under its legal mandate.[31] But the fact that the WHO issued a declaration in this uncertain context was still troubling for some Member States, and the precise obligations of the Chinese government according to international law were disputed.[32]

2 The 2009-2010 A(H1N1) Influenza Pandemic

On April 25, 2009,[33] the WHO's Director-General declared, for the first time, that the unusual cases of A(H1N1) influenza reported by Mexico and

---

26 Ibid., 369.

27 Heymann & Rodier, "SARS: A global response", above Fn. 22, 190.

28 Articles 50 to 75 of the 1969 IHR.

29 Hanrieder, T & Kreuder-Sonnen, C, "WHO decides on the exception? Securitization and emergency governance in global health" (2014), 45 *Security Dialogue*, 331 (336-338).

30 Schermers, H & Blokker, N, *International Institutional Law. Unity Within Diversity*, 5th edition, 2011, 180-182.

31 For the relationship between the doctrine of implied powers and the Constitution of the WHO, see Burci, G & Quirin, J, "Legality of the Use by a State of Nuclear Weapons in Armed Conflict, International Court of Justice, Advisory Opinion of 8 July 1996" in Ryngaert, C, Dekker, I F & Wessel, R A et al. (eds.), *Judicial Decisions on the Law of International Organizations*, 2016, 108-111.

32 A discussion of the reaction of China to this epidemic from an international law perspective can be seen in Reader, J, "The case against China. Establishing International Liability for China's Response to the 2002-2003 SARS Epidemic" (2006), 19 *Columbia Journal of Asian Law*, 519 (568-570).

33 WHO, *Swine influenza*, 2009, available at http://bit.ly/2nekbtY.

the United States of America constituted a PHEIC. Later, on June 11, 2009, there was also a declaration of the highest pandemic alert level (then level 6),[34] which led to criticisms from other countries that were not as affected by the virus as Mexico and the United States of America were.[35] Broadly speaking, after the "formal" end of the 2009-2010 influenza pandemic was declared in August 2010, the outcome was far less drastic than the previously feared scenario of a deadly avian-flu pandemic.

The main source of criticism against the WHO's reaction to the pandemic was the fact that pharmaceutical companies made huge profits as a result of the declaration of the maximum pandemic phase (level 6).[36] The backlash resulted in, among other things, an investigation within the Council of Europe[37] due to what was perceived as pernicious influence by the pharmaceutical industry. Although the eventual report presented at the Parliamentary Assembly of the Council did not yield evidence of malfeasance, it did include criticisms related to lackluster transparency in decision-making. Not disclosing the names of members of the Emergency Committee, which falls under the discretion of the WHO Director-General in the absence of any explicit legal provision in the IHR mandating it, was a notable point of controversy. An extensive report by an IHR Review Committee was issued.[38] Several recommendations for enhancing decision-making within the WHO were presented to the World Health Assembly in 2011. However, there were no calls for a reform of any of the provisions within the IHR.

---

34 WHO, *World now at the start of 2009 influenza pandemic. Statement to the press by the WHO Director-General Dr Margaret Chan*, available at http://bit.ly/1gIUU2R.

35 There is a formal distinction between a PHEIC and a Pandemic Declaration, as stipulated by the WHO itself in its latest edition of pandemic guidelines. See WHO, *Pandemic Influenza Risk Management. WHO Interim Guidance*, 2013, 7, available at http://bit.ly/2nengug; also, Villarreal, P, "Pandemic Declarations of the World Health Organization as an Exercise of International Public Authority: The Possible Legal Answers to Frictions Between Legitimacies" (2016), 7 *Göttingen Journal of International Law*, 95.

36 See the investigative report by Cohen, D & Carter, P, "WHO and the pandemic flu 'conspiracies'" (2010), 340 *The BMJ*, 1274 (1279).

37 Parliamentary Assembly of the Council of Europe, *Resolution 1749*, 2010, available at http://bit.ly/2mj1x5a.

38 WHO, *Strengthening Response to Pandemics and other Public Health Emergencies: Report of the Review Committee on the Functioning of the International Health Regulations (2005) and on Pandemic Influenza (H1N1) 2009*, 2011, 29, available at http://www.who.int/ihr/publications/RC_report/en/.

3 PHEICs as an Accelerator: The Push Against Poliomyelitis

On May 5, 2014,[39] a PHEIC was declared for the second time in relation to the spread of wild poliovirus throughout regions of Africa and the Middle East. This was considered a consequence of both an anti-vaccination sentiment,[40] as well as longstanding military conflict[41] that dramatically undermined the provision of health services throughout these regions. Here, the PHEIC declaration was a companion to the decades-old global polio eradication campaign. It has served as an accelerator for a previously existent threat, and not just as a reaction to a new, unprecedented event.

The legal justification for declaring a PHEIC in the fight for eradicating Poliomyelitis can contribute to understanding how the figure is more or less flexible in order to face different arrays of challenges. While the Poliomyelitis PHEIC did not generate the same level of criticism as the A(H1N1) influenza pandemic, caution and balance still have a role to play. Using the legal understanding of emergency too often could gradually erode its weight, as it is usually understood as an extraordinary event requiring equally extraordinary measures. Similarly, if its sole purpose is to enhance the effectiveness of previously deployed public health campaigns, it can lead, on one hand, to the dilution of the notion of emergency, like the "cry wolf" scenario. On the other hand, it can also lead to questioning the discretion of the authority in charge of the declaration.

4 Deadly Delay: The Ebola Outbreak in West Africa

Despite initial reports on March 2014 by Médecins Sans Frontières[42] and the government of Guinea about the out-of-control spread of Ebola virus

---

39 WHO, *Statement on the meeting of the International Health Regulations Emergency Committee concerning the international spread of wild poliovirus*, 2014, available at http://bit.ly/Q5J4qw.

40 See the Interactive Map of the Global Health Program at the Council of Foreign Relations, available at http://www.cfr.org/interactives/GH_Vaccine_Map/.

41 Gayer, M, Legros, D & Formenty, P et al., "Conflict and Emerging Infectious Diseases" (2007), 13 *Emerging Infectious Diseases*, 1625 (1628), available at http://wwwnc.cdc.gov/eid/article/13/11/06-1093_article.

42 Médecins Sans Frontières, *Pushed to the limit and beyond. A critical analysis of the global Ebola response one year into the deadliest outbreak in history*, 2015, available at http://www.msf.org/article/ebola-pushed-limit-and-beyond.

throughout the country, a PHEIC was only declared on August 8[43] of the same year. The WHO was then criticized for opposite reasons compared to the 2009 A(H1N1) influenza pandemic: It was now chastised for not raising the alarm fast enough.[44] While it is difficult to argue in terms of causality, it is asserted elsewhere that had this alarm been raised before, more resources could have been directed earlier for containing the spread of Ebola.[45]

As mentioned at the beginning of this article, on March 29, 2016, the WHO Director-General declared that the Ebola PHEIC had formally ended,[46] although the disease was still present in the West African region.[47] Failure to quickly respond to the spread of this disease can be considered as a consequence of both a flawed decision-making process within the WHO, as well as a prevalence of uncertainty within the community of experts. Deliberate choices by officials within the WHO cannot be overlooked. The conscious wait-and-see approach proved to be fatal in this case, leading to questions of why it took months for officials to sound the alarm.[48] Even if it is not measurable, the impact of the ill-fated reaction to the Ebola crisis on the institutional reputation of the WHO may affect future confidence by Member States towards its standards, guidelines and declarations. Considering how it is seen as an institution relying upon its technical expertise for enhancing observance with non-binding standards,[49] lack of trust can turn into a particularly dire hindrance.

As further argued in another section, the response – or lack thereof – of Regional Organizations of the WHO also needs to be taken into account. The contrast between the A(H1N1) Influenza pandemic and Zika, on one hand, and Ebola, on the other, could also be understood as a visible asymmetry between one Regional Organization and the other. The predominant

43 See WHO, *Statement on the 1st meeting*, above Fn. 2.

44 For an overview, see Moon, S, Sridhar, D & Pate, M A et al., "Will Ebola change the game? Ten essential reforms before the next pandemic. The report of the Harvard-LSHTM Independent Panel on the Global Response to Ebola" (2015), 386 *The Lancet*, 2204 (2206-2207).

45 The point is vehemently stated in the Report by Médecins Sans Frontières, *Pushed to the limit and beyond*, above Fn. 42, 11.

46 See WHO, *Statement on the 9th meeting of the IHR Emergency Committee*, above Fn. 1.

47 See WHO's Statement, *New positive case of Ebola*, above Fn. 3.

48 Moon, Sridhar & Pate et al., "Will Ebola change the game?", above Fn. 44, 2210-2211.

49 Burci, G & Vignes, C, *World Health Organization*, 2004, 155.

historical position of the Pan American Health Organization (PAHO), which precedes the WHO itself and is today the regional body for the Americas, is reflected in Article 54 of the Constitution of the WHO and is analyzed by other authors elsewhere.[50]

Unlike the other PHEICs mentioned herein, the magnitude of the Ebola crisis in West Africa also led to atypical resolutions within the general aegis of the United Nations. These consisted of Security Council Resolution 2177 (2014),[51] as well as General Assembly Resolution 69/1 (2014).[52] As discussed elsewhere in this book,[53] these resolutions were unprecedented in terms of its subject matter, contributing to the conceptualization of health as a security issue. Moreover, at the governance level, Resolution 69/1 sparked the creation of an ad hoc body, the United Nations Mission for Ebola Emergency Response (UNMEER), with a temporal mandate that lasted from September 19, 2014 until July 31, 2015. Nevertheless, its ad hoc nature has also been subject to criticisms, insofar as it was "superimposed"[54] on already existing structures without duly taking into account the ongoing operations.

---

50 Lee, K, *The World Health Organization (WHO)*, 2009, 30-34; Hanrieder, T, *International Organization in Time. Fragmentation and Reform*, 2015, 58-61.

51 United Nations Security Council, *Resolution 2177 (2014)*, available at http://bit.ly/1qidtMV.

52 United Nations General Assembly Resolution 69/1, *Measures to contain and combat the recent Ebola outbreak in West Africa*, available at http://www.un.org/en/ga/search/view_doc.asp?symbol=A/RES/69/1. For a more detailed analysis of both resolutions, see Burci, G & Kirin, J, "Ebola, WHO, and the United Nations: Convergence of Global Public Health and International Peace and Security" (2014), 18 *ASIL Insights,* available at http://bit.ly/2m5AFIF.

53 See particularly the contributions of *Robert Frau*, "Combining the WHO's International Health Regulations (2005) with the UN Security Council's Powers: Does it Make Sense for Health Governance?" and *Ilja Robert Pavone*, "Ebola and Securitization of Health: UN Security Council Resolution 2177/2014 and its Limits" in this volume.

54 See the Report of the United Nations High Level Panel on the Global Response to Health Crises, *Protecting Humanity from Future Health Crises*, 2016, para. 160.

5 The Race for Knowledge: The Zika Emergency of 2016

On February 1, 2016, the WHO's Director-General declared the Zika virus epidemic in the Americas a PHEIC.[55] The reasons for declaring this event as a PHEIC were not grounded on the severity of the disease in terms of fatalities.[56] Rather, the major source of concern was the then-suspected link between Zika virus and a surge in cases of microcephaly and a risk of developing Guillain-Barré syndrome.[57] To-date, Brazil has been the most affected country by the spread of the virus.

The criteria for assessing the justification for declaring a PHEIC can also be distinguished between Zika and the other instances mentioned above. Uncertainty can also be used as a legal argument: The Zika PHEIC Declaration was not made based upon what was known at the time, but rather because of what was unknown.[58] As stated at the beginning of this article, the Zika PHEIC was declared to be over in November 2016, despite how the virus itself is likely to linger throughout the coming years.[59] However, uncertainty surrounding the disease has been reduced perhaps as a result of the attention brought about by the PHEIC Declaration. The reorientation of resources towards research has yielded results that confirmed initial suspicions.[60] While there is still more to learn about the virus, the overall progress supports the usefulness of a PHEIC Declaration for the purpose of knowing more about a disease.

---

55 See WHO, *Fifth meeting of the Emergency Committee under the International Health Regulations (2005)*, above Fn. 5.

56 Illness caused by this virus is very rarely fatal, and it causes mild symptoms: rash, headaches, conjunctivitis, sometimes fever and joint pains. See the United States Centers for Disease Control and Prevention's factsheet on Zika, available at http://www.cdc.gov/zika/symptoms/index.html.

57 Heymann, Hodgson & Sall et al., "Zika virus and microcephaly", above Fn. 4, 719 (719-720).

58 Ibid.

59 See WHO, *Fifth meeting of the Emergency Committee under the International Health Regulations (2005)*, above Fn. 5.

60 There is a growing body of evidence confirming its link to microcephaly in newborns. For example see Brasil, P, José, P & Moreira, E et al., "Zika Virus Infection in Pregnant Women in Rio de Janeiro" (2016), 375 *New England Journal of Medicine*, 2321 (2332-2333).

6 Non-Emergencies as a Piece of the Puzzle

On par with the PHEIC declarations that have taken place, those occasions in which they have not been declared after an initial consideration merit further analysis. Information of why a situation did not constitute a PHEIC is just as relevant for clarifying its reach and applicability.[61] That being said, the appearance of Middle East respiratory syndrome in Saudi Arabia and South Korea since 2012, and the Yellow Fever crisis in Angola and the Democratic Republic of Congo in 2016[62] provide another piece of the puzzle. They were not determined to require a PHEIC declaration for their handling, despite being national emergencies on their own. And, unlike the West African Ebola crisis, such a cautious decision has thus far not yielded a devastating outcome, though this should by no means underestimate its danger.

To the question of which facts justify resorting to extraordinary measures, the narrative would be incomplete without addressing instances where the possibility of raising the alarm was discussed, but eventually discarded. It may be due to the epidemiological features of the corresponding viruses, or rather the social or economic context in which they took place. Whatever the reason, they also entail an exercise of authority through (technical) discretion on behalf of WHO officials. Decisions to not sound the alarm are just as consequential, and at times even moreso, than those to do so.

III Main International Legal Instruments Related to Disease Outbreaks

1 The Constitution of the WHO: The Core Mandate

According to its Constitution, and in light of its institutional history, responding to public health emergencies caused by communicable diseases is

61 In other instances, such as the spread of extensively drug-resistant tuberculosis, application of the IHR has been discussed outside of the WHO, but has not taken place. See the comment by Calain, P & Fidler, D, "XDR Tuberculosis, the New International Health Regulations, and Human Rights" (2007), 1 *Global Health Governance*, 1, available at http://bit.ly/2mYzBX8.

62 WHO, *Meeting of the Emergency Committee under the International Health Regulations (2005) concerning Yellow Fever*, available at http://www.who.int/mediacentre/news/statements/2016/ec-yellow-fever/en/.

one of the core functions of the WHO.[63] But the constant threat of epidemics and pandemics keeps raising questions as to which role the WHO already *has*, and which one it *should* have. For the purposes of this article, the descriptive and the normative elements are strictly distinguished. Any normative proposal should first be based on an accurate description, if it is to have any chance of succeeding *qua* proposal. As long as a steer in the leadership of the WHO can be accommodated within the basic legal framework, there can be diverging views on whether the WHO as an institution should have either an operative role or be limited to creating norms and standards.[64]

As a descriptive matter, the Constitution of the WHO has historically been understood as providing leeway in light of its broad wording.[65] Be that as it may, provisions within the Constitution constrain all of the WHO's bodies and officials. Therefore, concretely worded provisions cannot be circumvented, although the wording of several of the Constitution's Articles is vague, leaving ample room for their interpretation.[66] As seen during the SARS crisis, the established role of the WHO in its Constitution, as well as the broad definition of health in its Preamble, have led to it taking over emergency response even in the absence of an explicit mandate. It should be noted that this extended interpretation has not always been well received by Member States.[67]

2 The 2005 IHR

After the 2002-2003 SARS outbreak described above, a new consensus within the World Health Assembly emerged in order to revive the debate

63 Kamradt-Scott, *Managing Global Health Security*, above Fn. 21, 21.

64 For example see an opinion in favor of a normative role in Velasquez, G & Alas, M, "The slow shipwreck of the World Health Organization?" (2016), *Third World Network*, available at http://www.twn.my/title2/health.info/2016/hi160503.htm.

65 Lee, *The World Health Organization*, above Fn. 50, 16-21.

66 Making this point with regards to Article 18, see in this sense Burci & Vignes, *World Health Organization*, above Fn. 49, 56.

67 The idea of an overreach by the WHO was also raised in 1970 with regard to a cholera outbreak in Guinea. See Kamradt-Scott, A, "WHO's to blame? The World Health Organization and the 2014 Ebola outbreak in West Africa" (2016), 37 *Third World Quarterly*, 401 (402-403).

about reforming the 1969 IHR.[68] The result was a rarely seen[69] willingness to resort to the atypical[70] powers provided by Article 21 of the Constitution of the WHO. The outcome of this process was the approval in 2005 of the new version of the IHR, which is currently in force and represents the main international legal instrument for disease outbreak alert and response. The IHR are legally binding for WHO Member States,[71] as provided for in Articles 21-22 of its Constitution. State consent for being bound could then be traced back to an original delegation made through the approval of the Constitution itself, from 1946 onwards.

The underlying objective of the IHR, according to its Article 2, is the containment of the international spread of diseases through a public health response, whilst avoiding unnecessary interference with traffic and trade. This can be seen as the normative (in the sense of what *ought* to be) dimension of the IHR, and it is possible to interpret the descriptive part of its provisions with this lens. More specific arguments of whether particular public health measures, such as those foreseen in Part V of the IHR, are justified or not, can only be effectuated by contrasting available factual data with existing technical knowledge. It is not possible to ascertain whether a particular decision, such as denial of entry of persons or goods, are "more restrictive of international traffic [...] [or] more invasive or intrusive to persons than reasonably available alternatives" (Article 43 IHR), unless there is an assessment of the epidemiological features of a pathogen, which inevitably requires technical input from medical experts.

---

68 The debate had stagnated even after a World Health Assembly Resolution in 1995 called for such reforms in light of outbreaks of plague in India, and Ebola in Congo. See Resolution WHA48.7, World Health Assembly, 1998; also, Fidler, "From International Sanitary Conventions", above Fn. 25, 343; likewise, see the Editorial Comment, "Ebola: what lessons for the International Health Regulations?" (2014), 384 *The Lancet*, 1321 (1321).

69 See Aginam, O, "Mission (Im)possible? The WHO as a 'Norm Entrepreneur' in Global Health Governance" in Freeman, M, Hawkes, S & Bennett, B (eds.), *Law and Global Health. Current Legal Issues*, 2014, 559; labeling it a "cosmopolitan moment", see Kickbusch, I & Reddy, K, "Global health governance – The next political revolution" (2015), 129 *Public Health*, 838 (840).

70 Fidler, "From International Sanitary Conventions", above Fn. 25, 332-333.

71 However, this formal legal status can, of course, be detached from on-the-ground circumstances, as witnessed during the 2014-2016 Ebola crisis. See the contribution of *Susan L. Erikson*, "The Limits of the International Health Regulations: Ebola Governance, Regulatory Breach, and the Non-Negotiable Necessity of National Healthcare" in this volume.

The WHO's discretion in disease outbreaks is related to the way in which abstract legal norms of the IHR have been interpreted, so as to apply them to particular cases.[72] Interpretations are undertaken on a case-by-case basis, though it should be clarified that it is put into force through the application of rules of the IHR by what is generally referred to as "practice",[73] and not through dispute-settlement case law.[74] The broad wording of IHR provisions can give way to an expansion or reduction of its applicability in future instances, depending on who is interpreting them. A descriptive endeavor requires a broader approach in order to complete this picture. In this sense, the inclusion of expertise clauses within the IHR[75] leads to a specific type of leeway when applying a provision to a particular case. Consequently, in line with arguments put forward above, a descriptive statement of whether an IHR provision is legally applicable in a particular context can only be reached by resorting to the technical knowledge on the subject matter (such as Medicine, Public Health, Epidemiology).[76] The 2016 Zika emergency also shows how uncertainty can be invoked as sufficient grounds for declaring a PHEIC.[77]

a PHEIC Declarations

The legal definition of a PHEIC is a guiding axis in the legal role of the WHO *vis-à-vis* disease outbreaks. Once heralded as an innovative tool of

---

72 In Weberian terms, this would amount to a distinction between "lawmaking" and "lawfinding", wherein he also includes members of public administrations in charge of the application of a general rule to a particular case. Kennedy, D, "The Disenchantment of Logically Formal Legal Rationality, or Max Weber's Sociology in the Genealogy of the Contemporary Mode of Western Legal Thought" (2004), 55 *Hastings Law Journal*, 1031 (1040).

73 "Interpretation" is understood here in its wide sense, encompassing all applications of a rule to concrete cases. See on this matter Schermer, H & Blokker, N, *International Institutional Law*, above Fn. 30, 841 et seq.

74 See the contribution of *Leonie Vierck*, "The Case Law of International Public Health and Why its Scarcity is a Problem" in this volume.

75 Articles 47-49 of the 2005 IHR.

76 Articles 9 and 11(2) of the 2005 IHR.

77 Annex 2 of the IHR provides examples of diseases which will be notified to the WHO on the basis of their likelihood of being a PHEIC. It is an "open list" of diseases, as drawn upon the following clause: "including those of unknown causes or sources".

the 2005 version of the IHR,[78] its heterogeneous application between one case and another illustrates how its flexibility has been adopted by WHO public officials, namely its Director-General and the IHR Emergency Committee. This legal definition has thus far been used in events related to the international spread of an infectious disease (H1N1 influenza, Poliomyelitis, Ebola and Zika). Amidst the vague wording of its definition in Article 1 IHR,[79] every one of these PHEIC Declarations has had its own particular features, both from a legal and a medical perspective.

The question of how far this figure can be extended is a matter of interpretation by WHO officials. Public statements informing that a PHEIC has been declared may contain a more or less detailed description of the facts motivating this step. Yet explanations provided for doing so tend to be brief, with statements being nowhere near as thorough as, for example, a ruling by a Court would be. As case law related to PHEICs is mostly absent[80] despite there being a dispute-settlement mechanism established by Article 56 IHR, there is still no possibility to extract elaborate legal interpretations like those deriving from the reconstruction of facts by adjudicative bodies.

Additionally, the binary feature of either having a PHEIC or not has recently been revisited and subjected to criticism.[81] Attempts at reforming the current configuration of PHEIC declarations have not been fruitful,[82] even though, as explained in a subsequent section, there are ongoing changes to the internal WHO structure in the corresponding area. While the current formulation of PHEICs is riddled with questions concerning their relevance

---

78 Labeling it as one of the "major substantive" novelties of the 2005 IHR, see Fidler, "From International Sanitary Conventions", above Fn. 25, 358.

79 The definition of a PHEIC in Article 1 IHR reads as follows:
"[…] an extraordinary event which is determined, as provided in these Regulations:
(i) to constitute a public health risk to other States through the international spread of disease and
(ii) to potentially require a coordinated international response."

80 See the contributions of *Leonie Vierck*, "The Case Law of International Public Health and Why its Scarcity is a Problem" and *Susan L. Erikson*, "The Limits of the International Health Regulations: Ebola Governance, Regulatory Breach, and the Non-Negotiable Necessity of National Healthcare" in this volume.

81 WHO, *Report of the Ebola Interim Assessment Panel*, para. 23, available at http://bit.ly/1CYf2Yv.

82 WHO, *Report of the Review Committee on the Role of the International Health Regulations (2005) in the Ebola Outbreak and Response*, World Health Assembly document A69/21, 2016, para. 104-109.

for disease outbreak preparedness and response, the perils of being over- or underused can already be factually attested.

b Temporary Technical Recommendations

On par with a declaration of a PHEIC, the WHO Director-General can issue temporary recommendations after consulting the corresponding Emergency Committee. These tag-along recommendations issued during a PHEIC in light of Article 12(2) could not be considered as "new" legal obligations for Member States.[83] According to Article 18 IHR, temporary recommendations range from providing safety measures for medical personnel to placing persons under quarantine and isolation, as well as suggesting States to implement travel bans or, conversely, refraining from doing so.[84] As seen during the 2014-2016 Ebola epidemic in West Africa, Security Council Resolution 2177 (2014), declaring this outbreak a "threat to international peace and security" amounted to invoking chapter VII of the UN Charter.[85] This included a mention of the temporary recommendations issued by the WHO, for example abstaining from imposing general travel bans to the most affected countries.[86] Nevertheless, in this contribution they are not seen as having elevated technical recommendations to a binding level.[87]

---

83 See the contribution of *Robert Frau*, "Combining the WHO's International Health Regulations (2005) with the UN Security Council's Powers: Does it Make Sense for Health Governance?" in this volume. Also, see WHO, *Report of the Review Committee*, above Fn. 82, para. 68. However, in no way does this suggest that they are irrelevant. See Kamradt-Scott, "WHO's to blame?", above Fn. 67, 411; likewise, Benton, J, "Global Emergency Power in the Age of Ebola" (2016), 57 *Harvard International Law Journal*, 1 (23-26).

84 Technical recommendations issued when the West African Ebola crisis was declared a PHEIC on August 8, 2014, favored not implementing general travel bans to the affected countries, but rather to install individual screening processes for possible cases instead. See the WHO, *Statement on the 1st meeting*, above Fn. 2.

85 To this effect, see the contributions of *Robert Frau*, "Combining the WHO's International Health Regulations (2005) with the UN Security Council's Powers: Does it Make Sense for Health Governance?" and *Ilja Robert Pavone*, "Ebola and Securitization of Health: UN Security Council Resolution 2177/2014 and its Limits" in this volume.

86 United Nations Security Council Resolution 2177 (2014), para. 9.

87 See the contribution of *Robert Frau*, "Combining the WHO's International Health Regulations (2005) with the UN Security Council's Powers: Does it Make Sense for Health Governance?" in this volume.

Likewise, proposals to imbue them with a binding nature have not prospered, as this approach has been deemed by some as "recycled" and unlikely to be accepted by States.[88] Still other arguments deal with whether recommendations *are* (descriptively), in fact, more than that, or whether they *should* (normatively) be something more. After all, if disregarding technical recommendations issued on par with a PHEIC constitute a violation of the IHR per se, they might actually have a different legal status. To consider the status of temporary recommendations as legally binding[89] would thus render the WHO, and its Director-General in particular, into perhaps the most powerful of the specialized agencies of the UN. It would also entail that the more legally-intrusive recommendations, such as those promoting the declaration of national emergencies, might touch upon sensitive sovereignty issues. This debate, however, will not be further developed in this article. Suffice it to say, that the view considering the WHO's temporary recommendations as legally binding will not be adopted along these lines.

IV Functions of WHO's Bodies in the Context of Disease Outbreaks

The internal governance structure of the WHO does not differ dramatically in comparison to those of other International Organizations.[90] As mentioned before, most of its functions are directly drawn out from the Constitution of the WHO, whereas others derive from the IHR. A brief outline of each of the main bodies can be illustrative as an overview of the governance for disease outbreak alert and response within the WHO.

---

88 Namely, see Fidler, D, "Ebola Report Misses Mark on International Health Regulations" (2015), *Chatham House Expert Comment*, available at http://bit.ly/2lSS2Yk.

89 See for example Acconci, P, "The Reaction to the Ebola Epidemic within the United Nations Framework: What Next for the World Health Organization?" in Lachenmann, F, Röder, T & Wolfrum, R (eds.), *Max Planck Yearbook of United Nations Law*, 2014, 423.

90 For a general sketch of the structure of International Organizations, see Davies, M & Woodward, R, *International Organizations. A Companion*, 2014, 87-88.

1 The World Health Assembly

As the supreme decision-making authority of the WHO,[91] the World Health Assembly can assign new competences to the other organs, as well as limit their scope.[92] It is also the organ in charge of ultimately reforming the IHR. Insofar as it has a one member, one vote system, there is a *prima facie* democratic element to decisions within the WHO. In this sense, the World Health Assembly acts as a norm-creator, providing a general framework of action for other bodies to follow. For the purposes of this contribution, the most salient powers of the World Health Assembly are those inserted in Articles 21 and 22 of its Constitution, which grant the authority to adopt legally binding regulations for all Member States, unless they explicitly reject this within a determined period (opt out). Given how voting-based processes may make the World Health Assembly unsuitable for dealing with emergencies caused by disease outbreaks, executive decision-making can be justified on grounds of celerity. It is at this point where the role performed by the WHO's administrative branch enters the scene.

2 The Secretariat

a WHO Director-General

The degree of autonomy possessed by the WHO's Secretariat as established in Article 37 of its Constitution has led to it being considered, along with other International Organisations (IO) from the United Nations with legal mandates, as reaching beyond initial consent by Member States.[93] As a display of expedient decision-making in the context of emergencies, the

---

91 The list of its broad powers is enshrined in Article 18 of the Constitution of the WHO.

92 Perhaps the most telling example of this is how the World Health Assembly's reforms to its Rules of Procedure have led to limiting Director-General's reelection to only one additional term, despite the fact that the Constitution of the WHO contains no such limitation. See Rule 106 of the Rules of Procedure of the World Health Assembly.

93 Explained with more detail in Kamradt-Scott, *Managing Global Health Security*, above Fn. 21, 37; also Cortell, A & Peterson, S, "Dutiful agents, rogue actors, or both? Staffing, voting rules, and slack in the WHO and WTO" in Hawkins, D, Lake D A & Nielson, D L et al. (eds.), *Delegation and Agency in International Organizations*, 2006, 265.

Secretariat of the WHO, headed by the Director-General, is the organ with the exclusive authority in terms of the IHR for issuing PHEIC Declarations and temporary technical recommendations.

Similar to national administrative law, the head of the Executive body in the WHO performs an exclusive decision-making role in emergency settings. But, unlike several national constituencies,[94] there is no corresponding legal procedure for overturning Director-General's exercise of discretion when using the powers granted by Article 12 of the IHR. Aside from obligations to report to the World Health Assembly under Article 54 of the IHR, the Director-General's discretion does not foresee the possibility of legally challenging its decisions regarding PHEIC declarations. The only accountability mechanism is the option of creating ex-post Review Committees under Articles 50-53 of the IHR; that is, only *after* the emergency alert has been issued.

b Emergency Committee

Although the adoption of the IHR did not lead to a structural overhaul inside the WHO, it did lead to the creation of intermittent bodies such as the Emergency Committee. According to Articles 12 and 48 of the IHR, the WHO Director-General is obliged to "consult" an Emergency Committee before declaring a PHEIC. The Committee will be convened with specialists of the relevant fields chosen by the WHO Director-General, a feature that displays its technocratic nature.[95] Yet the Middle East respiratory syndrome outbreaks in Saudi Arabia and South Korea and the ongoing Yellow Fever crisis in African countries display how the process of declaring PHEICs is not necessarily streamlined after the WHO Director-General's preliminary assessment under Article 12 of the IHR. Hence, the Emergency Committee's autonomy is not just a theoretical possibility, since its mere summoning has not always led to a PHEIC Declaration. As seen in the cases described in previous paragraphs, the constant convergence between the Emergency Committee's advice and the Director-General's final decisions reaffirms the former's sway in determining whether a PHEIC should be declared or not.

---

94 This contrast between national and international administrative acts is also discussed in Benvenisti, E, *The Law of Global Governance*, 2014, 96-98.

95 Here, "technocracy" is understood as decision-making by a body of experts, which do not necessarily rely on their democratic credentials. See Barnett & Finnemore, *Rules for the World*, above Fn. 16, 83-85.

It is very difficult – though legally still possible – to imagine a scenario in which the Director-General disregards the input by the Emergency Committee altogether.

3 WHO Regional Organizations

In the cases of the 2009 A(H1N1) Influenza pandemic and the 2016 Zika outbreak, the governments of primarily affected countries,[96] particularly through their Ministries of Health, notified the WHO through their National IHR Focal Points. Conversely, at the outset of the Ebola crisis in April 2014, even though national authorities were in continuous communication with the WHO, it was a Non-Governmental Organization (Médecins Sans Frontières) insisting on the need to take more urgent measures.[97] As discussed above, the declaration only took place several months later, leading to widespread criticism of the WHO's response.

As mentioned elsewhere in this edited volume,[98] decision-making at WHO headquarters has been based on factual assessments of the severity of the outbreak. While the technical aspects of epidemiological surveillance are beyond the reach of this contribution, it is perhaps illustrative how complexities inherent to this task can mislead even renowned experts, casting light upon how complicated such an assessment may become.

Secondly, differences in expediency could also be attributed to diverging capacities of the national and regional health institutions in each of the affected regions.[99] The WHO receives regular notifications through the IHR National Focal Points, with the assumption that under Article 6 of the IHR, national authorities have the legal responsibility to notify the International Organization. The WHO itself does not have sufficient capacity to deploy

---

96 Specifically, in the case of A(H1N1) Influenza, the National IHR Focal Points of Mexico and the United States of America; in the case of Zika, Brazil's National IHR Focal Point.

97 Moon, Sridhar & Pate et al., "Will Ebola change the game?", above Fn. 44, 2206.

98 See particularly the contribution of *Wolfgang Hein*, "The Response to the West African Ebola Outbreak (2014-2016): A Failure of Global Health Governance?" in this volume.

99 For a study on the role of regional institutions in West Africa during the Ebola crisis, see the contribution of *Edefe Ojomo*, "Fostering Regional Health Governance in West Africa: The Role of the WAHO" in this volume.

on-the-ground surveillance in every country, as this would require considerably more resources than it currently has. It could also possibly lead to even more controversies related to interferences with State sovereignty.

Thirdly, and similar to the national levels, the WHO Regional Organizations' role is supposed to be that of a more direct operator in the countries of different regions. Article 44 of the IHR (2005) vaguely contemplates the possibility of "collaboration" of the WHO with its Member States on several fronts, which may also take place through the WHO Regional Organizations, each of them composed of Committees and Offices. Yet, aside from ample and unspecific collaborative possibilities enumerated in Article 44, there is no clear role for the Regional Organizations in the case of PHEICs.

The "federalist"[100] arrangement between WHO Headquarters and its Regional Organizations has also been criticized by virtue of the fragmentation of functions it caused, mainly during emergency settings.[101] After failed attempts at the beginning of the 2000s to unify decision-making processes within the WHO,[102] lack of oversight over decision-making within its Regional Organizations allowed for the appointment of several officials almost exclusively as political rewards, instead of the legally-based criteria of professional merits or technical expertise.[103] Thus, the lack of coordination witnessed during the West African Ebola crisis showcased how underlying shortcomings at the WHO's Regional Organizations can spill over to the central, broader institution.

---

100 Hanrieder, T, "The path-dependent design of international organizations: Federalism in the World Health Organization" (2015), 21 *European Journal of International Relations*, 215 (223-226).

101 Benton, "Global Emergency Power", above Fn. 83, 29-30.

102 The objectives and results of the "One WHO" campaign contribute to this understanding. See Lee, *The World Health Organization*, above Fn. 50; Hanrieder, T, *International Organization in Time. Fragmentation and Reform*, 2015, 93-116.

103 For a glimpse at these criticisms, see WHO, *Report of the Review Committee on the Role of the International Health Regulations (2005)*, above Fn. 82, para. 176 et seq.

V *The Promises and Pitfalls in the Governance of Disease Outbreaks*

1 Fleshing Out "Bad" Governance in Disease Outbreaks

A combination of factors have been interpreted as the source of the dysfunctional response to the surge of Ebola in 2014. The Ebola crisis displayed how on-the-ground assessments of the severity of outbreaks are not always streamlined, least of all when dealing with disagreements between experts on the subject matter.[104] Additionally, during the previous year when the Ebola crisis was declared as a PHEIC, there were severe budget cuts to the WHO's Emergency branch.[105]

The process that led to the current budgetary stagnation, starting from the 1980s, has been documented elsewhere.[106] Partly as a result of the chronic budgetary problems, there is a dominance of voluntary contributions, which are "earmarked" for favored donor projects.[107] Hence, the WHO bodies often have little to no say on where and how to allocate resources. This has been the source of many ailments within the WHO governance throughout the last three decades, and the governance of disease outbreaks is not exempt from this disruptive inertia.

Likewise, debates between Member States within the WHO, and specifically within the World Health Assembly, are likely to lead to occasional disagreements. It would not be a deliberative forum if this possibility did not exist. Still, there are concerns related to the constant paralysis and the varying level of discussions within this organ.[108] And, in effect, the afore-

104 Particularly, see the heated disagreement between Médecins Sans Frontières, on one hand, and WHO and Centers for Disease Control and Prevention (CDC) officials, on the other. For a more detailed description of the initial assessments of the magnitude of the Ebola crisis by several experts, see the contribution of *Wolfgang Hein*, "The Response to the West African Ebola Outbreak (2014-2016): A Failure of Global Health Governance?" in this volume.

105 Moon, Sridhar & Pate et al., "Will Ebola change the game?", above Fn. 44, 2210.

106 Mostly, it is the result of the decision of Member States to impose a policy of zero growth on its contributions to the United Nations system. See Beigbeder, Y, *The World Health Organization*, 1998, 154; see also the contribution of *Mateja Steinbrück Platise*, "The Changing Structure of Global Health Governance" in this volume.

107 Gostin, L, *Global Health Law*, 2014, 123-125.

108 Lee, K & Pang, T, "WHO: Retirement or reinvention?" (2014), 128 *Public Health*, 119 (122).

mentioned budgetary problems can themselves be seen as a result of political dysfunction within the WHO. In the context of the Cold War, ideological disagreements between the two competing powers led to stalemates at the UN level.[109] Belief in the possibility of having politically isolated decision-making in the WHO has been heavily contested.[110]

Furthermore, in tune with the understanding of International Organizations as bureaucracies,[111] legal analysis usually focuses on impersonal rules and norms, hence the personal dimension of discretion tends to be overlooked.[112] But the fact that there is a high degree of leeway in several provisions of the IHR makes paying attention to the personal dimension all the more necessary. Even if this falls beyond the limits of the current analysis, multiple calls for leadership renewal and a change of mindset have gained more relevance in several instances.[113] Persons in charge of interpreting norms matter as well. Until today, PHEIC Declarations have only been issued under one Director-General's mandate. The possibility for each Director-General to provide her/his own imprint under both the Constitution of the WHO and the IHR is reason enough for paying attention to the person occupying that post.

For instance, when comparing the 2009-2010 A(H1N1) influenza pandemic with the 2014-2016 Ebola crisis, both a premature and a delayed response can reflect upon the WHO Director-General's role at the helm of the institution. By questioning the appropriateness of the model of executive authority for declaring a PHEIC, the possibility of delegating this function on another organ was put forward on some fronts.[114] Even if these proposals

---

109 Notably, the backlash against the Alma-Ata Declaration of 1978. Lee, *The World Health Organization*, above Fn. 50, 14 (79-86).

110 Benton, "Global Emergency Power", above Fn. 83, at footnote 160.

111 Barnett & Finnemore, *Rules for the World*, above Fn. 16, 17-19.

112 The longstanding impersonal element in legal analysis is also linked to *Max Weber*'s conception of legally-legitimized authority. It should be noted, though, that Weber himself posited that the "pure" versions of authority are seldom to be found, allowing for a mixture of personal and impersonal modes. See Weber, M, *Max Weber on Law in Economy and Society (edited by Max Rheinstein)*, 1969, 334-337.

113 This includes literature within the medical community. See Moon, Sridhar & Pate et al., "Will Ebola change the game?", above Fn. 44, 2204.

114 See WHO, *Report of the Ebola Interim Assessment Panel*, above Fn. 81; see also WHO, *Report of the Review Committee on the Role of the International Health Regulations (2005)*, above Fn. 82, para. 160.

did not prosper, it might reflect a loss of confidence towards the unipersonal model.

2 In Search of Normative Answers to Technical Discretion

The legal framing of PHEICs, as envisioned by the 2005 version of the IHR, can be construed as granting leeway to the WHO, and particularly to its Director-General. One of the main reasons for the obsolescence of the 1969 version of the IHR was its rigid approach towards diseases, which left new and reemerging pathogens out of its purview.[115] Given how uncertainty is an ever-present factor in disease outbreak preparedness and response, a broad approach can be justified. The complexities of every outbreak entail that a definite, "one-size-fits-all" legal category is a long shot. Existing knowledge in the field of Epidemiology has not reached the level of complete foresight. To the contrary, uncertainty and risk regarding communicable diseases are a constant, as witnessed with the spread of Zika virus.

The powers of the WHO's Director-General deriving from the IHR do not constitute a "blank check". The conundrum has been, and will continue to be, how to draw a clear line between over- and underreacting. An overarching challenge is how to better ensure the justified use of powers when authorities such as the Director-General and the Emergency Committee engage in interpretation. In light of the heterogeneous set of events that can fall under the purview of PHEIC declarations, a more fine-tuned predetermined framework is currently not available.[116] Devising one would also require a technical-medical assessment which, in fact, acquires a legal dimension at the same time. The broad wording of the IHR can be seen as factually justified amidst prevailing uncertainties. As exemplified by the contrast between the controversy surrounding the cases of H1N1 influenza and Ebola, flexibility also entails granting more room for wrongful assessments with fatal consequences.

If a higher level of discretion is directly proportionate to the need for its normative assessment, the fact that flexibility is justified on technical grounds is not enough on its own to settle the normative discussion. Exercises of authority by International Organizations need to be subjected to

115 For more on this matter, see Villarreal, "Pandemic Declarations as an Exercise", above Fn. 35.

116 Benton, "Global Emergency Power", above Fn. 83, 35-36.

normative standards, with corresponding responses deriving from legal approaches.[117] Even if authority exercised by WHO officials is not deliberation-based in the same democratic vein as that of other institutions,[118] it does not mean normative assessments are pointless.[119] The current accountability model contemplates an ex-post evaluation by an External Review Committee. Moreover, reviews do not have a legally binding nature by themselves. At most, they can lead to an adverse resolution by the World Health Assembly and the legal nature of these acts *vis-à-vis* Member States can be contested.

The political momentum created by the catastrophic magnitude of the West African Ebola epidemic has thus far led to noticeable, albeit not dramatic, internal reforms. For instance, further adding to the existing governance framework, the creation of a Health Emergency Programme was proposed at the 69th World Health Assembly in May 2016, including delegation of logistical but not decision-making functions to other administrative posts.[120] This, of course, is a minor step towards addressing the roots of the "bad" governance issues underlying disease outbreak preparedness and response in the WHO.

One proposal for enhancing the governance related to emergency decision-making in the WHO would be to introduce a series of additional *ex ante* assessments that aim at guaranteeing that these declarations have justified grounds.[121] The problem is its practical feasibility: The WHO reportedly receives more than three hundred yearly notifications of events that might constitute a PHEIC.[122] Additional hurdles could effectively overload an already overburdened structure, which might prove to be untenable resource-wise.[123]

Likewise, there have been discussions related to the legal responsibility of the WHO when declaring a PHEIC. Despite their current embryonic

---

117 Bogdandy, Dann & Goldmann, "Developing the Publicness", above Fn. 12, 13-16.

118 Already posited by Stein, E, "International Integration and Democracy: No Love at First Sight" (2001), 95 *American Journal of International Law*, 489 (497-499 and 532).

119 Delbrück, "Exercising Public Authority", above Fn. 18, 42.

120 See the Report by Direct-General to the 69th World Health Assembly, *Reform of WHO's work in health emergency management,* May 5, 2016, particularly para. 5.

121 Benton, "Global Emergency Power", above Fn. 83, 40.

122 See WHO, *Report of the Review Committee on the Role of the International Health Regulations (2005)*, above Fn. 82, para. 91.

123 Ibid., para. 88 and 107.

stage, the (Draft) Articles on the Responsibility of International Organizations provide a parameter for this matter. According to *Burci* and *Feinäugle*, declaring a PHEIC without following the steps stipulated within the IHR for doing so could possibly lead to responsibility on behalf of the WHO.[124] There is still a long way ahead for reaching this goal, as determining the existence of responsibility would give way to lengthy procedures filled with countless bureaucratic obstacles and fact-finding tasks consuming essential economic resources. Therefore, a formal proposal of this kind, logically and legally sound as it may be, would have to first circumvent the factual limitations present in the complicated scenario of the responsibility of Inter-national Organizations in general,[125] a problem ranging far beyond the WHO.

VI Conclusion

The failure to effectively respond to the 2014-2016 West African Ebola crisis put several structural shortcomings of the WHO into the fore. Among them, the governance framework for dealing with epidemics and pandemics stands out. Insofar as disease outbreak preparedness and response is one of the pillars of international cooperation in the field of health, it is all the more reason to be concerned with the status of affairs as it stands.

It is only after reaching an understanding of the governance framework from a descriptive perspective that normative work can aim at successfully tackling a problem. Given how public health emergencies do not wait for the "appropriate" moment, discussions of legal reforms take place as the subject matter is in motion. For the time being, the exercise of international public authority in the case of disease outbreaks relies mostly upon technical expertise, under the assumption that it is more likely to lead to an accurate result. Consequently, assessments on the justification of the use of

---

124 Although issuing a PHEIC Declaration falls under the authority of WHO Director-General, according to Article 6 of the Draft Articles on the Responsibility of International Organizations, legal responsibility for actions of an organization's organs or agents falls upon the organization itself. See Burci, G & Feinäugle, C, "The ILC's articles seen from a WHO perspective" in Ragazzi, M (ed.), *Responsibility of International Organizations. Essays in memory of Sir Ian Brownlie*, 2013, 186.

125 The challenge of determining when exactly an International Organization has acted wrongfully in legal terms is also presented in Blokker, N, "Member State Responsibility for Wrongdoings of International Organizations" (2015), 12 *International Organizations Law Review*, 319 (324).

legal powers cannot be untangled from the technical dimension of decisions. Even if not all facts can be interpreted under the aegis of causality, there will be no lessons learned unless there is explicit recognition of what went wrong, including, among other things, the scientific input of experts.

Claims against the WHO's lack of celerity in the 2014 West African Ebola crisis shed light on the fact that legal acts such as a PHEIC declaration can fulfill vital functions for addressing an initially local outbreak. As discussed throughout the article, the process leading to this declaration is not necessarily straightforward. Obstacles may result from either a wrongful assessment of the situation by decision-makers, or a long-standing pathological governance permeating across the whole of the institution.

In sum, the flexibility of norms within the IHR require balancing between the weight of the governance framework, and the particular acts by officials. Although this article focuses more on the first aspect, the latter dimension should not be underestimated when engaging in further analysis. An overview of the governance issues can help to incorporate additional elements for obtaining a more complete picture of what goes wrong during public health emergencies, and to what extent the shortcomings can be attributed to the framework of disease outbreak preparedness and response. Normative appraisals for improvements need to be solidly grounded on accurate factual and legal diagnostics. Otherwise, future attempts at improvements may amount to trying to construct a skyscraper without noticing its fragile foundations: By the time the problem is identified, it may already be too late to change course.

Fostering Regional Health Governance in West Africa: The Role of the WAHO

*Edefe Ojomo**

Abstract

Global, regional and national responses to the recent Ebola crisis revealed considerable gaps in the various health governance frameworks, leading to calls for reform. While most analyses have focused on national and global institutions and challenges, this paper discusses the role of regional institutions and their governance challenges. It argues that regional institutions can make up for weaknesses in national governance systems. However, they must overcome governance challenges that flow from state control over regional processes, especially where such states have capacity and legitimacy deficits. It discusses the role of the West African Health Organisation (WAHO), the specialized institution of the Economic Community of West African States responsible for health governance in the region. This article is part of a broader research frame on regional governance in areas with governance challenges caused by capacity and legitimacy deficits.

This research proposes new ways of thinking about and practicing regional (health) governance in West Africa, by focusing not only on capacity building but also on enhancing the legitimacy of governance actors. Regional institutions occupy a particularly important position, where they can provide a larger pool of resources that creates an insurance scheme for states

---

* Lecturer, Faculty of Law, University of Lagos, and JSD Candidate, New York University School of Law.
I gratefully acknowledge the useful comments of and discussions with Professors *Eyal Benvenisti*, *Benedict Kingsbury*, *Grainne De Burca*, *Thomas D'Aunno*, *Kevin Davis*, *Lewis Kornhauser*, and *Daniel Abebe*, as well as the very helpful comments and assistance of *Edema Ojomo*, *Thomas Streinz*, *Leonie Vierck*, *Daniel Stewart*, *Margaret Kadiri*, *Ryan Liss*, *Joanna Langille*, and *Sumeya Mulla*, and feedback from participants of the "Comparative Law, International Law in US Law & IR/IL" session at the 2015 Salzburg Cutler Seminar, the 2015/2016 Legal Theory Thesis Seminar at NYU Law, and the 2016 Workshop on International Health Governance organized by the Max Planck Institute for Comparative Public Law and International Law. All websites last accessed November 18, 2016.

in the event of crises. They can also enhance the legitimacy of national and global processes and institutions by supplying an alternative governance structure that regulates relations amongst governance actors and targets.

I Introduction

International cooperation, involving global and regional intergovernmental institutions, states acting unilaterally, as well as prominent international Non-Governmental Organizations (NGOs), was central to the response to the 2014 Ebola outbreak in West Africa.[1] While international cooperation is a critical and inevitable element of the current interdependent international community of states, it is more so in the case of states with weak institutions whose citizens can no longer rely on them for the supply of basic needs. Citizens of these states must look beyond the state for governance solutions, and regional institutions might be able to enhance the legitimacy and capacity required to meet their needs. However, in the context of such states, regional institutions must also overcome the control of states in order to be effective, and this has not been the case in West Africa, as the response to the Ebola outbreak revealed.

National and international efforts to contain the spread of the Ebola virus reveal significant gaps in the global framework for the promotion of public health, such as funding deficits in the World Health Organization (WHO), questionable response mechanisms at the national, regional and global levels, and poor coordination of efforts by authorities at different levels;[2] but, a prominent issue that has remained at the core of such discussions is the governance deficit in the countries most affected by the outbreak, the re-

1 This paper adopts a global governance approach to the study of international institutions, thus looking beyond traditional subjects of international law to investigate sites of power, capacity and legitimacy. See Kingsbury, B, Kirsch, N & Stewart, R, "The Emergence of Global Administrative Law" (2005), 68 *Law & Contemporary Problems*, 15; Slaughter, A, *The New World Order*, 2004; Mattli, W & Buthe, T, *The New Global Rulers: The Privatization Of Regulation In The World Economy*, 2011.

2 See Moon, S, Sridhar, D & Pate, M A et al., "Will Ebola change the game? Ten essential reforms before the next pandemic. The report of the Harvard-LSHTM Independent Panel on the Global Response to Ebola" (2015), 386 *The Lancet*, 2204; McKay, B & Wonacott, P, "After Slow Ebola Response, WHO Seeks to Avoid Repeat" (December 29, 2014), *The Wall Street Journal*, http://on.wsj.com/13Px9Et.

sultant spillover effects, and how these can be addressed. The focus on national institutions appears to overlook important subnational, transnational and regional governance structures.

This paper addresses questions related to regional governance that arise from the Ebola epidemic in West Africa. It seeks to show how the severity of the outbreak was closely linked to the weakness of governance structures that have been unable to fulfill their objectives, particularly with regard to healthcare. Rather than focus on traditional state-building and global governance mechanisms, which have been – and continue to be – prevalent in some of the countries affected by the outbreak, this paper goes further and proposes a more comprehensive approach to fostering governance for the citizens of countries with weak national institutions. The main argument is that regional institutions have significant governance roles that are shaped by the condition of other governance structures. This study provides a basic introduction to the possibilities of focusing on regional institution building to address governance challenges.

This is not a discussion of the technicalities of national, regional or global public health issues. The paper simply uses the Ebola outbreak and the related narratives and responses as a backdrop for discussing issues relating to governance and institutional performance. The choice of the Ebola outbreak as a case study was dictated by the dire nature of the outbreak, as it revealed quite vigorously how national crises can affect regional and global communities and how the latter respond. The relevant themes of state fragility, interacting governance orders, and development assistance and intervention are potent in the Ebola narratives and subsequent evaluations of the experience.

Part II of the paper provides a brief narrative about the outbreak of the Ebola epidemic in West Africa. Part III discusses the response of national and global health governance structures to the epidemic and analyzes the underlying governance implications. Part IV examines the current practice of regional governance in West Africa within the context of the Ebola outbreak, pointing out weaknesses in the existing framework. The paper then discusses the importance of enhancing capacity and legitimacy in regional institutions to develop effective governance structures, and identifies possible challenges to the establishment of such a system. Part V concludes with a summary of the discussions and argument.

II Ebola: An Infection of Sovereign Statehood

The 2014 Ebola outbreak in West Africa began with the death of a child in Guinea in December 2013. Over the course of four months, the disease spread to neighboring Liberia and Sierra Leone, and by the end of the year, there were reported incidents in Nigeria, Mali, Senegal, Spain and the United States. In August 2014, the WHO declared the crisis a "public health emergency of international concern", which lasted until March 2016.[3]

This analysis identifies three factors as having contributed to the spread of the disease in Guinea and amongst its neighbors, Liberia and Sierra Leone, namely: poor health care and infrastructure; slow government intervention in rural areas; and the porosity of borders. While the disease also spread into Mali, Nigeria and Senegal in West Africa, the outbreak was more effectively contained in these countries; interestingly, the second element, absence of government in rural areas, did not come into play in those states because the identified incidents happened in cities.

1 The Infrastructure and Personnel Deficit

Guinea, Liberia, and Sierra Leone, the countries most affected by the Ebola outbreak and the consequent epidemic, have endured severe political crises over the past three decades, resulting in civil wars in Liberia and Sierra Leone with spillover implications for Guinea.[4] These situations depleted gravely scarce resources and led to the destruction of already limited infrastructure. In addition to the infrastructure deficit, there is also a shortage of qualified health care workers in the countries affected. Consequently, the domestic healthcare system that should have provided a first response to the outbreak was severely broken down and, therefore, insufficient to provide

---

3 The contributions of *Wolfgang Hein*, "The Response to the West African Ebola Outbreak (2014-2016): A Failure of Global Health Governance?" and *Michael Marx*, "Ebola Epidemic 2014-2015: Taking Control or Being Trapped in the Logic of Failure – What Lessons Can Be Learned?" in this volume provide details of the timelines and narratives about the conditions under which the outbreak occurred.

4 See Olonisakin, F, "Children and Armed Conflict" in Adebajo, A & Ismail Rashid, I (eds.), *West Africa's Security Challenges: Building Peace in a Troubled Region*, 2004, 245 (252); Lowenkopf, M, "Liberia: Putting the State Back Together" in Zartman, W (ed.), *Collapsed States: The Disintegration and Restoration of Legitimate Authority*, 1995, 91 (95).

the necessary healthcare assistance required to address an epidemic of such proportions.[5] Notably, these profoundly underequipped systems were also dealing with other severe disease outbreaks such as cholera, dengue fever, Lassa fever, malaria, yellow fever and HIV/AIDS.[6]

The situation revealed serious capacity deficits in these countries, with external assistance providing the bulk of national healthcare needs.[7] Thus, the state, in these instances, has been unable to provide basic healthcare services to the majority of its population, generating significant implications for the relationship between the state and its citizens.

2 Absence of Government in Rural Areas

African states were built upon a system established to dominate local societies and extract resources for the benefit of non-locals,[8] and governance is built upon the existence of formal, non-indigenous and informal, indigenous systems.[9] The resultant rural-urban divide reveals, in geographical terms, where the state begins and where it ends, not just in influence and penetration but also in legitimate control. Legitimacy in most poor and rural societies lies in informal systems that are usually based on ethnic affiliations while the state and its formal institutions are regarded with suspicion and

5 For details of the health governance deficits in these countries, see the contribution of *Michael Marx*, "Ebola Epidemic 2014-2015: Taking Control or Being Trapped in the Logic of Failure – What Lessons Can Be Learned?" in this volume.

6 Garrett, L, "Ebola's Lessons: How the WHO Mishandled the Crisis" (September/October 2015), *Foreign Affairs*, https://www.foreignaffairs.com/articles/west-africa/2015-08-18/ebolas-lessons.

7 See Sayegh, J, "Ebola and the Health Care Crisis in Liberia" (October 2014), *Cultural Anthropology*, http://bit.ly/2mfhA6Q; Hughes, J, Glassman, A & Glenigale, W, "Innovative Financing in Early Recovery: The Liberian Health Sector Pool Fund" (February 2012), *288 Working Paper, Centre For Global Development*, http://bit.ly/2lEXFN9.

8 See Nkrumah, K, *Africa Must Unite*, 1963.

9 See Davidson, B, *The Black Man's Burden: Africa and The Curse of the Nation State*, 1992; Mamdani, M, *Citizen And Subject: Contemporary Africa And The Legacy Of Late Colonialism,* 1996; Young, C, *The African Colonial State in Comparative Perspective*, 1994; Okafor, O, *Redefining Legitimate Statehood: International Law and State Fragmentation in Africa*, 2000, 32.

hostility. Legitimacy, in the current analysis, refers to sociological legitimacy, especially where parallel institutions perform similar roles.[10]

When the outbreak began in Guéckédou, the distance between the state and the people was depicted by the difficulty faced by institutional bureaucracies in linking resources in the urban capital with those in the hinterlands. Rural and poor communities in Liberia and Sierra Leone suffered a similar fate. But, in Nigeria and Senegal, the first cases occurred in Lagos and Dakar, where there were medical facilities to quickly identify and handle the cases.[11] In Liberia and Sierra Leone, urban slums and rural communities were physically cordoned off and residents "imprisoned" in their communities by gates and "check points" that kept them separate from "the state".[12] Thus, an important theme in the relationship between state and society in many African countries was depicted in the Ebola outbreak. It is not only that the state is separate from the people, but that the people are hostile towards the state, its institutions and officials.[13] In addition, the absence of the state in vast areas of the physical – as well as social, economic, and political – territory makes it less effective to control its "sovereign territory", leading to practically and normatively meaningless border demarcations between countries.[14]

10 This paper focuses on sociological legitimacy in Weberian terms, following the definition of legitimacy as the acceptance of the validity of exercise of power. "[…] the legitimacy of a system of control has far more than a mere 'ideal' significance […]. What is important is the fact that in a given case the particular claim to legitimacy is to a significant degree and according to its type treated as 'valid'; that this fact confirms the position of the persons claiming authority and that it helps to determine the choice of means of its exercise." Weber, M, *Economy And Society* (Roth, G & Wittich, C (eds.)), 1978.

11 WHO, *The Outbreak of Ebola Virus Disease in Senegal is Over*, 2014, available at http://www.who.int/mediacentre/news/ebola/17-october-2014/en/.

12 See McNeil, Jr., D, "Using a Tactic Unseen in a Century, Countries Cordon off Ebola-Racked Areas" (August 12, 2014), *New York Times*, http://nyti.ms/2muOX11.

13 Wilkinson, A & Leach, M, "Briefing: Ebola – Myths, Realities, and Structural Violence" (2014), *African Affairs*, 1.

14 See Herbst, J, *States and Power in Africa: Comparative Lessons in Authority and Control*, 2000.

3 Porous Borders

The spread of the Ebola virus from Guinea to neighboring countries has been attributed to the porosity of the borders purportedly separating these countries.[15] Just as in Guinea, the communities where the first cases occurred in Liberia and Sierra Leone were border communities with limited infrastructure and government presence.[16] And, just as in Guinea, it did not take much time before cases were being reported in the capitals and urban areas, especially in slums where the underserved poor lived.[17]

The combination of poor infrastructure, absence and rejection of the state in societies, and porous borders are related issues that depict state fragility.[18] These factors reveal deficits in the capacity and legitimacy of states. In the Ebola case, these deficits triggered the outbreak and contributed to the difficulty in containing it, but the focus on state deficit has been with regard to capacity, ignoring the critical legitimacy deficit that lies at the root of the state's malfunction.

Based on the above, this paper argues that it is important to address the governance challenges of states in ways that go beyond capacity building. The current state-building framework, comprising external efforts to build capacity, is evidently inadequate for addressing legitimacy gaps. Liberia is a clear example, where despite more than a decade of intense international engagement and participation in governance, most of the citizens live outside the reach of the state and continue to suffer deficient living conditions without access to basic amenities and infrastructure.[19] Regionalism, it is argued here, if properly revised within the West African context, might present an effective alternative that brings together the collective resources of states and external partners while also deconstructing barriers to legitimate communities that exist within and across states.

---

15 Wilkinson & Leach, "Briefing: Ebola – Myths, Realities", above Fn. 13, 10.

16 Ibid.

17 See Garrett, "Ebola's Lessons: How the WHO Mishandled the Crisis", above Fn. 6.

18 See OECD, *Glossary of Statistical Terms*, 2007, 314; Zartman, W, "Introduction: Posing the Problem of State Collapse" in Zartman, W, *Collapsed States*, above Fn. 4, 9; Call, C, "The Fallacy of the 'Failed State'" (2008), 29 *Third World Quarterly*, 1491; Call, C, "Ending Wars, Building States" in Call, C & Wyeth, V (eds.), *Building States to Build Peace,* 2008, 1.

19 See Dwan, R & Bailey, L, "Liberia's Governance and Economic Management Assistance Program (GEMAP)" (2007), *A Joint Review by the Department of Peacekeeping Operation's Peacekeeping Best Practices and the World Bank's Fragile States Group*, available at http://bit.ly/2ljLyT7.

III Deconstructing Health Governance: National and Global Responses

Two main points that came under scrutiny during and following the Ebola epidemic were its implications for global health governance, particularly in relation to the role of the WHO, and its revelations about national health governance, especially concerning states with weak institutional capacity. Regarding the first, there has been immense criticism of the WHO and its methods – or the lack thereof – in responding to global public health emergencies. The poor performance of the WHO in areas such as fundraising for its projects and clearly defining its goals and priorities, the Organization's inability to coordinate its efforts with those of national, regional and other global organizations as well as NGOs and other private entities, and its inability or unwillingness to rise above the politics of its Member States, have been identified as some of the weaknesses that hampered its response to the Ebola epidemic.[20] On the second issue, the national health infrastructure in the countries that were most affected by the Ebola epidemic has been recognized as fundamentally deficient and incapable of protecting the lives and wellbeing of citizens.

This paper takes a rather broad notion of governance that does not limit itself to public authority but rather covers both functional and relational elements of the concept.[21] As such, the deconstructive stance of new governance theories, which looks beneath and beyond traditional realms such as the state, provides a foundational base for this study.[22]

The state has usually served as the main actor in national and global health governance, but this does not mean that there are no alternative institutions through which other actors can – and do, in many cases – provide

20 See Garrett, "How the WHO Mishandled the Crisis", above Fn. 6.; see also Gostin, L, "A Proposal for a Framework Convention on Global Health" (2007), 10 *Journal of International Economic Law*, 989.

21 See above Fn. 1. See, for a contrast, Bogdandy, A von, Dann, P & Goldmann, M, "Developing the Publicness of Public International Law: Towards a Legal Framework for Global Governance Activities" in Bogdandy, A von, Dann, P & Goldmann, M (eds.), *Exercise of International Public Authority by International Institutions: Advancing International Institutional Law*, 2010, 10.

22 See Bevir, M, "Governance as Theory, Practice, and Dilemma" in Bevir, M (ed.), *The Sage Handbook of Governance*, 2010; Lobel, O, "New Governance As Regulatory Governance" in Levi-Faur, D (ed.), *The Oxford Handbook of Governance*, 2012; Risse, T, "Governance in Areas of Limited Statehood: Introduction and Overview", in Risse, T (ed.), *Governance Without a State? Policies and Politics in Areas of Limited Statehood*, 2011.

related functions. Private entities such as hospitals, NGOs, and corporations, have become an integral part of the national and global health order.[23] Governance actors – particularly states and International Organizations – exercise authority through the creation of rules that seek to influence or control the behavior or conditions of other players, the targets of such exercise of authority. Governance targets in the health sector include individuals, private-for-profit organizations, NGOs, and states, and they are usually on the receiving side of governance efforts. The relationship between governance actors and their targets is dictated by the exchange of capacity and legitimacy. The focus of this section is on how capacity and legitimacy influence the performance of governance institutions.

1 National Health Governance

The Ebola case reveals significant capacity gaps in the national health governance structures involved. The health sector capacities of Guinea, Liberia, and Sierra Leone were among the lowest in the world. Much of their governance capacity was externally derived and sustained through external funding, research facilities, and, in some cases, manpower.[24]

In addition to this capacity deficit, there was also an important legitimacy dynamic that contributed to the governance challenges that impacted the onset of and response to the Ebola outbreak.[25] The state was not the primary governance actor within the national order. It shared this role with social and cultural institutions that determined how societal life, including healthcare, was regulated in poor and rural communities.[26] In most of the countries in West Africa, more than half of the population who live in rural and urban poor communities have limited access to public facilities and services. These citizens exist within alternate governance structures, ranging

---

23 See Reich, M, "Introduction: Public-Private Partnerships for Public Health" in Reich, M (ed.), *Public-Private Partnerships For Public Health*, 2002, 1 (12).

24 See generally, the contribution of *Michael Marx*, "Ebola Epidemic 2014-2015: Taking Control or Being Trapped in the Logic of Failure – What Lessons Can Be Learned?" in this volume, describing the infrastructure and personnel deficits in the most affected countries.

25 See Weber, *Economy And Society*, above Fn. 10; Shany, Y, *Assessing the Effectiveness of International Courts*, 2014, 139.

26 See Garrett, "How the WHO Mishandled the Crisis", above Fn. 6.

from families to religious institutions, which they accept as having legitimate authority over them, while they "avoid" the state as much as they can.[27] The relationship between the state and alternate governance structures within the state is not the focus of this study but it depicts an important legitimacy deficit that reveals gaps in the notion of the state as governance structure that are more than just capacity gaps. It also forms part of the narrative of how the state functions with this internal legitimacy deficit by relying on external legitimacy.

The state relies on external actors to confer legitimacy on it, so those actors determine the rules that govern state existence and performance. The state is, therefore, subject to external influence that is responsible not only for its capacity but also for determining its legitimate existence and performance.[28] Institutions such as the World Bank, the WHO, and other International Organizations, recognize and evaluate the legitimacy of developing countries as governance actors, and they come up with ways to measure state capacity while they make states undertake efforts to enhance their governance capital, but most of this is externally driven and may not enhance internal legitimacy.[29] Consequently, external governance actors are responsible for evaluating the performance of states and thus determining their legitimate status as suppliers of pubic goods in different fields such as healthcare, economic development, security, and so on.[30] Two important points to note are that, first, legitimacy here is usually based on normative standards, which relegates sociological legitimacy to the background.[31]

---

27 See Azarya, V & Chazan, N, "Disengagement from the State in Africa: Reflections from the Experience of Ghana and Guinea" (1987), 29 *Comparative Studies in Sociology and History*, 106; Azarya, V, "Reordering State-Society Relations: Incorporation and Disengagement" in Rothchild, D & Chazan, N (eds.), *The Precarious Balance: State and Society in Africa*, 1988, 3.

28 See Krasner, S, *Power, the State and Sovereignty: Essays on International Relations*, 2009, 241.

29 Davis, K, Kingsbury, B & Merry, S, "Indicators as a Technology of Global Governance" (2012), 36 *Law & Society Review*, 73; Davis, K, Kingsbury, B & Merry, S, *Governance By Indicators: Global Power Through Quantification And Rankings*, 2015.

30 This represents a global governance structure in which International Organizations, governance networks, NGOs and so on are governance actors and states, private corporations and individuals are governance targets.

31 Buchanan, A, *Justice, Legitimacy and Self-Determination: Moral Foundations of International Law*, 2009, 146; Sadurski, W, "Supranational Public Reason: On Legitimacy of Supranational Norm-Producing Authorities" (2015), 4 *Global Constitutionalism*, 396.

Second, significant focus is placed on enhancing the legitimacy of states through capacity building initiatives that focus on meeting a set of normative standards.[32] Thus, domestic constituents who are the final targets of many governance measures have superficial connections to and power over the state as they are not the primary constituents in the contemplation of the state when the latter is making governance decisions.[33] This describes, to some extent, the national health governance structure, which is generally overseen by state institutions but which really derives much of its capacity and legitimacy from actors such as the WHO and external donors that form part of a complex global health governance structure.[34]

2 Global Health Governance[35]

The WHO remains the face of global health governance, but its capacities have also been greatly undermined.[36] States exercise political leadership over the WHO, voting on the organization's agenda at the annual World Health Assembly (WHA). States are also targets of WHO governance, since the organization regulates state activities by prescribing rules and norms for the promotion of national and global health.[37] In addition to this, the WHO

32 See, for instance Pritchett, L, "Fragile States: Stuck in a Capability Trap?" (2010), *World Development Report 2011, Background Paper*, available at http://bit.ly/2mnhwPb.

33 Of course, governments may use domestic constituents as leverage to evade responsibilities from their other constituencies, so the legitimacy-conferring status of domestic constituents is not altogether pointless, but it is, in many cases, superficial.

34 See Reich, "Introduction: Public-Private Partnerships for Public Health", above Fn. 23.

35 The contributions of *Pedro A. Villarreal*, "The World Health Organization's Governance Framework in Disease Outbreaks: A Legal Perspective" and *Wolfgang Hein*, "The Response to the West African Ebola Outbreak (2014-2016): A Failure of Global Health Governance?" in this volume provide a more comprehensive discussion of the WHO and its governance challenges.

36 See Garrett, "How the WHO Mishandled the Crisis", above Fn. 6; Gostin, "A Proposal for a Framework Convention", above Fn. 20; Fisher, A, "From Diagnosing Under-immunization to Evaluating Health Care Systems: Immunization Coverage Indicators as a Technology of Global Governance" in Davis, Kingsbury & Merry, *Governance By Indicators*, above Fn. 29.

37 See Gostin, "A Proposal for a Framework Convention", above Fn. 20.

is supposed to provide leadership in a sector that has seen increased participation by other International Organizations, NGOs, and private for-profit organizations, many of which have significantly more resources than the WHO and whose resources are used to influence health policy and programs in the WHO and in its Member States.[38] Unsurprisingly, the WHO has fallen short in its leadership role with the cacophony of powerful governance voices in its domain.

Non-state entities provide capacity and determine the legitimacy of national health governance structures in many developing countries. They do this because they are able to fill a capacity gap in these countries. However, their legitimacy has been called into question by many observers, as they are recognized as governance actors that affect the decision-making of states and control the activities of target populations in the countries they support.[39] Consequently, in 2009, the WHO convened a forum to define policy options to enhance collaborative efforts amongst stakeholders. The result of this meeting was the Venice Concluding Statement on Maximizing Positive Synergies between Health Systems and Global Health Initiatives, which affirmed the central role of the WHO and acknowledged the need for collaborative work.[40] However, the targets of the policies and programs initiated and executed by these "stakeholders" usually do not have a say in how or what policies and programs are adopted or undertaken. Therefore, there is a legitimacy deficit in the global health governance system that is akin to the legitimacy deficit recognized in global governance systems generally.[41]

This legitimacy deficit is revealed in at least two ways. First of all, global governance organizations are not accountable to the publics whose lives or activities their influence affects. Secondly, the inequality in capacity of states means that not all members of the global community or of global

---

38 Ibid.; Fisher, "From Diagnosing Under-immunization to Evaluating Health Care Systems", above Fn. 36; Sridhar, D & Gostin, L, "Reforming the World Health Organization" (2011), 305 *Journal of the American Medical Association*, E2.

39 See above Fn. 38.

40 See World Health Organization Maximizing Positive Synergies Collaborative Group, "Venice Statement: Global Health Initiatives and Health Systems" (2009), 374 *Lancet*, 10; World Health Organization Maximizing Positive Synergies Collaborative Group, "An Assessment of Interactions between Global Health Initiatives and Country Health Systems" (2009), 373 *Lancet*, 2137.

41 See Kingsbury, Kirsch, & Stewart, "The Emergence of Global Administrative Law", above Fn. 1, 15.

governance organizations have an equal say in how global standards are established or implemented.

On the one hand, global governance structures must be held accountable for their exercise of authority, especially where it affects targets who have no direct say in the constitution or operations of the global governance system in question.[42] These targets could be individuals, private corporations, or even states. This is mainly a question of representation of the target by the governance actor, so there is a democratic element to the legitimacy questions it raises. Responses would focus on participation and efforts at increasing representation through democratic processes.[43] On the other hand, global governance structures are sometimes improperly constituted so that there are inequalities within their ranks that raise legitimacy concerns. Here, questions of equality are at the fore, as states are expected to represent themselves as equal participants in international institutions, based on the concept of sovereignty enshrined in the UN Charter and embedded in international legal practice.[44] However, the unequal capacity of states determines the role that they play in international institutions, raising legitimacy concerns within organizations.[45]

These two legitimacy questions are indistinguishable where some states, which are targets of governance action, have limited say in the decision-making process of those governance organizations. Nevertheless, where there are national governance challenges caused by grave capacity and legitimacy deficits, the legitimacy deficit of global governance institutions must be deconstructed to the above two levels, since it is not clear that states can or will represent their populations if their capacity is enhanced. Therefore, legitimacy must be leveraged for both national and global governance processes through a remedial governance structure that will play a dual role

42 See ibid.; Bogdandy, Dann, & Goldmann, *Exercise of International Public Authority*, above Fn. 21.

43 See Sadurski, "Supranational Public Reason", above Fn. 31.

44 See Franck, T, "Legitimacy in the International System" (1998), 82 *American Journal of International Law*, 705 (731); Franck, T, *The Power of Legitimacy among Nations*, 1990, 101; Kingsbury, B, "Sovereignty and Inequality" (1998), 9 *European Journal of International Law*, 599.

45 See Krasner, *Power, the State and Sovereignty*, above Fn. 28; Krasner, S, *Sovereignty: Organized Hypocrisy*, 1999; Jackson, R, *Quasi-States: Sovereignty, International Relations, and the Third World*, 1990.

of improving representation of targets and participation in global governance institutions. This paper proposes that regional governance structures might serve this purpose.

IV Regionalism: Arguments for a Remedial Governance Structure

Regional integration in Africa has been regarded as a necessary step towards accelerated development on the continent. The belief is that greater gains would be made if states pooled their resources together instead of acting individually. The common history of colonialism, global marginalization, and underdevelopment, is expected to form an important basis for this shared effort.[46] But, in the past half-century, as more efforts have been made towards integration, the expected development has not followed.[47] Despite elaborate regional goals and objectives, regional institutions in Africa have not been effective in facilitating development, for two major reasons. First, they have also suffered significant capacity deficits, especially considering the weak status of their members in this regard. Second, regional institutions have not been effectively utilized as a legitimacy-enhancing mechanism to engage citizens and global actors for effective institutional development.

This section describes the current framework for regional integration in West Africa, using the Economic Community of West African States (ECOWAS) to illustrate the regional response to the Ebola outbreak. Then, it examines the governance challenge of regional institutions. Finally, it discusses the need to enhance the capacity of and leverage legitimacy through regional institutions.

1 The Current Regional Framework

ECOWAS is the primary regional institution in West Africa, established by treaty in 1975 with the primary purpose of promoting economic development in West Africa. Membership consists of 15 countries, most of which

---

46 Nkrumah, *Africa Must Unite*, above Fn. 8, 170.

47 See Senghor, J, Ashurst, M & Bhalla, J et al., *Going Public: How Africa's Integration can Work for the Poor*, 2009.

have experienced violent conflict, military coups, and authoritarian governments within the past five decades.[48] Consequently, in a revised treaty in 1993, ECOWAS expanded its mandate and institutions to include non-economic principles such as the promotion of democracy, maintenance of peace and security and respect for human rights.[49]

ECOWAS functions through political and administrative institutions with general functions as well as specialized institutions with particular functions. It has an executive, a legislative, and a judicial arm. Community institutions rely on states for implementation of Community policies and decisions, while they provide administrative and technical guidance and support. It is a largely state-driven process that involves limited collaboration with and no room in essential decision-making for civil society and the private sector. This is the framework within which a regional response was crafted to address the Ebola crisis.

The two main institutions responsible for managing the response to the Ebola crisis were the Commission and the West African Health Organisation (WAHO).[50] WAHO, the specialized institution responsible for health matters within the region, was established in 1987 and came into operation in 1998 when its Headquarters was instituted in Bobo-Diolassou, Burkina Faso, but it did not begin active operations until 2000. It was established in an effort to create a health institution that would serve francophone and non-francophone states in West Africa. The ECOWAS Commission, which was also responsible for providing a response to the Ebola outbreak, is described as "the main engine room for all ECOWAS programmes, projects and activities",[51] and its Directorate of Humanitarian and Social Affairs is also responsible for regional health matters.

Although WAHO regards itself as financially autonomous, its funding comes from the ECOWAS budget, which is approved by the recommendation of the Council of Ministers (the Council),[52] and from donors. Its governance framework is also tied to the ECOWAS political leadership.[53]

---

48 The Republic of Benin, Burkina Faso, Cape Verde, the Gambia, Ghana, Guinea, Guinea Bissau, Liberia, Mali, Niger, Nigeria, Senegal, Sierra Leone, Togo.

49 See Kufuor, K O, *The Institutional Transformation of the Economic Community of West African States*, 2006; Ogwu, J & Alli, W (eds.), *ECOWAS: Milestones in Regional Integration*, 2009.

50 See Article III, Protocol of WAHO (1987).

51 About the Commission see, http://www.comm.ecowas.int/about-ecowas/.

52 See Articles 10 and 69 of the 1993 Revised ECOWAS Treaty.

53 See Article IX of the Protocol on the Establishment of a West African Health Organisation (A/P.2/7/87).

WAHO also relies significantly on states for the implementation of regional health policies and plans, including health financing.

Under this framework, WAHO informed Member States of its critical capacity deficit and its consequent inability to provide an adequate response to the Ebola outbreak. In addition to this capacity deficit, it was also constrained by the institutional hierarchy of ECOWAS, as it could not execute a comprehensive plan to control the outbreak without clear approval from the Authority. Approval was given at the July Summit of the Authority, about four months after the diagnosis was made. At the Summit, the Authority directed WAHO and the Commission to adopt a regional approach to contain the spread of the virus, and it established a solidarity fund for Member States to contribute towards these efforts.[54] The consequent regional approach devised by WAHO consisted of policy, advocacy and intervention strategies, described below.

After the July Summit of the Authority, WAHO convened a meeting of the Health Ministers of the region to develop a regional response. This response involved setting up institutional structures to address the crisis as a regional rather than a national challenge.[55] Non-state actors were also involved in implementation mechanisms set up by WAHO but not in the decision-making that was to drive the regional response. The strategy was meant to assist states to coordinate their response through information campaigns and workshops to foster community responses. However, weaknesses in the broader regional structure were revealed by the incidence of border closures, quarantines and travel bans, which affected citizens who were ordinarily used to crossing the borders freely for economic, social and cultural reasons. These border closures also constrained regional efforts at addressing the crisis. This affected two core aspects of the integration mandate – open borders and Community citizenship. The free movement of persons, capital, and goods across borders is a core component of the West

---

54 Final Communiqué: Forty Fifth Ordinary Session of the Authority of ECOWAS Heads of State and Government (July 10, 2014), No. 134/2014, available at http://news.ecowas.int/presseshow.php?nb=134&lang=en&annee=2014.

55 See Traore, M, "Ebola in West Africa: ECOWAS Health Ministers Pledge for Synergy of Appropriate Strategies and Efficient Response to Ebola Virus Disease (EVD) outbreak in ECOWAS Member States" (August 2014), *WAHO Press Release*, available at http://www.wahooas.org/spip.php?article731&lang=en.

African integration agenda.[56] In fact, ministers of Member States declared ECOWAS a borderless region in 2001, because national borders were to be open to Community citizens, who were entitled to the rights of free movement, residency and establishment in all states within the region.[57] However, in the wake of the epidemic, the regional obligation of states to respect the right of free movement of Community citizens was violated by Member States that were, in reality, accountable only to themselves.[58] While the right to free movement is not an absolute right, the Community's legal and policy framework has not been clear as to its boundaries. One of the guiding principles of WAHO is that it will avoid the spread of diseases in the region that may arise from the free movement of persons, but the Organization has no clear mechanism in its latest strategic plan on how to do this, and when Member States responded with unilateral border closures, WAHO did not appear to have provided any guidance on appropriate responses.[59] Thus, regional efforts to control the outbreak were undermined not only by unilateral national actions but also by unclear regional mechanisms to guide members in their response. These factors have made it difficult for regional institutions to compel state compliance with regional obligations.

The advocacy aspect of the regional response involved organizing cross-border initiatives that brought together stakeholders from different countries to provide information and support for border communities.[60] But these efforts were thwarted by national responses to the crisis which, as explained above, undermined the regional response.

As part of the intervention strategy, WAHO was to deploy personnel to the affected countries. The Organization sent out fewer than ten technical officials into the field after the outbreak began. It was not until December 2014, a year after the first case and more than half a year after the diagnosis was made, that WAHO sent out its first robust team of 150 trained medical

---

56 Article 27 of the 1975 ECOWAS Treaty, Article 1 of the 1993 Revised Treaty, a 1979 Protocol on Free Movement of Persons, and subsequent Decisions and Declarations of the Authority of Heads of State and Government and the Council of Ministers guarantee a right of free movement to Community citizens.

57 Community citizenship was defined in the 1982 Protocol on the Definition of Community Citizenship.

58 For restrictions on the right, see Article 4 of the 1979 Protocol Relating to the Free Movement of Persons, Residence and Establishment.

59 WAHO, *Strategic Plan 2009-2013*, 2009, 25.

60 Ibid.

professionals from Member States (Cote d'Ivoire, Ghana, Mali, Niger, Nigeria, and Togo) to assist with the medical response.[61] WAHO worked with the African Union in the implementation of its African Union Support to the Ebola Outbreak in West Africa (ASEOWA), which deployed more than 700 national and regional health workers. Meanwhile, at this point, the international NGO, *Médecins Sans Frontières* (MSF), had already engaged more than 300 international medical professionals and more than 3000 locals to tackle the outbreak.[62] However, there has been no evidence of coordination between the regional workers and NGOs responding to the crisis. In fact, responders complained about the poor coordination and the absence of a central leadership.[63] Needless to say, the intervention strategy of WAHO did not reveal an effective regional response.

In addition to policy constraints, WAHO complained of funding and staffing shortages, amongst other things. So, while a paper strategy was being developed by the Organization, actual implementation was not underway – nor was it realistically foreseeable – as the resources for any such intervention were unavailable. Hence, WAHO has not featured significantly in discussions about the response to the epidemic because its role on the ground was minimal at best.[64]

From the above, the limitations placed on the regional response can be attributed to a regional capacity deficit as well as lack of accountability of Member States towards the fulfillment of their regional (and national) obligations.[65] The control of WAHO by ECOWAS states, in terms of both participation and output, has meant that the governance deficit of those states

---

61 See WAHO, *WAHO Recruited Medical Personnel Finally Deployed to Boost EBOLA Response Effort*, http://www.wahooas.org/spip.php?article836&lang=en; WAHO, *Fact Sheet: African Union Response to the Ebola Epidemic in West Africa, as of 1/26/2015*, available at http://bit.ly/2mOCh5D.

62 See Doctors without Borders, *Ebola*, http://www.doctorswithoutborders.org/our-work/medical-issues/ebola.

63 See Garrett, "How the WHO Mishandled the Crisis", above Fn. 6.

64 An exception is Bappah, Y H, "In Ebola Response, ECOWAS Offers Best Hope of Success" (August 2015), *IPI Global Observatory*, https://theglobalobservatory.org/2015/08/ebola-ecowas-manu-river-union-liberia-sierra-leone/.

65 See El-Ayouty, Y & Zartman, W (eds.), *The OAU after Twenty Years*, 1984; Asante, S K B, *The Political Economy of Regionalism in Africa: A Decade of The Economic Community of West African States*, 1986; Kufuor, *The Institutional Transformation Transformation of the Economic Community*, above Fn. 49; Bach, D, *Regionalism in Africa: Genealogies, Institutions and Trans-State Borders*, 2015.

has been transferred to the regional level.[66] Therefore, regional institutions like WAHO are unable to provide a buffer for states to overcome domestic and global challenges. In order to improve the performance of regional institutions, it is important to address capacity and legitimacy challenges through the regional framework to build strong alternative institutions in regions with significant governance challenges.

2 Why Regional Governance?

Alesino and Spolaore note that, "borders [...] are the outcome of choices and interactions by individuals and groups who pursue their goals under constraints".[67] They argue that "the sizes of national states (or countries) are due to trade-offs between the benefits of size and the costs of heterogeneity of preferences over public goods and policies provided by government".[68] The authors try to produce an economic analysis of optimal state effectiveness based on considerations relating to size. This is important for the study of African states because the borders have defined not just the legitimacy but also the capacity of those states.[69] Control over territory in Africa has been undermined by limited infrastructure, governance deficits, and low citizen loyalty, and the size of the states has, along with their historical, economic and political development, contributed to their lack of control. There are indeed domestic collective action problems because the central state is unable – sometimes unwilling – to supply public goods, and individual (or group) incentives to cooperate are greatly limited. Therefore, the capacity and legitimacy deficit of African states are inextricably linked.

Regional institutions can provide the opportunity to combine big development with small development by raising resources to support members to cover risks that they face from capacity and legitimacy deficits, in areas such as healthcare, financial security, peace building, and infrastructure.[70] The incentive for states to participate would be access to this increased capacity, which will help alleviate their capacity deficits. Citizens will also

---

66 See WAHO, *ECOWAS Launches Full Scale Fight against Ebola*, http://www.wahooas.org/spip.php?article802&lang=en.

67 Alesina, A & Spolaore, E, *The Size of Nations*, 2003, 2.

68 Ibid., 3.

69 See Ibid., 11. Okafor, *Redefining Legitimate Statehood*, above Fn. 9, 127; Herbst, *States and Power in Africa*, above Fn. 14.

70 See Pritchett, "Fragile States: Stuck in a Capability Trap?", above Fn. 32.

benefit from increased capacity where regional institutions are not focused on upholding unaccountable states but rather on fostering communities that exist within states and across borders. Thus, regional institutions must provide access to resources that are not available at the national level.[71] This is one of the objectives of WAHO in its strategic plan, but as the Organization recognized even before the outbreak, it did not have the resources to play this role in the region.[72]

In addition to capacity enhancement, regional institutions can also enhance state legitimacy and tackle fragmentation by deemphasizing borders and providing citizens with access to resources across borders. Migration and trade policies as well as cross-border programs have the binary effect of facilitating regional trade while also bringing together societies and giving citizens greater freedom to develop their capacities. Although functioning regional institutions are detrimental to certain rent-based interests in Member States that seek to consolidate power by strengthening the borders and undermining regional policies,[73] the growing participation of non-state actors, foreign states and International Organizations in national, regional and global processes can bring multidimensional power dynamics into play in regulating the control of states and other political interest groups in regional institutions.

Therefore, regional institutions can serve two very important functions in addressing the governance challenges of Member States. First, with regard to the capacity deficit, regional institutions will pool together the resources of Member States as, amongst other things, a premium for indemnifying states against losses that may arise from national and regional challenges. Second, the legitimacy deficit of states can be addressed by providing a venue for citizens to seek public goods that cannot or will not be supplied by other governance actors, including states. Although WAHO sees itself as playing an important coordination role among stakeholders, the Organization does not appear to recognize its role as a legitimizer of its

---

71 See Karen, A K, Helfer, L, & MacAllister, J, "A New International Human Rights Court for West Africa: The ECOWAS Community Court of Justice" (2013), 107 *American Journal of International Law*, 1; Ojomo, E, "Competing Competencies in Adjudication: Reviewing the Relationship between the ECOWAS Court and National Courts" (2014), 7 *African Journal of Legal Studies*, 87.

72 See WAHO, *Strategic Plan 2009-2013*, above Fn. 59.

73 See Herbst, *States and Power in Africa*, above Fn. 14, 253; Englebert, P & Hummel, R, "Let's Stick Together: Understanding Africa's Secessionist Deficit" (2005), 104 *African Affairs*, 399.

Member States and of global institutions like the WHO. Instead it has focused mainly on building its own capacity by enhancing its resources.[74]

3 Addressing the Capacity Deficit in Regional Institutions

When the officials of WAHO were faced with the Ebola outbreak in ECOWAS Member States, they had to rely, to a large extent, on national institutions in Member States to provide a response.[75] Also, since WAHO relies significantly on ECOWAS for its budget, the capacity deficit that makes ECOWAS Member States unable to handle the outbreak also exists at the regional level, creating a challenge for WAHO to provide the adequate response to tackle the epidemic.[76] This capacity deficit has been recognized as a major hindrance to WAHO's fulfillment of its objectives of fostering national and regional health governance.

While regional institutions can be relied upon for the supply of national public goods, especially in small states or weak states that are unable to supply those goods by themselves, they must incentivize states to participate in the regional enterprise.[77] Since the pursuit of individual interests will usually outweigh the pursuit of collective interests, weak states are more likely to cooperate to gain from the benefits of collective action, especially if their contributions are minimal and if the goods in question are exclusive public goods, which do not require "jointness of supply".[78] Public health issues such as the eradication of contagious disease involve the supply of weakest link public goods so that the supply of the good depends on the

74 Institution building of WAHO has been a part of the Organization's two strategic plans, in 2003 and 2009.

75 See Asante, S K B, *Report on a Study on National Focal Pints for ECOWAS and NEPAD Initiatives*, July 2004, (On File with Author).

76 See WAHO, *Strategic Plan 2009-2013*, above Fn. 59; WAHO, *Programme – Diversification of Health Financing Mechanisms*, (On File with Author).

77 See Snidal, D, "Relative Gains and the Pattern of International Cooperation" (1991), 85 *American Political Science Review*, 701.

78 See Olson, M, *The Logic of Collective Action: Public Goods and the Theory of Groups*, 1965, 38; Ostrom, E, *Governing the Commons: The Evolution of Institutions for Collective Action*, 1990, 6.

participation of the weakest link.[79] However, where the members of regional organizations consist of relatively small and large states, the large states may be expected to bear the bulk of the cost of providing the collective goods if cooperation provides sufficient incentives for them to do so.[80] Large states, like Nigeria, with significant interest in the regional integration process, have invested remarkable capacity, including funding and personnel, towards the initiation, development and maintenance of regional integration in West Africa.[81] However, smaller states with access to fewer resources are more committed to the integration process for their individual benefits and may not be committed to the supply of regional public goods. Consequently, where there are opportunities to develop state capacity, smaller states will pursue such opportunities instead of opportunities for regional capacity development.[82] This would mean that, in regions with fragile states, the regional system is held together by large states with governance challenges, while the smaller states rely on the regional system, the larger states, and whatever other external capacity they can generate to boost their weak capacity, thus placing added strain for the supply of weakest link public goods on larger states. In other words, the hegemon must provide incentives to hold together the collective, and this includes providing rewards to smaller states for cooperating, usually through its significant contribution to the regional project.[83] In the West African context, Nigeria has played this role, but, the country's desire to play a leadership role in the region, its interest in limiting the influence of extra-regional powers such as Gaddafi's Libya, and its pursuit of regional stability have shaped its commitment to making significant unilateral contributions to the West African

79 See Barrett, S, *Why Cooperate? The incentive to Supply Global Public Goods*, 2007; Bodansky, D, "What's in a Concept? Global Public Goods, International Law and Legitimacy" (2012), 23 *European Journal of International Law*, 651.

80 See Snidal, "Relative Gains and the Pattern of International Cooperation", above Fn. 77.

81 See Bach, D, "The Politics of West African Economic Cooperation: CEAO and ECOWAS" (1983), 21 *Journal of Modern African Studies*, 605 (616); Vogt, M A, "The Involvement of the Economic Community of West African States in Liberia's Peace-keeping" in Vogt, M & Aminu, L S (eds.), *Peace Keeping as a Security Strategy in Africa*, vol. 1, 1996, 342, for a discussion of the role of Nigeria in the peace-keeping intervention.

82 See Olson, *The Logic of Collective Action*, above Fn. 78.

83 See Snidal, "Relative Gains and the Pattern of International Cooperation", above Fn. 77.

regional process.[84] Additionally, Nigeria's own governance challenges mean that its commitment to and engagement in the regional process is not consistent. In the case of health, Nigeria has not shown as much interest as it has in other areas, such as collective security and money laundering. This has meant that, until recently, regional health governance has remained underfunded and under-resourced.

In West Africa, capacity deficits make it difficult to set up the kind of "insurance scheme" required at the regional level to "share the risk of an uncertain environment" [85] caused by state weakness, as can be seen from the spillover of regional crises in areas ranging from health to terrorism. The insurance benefits of regional integration are many, but states must determine "whether such insurance benefits [...] can be sufficient to offset the political and economic costs associated with [... cooperation]".[86] Thus, regional integration must provide added incentives for states to not only channel their limited resources towards the supply of regional public goods for collective interests, but also give up limited external resources to regional development.[87] One way for regional institutions to provide the incentives required for states to invest in the regional process is by protecting individual states from the cross border risks associated with the weakness of national institutions. This way, the collective interest will be tied to addressing individual interests of states by providing a security against domestic and external risks.[88] This is a driving force for WAHO's current health financing program which seeks to enhance and diversify funding opportunities for national and regional health programs, as well as its capacity building program that aims to build its personnel and infrastructure to enable it to fulfill its objectives.[89]

Based on the foregoing, WAHO has recognized its capacity deficit and emphasized the role of capacity for fostering regional health governance in West Africa, but it has neglected to discuss national, global and regional legitimacy concerns that must also be addressed. This paper introduces the

---

84 See Bach, "The Politics of West African Economic Cooperation", above Fn. 81; see also Nwokedi, E, "Sub-Regional Security and Nigerian Foreign Policy" (1985), 84 *African Affairs*, 195; Babangida, I B, "Reaffirming the Raison D'etre of the ECOWAS" in Nwachukwu, I (ed.), *Nigeria and the ECOWAS since 1985: Towards a Dynamic Regional Integration*, 1991.

85 Ostrom, *Governing the Commons*, above Fn. 78, 13.

86 Alesina & Spolaore, *The Size of Nations*, above Fn. 67, 6.

87 Olson, *The Logic of Collective Action*, above Fn. 78.

88 See Alesina & Spolaore, *The Size of Nations*, above Fn. 67.

89 See generally, WAHO, *Strategic Plan 2009-2013*, above Fn. 59.

argument that it is important to build the capacity of regional institutions while also leveraging their legitimacy in order to make them more effective to deal with the governance challenges in Member States.

4 Effectiveness, Control and the Legitimacy Deficit: Leveraging Legitimacy through Regional Institutions

As noted above, legitimacy here refers to sociological legitimacy; thus, it is the acceptance by a governance target of the exercise of power by a governance actor.[90] If we think of citizens as the main governance targets affected by the exercise of power by national, regional and global health governance actors, then they are legitimate to the extent that these targets accept them as such. This is quite distinct from legitimacy based on effectiveness, capacity or some other normative value.[91] Acceptance, for the current purpose, can be based on historical, cultural or some other sociopolitical affiliation, and it is an origin-based phenomenon more than it is a goal- or consequence-based phenomenon.[92]

In the Ebola case, where the state lacks the resources to foster the supply of public goods, this is not the basis for the absence of its legitimacy but only further entrenches the legitimacy gap. On the other hand, the legitimate communities that form the basis for cooperation amongst citizens do not derive their legitimacy from being effective at fostering the supply of public goods, so, their capacity deficit does not diminish their legitimacy. Finally, external actors such as intergovernmental organizations and NGOs that have significant capacity cannot accumulate legitimacy simply by being effective. Hostility towards health workers in rural communities is evidence of this.[93]

90 See Weber, *Economy And Society*, above Fn. 10.

91 See Buchanan, *Justice, Legitimacy and Self-Determination*, above Fn. 31.

92 Weber distinguished between *zweckrational* and *wertrational*, the former referring to rational action influenced by the expectation of outcomes and the latter referring to that influenced by the belief in the absolute value of an action or condition. Origin-based legitimacy is rational in the second sense. Weber, M, *The Theory of Social and Economic Organization*, (translated by Henderson, A M and Parsons, T), 1947, 115.

93 See, for instance, Sandner, P, "Attacks on Health Workers Hamper Ebola Fight" (Februar 18, 2015), *DW*, available at http://bit.ly/2mi9Y31.

The legitimacy of regional institutions in this context flows from two realities: first, the citizen, marginalized by the state and without access to basic resources, is constantly in search of an alternative system for the supply of public goods – a parallel system, if you will; second, the trans-border realities of African societies whose social, cultural and political networks are not adequately represented within clear border territories are better represented within a "borderless" framework.[94] Thus, the regional system provides an alternative governance structure that focuses more on inclusion than on sovereign power or effectiveness, thus diffusing the central power of the state without undermining it.[95]

Where regional institutions serve as instruments for the facilitation of free flowing relations amongst communities, they would enhance legitimacy by diffusing the central power of the state.[96] For instance, if ECOWAS institutions had been effective in maintaining border flows and fostering cross border activities, they would have enhanced not only regional institutional legitimacy but also state legitimacy by fostering relations between subnational and transnational groups, sites of legitimacy, on the one hand, and national, regional and global institutions on the other. Furthermore, regional institutions can also serve as a buffer between national and global institutions, to address issues of legitimacy where states are governance targets.[97] In this regard, WAHO had an opportunity to coordinate the multitude of governance actors that intervened in responding to the outbreak. The affected states were not in a position to provide such coordination, and ECOWAS should have provided not just an intervention mechanism but a coordinating mechanism, being representative of the affected states and other states in the region as well as of the communities that were being affected within and across state borders. In other words, regional institutions could address different levels of the legitimacy gap in health governance.

---

94 Okafor, *Redefining Legitimate Statehood*, above Fn. 9; Kaplan, S, *Fixing Fragile States: A New Paradigm for Development*, 2008; Young, *The African Colonial State in Comparative Perspective*, above Fn. 9; Herbst, *States and Power in Africa*, above Fn. 14.

95 See above Fn. 27.

96 See Kaplan, *Fixing Fragile States*, above Fn. 94; Joseph, R & Herbst, J, "Responding to State Failure in Africa" (1997), 22 *International Security*, 175 (182).

97 See Loevy, K, "The Legal Politics of Jurisdiction: Understanding ASEAN's Role in Myanmar's Disaster, Cyclone Nargis" (2014), 5 *Asian Journal of International Law*, 1.

The regional system can serve as a means of diffusing national and global power by fostering decentralized and collective systems of power, respectively. It does this without necessarily challenging the central systems of power at the national and global level, so national ministries and IGOs would still play a significant role in region-led processes. But, by allowing their processes to pass through regional institutions, they help overcome fear of domination by governance targets that they seek to influence.[98] Where regional institutions build capacity without addressing these legitimacy concerns, they run the risk of alienating citizens and communities and providing even fewer incentives for cooperation amongst their Member States.

5 Challenges to a Regional Alternative

The greatest challenge to constructing a regional alternative is in providing incentives for states to participate in a process that might be seen as undermining their power by fostering alternative institutions that compete with them for authority and for scarce resources. The current reality is that states control the regional process. States control the level of accountability that regional institutions can promote as well as the level of competition between national institutions and regional institutions for scarce global resources. Thus, in order for states to allow greater cooperation in the regional process, the regional enterprise must provide significant individual benefits for states. Additionally, the bulk of the cost must be borne by state and non-state actors with greater incentives to cooperate than to deflect. Realistically, the cost of forfeiting political supremacy and capacity building resources should not surpass the benefit of building strong regional institutions that foster the supply of regional public goods not just to national institutions but to citizens. One way to address this challenge is by providing regional frameworks in selected areas of intervention that would pose the least challenge to states and provide significant gains to them and their citizens.[99] This paper provides broad conceptions of the issues to be considered in developing such a system in the hope that this would serve as a starting point for thinking differently about the development of innovative

---

98 This is Weber's definition of power without legitimacy. See Weber, *Economy And Society*, above Fn. 10.

99 Alesina & Spolaore, *The Size of Nations*, above Fn. 67, 210.

regional systems that comprehensively address the weakness of state institutions in West Africa and similar regions.

V Conclusion: Rethinking Regional Governance

As the Ebola epidemic comes to an end in West Africa and development actors focus their attention on building the capacity of the states most affected, especially in healthcare provision, it is important to place significant focus on the comprehensive governance deficits in those states and the development of innovative frameworks for overcoming those deficits. The current international legal system does not address state legitimacy as it places critical importance on the territorial sovereignty of states, thus underpinning the state as the primary locus of political community. However, in many instances, the state has come under attack from within and without. Regional institutions were meant to address this crisis by innocuously deemphasizing the borders – and in effect the territorial dominance of the state – and leveraging the legitimacy of systems that are recognized by citizens as valid representation of their interests and identities. They are also meant to serve as buffers against external "attacks" against the state. However, the current regional framework is undermined by governance challenges that reveal capacity and legitimacy gaps, mostly flowing from the control of regional processes by troubled states.

In order to address the shortcomings of the current regional system, it is important to focus on enhancing the capacity and harnessing the legitimacy of regional organizations such as ECOWAS so that they can foster the valid exercise of power by political institutions, which is lacking in the current governance system.

Ebola and Securitization of Health: UN Security Council Resolution 2177/2014 and Its Limits

Ilja Richard Pavone[*]

Abstract

The Security Council's Resolution 2177/2014 on the Ebola Outbreak represented a landmark in the evolution of the notion of security, positioning it alongside modern threats to peace and security. Indeed, for the first time in its practice, the Security Council qualified an infectious disease as a "threat to international peace and security" according to Article 39 of the UN Charter. The present paper deals with whether this resolution represented the culmination of a process of securitization of health started in 2000, or if it was just an isolated event. Did it mark an evolution of the activities and modalities of response of the Security Council to new global threats, or was it no more than a mere flash in the pan? In addition the legal and theoretical foundations of this highly innovative practice of the Security Council, and its relation with the Human Security concept are also discussed.

I Framing the Issue

The last quarter-century registered the resurgence of a phenomenon – infectious diseases – that the medical community deemed to have defeated with the global vaccination campaign, which eradicated Smallpox in the Seventies-Eighties and is now close to doing so with Poliomyelitis.

This had determined the idea that the main challenges to public health in industrialized countries were by then mainly represented by diseases not related to viruses, such as tumors and neurodegenerative diseases (i.e.

---

* PhD in International Law and Human Rights at Sapienza University of Rome, Researcher of International Law at the National Research Council of Italy (CNR), Rome, and Professor of Environmental Law, Tuscia University, Viterbo. Visiting Scholar at the Max Planck Institute for Comparative Public Law and International Law, Heidelberg. All websites last accessed April 3, 2017.

Amyotrophic Lateral Sclerosis, Alzheimer's Disease and Parkinson's Disease) associated with the process of aging of the population ("epidemiological transition model").[1]

The world medical community is now instead facing the emergence of new infectious diseases, the re-emergence of old infectious diseases and the persistence of intractable infectious diseases, that required a re-evaluation of the epidemiological transition model. Those global health challenges, represented by epidemics and pandemics such as HIV/AIDS, SARS, Ebola and Zika that arose in developing countries (in South-East Asia, Sub-Saharan Africa and Latin America), and associated with a high risk of spread in developed countries, resulted in the emergence of a collective interest in the protection of health.[2]

The global health governance architecture, based on the leading role of the World Health Organization (WHO), was heavily challenged by the 2014 Ebola Outbreak in West Africa. Many states (partially or completely) ignored the Temporary Recommendations issued by WHO, and the weakness of the International Health Regulations (IHR) became visible, given the lack of an enforcement mechanism. Therefore, in light of the failure of the IHR to provide an adequate and early response to the epidemic, the United Nations Security Council (UNSC) acted as a "Global Health Keeper"[3] and heavily questioned the central role of WHO in dealing with health emergencies, as it is further discussed in the present book by *Robert Frau*'s paper.[4]

In this framework, within a process described as "securitization of health", the UNSC assumed the role of a "securitization actor" by adopting Resolution 2177/2014 on the Ebola Outbreak. The joint efforts by the Security Council in a strict and successful cooperation with WHO and other

---

1 Indeed, according to Proposition Two (Shifts in Mortality and Disease Patterns) of the "epidemiologic transition" model, degenerative and man-made diseases would have gradually displaced infectious diseases. See, Omran, A, "The epidemiologic transition: A theory of the epidemiology of population change" (2005), 83 *The Milbank Quarterly*, 731.

2 Fidler, D P, *International Law and Infectious Diseases*, 1999, 6.

3 Arcari, M & Palchetti, P, "The Security Council as a global 'health-keeper'? Resolution 2177 (2014) and Ebola as a threat to the peace" (2014), 1 *Questions of International Law – Zoom In*, available at http://bit.ly/2mdd3AK.

4 On the role of WHO during the Ebola Outbreak, see Villarreal, P A, "Cuando los derechos humanos chocan entre sí. Las recomendaciones de la Organización Mundial de la Salud frente a la crisis del Ébola en África de 2013-2015" (2015), 2 *Revista del Posgrado en Derecho de la UNAM*, 181.

international and regional organizations[5] resulted in the defeat of the disease in the most affected countries[6] (zero cases for at least 42 days were declared by WHO on March 17, 2016 in Sierra Leone, on June 1st, 2016 in Guinea, and on June 9, 2016 in Liberia).[7]

Resolution 2177 implicated what would initially appear to be a turning point in defining roles, functions and powers of the UNSC in the field of health; indeed, for the first time in its practice it classified an infectious disease as a "threat to peace and security", according to Article 39 of the UN Charter.[8] This resolution marks the culmination of a trend of securitization of health, which started with two previous resolutions of 2000 and 2011 on HIV/AIDS in Sub-Saharan Africa (Resolutions 1308 and 1983). It is not a case that some scholars discussed concerning the possibility to extend the concept of Responsibility to Protect (R2P) to the health sector, indicating to the UN Members States, acting through the UNSC or *uti singuli*, a duty to protect the health of populations affected by a health pandemic with potential repercussion on a global scale ("Responsibility to Practice Public Health").[9] According to this theory, if and when the most affected countries are not able to respond adequately in the presence of global epidemics/pandemics and to protect the right to health of their citizens, the UNSC would be the only organ within the UN system in charge of providing a collective response. In this case, it would act as bearer of the interest

---

5 Alvarez J E, *The Impact of International Organizations on International Law*, 2016, 232.

6 On the interaction between these two actors, Agnes, A, "A Combative Disease: The Ebola Epidemic in International Law" (2016), 39 *Boston College International and Comparative Law Review*, 97; see also the contribution of *Robert Frau*, "Combining the WHO's International Health Regulations (2005) with the UN Security Council's Powers: Does it Make Sense for Health Governance?" in this volume.

7 WHO, *Ebola Outbreak 2014-2015*, http://www.who.int/csr/disease/ebola/en/. Some flare ups of the disease have, however, been registered and are still expected, see WHO, *Latest updates on the Ebola outbreak*, http://who.int/csr/disease/ebola/top-stories-2016/en/.

8 Burci, G L & Quirin, J, "Ebola, WHO and the United Nations: Convergence on Global Public Health and International Peace and Security" (2014), 18 *ASIL Insight*, available at http://bit.ly/2m5AFIF; Pavone, I R, "The Human Security Dimension of Ebola and the Role of the Securi-ty Council in Fighting Health Pandemics: Some Reflections on Resolution 2177/2014", (2014), 39 *South African Yearbook of International Law*, 56.

9 Fidler, D P, "The UN and the Responsibility to Practice Public Health" (2005), 2 *Journal of International Law & International Relations*, 41.

of the international community to protect public health, even with the power to adopt measures *ex* Chapter VII of the UN Charter.

In the present paper, the background of the trend to securitize health issues by the UNSC will be discussed, suggesting that Resolution 2177, although innovative in expanding the notion of threats to peace and security, did not eventually modify roles and functions of the Security Council in a sensible manner. In particular, it can be argued that Resolution 2177 was in reality a missed opportunity to extend the R2P concept to the health sector, given that the UNSC did not expressly act under Chapter VII missing to mention R2P, nor did it adopt concrete measures under Articles 41 or 42 of the UN Charter.

For structural purposes, this article is divided into two parts. The first section investigates the theoretical foundations of Resolution 2177, exemplified by the securitization theory and the Human Security concept. The second part engages with the practice on securitization of the United Nations, focusing attention on the content of the three UNSC Resolutions that dealt with health issues under a security paradigm. In this part, it will also be explained why Resolution 2177 was not as revolutionary as it might have seemed at a first glance, arguing that in this case the UNSC did not intend to act *ultra vires* in extending its powers and functions to the health sector or to set a precedent.

II New Threats to Peace and Security

The main global challenges to peace and security in the 21st Century are new and unpredictable events that defined a reshaping of the concept of security. The globalized world must face emerging and unpredictable threats, such as the re-emergence of infectious diseases, the rise of ISIS, environmental degradation and climate change.

Those menaces, which were of course not envisaged when the UN Charter was adopted, came out gradually after the end of the Cold War. The different threats are less predictable than "classical" military perils represented by a single enemy state and have different sources: non-state actors (groups of individuals linked to terrorist groups, pirates or insurgents), and intangible actors such as infectious diseases and global warming (even though one could argue that climate change is also the result of the economic activities of states, leading to their refusal to subscribe and implement environmental regulations).[10]

The classical notion of security was strictly related to the realist view of international relations, developed at the beginning of the Cold War. The theory of realism represents an interpretation of international relations that points out their most conflictual and controversial aspects. It identifies the world order as a system dominated by anarchy, whereas a cluster of states – merely concerned with their own domestic security and national interests – are in competition amongst themselves for the pursuit of power.[11] According to this view, security is the protection of the homeland from aggressions or attacks caused by foreign troops. This classical interpretation of national security was then recognized by Article 51 of the UN Charter (the right to individual or collective self-defense in response to an act of aggression).

Today the notion of security has radically changed if compared to the "realist view". It is generally accepted that security agendas should no longer be limited to resisting armed attacks by hostile troops and preventing armed conflict, because the array of risks to the survival of the population of a state has multiple sources. In fact, the classical conception of security failed to protect human populations against the new menaces related to the process of globalization endangering their lives.[12]

The nature of the threats and their source have radically changed together with their object. As a matter of fact, it is no longer the state that needs protection, but the individuals and their health (and the environment in which they live), according to the emerging concept of Human Security, which considers "security" as something more that the defense of the territory by an armed attack.[13] The end of the Cold War attested the idea that if the states were safer than before, their citizens were not in the same situation.

---

10 Farrell, G, "Network structure and influence of the climate change counter-movement" (2016), 6 *Nature Climate Change*, 370.

11 Amongst the most influential writings on "realism", see Morgenthau, H G, *Politics among Nations: The Struggle for Power and Peace*, 1948; Kissinger, H, "Documentation: Foreign Policy and National Security" (1976), 1 *International Security*, 182; Walz, K N, *Theory of International Politics*, 1979.

12 Wellens, K, "The UN Security Council and New Threats to the Peace: Back to the Future" (2003), 8 *Journal of Conflict and Security Studies*, 15.

13 Oberleitner, G, "Human Security: A Challenge to International Law?" (2005), 11 *Global Governance*, 185.

The UNSC practice reveals a trend to determine non-conventional "threats to peace and security" under Article 39 of the UN Charter and to align more closely with the Human Security paradigm. A significant moment of this extension is represented by Resolution 688/1991 on the repression of the Kurds in Northern Iraq, whereby the Council considered "the massive flow of refugees towards and across international frontiers and to cross-border incursions, as a threat to international peace and security in the region" (Preamble, Recital 3).[14] The most consistent developments have been registered through Resolution 794/1992 on Somalia,[15] Resolution 965/1994 on Rwanda[16] and Resolution 1529/2004 on Haiti.[17]

This tendency by the Security Council of gradual extension of the notion of threat to international peace since the cessation of the Cold War found its "ideological" foundations in the well-known Presidential Statement of January 31, 1992,[18] through which, for the first time, a UN body emphasized forms of instability different from armed conflicts.[19] Indeed, non-military sources of instability in the economic, social, humanitarian and ecological field have been qualified as "threats".

A further expansion in the meaning of a threat took place with regard to international terrorism; in particular, Resolution 1368/2001 at the aftermath of the Al-Qaeda terrorist attack against the World Trade Center qualified this event, as well as *any other act* of international terrorism, as a threat to international peace and security (Preamble).[20] Therefore, international terrorism was considered as a threat in general terms, regardless of specific

---

14 UNSC Resolution 688 of April 5, 1991.

15 UNSC Resolution 794 of December 3, 1992, on the situation in Somalia. The Council recognized a humanitarian disaster, consisting in gross violations of human rights and of the rules of international humanitarian law as a threat to peace and security (Preamble).

16 UNSC Resolution 955 of November 8, 1994, on the establishment of an International Tribunal and adoption of the Statute of the Tribunal. The UNSC qualified genocide and the systematic violations of human rights as a threat to peace and security (Preamble).

17 UNSC Resolution 1529 of February 29, 2004, on the situation in Haiti. The UNSC invoked "the deterioration of the political, security and humanitarian situation in Haiti" and established that "the situation in Haiti constitutes a threat to international peace and security, and to the stability of the Caribbean" (Preamble).

18 UN Doc. S23500, Decision of January 31, 1992 (3046th meeting), Statement by the President.

19 Bailliet, C M, *Security: A Multidisciplinary Normative Approach*, 2009, 13.

20 UNSC Resolution 1368 of September, 12, 2001, on Threats to international peace and security caused by terrorist acts. See also Resolution 1373 of September, 28,

states or specific crises, and it was the first time that such an abstract phenomenon was included within the concept of international threats.[21]

In line with this tendency, Resolutions 2134 and 2136, adopted on January 28 and 30, 2014, concerning respectively the crisis in the Central African Republic and the equally serious situation of conflict in the Eastern part of the Democratic Republic of Congo, have – incidentally but rather significantly – pointed out the linkage between wildlife poaching and trafficking, ongoing civil wars in the African continent and the activities of criminal networks and terroristic organizations that operate on an international scale.[22] The strict relationship between natural resources and conflicts, although an object of growing interest,[23] had until now remained unrelated to the UNSC practice, at least as regards the significance raised by living natural resources. In these resolutions in particular, the UNSC considered illegal poaching of elephants and smuggling of their ivory as a fuel factor of armed conflicts, because it is an illicit source of financing for various armed groups often linked to international terrorism.[24] These two resolutions – alongside Resolution 2177 – represent a very innovative development of the UNSC practice concerning the notion of threats to peace and security, and in particular on the same qualification of the legal concept of international security.

Conceptually, the aforementioned trend to expand the notion of security matters to the domains of environment and health reflects the new challenges emerging from the process of globalization and, as underlined by some scholars, echoes the point of view of the Copenhagen School theory

---

2001on Threats to international peace and security caused by terrorist acts, which states in the Preamble that "*any act* of international terrorism, constitute a threat to international peace and security". In this regard, see Cadin, R, I presupposti dell'azione del Consiglio di sicurezza nell'articolo 39 della Carta delle Nazioni unite, 2008, 278; Värk, R, "Terrorism as a Threat to Peace" (2009), 16 *Juridica International*, 216.

21 Conforti, B & Focarelli, C, *Le Nazioni Unite*, 2010, 213.

22 Peters, A, "Novel practice of the Security Council: Wildlife Poaching and Trafficking as a Threat to the Peace" (2014), *EJIL Talk*, http://bit.ly/1cQ5gtX.

23 For instance, Öberg, M & Strøm, K, *Resources, Governance, and Civil Conflict*, 2008.

24 Pontecorvo, C M, "Consiglio di sicurezza e risorse naturali viventi: il wildlife trafficking come fuelling factor dei conflitti armati" (2014), 5 *Ordine internazionale e diritti umani*, 938.

of securitization,[25] representing the decline of the "realist thinkers in international relations".[26]

In the next paragraphs, the theoretical framework of Resolution 2177, focusing on the concepts of securitization of health and Human Security as its theoretical foundations, will be analyzed.

III Securitization Theory and Health

The term "Securitization" refers to "things discussed in security terms" or "things identified as requiring exceptional response".[27] This concept draws its theoretical foundations from the Copenhagen School's securitization theory that, for the first time, gained the attention on the need to go beyond the traditional concept of security centered on the defense of the territory of the state by foreign military threats. *Buzan*, considered as the founder of the Copenhagen School, highlighted that the state cannot be considered as the only referent of security policies and also that – in particular in the context of fragile or failed states – non-state actors must be taken into account as the target of security policies.[28]

The Copenhagen School identified five domains of security that comprise not only military security, but also environmental, economic, social and political security, therefore differentiating itself from the "realist thinkers". In particular, it highlighted a multitude of security threats originating from state as well as non-state actors and non-tangible entities, such as environmental degradation or infectious diseases.

In this framework, securitization is described as a process in two phases, through which states recognize an issue as a threat to their security.[29] In brief, phase I requires the use of the "language of security" that initiates the securitization process, labeling a determined issue or event as menace

25 The theory of international relations developed by the Copenhagen School, which emphasizes in particular the social aspects of security, is based upon the study of Buzan, B, *People, States and Fear: The National Security Problem in International Relations*, 1983. For further discussions, see Buzan, B, Waever, O & Wilde, J de, *Security: A New Framework for Analysis*, 1998, 23.

26 Swain, A, *Understanding Emerging Security Challenges*, 2013.

27 Hindmark, S, *Securing Health: HIV and the Limits of Securitization*, 2016, 22.

28 Buzan, B, *People, States and Fear: The National Security Problem in International Relations*, 1983.

29 Buzan, Waever & de Wilde, *Security: A New Framework for Analysis*, above Fn. 25.

(speech act). Indeed, as argued by *Austin* since 1962, language is a key instrument whose function is not limited to the delivery of information, but it is a real form of action or social activity.[30] During phase II, the audience and the stakeholders involved are convinced that they are facing a threat; the issue is accordingly widely and commonly accepted as a risk for security (act of securitization). Thus, the securitization actor is legitimized to adopt extraordinary measures.[31] Ebola – which can be considered as a "social threat" – passed through this process of securitization and the UNSC became the securitization actor by adopting Resolution 2177.

The securitization of health dates back to the end of the Cold War with the rise of global health risks, such as the emergence of new infectious diseases (HIV/AIDS), the menace of bioterrorism, environmental degradation and global warning and mass migrations. The globalization process and the increased mobility of persons and animals around the globe accelerated the diffusion of infectious diseases, rendering them a global threat.[32] In particular, developed countries found themselves vulnerable to the spread of health pandemics generated in the Third World.

At the political level, the drive of change in the perception of infectious diseases as a global security issue was led by the US under the Bill Clinton administration. The US National Intelligence Council Report of 2000 ("The Global Infectious Disease Threat and its Implications for the United States") recognized for the first time that new and re-emerging infectious diseases could pose a rising global health threat and could have a negative impact on US and global security.[33] The document asserted then that the consequences of epidemic outbreaks will lead to conflict or increase the

30 Austin, J L, *How to do Things with Words*, 1962, 1. On the role of language in the securitization process, see Elbe, S, *Security and Global Health. Towards the Medicalization of Insecurity*, 2010, 11.

31 Emmers, R, "Securitization", in Collins, A (ed.), *Contemporary Security Studies*, 2007, 112.

32 Fidler, D P, "Globalization, International Law, and Emerging Infectious Diseases" (1996), 2 *Emerging Infectious Diseases*, 77.

33 The text of the report is available at https://www.dni.gov/files/documents/infectiousdiseases_2000.pdf. As evidence of the growing concern in the United States regarding biological threats (including infectious diseases), we can refer to then-US President *Barack Obama*'s Executive Order of November 4, 2016 ("Advancing the Global Health Security Agenda to Achieve a World Safe and Secure from Infectious Disease Threats"). This Executive Order gives public authorities special powers to respond to infectious diseases that could represent a threat to national security. See http://bit.ly/2mwRexg.

likelihood of conflict.[34] It was a turning point for the definitive emergence of public health as a security matter at the domestic level, since the previous security strategy of 1998 ("A National Security Strategy for a New Century"), included public health only amongst the secondary threats, and HIV/AIDS, for instance, was mentioned only once.

All these chain of events constituted the move towards securitization within different spheres (academic and political) and came to the decisive moment for the acceptance of health as a security threat within the United Nations, represented by the report of the Secretary-General's High Level Panel on Threats, Challenges and Change (2004). It highlighted global security threats such as civil wars, the spread of Weapons of Mass Destruction (WMD) and international terrorism. In particular, para. 67 of the Report explicitly referred to health threats ("The Security Council, should host a second special session on HIV/AIDS as a threat to international peace and security"). Indeed, a key element of the Report is represented by the holistic approach it took to health and security, posing at the same level of "threats" naturally occurring outbreaks as well as pandemics generated by biological or chemical agents voluntarily released in the atmosphere (bioterrorism).

The Report recommended that the Security Council consult with the Director-General of the WHO "to establish the necessary procedures for working together in the event of a suspicious or overwhelming outbreak of infectious disease" (para. 70) and, in turn, that WHO Director-General "keep the Security Council informed during any suspicious or overwhelming outbreak of infectious disease" (para. 144).[35] Furthermore, this document speculated for the first time the necessity for the Security Council to provide a concrete support to the action of WHO personnel ("if existing [IHR] do not provide adequate access for WHO investigations and response coordination, the Security Council should be prepared to mandate greater compliance", para. 144); it could also imply the use of its powers *ex* Chapter VII, in order to realize efficient quarantine measures.

Conferring upon the Security Council the main responsibility of dealing with potential global spread of a virus in case of failure of the WHO, meant that the UNSC acquired a central role triaging health emergencies.[36] Now

34 Washer, P, *Emerging Infectious Diseases and Society*, 2010, 149.

35 Report of the Secretary-General's High-Level Panel on Threats, Challenges and Change, *A More Secure World: Our Shared Responsibility*, UN Doc. A/59, 2004. Odello, M, "Commentary on the United Nations High-Level Panel on Threats, Challenges and Change" (2005), 10 *Journal of Conflict and Security Law*, 231.

36 Davies, S E, "Is There an International Duty to Protect Persons in the Event of an Epidemic?" (2010), 2 *Global Health Governance*, 1.

would its extended mandate also imply the possibility to adopt measures within the framework of Chapter VII of the UN Charter in order to protect human populations from health menaces derived from infectious diseases – that can be generated naturally or voluntarily by the human being (bioterrorism) – with a potential global diffusion?

The next paragraphs deal with why this extended mandate – even if it sounded as if there was a danger of *ultra vires* – did not imply, under a practical point of view, the emergence of a new norm of international law recognizing a new power to the UNSC to intervene in order to protect the health of populations in the presence of health epidemics or pandemics. The failure to include Resolution 2177 within the Human Security paradigm, which will now be explained, will contribute to support this position.

IV The Human Security Paradigm

In general terms, the 'Human Security' paradigm, which encompasses the above mentioned modern threats to peace and security and added a new dimension to the debate on the notion of security, traces back to the writings of eminent scholars in the early 1980s (*Ullman*) and encompasses health within the security paradigm.

Ullman affirmed that non-conventional threats, including economic and environmental issues, could be just as dangerous as traditional military ones, and therefore should deserve consideration as "security issues". *Ullman* defined a threat to security as

> "an action or sequence of events that (1) threatens drastically and over a relatively brief span of time to degrade the quality of life for the inhabitants of a State, or (2) threatens significantly to narrow the range of policy choices available to the government of a State or to private, nongovernmental entities (persons, groups, corporations) within the State".[37]

Wars of an international or an internal character, terrorism and natural disasters can be included within the first category. A situation with few opportunities for trade, investment and cultural exchange, and in which important values are threatened falls within the second category.

Along the same line of thought, *Mathews* argued that environmental degradation should be considered as a priority in national security strategies, even if she still considers the state, rather than the human being, as the main

37 Ullman, R, "Redefining Security" (1983), 8 *International Security*, 133.

object of security policies.[38] The 1987 "Brundtland Report" drafted by the United Nations World Commission on Environment and Development (WCED) entitled *Our Common Future*, which was known for having elaborated the concept of sustainable development relevant for the current UN debate, also referred to environmental degradation as a threat to national security (para. 22). Therefore, according to this point of view, damages to the environment and the related consequences on the health and well-being of populations can be a source of political and social instability and conflict.

This position was then confirmed by the notion of Human Security, promoted by Canada and officially endorsed by the United Nations through the UN Development Programme (UNDP), which contributed significantly to the evolution of the security concept and "translated into practice" the thoughts of *Ullman*. UNDP defined Human Security in its 1994 Human Development Report, drafted by *Mahbub ul Haq* and influenced by eminent scholars such as *Martha Nussbaum* and *Amartya Sen*, as "safety from chronic threats, hunger, disease and repression" and "protection from sudden and hurtful disruption in the patterns of daily life". In delineating Human Security, the UNDP highlighted seven dimensions: economic security, food security, environmental security, energy and resource security, bio-security and health security. Therefore health is considered as one of the core values to be secured. Indeed, according to the proponents of the Human Development Report, the Human Security concept would better respond to the health needs of populations; in a few words, traditional military means are not the most appropriate tool to protect people against the spread of a pandemic.

Strictly related to the Human Security discourse is the distinction between negative and positive peace, drawn by an eminent Norwegian scholar, *Johan Galtung*.[39] Negative peace generally means the absence of an armed conflict and of physical violence, while the concept of positive peace is more articulated. It refers to the presence of conditions that enable a major political equality and social and economic justice. In this regard, the promotion of Human Security can be an important tool in the achievement of positive peace and in the prevention of conflicts.[40]

---

38 Mathews, J T, "Redefining Security", in Owen, T (ed.), *Human Security*, 2013, 37.

39 Galtung J, "An Editorial" (1964), 1 *Journal of Peace Research*, 1.

40 Turan, T, *Positive Peace in Theory and Practice Strengthening the United Nations Pre-Conflict Prevention Role*, 2015, 70.

A second influential report was adopted in 2003 ("Human Security Now") by the Commission on Human Security, co-chaired by *Sadako Ogata* and *Amartya Sen*. It identified three health challenges strictly related to Human Security: global infectious disease, poverty-related threats and violence and crisis.[41] The report contained a strategy for a "people-centered approach to global health" based on empowerment and protection. Empowerment requires adequate policies with the aim of increasing individual and community capacity, while protection entails prevention of diseases through adequate health strategies. As far as we are concerned, the key element of the 2003 report is given by the incorporation of health within the Human Security discourse.[42]

The novelty of the notion of Human Security is given by the change of perspective in entailing not only the territory of a state, but also the populations as bearers of a right to be protected against threats. It also comported a shift in the approach: in fact, security should no longer be achieved through military means but also through sustainable human development.[43]

This extensive and comprehensive catalogue of sources of Human Security focuses on the potential of harm to individuals and paved the way to the concept of Responsibility to Protect, whose efficiency has been widely challenged due to the failures it met facing the humanitarian crises in Libya and in Syria.[44]

The former UN Secretary-General *Kofi Annan* in his 2005 Report ("In Larger Freedom") included deadly infectious diseases amongst the threats to peace and security of the 21st Century (para. 78), providing moral and legal value to the extension of the Human Security concept to health.

Ebola was a Human Security crisis in all respects, because – given its unprecedented nature – it endangered the life of entire populations of Western Africa. However, the notion of Human Security, even though it certainly contributed to the drafting process of Resolution 2177, was not pivotal. Indeed, in Resolution 2177 the predominant concerns were for the potential impact of Ebola on the political and economic stability of the most affected

---

41 Tigerstrom, B von, *Human Security and International Law*, 2008, 178.

42 Chen, L & Narasimhan, V, "Human Security and Global Health" (2003), 4 *Journal of Human Development*, 181.

43 Tadjbakhsh, S & Anuradha, C, *Human Security: Concepts and implications*, 2007, 21.

44 Pavone, I R, "The Crisis oft he Responsibility to Protect Doctrine in the Light oft he Syrian Civil War" (2014), *The Global Community Yearbook of International Law and Jurisprudence*, 103.

countries, and consequently of the African region, compared to concerns for the welfare and well-being of the populations affected by the disease.

V Human Security and Securitization of Health

The Human Security concept and the ongoing process of securitization of health, both recognizing that health epidemics and pandemics pose a threat to peace and security, would seem at a first glance as similar concepts. The securitization of health is instead, for some aspects, at odds with the Human Security concept. Indeed, securitization means that health epidemics and pandemics are no longer considered as a humanitarian issue that must be handled uniquely by the instruments and means provided by development cooperation and by international human rights law, but as a security matter that could also require military means.[45]

Therefore, the Human Security concept and securitization are two sides of the same coin. Both the concepts recognize the nexus health-security, but the means they rely on to protect security against an outbreak are, at least theoretically, quite different.

The Human Security concept is based on the idea that the respect of human rights and human dignity are the main tools to avoid a potential global spread of an infectious disease. In short, if the right to health is adequately fulfilled and promoted – which means access to timely, acceptable, and affordable health care of appropriate quality – a regional health epidemic can be successfully contained. Indeed, all West African countries that have been affected by the Ebola outbreak are listed on the "Fragile States Index".[46] This means that the root causes of the outbreak of the disease and of the failure to contain the epidemic since its beginning are due to fragile or broken health systems, densely populated urban areas, poverty and malnutrition. Therefore, the security-development nexus was satisfied in this case (fragile States pose a threat to peace and security, providing fertile ground

---

45 Floyd, R, "Human Security and the Copenhagen School's Securitization Approach: Conceptualizing Human Security as a Securitizing Move" (2007), 5 *Human Security Journal*, 38.

46 The Fragile State Index is an annual report published by the Fund for Peace. Guinea is at the "high alert" level (12th of 178 countries in the Fragile States Index Rank), Liberia and Sierra Leone are at the "alert" level. The Report is available at http://fsi.fundforpeace.org/.

for tangible and intangible threats, such as terrorism and/or infectious diseases). Thus, those threats are often generated by the failure of a country's efforts towards development, and more security can only be achieved through the fulfillment of the Sustainable Development Goals (2015-2030).[47]

In light of this brief analysis, does it really make sense to frame an infectious disease as a security matter? Advocates of securitization of health retain that a public health emergency – posing a threat to national security – should be treated in the same manner as a traditional military menace, therefore implying a military response. The value of securitizing health issues, according to *Enemark*, is that it "promises to attract greater political resources and attention for protecting human health and human lives in the face of specific infectious disease threats".[48] In other words, since governments fear exposure to serious threats affecting their homeland security, they are willing to invest more resources and funds against a health epidemic.[49]

However some scholars raised concerns of the equivalence between infectious diseases and national and international security threats, focusing on the risk of overriding human rights and civil liberties.[50] Likewise, there is an underlying lack of historical evidence on the link between infectious diseases and political crises.

The next paragraphs explain that the Security Council's practice of securitization of health never implied military measures nor the limitation of human rights and personal freedoms. However, the WHO's technical recommendations hinted at the latter type of measures; indeed, Resolution 2177 contains a coordination clause which *urges* Member States to comply with these recommendations (para. 9),[51] as explained by *Pedro A. Villarreal* and *Robert Frau* elsewhere in this book. Therefore, the concerns over the ongoing process of securitization of health have been discredited by the

---

47 See United Nations, *Sustainable Development Goals,* available at https://sustainabledevelopment.un.org/?menu=1300.

48 Enemark, C, *Disease and Security: Natural Plagues and Biological Weapons in East Asia*, 2007, 20.

49 In this sense, see DeLaet, D L & DeLaet, D E, *Global Health in the 21st Century: The Globalization of Disease and Wellness*, 2015, 128.

50 Elbe, S, "Should HIV/AIDS Be Securitized? The Ethical Dilemmas of Linking HIV/AIDS and Security" (2006), 50 *International Studies Quarterly*, 119.

51 Para. 9 of Resolution 2177 "urges Member States to implement relevant Temporary Recommendations issued under the International Health Regulations (2005) regarding the 2014 Ebola Outbreak in West Africa".

cautious policy of the Security Council. Indeed, it managed to contain the disease in a balanced way without overlapping the roles and functions of other UN bodies and Specialized Agencies through a coordinated action with the General Assembly (GA) and the WHO. In addition, it avoided authorizing measures under Article 41, which would have meant imposing quarantine measures and Article 42, which would have implied the authorization to measures requiring the use of force (even though single states such as the United States and United Kingdom sent military troops on the ground)[52].

VI UNSC Resolutions 1308 and 1983

The UNSC meeting of January 10, 2000 devoted to "The situation in Africa: the impact of AIDS on peace and security in Africa", is represented by the literature on securitization as the official endorsement by the Security Council of the nexus health pandemics-security.[53] Promoted by the former UNAIDS Executive Director *Peter Piot* and the US Ambassador *Richard Holbrooke*, the meeting was an occasion to gain worldwide attention on the impact of HIV/AIDS on the development and security of Sub-Saharan Africa, the continent most deeply affected by the pandemic. The former US Vice-President, *Al Gore*, in his Opening Statement before the Security Council, stressed the need of a reform of the UNSC security agenda, that should have included the plague of HIV/AIDS, given the huge amount of deaths it caused.[54] *Gore*'s historical discourse laid the foundation for the adoption on July 17, 2000 of UNSC Resolution 1308/2000 on HIV/AIDS, which serves as a "precedent-setting" because it is the first resolution ever

52 Military personnel from United States (Operation United Assistance) and United Kingdom (Operation Gritrock) was deployed in West Africa, with the task of co-operating with the domestic authorities in containing the spread of the disease. See the report by Scott, A K, "Saving Lives: the Civil-Military Response to the 2014 Ebola Outbreak in West Africa" (2015), 14, available at http://bit.ly/2nOXOzO; see also https://obamawhitehouse.archives.gov/ebola-response.

53 See, for instance, Altman, D, "AIDS and Security" (2003), 17 *International Relations*, 417; Elbe, S, "AIDS, security, biopolitics" (2005), 19 *International Relations*, 403; Prins, G, "AIDS and global security" (2004), 80 *International Affairs*, 931.

54 Vice President Al Gore, *Opening Statement in the Security Council Meeting on AIDS in Africa*, SC/6781, of January 10, 2000, available at www.un.org/News/Press/docs/.

adopted by the UNSC dealing with an infectious disease.[55] However, it impersonated a change of perspective on HIV/AIDS: its scope was not addressed to the impact of HIV/AIDS on the security and development of the African continent, but it was limited to the impact of the virus on the health of peace-keepers. In fact, the resolution aimed to pursue the goal related to the health of UN Blue Helmets deployed in humanitarian missions in Sub-Saharan Africa, considered as subjects both at risk of infection and as potential vectors for the transmission of HIV. Indeed, the UNSC expressed concern about the potential damaging impact of HIV/AIDS on the health of peacekeeping forces and recommended they receive voluntary testing and counseling (para. 2) and participation in training and educational programs on HIV prevention (para. 3).

In Resolution 1983/2011 of June 7, 2011, the UNSC underlined that HIV/AIDS represents "one of the most formidable challenges to the development, progress and stability of societies", and therefore demanded "an exceptional and comprehensive global response" (para. 6 of the Preamble). The UNSC then reiterated that Peacekeeping operations can be "important contributors to an integrated response to HIV and AIDS" (para. 4), encouraging the inclusion of "HIV prevention, treatment, care and support" in the mandates of UN missions (para. 7).

Those two resolutions represent a step back when compared to the premises of the UNSC meeting of January 2000, because they narrowed their scope exclusively to the health of peace-keepers. In addition, those resolutions were not passed under Chapter VII and did not expressly qualify HIV/AIDS as a threat to peace and security. Indeed, the concrete impact of these resolutions on the securitization of HIV/AIDS has been heavily questioned.[56] *Garrett* stated, for instance, that except in cases where rape and

---

55 Resolution 1308/2000, S/RES/1308, "The responsibility of the Security Council in the maintenance of international peace and security: HIV/AIDS and international peacekeeping operations". In this regard see, Wet, E De, *The Chapter VII Powers of the United Nations Security Council*, 2004, 172; Poku, N K, "HIV/AIDS, State Fragility, and United Nations Security Council Resolution 1308: A View from Africa" (2013), 20 *International Peacekeeping*, 521. More in general, on the potential impact of HIV/AIDS on military troops, see Heinecken, L, "Facing a Merciless Enemy: HIV/AIDS and the South African Armed Forces" (2003), 29 *Armed Forces & Society*, 281.

56 McInnes, C & Rushton, S, "HIV/AIDS and Securitization Theory" (2013), 19 *European Journal of International Relations*, 115; Rushton, S, "AIDS and international security in the United Nations System" (2010), 25 *Health Policy and Planning*, 495.

sexual violence were committed as instruments of war, there was little evidence that HIV transmission was caused by a conflict and that the UN "blue helmets" were persons at high risk of being infected by HIV.[57] As analyzed in the next paragraphs, Resolution 2177/2014, although it expressly qualified Ebola as a threat to peace and security, does not represent a real "step beyond" in the securitization process either.

VII Resolution 2177/2014

Facing the challenge of finding the most appropriate strategy which would have allowed a worldwide mobilization against Ebola, the UNSC adopted a first resolution on the matter on September 15, 2014 (Resolution 2176), where it showed itself heavily concerned over the "current outbreak of the Ebola virus in some countries in Western Africa" (Preamble). In this resolution the SC declared, *inter alia*, the primary responsibility of the concerned government (Liberia) to maintain peace and security and to protect its own population (this important reference to the Responsibility to Protect Doctrine has been subsequently omitted in Resolution 2177). Resolution 2176 enunciated the key elements that then structured the position of the UNSC. It had, in particular, underlined the nexus between the Ebola epidemic and the "lasting stability" of Liberia. However, in this first phase the SC did not make any mention of the subsistence of a threat to peace and security, although it used the wording "acting under Chapter VII of the United Nations" (Preamble, Recital 12).

Subsequently, in response to a request of aid issued by the presidents of Guinea, Liberia and Sierra Leone with a joint letter of August 29, 2014 transmitted by the Secretary-General,[58] the UNSC held an emergency meeting on September 18, 2014, which led to the adoption by consensus of Resolution 2177, supported by 130 Member States (a number never registered before in the SC practice).[59] The majority of Member States, well

57 Garrett, L, "The Lessons of HIV/AIDS" (2005), *Foreign Affairs,* available at https://www.foreignaffairs.com/articles/2005-07-01/lessons-hivaids.

58 Letter dated September 15, 2014 from the Secretary-General addressed to the President of the Security Council, S/2014/669.

59 See Statement by the US Ambassador to the United Nations, Samantha Power, UN Doc. S/PV.7268, 8. See also the Statement by the President of the Security Council of November 21, 2014, UN Doc. S/PRST/2014/24.

aware that health issues do not fall traditionally within the domain of Chapter VII of the UN Charter, maintained, however, that the emergency situation caused by the rapid spread of this disease required extraordinary measures as well as a rapid reaction. The situation of emergency bypassed the debate on the re-partition of powers between the Assembly and the Council, which had been raised as a result of the previous discussion concerning climate change as a threat to peace and security.[60] Only few States raised concerns.[61] Argentina, a State traditionally critical towards the action of the Security Council, stated that

> "Argentina believes that Ebola is not merely a health problem. It is a multidimensional reality [...] eroding the possibilities of human social and economic development, which is at the root of most of the conflicts we deal with in the Council, and which may have consequences for security".[62]

The delegate of Brazil considered Ebola as a matter that should have been better addressed within the framework of development cooperation rather than within Chapter VII of the Charter.[63]

In line with the classical scheme of resolutions adopted within Chapter VII, the UNSC classified Ebola as a *threat* to international peace and security, and noted that the outbreak could have threatened the "peace-building and development gains" of Guinea, Liberia and Sierra Leone.[64] In fact, it is relevant to clarify that the hardest-hit countries were recovering from civil

60 Scott, S V, "Securitizing Climate Change: International Legal Implications and Obstacles" (2008), 21 *Review of International Affairs*, 614.

61 For the debates within the Security Council during the adoption of Resolution 2177, see http://outreach.un.org/mun/files/2014/11/SPV7268_ebola.pdf.

62 Intervention of the Representative of Argentina, Mrs. Perceval, UN Doc. S/PV.7268 20-21.

63 Intervention of the Representative of Brazil, Mr. Patriota, UN Doc. S/PV.7268 28-29. Similarly, the delegate of Colombia raised some criticism about the fact that Ebola was debated within the SC, arguing that this issue should have instead been within the competency of the GA (Intervention of the Representative of Colombia, Mr. Ruiz, UN Doc. S/PV.7268 45).

64 Some scholars retain, however, that Resolution 2177 was adopted not within Chapter VII, but within Chapter VI of the UN Charter. See, Hübler, A K J, "Ebola – International Disaster Response to a Global Health Emergency" (2015), 6 *Freiburger Informationspapiere zum Völkerrecht und Öffentlichen Recht*, 21, available at http://bit.ly/2mx9Lt5. For a different position, arguing that Resolution 2177 can be placed in Chapter VII, see Poli, L, "La risoluzione n. 2177 (2014) del Consiglio di sicurezza delle Nazioni Unite e la qualificazione dell'epidemia di ebola come minaccia alla pace ed alla sicurezza internazionale", (2015), 9 *Ordine internazionale e diritti umani*, 238.

wars and were facing a process of peace consolidation, whose efforts seriously risked being undermined by the viral epidemic. In addition, in Recital 4 of the Preamble, the SC dwelled upon the transboundary implications of Ebola and on the potential impact on regional and international security.

As to the operative part of the resolution, it enclosed important dispositions. The UNSC urged Member States to provide additional resources in the struggle against Ebola, to respond urgently to the crisis and to refrain from isolating the affected countries. The UNSC in particular encouraged

> "the governments of Liberia, Sierra Leone and Guinea to accelerate the establishment of national mechanisms to provide for the rapid diagnosis and isolation of suspected cases of infection, treatment measures, effective medical services for responders, credible and transparent public education campaigns, and strengthened preventive and preparedness measures to detect, mitigate and respond to Ebola exposure, as well as to coordinate the rapid delivery and utilization of international assistance" (para. 1).[65]

The Security Council also blamed private entities, like airlines and shipping companies, for their decision to curb trade and travel to and from the most affected countries, asking the first to lift general travel and border restrictions and the latter to maintain trade and transport links with the affected countries and the wider region (para. 4).[66] Through this resolution, the UNSC requested that the Secretary-General ensure that all relevant United Nations sections accelerated their response to the outbreak, encouraging the WHO to strengthen its technical leadership and operational support to Governments and other partners in that effort (para. 12).[67]

---

65 In addition, it encouraged "the governments of Liberia, Sierra Leone and Guinea to continue efforts to resolve and mitigate the wider political, security, socioeconomic and humanitarian dimensions of the Ebola outbreak, as well as to provide sustainable, well functioning and responsive public health mechanisms" (para. 2). It also called on Member States "to provide assistance in response to the Ebola outbreak, to enhance efforts to communicate to the public, as well as to implement, the established safety and health protocols and preventive measures to mitigate against misinformation and undue alarm about the transmission and extent of the outbreak among and between individuals and communities" (para. 6).

66 The resolution "expresses concern about the detrimental effect of the isolation of the affected countries as a result of trade and travel restrictions imposed on and to the affected countries" (para. 3) and "calls on airlines and shipping companies to maintain trade and transport links with the affected countries and the wider region" (para. 4).

67 A Statement by the UNSC President of 21 November 2014 welcomed progress in slowing the spread, confirming that the response capacities available to the affected countries had "expanded substantially", warning however that much remained to be done to end the epidemic.

The recommendations contained in Resolution 2177 had three goals: (1) to answer in an appropriate manner to the humanitarian emergency caused by the spread of the virus, and (2) to prevent a further aggravation and a wider diffusion of the disease, (3) while limiting side effects (for example a health crisis) that – as previously underscored – might impact political, social, economic and humanitarian spheres, not just on a local scale, but potentially extending to a regional or even a global level. With this resolution, the UNSC further confirmed its recent trend to act on emerging global threats recommending specific measures that are intended to stimulate and to address the action of the states and of the stakeholders involved in a crisis, by limiting the possible associated security repercussions.

VIII Consequences arising from the adoption of Resolution 2177

Resolution 2177 was a landmark in the history and practice of the Security Council, contributing to align its functions and powers with emerging threats to peace and security. The key issue is now to evaluate if this new practice of the Security Council is conceptually based on the Human Security paradigm, and if it therefore implies a duty under international law to protect the health of populations affected by epidemics and pandemics in line with the R2P Doctrine, echoing the "Responsibility to Practice Public Health" theorized by *Fidler*.[68]

Indeed, R2P is strictly related to the Human Security discourse, given that massive violations of human rights fall within the category of Human Security, as well as health is a Human Security matter. R2P is based on two assumptions.[69] First, states have an international responsibility to protect their own populations from gross violations of human rights, such as genocide, war crimes, ethnic cleansing and crimes against humanity (labeled as "mass atrocities crimes"). This duty is deeply embedded in existing international customary law and is well established in universal and regional human rights treaties. Secondly, if the host state is unwilling or unable to do so, or if it commits a violation of *erga omnes* obligations (mass atrocities amounting to a violation of *jus cogens*) incurring in an aggravated regime of responsibility, the UN Member States are entitled to intervene (including through use of force) in order to protect these populations.

---

68 See above Fn. 2.
69 GA Resolution 60/1 of October 24, 2005 ("World Summit Outcome Document"), para. 139. Text available at http://www.ifrc.org/docs/idrl/I520EN.pdf.

R2P is founded on a Three-Pillar Strategy: Pillar One regards the responsibility of states to protect their populations from genocide, war crimes, ethnic cleansing and crimes against humanity and from their incitement. Pillar Two is the commitment of states to assist – through capacity-building – other states that are willing, but weak and unable, to uphold their Pillar One responsibilities. Pillar Three foresees the duty of the international community to react when a state is manifestly failing to provide such protection. Accordingly, the R2P doctrine allows the use of force as an *extrema ratio* (authorized by the UNSC) if diplomatic efforts have failed and non-forceful measures, such as sanctions, were unsuccessful in ending mass atrocities.[70]

One could therefore discuss – in light of Resolution 2177 – an extensive interpretation of those categories in order to include health epidemics and pandemics within the categories covered by R2P. However, considering a careful analysis of the content of Resolution 2177, it is premature to identify a norm in international law that establishes a clear duty to protect populations in the event of pandemics. Indeed, as already observed, Resolution 2177 did not contain any reference to the primary responsibility of affected States to protect the health of their populations (unlike Resolution 2176), and no official document adopted within the United Nations explicitly mentioned R2P with reference to health emergencies. It must not be underestimated that ultimately it was not Ebola itself, but the political instability that it could have generated in the hardest hit countries that led the Security Council to act. Therefore, the Security Council did not directly address the disease and its implications for the health of the populations affected, but rather its political consequences in terms of possible civil unrests and riots that could have led to the collapse of the fragile political institutions in the hardest hit countries.[71] Accordingly, even though the 2014 Ebola outbreak was first and foremost a serious human rights crisis, the risks for security were predominant with respect to the aspects related to the violation of fundamental human rights. Rather, Resolution 2177 failed to address the main human rights issues raised by the disease, such as the discrimination and stigmatization of the persons affected by the virus, the violation of the right to health, the right to food and the right to education, and restrictions to the right of free movement. This is the reason why it can be assumed that

---

70 In general, on R2P, see Peters, A, "The Security Council's Responsibility to Protect" (2011), 8 *International Organizations Law Review*, 15.

71 In this sense, Hood, A, "Ebola: A Threat to the Parameters of a Threat to Peace?" (2015), 16 *Melbourne Journal of International Law*, 29 (40).

Resolution 2177 can more easily be related to a securitization discourse than to the Human Security paradigm.

In particular, Resolution 2177, although it explicitly referred to Ebola as a threat to peace and security using the Chapter VII language, did not contain any practical decisions. For instance, the UNSC could have authorized Member States to deploy troops to protect and to surveil the borders and/or to enforce quarantine measures, but it decided not to act in this way. Indeed, this was related in an indirect way to the WHO technical recommendations, as explained by *Pedro A. Villarreal* in this book. Instead, this resolution, given its declaratory rather than mandatory nature (it contains recommendations and not decisions), could have also been adopted by the General Assembly.

In addition, the mandate of United Nations Mission in Liberia (UNMIL), a peacekeeping force already present in Liberia, was extended with Resolutions 2215/2015, but it did not mention, amongst the task of UNMIL, the coverage of the outbreak.[72] On its own, it was the General Assembly and not the Security Council that established with Resolution No. 69/1 of September 19, 2014, the first UN Peacekeeping force with a specific mandate concerning health, the United Nations Mission for Ebola Emergency Response (UNMEER).[73]

In this regard, one could also argue that the Ebola outbreak, and more generally health epidemics and pandemics, could be classified as natural disasters, at the same level as natural hazards such as an earthquake or a flood.[74] It would entail a duty by the international community to protect the persons involved in a disaster if the host state is unable to protect them.[75] It would imply that, in case of failure by the domestic authorities to protect

72 Davies, E S & Rushton, S, "Public health emergencies: a new peacekeeping mission? Insights from UNMIL's role in the Liberia Ebola outbreak" (2016), 37 *Third World Quarterly*, 419.

73 UN Doc. A/RES/69/1. The mission ended its mandate on July 31, 2015.

74 This varies throughout several levels. In some national (and possibly international) jurisdictions they have been assembled under the aegis of "emergencies". However, in the case of theoretical debates they are consistently and commonly distinguished. See Acconci, M P, *Tutela della salute e diritto internazionale*, 2011, 334; Bartolini, G, "La definizione di disastro nel progetto di articoli della Commissione del diritto internazionale" (2015), 98 Rivista di diritto internazionale, 55; Breau, S C & Samuel, K L H, *Research Handbook on Disasters and International Law*, 2016.

75 On this topic: Davies, E S, "Is There an International Duty to Protect Persons in the Event of an Epidemic?" (2010), 2 *Global Health Governance*, 1.

the health of their populations in the presence of a disaster, the Security Council could intervene, even adopting military measures under Pillar Three of R2P.

However, this position raises two issues. First, the scope of the R2P Concept is restricted to "massive human rights violations", or "core crimes" that are defined in Articles 6-8 of the Statute of the International Criminal Court (genocide, crimes against humanity, war crimes, aggression) committed during or as a consequence of a civil war or of a disaster. This narrow application of the R2P Concept, confirmed both by the UN Secretary-General[76] and by the International Law Commission (ILC) Special Rapporteur on the Protection of Persons in the Event of Disasters,[77] limits, as a consequence, any enlargement of this notion to the health domain. Secondly, even assuming an application of R2P to disasters, the linkage between health pandemics and natural disasters has not yet been clarified. The definition of "disaster" provided by the ILC in the draft Articles on the protection of persons in the event of disasters, is not limited to natural disasters.[78] This definition could therefore also apply to events such as infectious diseases and/or nuclear incidents, although it does not expressly mention health epidemics or pandemics. Therefore, the UNSC should have specified in Resolution 2177 the possible nexus between Ebola and natural disasters, recalling disaster law and the duty of the hosting state to protect their populations, but this did not happen.

As a conclusion of this brief analysis, one can ask why the wording of Resolution 2177 was so cautious, why any reference to R2P was eventually

---

76 2009 report of the Secretary-General on implementing the responsibility to protect A/63/677, para. 10 (b).

77 International Law Commission, "Report of the International Law Commission on the work of its Sixty-first session" – Chapter IX: Protection of persons in the event of disasters, (May 5, June 5, July 6, August 7, 2009) UN Doc. A/64/10 para. 156. As regards the concept of 'responsibility to protect', the Special Rapporteur recalled the 2009 report of the Secretary-General on implementing the responsibility to protect, which clarified that "*the concept did not apply to disaster response*".

78 Article 3 of the draft Articles states that "disaster means a calamitous event or series of events resulting in widespread loss of life, great human suffering and distress, mass displacement, or large-scale material or environmental damage, thereby seriously disrupting the functioning of society". International Law Commission, Sixty-eight session, Geneva, May 2 - June 10, and July 4 - August 12, 2016, Protection of persons in the event of disasters. Titles and texts of the preamble and draft Articles 1 to 18 of the draft Articles on the Protection of persons in the event of disasters adopted, on second reading, by the Drafting Committee (Doc. A/CN.4/L.871).

deleted, why this resolution did not formulate any duty upon Member States but it simply recommended measures, or why the Security Council decided not to adopt any concrete measure under Chapter VII. Probably, if the content of the resolution would have been more cogent, it would not have been possible to reach unanimity within the Security Council; some Member States would have raised objections and the great momentum reached would have failed. Put simply, it was not the intention of the drafters of Resolution 2177 to adopt a legislative act with such wide implications on roles and functions of the Security Council as initially speculated.

IX Conclusions

Much has been debated on the role the Security Council played in the 2014 Ebola Outbreak, evaluating positive and negative aspects of Resolution 2177 on global health governance and UNSC powers.[79] It is undeniable that the steps for the securitization of Ebola – as described by the Copenhagen School's Theory – have been fully respected, and therefore the UNSC became the "securitization actor" charged with adopting extraordinary measures if necessary.

In practice, however, the culmination of the trend of securitization of health within the UNSC represented by Resolution 2177 never implied a real "militarization" of Ebola (nor a "militarization" of HIV/AIDS if we analyze the content of the two previous resolutions on HIV/AIDS). Although Resolution 2177 was an extraordinary response to an extraordinary event, it did not empower the UNSC to act as a "Global Legislator", as it did with the two historical Resolutions 1373/2001 and 1540/2004 concerning WMD and international terrorism, for instance.[80] In the case of Ebola,

79 See for instance, Elbe, S, "Health and Security", in Collins, A (ed.), Contemporary Security Studies, 2016, 379; Lappin, R, "Ebola and Understanding Health Crises as Threats to International Security" (2016), Oxford Human Rights Hub Blog, available at http://bit.ly/2me1IAx; Roemer-Mahler, A & Elbe, S, "The race for Ebola drugs: pharmaceuticals, security and global health governance" (2016), 3 *Third World Quarterly*, 487.

80 With the adoption of Resolutions 1373 and 1540, the UNSC obliged all UN Member States to adopt some measures against the phenomenon of international terrorism and in order to prevent terrorists to accede to WMD. It was a novelty, given that usually the UNSC imposes duties upon states in relation to a very specific dispute or situation. See Rosand, E, "The Security Council as Global Legislator: Ultra Vires or Ultra Innovative?" (2004), 28 *Fordham International Law Journal*, 549.

it would have mandated the imposition of specific obligations upon Member States and the adoption of measures under Articles 41 and/or 42 of the UN Charter.

Therefore, the drafters of Resolution 2177 did not set out to create a precedent that could have had long-term implications on the roles and functions of the UNSC, by establishing new duties upon Member States; they simply aspired to reach a stricter cooperation amongst UN Member States and to gain additional financial resources while facing an exceptional event. A key element in support of this view is given by the fact that Resolution 2177 did not directly target Ebola and its potential devastating impact on public health; rather it referred to the likely negative consequences of the disease in terms of increasing social and political instability in the most affected countries, which were still recovering from civil wars. In conclusion, the concerns on the trend of securitization of health and on the excessive extension of the powers of the Security Council during the Ebola Outbreak at the expense of the WHO and other UN bodies have been retracted by its practice: "draconian measures" on the population aimed at limiting civil rights and personal freedoms were never imposed nor were "boots on the ground" under UNSC mandate ever deployed (although they were certainly deployed by Western governments under the form of foreign military assistance). The securitization policy implemented by the Security Council in the Ebola crisis was for the most part symbolic and helped to coordinate international efforts and build momentum in the global community, ultimately proving itself successful in containing the worldwide spread of the disease.

Combining the WHO's International Health Regulations (2005) with the UN Security Council's Powers: Does it Make Sense for Health Governance?

Robert Frau[*]

Abstract

Does it make sense to modify and adapt the International Health Regulations (2005) (IHR) in light of the recent crises? Does it make sense to create legally binding effect for the World Health Organization's (WHO) temporary recommendations? Does it make sense to engage the United Nations Security Council? How can both be combined?

This article attempts to answer these questions. It addresses the pluriverse of actors in health governance with an emphasis on the WHO and the UN Security Council.

The assessment by the WHO's internal review may lead one to assume that it simply does not matter. During the Ebola-outbreak 2014, states disregarded the WHO's non-binding temporary recommendations. This article suggests that creating binding effects may not matter as much as lawyers would hope: Other issues are more pressing in times of crises. Creating legal effect may be theoretically possible, but it would probably not matter much during the next epidemic. A more sophisticated approach may be found in the WHO's IHR 2005, if states are prepared to re-interpret the existing law.

Engaging the Security Council is a good idea only for epidemics with negative impacts on a region's security. This is due to the mandate of the Security Council. In addition, legitimacy concerns with regard to the Security Council could be raised.

In contrast, it makes sense to focus on human rights law, which protects against the exercise of international public authority. It could lead to comprehensive international health governance, with the WHO at its core and the Security Council providing support where needed. Keeping the human

* Dr., Senior Research Associate at the Chair for Public Law, especially International Public Law, European Law and Foreign Constitutional Law, European-University Viadrina, Frankfurt (Oder), frau@europa-uni.de. All websites last accessed December 1, 2016.

right to the highest attainable standard of health care at the heart of health governance highlights for whom health governance works: the individuals affected by a pandemic.

I Introduction: The Ebola-Outbreak 2015 as a Global Health Crisis

Globalization exacerbates domestic health problems:[1] Diseases spread more easily to other parts of the world. Most recently, the outbreak of the Zika-virus in Latin America and the Caribbean, suspected to be connected to an observed increase in neurological disorders and neonatal malformations (2016),[2] caused worldwide fears.

The one example that stands out, however, is the Ebola-crisis starting in 2014. Starting with "patient zero", a two-year-old toddler, in a small village in Guinea,[3] the virus spread quickly through a region where Ebola was previously unknown. After affecting Guinea, Sierra Leone and Liberia and other states throughout the world, more than 11.323 lives were lost and more than 28.600 persons were infected.[4] Eventually, it turned out to be the biggest Ebola-outbreak in history by far.

---

1 Instructive Aginam, O, "Mission (Im)possible? The WHO as a 'Norm Entrepreneur' in Global Health Governance", in Freeman, M, Hawkes, S & Bennett, B (eds.), *Law and Global Health*, 2014, 559 (564 et seq.), who explains the shift from "international" to "global" health. Meier, B M & Mori, L M, "The Highest Attainable Standard: Advancing a Collective Human Right to Public Health" (2005), 37 *Columbia Human Rights Law Review*, 101 (105 et seq.) and UN High-level Panel on the Global Response to Health Crises, *Protecting Humanity from Future Health Crises*, January 25, 2016, para. 40.

2 On February 1, 2016 the WHO determined the Zika-outbreak a public health emergency of international concern, see WHO, *Statement on the first meeting of the International Health Regulations (2005) (IHR 2005) Emergency Committee on Zika virus and observed increase in neurological disorders and neonatal malformations*, available at http://bit.ly/1STUtYL.

3 UN High-level Panel on the Global Response to Health Crises, *Protecting Humanity from Future Health Crises*, above Fn. 1, para. 9.

4 Data up to March 27, 2016 taken from the World Health Organization, available at http://apps.who.int/ebola/ebola-situation-reports. For a historic overview see Gostin, L O & Friedman, E, "A Retrospective and Prospective Analysis of the West African Ebola Virus Disease Epidemic: Robust National Health Systems at the Foundation and an Empowered WHO at the Apex" (2015), 385 *The Lancet*, 1902 (1902 et seq.).

Notwithstanding its severity, the number of victims, the region affected by the outbreak, and not the least the media's fear-mongering coverage regarding Ebola being a threat to Europe,[5] the international response has not been speedy and comprehensive.[6] Even while the outbreak continued, several review processes were initiated and tasked to look at how international health governance could be improved.[7] This paper attempts to review two contributions to the fight: Temporary recommendations by the WHO and Resolution 2177 (2015) by the UN Security Council. After stocktaking, improvements are suggested for the respective instrument. As a third way forward, the paper proposes to utilize human rights law as catalyst for health governance and health law.

---

5 This holds true even for respectable news sources, see Elger, K, Hackenbroch, V & Knaup, H et al., "Gateway to Hell: The Threat of Ebola grows Worse" (September 8, 2014), *Spiegel Online International*, available at http://bit.ly/2lB67K0; Walker, T & Schmidt-Chanasit, J, "Is Europe taking the Ebola Threat seriously?" (Oktober 7, 2014), *Deutsche Welle*, available at http://www.dw.de/is-europe-taking-the-ebola-threat-seriously/a-17980662; "WHO warns of Ebola health care risks" (October 8, 2014), *BBC*, available at http://www.bbc.com/news/world-europe-29531671.

6 See Médecins Sans Frontières, *Ebola: Pushed to the limit and beyond. A critical analysis of the global Ebola response one year into the deadliest outbreak in history*, 2015, available at http://bit.ly/1OrjgQ8; Meier & Mori, "The Highest Attainable Standard", above Fn. 1, 101 (105 et seq.) as well as internal WHO documents published by The Associated Press dealing with the WHO's flawed attempts to combat the outbreak, available at http://apne.ws/1bGeijD. Criticism was also raised within the UN Security Council, Record of the 7502nd meeting of the Security Council, UN Doc. S/PV.7502 of August 13, 2015. The motifs for delaying response were already forecast by Davies, S & Youde, J, "The IHR (2005), Disease Surveillance, and the Individual in Global Health Politics" (2013), 17 *The International Journal of Human Rights*, 133 (134 et seq.); Silver, A, "Obstacles to Complying with the World Health Organization's 2005 International Health Regulations" (2009), 26 *Wisconsin International Law Journal*, 229 (235 et seq.).

7 See for example the UN Secretary General's High-Level Panel on Global Response to Health Crises or the WHO's own Ebola Interim Assessment Panel and Review Committee on the Role of the IHR (2005) in the Ebola Outbreak and Response.

II Pluriverse of Actors (1): The World Health Organization

1 Stocktaking

In international health governance, a pluriverse of actors undertakes the task of improving health: states, International Organizations as well as non-state actors work alone or together to combat diseases. Most prominently, the World Health Organization is tasked to attain for all peoples the highest possible level of health (Article 1 WHO Constitution).[8]

In order to do so, it has several possibilities at hand. In addition to the rather traditional and common possibilities to adopt conventions or agreements (Article 19 WHO Constitution) and to make recommendations (Article 23 WHO Constitution) there is a unique feature in WHO law: The authority of the WHO to issue legally binding regulations under Article 21 WHO Constitution.[9] This provision empowers the organization to adopt regulations concerning aspects specified in literae a-e. The key aspect is the entry-into-force: A convention or agreement adopted under this provision enters into force for all members after due notice has been given of its adoption (Article 22 WHO Constitution) – explicit consent is not required. As consequence, regulations adopted under Article 21 WHO Constitution are binding for Member States.[10] The only way to opt out of such an agreement for the state is to notify the Director-General of the rejection or a reservation by that state.

This is the legal ground for the International Health Regulations of 2005, or IHR (2005), which entered into force in 2007.[11] The IHR (2005) were the result of a reform process after the outbreak of the Severe Acute Respiratory Syndrome (SARS) in 2003 that affected more than 8.000 people

---

8 See Acconci, P, "The Reaction to the Ebola Epidemic within the United Nations framework: What Next for the World Health Organization?" in Lachmann, F, Röder, T J & Wolfrum, R (eds.), *Max Planck Yearbook of United Nations Law* 2014, 405 (406 et seq.).

9 Gostin, L O, *Global Health Law*, 2014, 111; Aginam, O, "Mission (Im)possible?", above Fn. 1, 559 (561).

10 Ruger, J, "Toward a Theory of a Right to Health: Capability and Incompletely Theorized Agreements" (2006), 18 *Yale Journal of Law & the Humanities*, 273 (312).

11 WHO, *International Health Regulations*, 2005, 2509 UNTS 179, thereinafter IHR (2005).

and killed 774 persons in 27 countries.[12] The preceding instruments were the IHR (1969),[13] which, as the name suggests, were adopted in 1969. After two modifications in 1973[14] and 1981[15] the scope of the IHR (1969) was limited to cholera, yellow fever and the plague. Before that, the WHO adopted the International Sanitary Regulations in 1951.[16] The current version is not limited to specific diseases.

In "Public Health Emergencies of International Concern", as defined in Article 1 IHR (2005), the WHO's Director-General has the power to issue temporary recommendations. These recommendations are non-binding in nature (Article 1 IHR [2005]). As a preparatory measure for further health crises, it may be useful to give the IHR (2005) and temporary recommendations more teeth.[17] This may be achieved by either creating explicit legal effect or by re-interpreting the law.[18]

2 No Case for a Binding Nature of Temporary Recommendations

De lege lata, temporary recommendations are non-binding, as stated in Article 1 (1) IHR (2005).[19] This does not lead to conclude that those recommendations are automatically without effect. On the contrary, due to the authority of the WHO, its aggregated expertise and the risk faced by states for defiance ensure compliance with emergency recommendations[20] – or at least *should* ensure compliance. In this sense, the WHO is supposed to work through its expertise. Theoretically, the mechanism regarding public health emergencies of international concern is an essential tool to address global

---

12 See WHO, *Summary of probable SARS cases with onset of illness from 1 November 2002 to 31 July 2003,* 2003, available at http://bit.ly/2lljjaE.

13 International Health Regulations, 1969, 764 UNTS 3, thereinafter IHR (1969).

14 WHO, *Health Assembly Resulution WHA26.55*, May 23, 1973.

15 WHO, *Health Assembly Doc. WHA34/1981/REC/I. at 10 (Resolution WHA34.13)*; see WHO, *Official Records, No. 217*, 1974, at 21, 71, and 81.

16 International Sanitary Regulations, 1951, 175 UNTS 215, thereinafter ISR (1951).

17 Villarreal, P A, "Reforms of the World Health Organization in light of the Ebola crisis in West Africa: More delegation, more teeth?" (August 26, 2015), *voelkerrechtsblog.com*, available at http://bit.ly/2m2NIYj.

18 See section II.4. The Way forward for the IHR (2005)?

19 Likewise Vierheilig, M, *Die rechtliche Einordnung der von der Weltgesundheits-organisation beschlossenen regulations*, 1984, 34.

20 Burci, G L & Quirin, J, "Ebola, WHO, and the United Nations: Convergence of Global Public Health and International Peace and Security" (2014), 18 *ASIL Insights*, available at http://bit.ly/2m5AFIF.

threats that utilizes international law without creating new obligations on the actors involved.

3 Evaluation within WHO

Despite the idea behind a non-binding character of temporary recommendations and its benefits, in fact many states ignored temporary recommendations during the Ebola-crisis 2014.[21] As stated earlier, there may be two solutions to this problem at hand.

Within the WHO two bodies identified Member States, whose lack of understanding of the IHR (2005) and respect for temporary recommendations, provided major obstacles.

a Ebola Interim Assessment Panel

Foremost, the Ebola Interim Assessment Panel was of the opinion that significant changes throughout the WHO were needed to re-establish the WHO's authority:[22] The panel found that the WHO lacked both, the capacity as well as the "organizational culture to deliver a full emergency public health response".[23] This went so far as to discuss a proposal to either establish a new health emergency organization or confer the lead in such cases to another UN agency.[24] As both would certainly have meant the end of the WHO as such, the panel urged the WHO to invest in its emergency operational capacity. In doing so, improvements were needed in governance and leadership, financing, organizational culture and procedures, as well as the work force and regional and international collaboration. In addition, research and development should be focused. The panel recalled that Member States of the WHO were responsible for raising the funds of the WHO. Without increased funding, all attempts of reform and improvement would

21 See WHO, *Report of the First Meeting of the Review Committee on the Role of the IHR (2005) in the Ebola Outbreak and Response*, August 25, 2015, para. 13.

22 WHO, *Report of the Ebola Interim Assessment Panel*, July 2015, 5.

23 Ibid., para. 26.

24 Ibid., para. 27.

be futile.[25] The Ebola Interim Assessment Panel also found shortcomings within the IHR (2005), which were implemented not strongly enough. First, the declaration of a public health emergency of international concern was too late. The panel highlighted that to declare a situation a public health emergency of international concern, the Director-General and her staff need to be independent and courageous.[26] However, this was absent during the first months of the crisis.[27] In addition, neither the Director-General nor the Member States took the IHR (2005) serious enough.[28] For example, Member States have failed to fulfill their obligations under the IHR (2005) to develop a preparedness strategy that could be independently evaluated.[29] As under the current IHR (2005), States will be penalized in practice by other countries if they report outbreaks quickly and transparently. Even though the IHR (2005) oblige States to act responsibly in case of an outbreak, the closing of borders and travel and trade restrictions hurt the countries affected by the crisis without benefiting anyone.[30] Here, the weakness of the IHR (2005) became very visible: Without any means to enforce its recommendations, States will most likely continue to defy temporary measures in situations of a public health emergency of international concern.[31] The panel proposed possible sanctions "for inappropriate and unjustified actions".[32] It also introduced the idea of calling on the Security Council in such cases.[33]

To summarize, the panel found shortcomings in leadership, organization and the behaviour of Member States. The IHR (2005) are, in the view of the panel, too soft and without any necessary enforcement mechanism.

25 WHO Ebola Response Team, "Ebola Virus Disease in West Africa — The First 9 Months of the Epidemic and Forward Projections" (2014), 371 *New England Journal of Medicine*, 1481 (1482).

26 WHO, *Report of the Ebola Interim Assessment Panel*, above Fn. 22, para. 8.

27 See also ibid., para. 20 et seq.

28 Ibid., para. 10.

29 Ibid., para. 11 et seq.

30 Ibid., para. 16.

31 Gostin & Friedman, "A Retrospective and Prospective Analysis of the West African Ebola Virus Disease Epidemic", above Fn. 4, 1902 (1904).

32 WHO, *Report of the Ebola Interim Assessment Panel*, above Fn. 22, para. 19.

33 Ibid., para. 19.

The Secretariat responded with an official paper.[34] With regard to the IHR (2005) the Secretariat announced a review process, albeit without going into detail on what changes could be imagined. It envisaged an intermediate stage before declaring a public health emergency of international concern.[35] With regard to possible disincentives or even sanctions for ignoring either the IHR (2005) or the temporary recommendations, the Secretariat kept rather quiet. It referred to its internal review process of the IHR (2005), which did focus on these issues.[36] Still, it is unfortunate that the Secretariat did not take a stand on such a crucial issue. For example, it could have envisaged a role of the Security Council, as recommended by the Ebola Interim Assessment Panel and the African Union.[37] In essence, it promised to work more efficiently and signalized institutional reforms to be prepared by several advisory bodies.

The Ebola Interim Assessment Panel has raised several important factors. From a legal perspective, the effectiveness of both, the IHR (2005) and the temporary recommendations issued in a concrete public health emergency of international concern needs to be increased. This could happen first through making the recommendations legally binding or by introducing a sanctions mechanism. Given that there is no such mechanism currently in place, even a soft one would be an improvement. Here, the Security Council could play a pivotal role. However, given that already the recommendations of 2011[38] to adapt the IHR (2005) in response to the swine flu pandemic of 2009 were ignored by the WHO and its Member States, it is not very likely that those regulations will be updated soon.

---

34 WHO, *Secretariat response to the Report of the Ebola Interim Assessment Panel*, August 2015, available at http://bit.ly/25dvmaA.

35 Ibid., para. 10. Likewise WHO, *Review Committee on the Role of the IHR (2005) in the Ebola Outbreak and Response, Implementation of the International Health Regulations (2005), A69/21*, May 13, 2016, recommendation 6, 64.

36 WHO, *Secretariat response to the Report of the Ebola Interim Assessment Panel*, above Fn. 34, para. 8; WHO, *Review Committee on the Role of the IHR (2005)*, above Fn. 35.

37 WHO, *Report of the Ebola Interim Assessment Panel*, above Fn. 22, para. 19; Statement of the representative of the AU, *Record of the 7502nd meeting of the Security Council*, UN Doc. S/PV.7502 of August 13, 2015, 8.

38 WHO, *Implementation of the International Health Regulations (2005) – Report of the Review Committee on the Functioning of the International Health Regulations (2005) in relation to Pandemic (H1N1) 2009, A64/10*, 2011.

b Review Committee on the Role of the IHR (2005) in the Ebola Outbreak and Response

Similar to the findings by the Ebola Interim Assessment Panel, the WHO's Review Committee on the Role of the IHR (2005) in the Ebola Outbreak and Response identified the lack of knowledge or understanding of the IHR (2005) and the need for further implementation (and not amendment) of the regulations as key issues for future reform.[39] Among others, it recommended to "incentivize compliance"[40] by supporting countries more which adhere to the IHR (2005) and to increase transparency and publicity about compliance with IHR (2005) and temporary recommendations.[41]

4 The Way forward for the IHR (2005)?

As stated earlier, there are two possibilities to enhance compliance with the IHR (2005) and temporary recommendations.

a Updating the IHR (2005)

First and most obvious, the WHO may modify the IHR (2005) in light of the recent defiance by states. If states are not ready to follow temporary recommendations, it may help if these recommendations became binding.

This would be a rather ingenuous way: Just a small modification is needed. In detail, Article 1 IHR (2005) could be modified to the extent that temporary recommendations are defined as "binding" measures. It would make sense to update the IHR (2005) in other ways as well. Most importantly, temporary recommendations should be relabelled as "temporary regulations" to make the binding nature transparent. By letting them expire after three months (as is today the case with temporary recommendations), states may be convinced not to opt-out of the modified IHR (2005). The binding nature would come with a price, in essence an expiration date. A

39 WHO, *Review Committee on the Role of the IHR (2005)*, above Fn. 35, para. 4 et seq., 154 et seq.

40 Ibid., para. 78.

41 Ibid., para. 66.

further vigorous addition would be a sanction mechanism for non-compliance with temporary recommendations. Of course, this would only make sense if the recommendations became binding.

However, the WHO's own review committee on the IHR (2005) advises against any modification of the existing law but suggests to better implement the existing law.[42] Especially a sanctions mechanism is highly unlikely. Given the WHO's reluctance to even name the states that have ignored past temporary recommendations,[43] an even more vigorous approach than under existing law is improbable.[44] It seems as if even the small obliteration of "non" in "non-binding" could not be achieved politically.

This questions the importance of law as in instrument in health governance: Legal tools are not the most important tools available in the fight against diseases.[45] What matters most are public health measures such as the improvement of hygiene, distribution of medication, development of antidotes. Whether or not an act is equipped with legal consequences is rather unimportant in the international arena and in the fight against a disease. Health governance relies on other mechanisms. Still, international law is not without any relevance and lawyers may nevertheless contribute in this effort. A purely source-based approach may stop short of the possibilities that international law and legal scholarship have to offer. In the end, rather than a change of the existing law, a new approach to the existing law is advisable and more likely. This more sophisticated approach is addressed in the following.

---

42 Review Committee on the Role of the International Health Regulations (2005) in the Ebola Outbreak and Response, Progress Report, January 25, 2016, 15; WHO, *Review Committee on the Role of the IHR (2005)*, above Fn. 35, para. 4 et seq., 154 et seq.

43 Kamradt-Scott, A, "WHO's to blame? The World Health Organization and the 2014 Ebola outbreak in West Africa" (2016), 37 *Third World Quarterly*, 1 (11).

44 As a somewhat lesser modification, the IHR (2005) could envisage a role for the UN Security Council. Currently, the IHR (2005) do not reference the Council overall. A modification could be made which entitles the Security Council to render those measures binding. In essence, this would not be needed, for the Security Council may do so already today: It is not a question of WHO-law, but of the UN Charter, more specifically of Article 41 UN Charter. It will be dealt with infra.

45 See Frau, R, "Law as an Antidote? Assessing the Potential of International Health Law Based on the Ebola-Outbreak 2014" (2016), 7 *Göttingen Journal of International Law*, 225 (228 et seq.).

b Article 43 IHR (2005) as a Means to Ensure Compliance

A smarter possibility to bring temporary recommendations to full effect may be to utilize Article 43 IHR (2005). This provision stipulates a very sophisticated process for additional health measures by states. In general, State Parties are not precluded from implementing additional health measures (Article 43 [1] IHR [2005]). However, the IHR (2005) are clear and repetitive on one thing: those additional measures may not be more restrictive on international traffic and not more intrusive on persons than reasonably available alternatives which achieve the appropriate level of health protection. If a state wants to adopt additional measures, this state shall provide the WHO with information. The WHO, in turn, assesses these measures and may request the state to reconsider its plans (Article 43 [4] IHR [2005]). In other words, additional measures must be justified by a State Party. If a state plans to adopt measures contrary to temporary recommendations already in place, those measures would contravene the conditions set at the end of Article 43 (1). If the WHO, for example, recommends to not restrict trade and travel, any trade and travel restrictions by states are more restrictive on international traffic and are more intrusive on persons. Thus, they fail to meet the threshold. Nevertheless, under international law, those national measures remain in force; the IHR (2005) cannot void any national measure. Still, the state is under the treaty obligation to report such measures (Article 43 [3], [5], [6] IHR [2005]). Thus, this requirement may push the state to adhere to the temporary recommendation and at least nudge him to refrain from contravening them. To be perfectly clear: This is in no way a legal enforcement mechanism, it may work for policy reasons only. From a public relations standpoint, it may sell well with local constituencies to adhere to the WHO's recommendation. If the WHO is recognized as an important and trustworthy actor, following its advice makes sense. But yet again, even though Article 43 IHR (2005) does not change the law, it may be advantageous for states to comply with the WHO's statement, thus, the WHO exercises public authority also in this field.[46]

46 Bogdandy, A von, Dann, P & Goldmann, M, "Developing the Publicness of International Law: Towards a Legal Framework for Global Governance Activities" (2008), 9 *German Law Journal*, 1375 (1382).

c Human Rights Law as Catalyst

Yet another possibility would be to interpret a state's obligation to progressively realize the human right to health in line with the temporary recommendations. In order to assess this possibility, a closer look at the human rights dimension is indispensable.

5 Changing Role of the WHO as a Price to Pay

Before addressing the human rights dimension, however, one further aspect needs to be emphasized: Be it the straightforward approach of changing the existing law or the more sophisticated approach of re-interpreting current law, both come with a price-tag. The WHO is supposed to function through its expertise. This organization is tasked to convince, not coerce by legal means. Conferring legally binding effects on acts (i.e. temporary recommendations) changes the perception of this organization. The WHO ceases to be seen as a health actor and takes the role of a norm-creator. Already existing legitimacy concerns towards the WHO would increase. Similar concerns exist towards the UN Security Council, the second actor which is analysed by this paper.

III Pluriverse of Actors (2): The UN Security Council

1 The UN and UNMEER

The UN were actively involved in the fight against Ebola with rather innovative measures. The Secretary General as well as the Security Council took unprecedented steps to counter the threat posed by Ebola. UNMEER, the United Nations Mission for Ebola Emergency Response, will be left out of the present analysis.[47]

---

47 See Frau, R, "Law as an Antidote?", above Fn. 45, 225 (253).

2 The UN Security Council and Resolution 2177 (2014)

a Article 41 UN Charter

In one astonishing move, the Security Council addressed the Ebola-outbreak in a resolution under chapter VII. In Resolution 2177 (2014) the Security Council highlighted the severity of the Ebola-outbreak. Taking note of the different actors, i.e. the countries affected, neighbouring states, UN-organs and organizations, Non-Governmental Organizations as well as first-line responders, the Security Council called upon them to collectively address the threat posed by the epidemic. In the operative part of said resolution, the Council commended the actors for their contributions but also "encouraged", "called" and "urged" these actors to do even more. Noteworthy is not the fact that the Council was not satisfied with the efforts to date, but that the Council did not "decide" on a common strategy, nor did it "demand" specific measures or "requested" concrete actions. It could have done so in regard to travel and trade restrictions, border management or access of health care workers to affected countries or regions – issues that are addressed by the WHO as well as by the Council, but only as recommendations.[48] Also, the recommendations by the WHO were not transformed into legally binding obligations by virtue of Security Council actions under chapter VII UN Charter. The Council could have easily demanded from Member States that they keep open their borders to affected countries, cooperate with them with regard to border management (exit and entry screenings that is) or address domestic actors to continue travel and transport to and from West Africa.[49] In essence, the Council refrained from addressing the epidemic by legal means and issued mere recommendations.

b Article 39 UN Charter

Audaciously the Council determined "that the unprecedented extent of the Ebola outbreak in Africa constitutes a threat to international peace and security", thus opening its powers under chapter VII. This is an innovative approach. Given, there is a large discussion about the scope of the notion

48 See preambular para. 9 and 17 of Resolution 2177 (2014).
49 Similar Gostin & Friedman, "A Retrospective and Prospective Analysis of the West African Ebola Virus Disease Epidemic", above Fn. 4, 1902 (1906).

"threat to international peace and security" under Article 39 UN Charter. As is well known, scholarship is divided on the interpretation of "peace" in Article 39 UN Charter. Some[50] argue for a wide understanding of "peace", which includes aspects of positive peace, for example "broader conditions of social development".[51] Others take a more cautious approach, understanding the term to cover only negative peace, in other words the absence of armed violence between states.[52]

With the Security Council understanding the Ebola-outbreak as a "threat to international peace and security", one could assume that the Council now opts for a wider interpretation of that notion as before. Is there any merit to this claim? Is that the way forward for the Security Council?

3 The Way forward for the Security Council?

a Article 39 UN Charter (1): Health Crises as a Threat to the Peace

First of all, the Security Council has never before understood Article 39 UN Charter as to include health aspects. While the Council prudently hinted that HIV/AIDS "may pose a risk to stability and security",[53] the Council did not dare to make that recommendation in the decades that followed this suggestion.[54] In addition, the human right to health is not closely related to negative peace, it is a part of positive peace. Also, the Council highlights the vast challenges, which are posed by the Ebola-outbreak, beginning with care for infected persons, safe burials of victims, misinformation about the virus and its transmission, food insecurity, a functioning domestic health care system and other. Contrary to its usual practice, the Council did not address the question of refugees explicitly as constituting a threat. This could be understood as a move away from the fear of refugees as a destabilizing factor. More than 130 States co-sponsored the draftresolution, mak-

---

50 See ibid.

51 Akehurst, M & Malanczuk, P, *A modern introduction to international law*, 1987, 219.

52 See only Tomuschat, C, "Obligations arising for States without or against their will" (1993), 241 *Recueil des Cours de l'Academie de droit international de la Haye*, 195 (334 et seq.).

53 Security Council Resolution 1308 (2000).

54 Security Council Resolution 1983 (2011), which repeats the phrasing of Resolution 1308 (2000).

ing it the most supported chapter VII resolution ever. This seems to demonstrate a unanimous understanding between Member States of the UNO as authorized interpreters of Article 39 UN Charter to include positive peace aspects in this notion.

Interpreting Resolution 2177 (2014) in this way, however, ignores the wording of the resolution. First of all, the Council clearly states that the "unprecedented extent" of the outbreak constitutes the threat and not the mere existence of an epidemic. Granted, the claim that something is unique may be made quite easily and is not decisive. Second, and most importantly, the Council relates the Ebola-outbreak to international peace and security in a rather traditional way: its preambular paragraphs emphasize such aspects repeatedly. The Council not only reiterates the international dimension of the disease, affecting several countries in the region, but links the disease directly to international security issues: The Security Council recognizes

> "that the peacebuilding and development gains of the most affected countries concerned could be reversed in light of the Ebola outbreak and underlining that the outbreak is undermining the stability of the most affected countries concerned and, unless contained, may lead to further instances of civil unrest, social tensions and a deterioration of the political and security climate."[55]

The meeting record is affluent with references to the instable situation in the most affected countries and the region.[56] Voices that based Resolution 2177 (2014) on the health crisis alone are minor.[57]

In this sense, the members of the Security Council did not interpret Article 39 UN Charter in an innovative way, Resolution 2177 (2014) keeps in line with the conservative understanding of the notion "threat to inter-

---

55 Preambular para. 4 Resolution 2177 (2014).

56 See for example the statements by the representatives of the Security Council Member States Argentina (20), Australia (16), Chad (19), Chile (22), China (16), France (10), Jordan (21), Lithuania (14), Luxembourg (18), Republic of Korea (13), Rwanda (12) and United Kingdom (17), as well as participating States under rule 37 of the Security Council's provisional rules of procedure Brazil (29), Canada (32), Colombia (45), Estonia (41), Germany (44), Guinea (24), Guyana (47), Italy (39), Japan (33), Morocco (29), Netherlands (35), Norway (42), Sierra Leone (26), Spain (38), Switzerland (30), Turkey (32) and International Organizations as the African Union (37), all in UN Doc.S/PV/7268. As a side note, the traditional aspects were already highlighted in Annex to the Letter dated September 15, 2014 from the Secretary-General addressed to the President of the Security Council, UN Doc. S/2014/669.

57 Statement by the representative of the United States, UN Doc. S/PV/7268, 7. See also the statement by the representative of France, UN Doc. S/PV/7268, 30.

national peace and security".[58] Ultimately, it is not Ebola that led the Security Council to act, but the anticipated instability of the region due to Ebola.

In addition, if states ignore the temporary recommendations issued by the Director-General, this may pose a threat to international peace and security. Thus, the Security Council may determine defiance as such and is at least in theory able to take measures under chapter VII UN Charter.

b Article 39 UN Charter (2): Safeguarding the Human Right to Health

Even if health crises per se do not fall under the notion of peace as intended by Article 39 UN Charter, the danger to the human right to the highest attainable standard of health, Article 12 ICESCR, could enable the Security Council to act. Precondition, however, is the existence of a threat to international peace and security. If, and only if, a danger to Article 12 ICESCR has some cross-border effects (or is feared to have such effects), Article 39 UN Charter is fulfilled and the Security Council may act.

c Article 41 UN Charter: Possible Measures by the Security Council

If the Security Council determines a situation to be a threat to peace and security, it opens the doors to chapter VII measures. These measures may include peaceful and coercive measures.

In the case of Ebola, however, the Security Council missed an opportunity to act swiftly and effectively and re-shape international health law or at least facilitate its development. Once the Council had determined that the unprecedented extent of the Ebola outbreak in Africa constituted a threat to international peace and security,[59] it could have issued binding decisions under Article 41 and 42 UN Charter and not mere recommendations under Article 40 UN Charter. The need for effective action was evident, at least by the repeated calls of the Emergency Committee regarding Ebola to address border management, exit and entry screening as well as a lift to trade and travel bans. Given the fact that the majority among the UN Member States was willing to deal with the crisis under chapter VII UN Charter,

58 See Acconci, "The Reaction to the Ebola Epidemic within the United Nations framework", above Fn. 8, 405 (419 et seq.) for a different approach.

59 Preambular para. 5 of Resolution 2177 (2014).

including all permanent and elected members of the Security Council, binding measures seemed to be a viable option.

The Council could have used its far-reaching powers under Article 41, 42 UN Charter in the following ways: For example, it could have authorized the deployment of troops in order to provide much needed staff for safe burials of victims or border management, i.e. to conduct exit or entry screenings. Furthermore, it could have elevated the WHO's temporary recommendations as proposed by the Emergency Committee regarding Ebola to legally binding obligations, where applicable. Surprisingly, the IHR (2005) do not reference the Security Council in any way and neither did the Security Council establish any relations to the WHO.[60] Also, it could have decided that borders to the three most affected countries had to stay open in order to halt the isolation of these countries and communities and subsequent protests and violence, which challenged the three states. After all, all the factors that the members of the Security Council feared contributed to the likelihood of new civil wars in the region.[61]

In the aftermath of the Ebola-crisis, experts suggested to install a permanent Global Health Committee.[62] This commission should be established by the Security Council and should be a subsidiary organ. As such, it could monitor health situations all over the world and advice the council on dangers and possible counter measures. The UN Charter would allow for that. It is up to the Security Council to organize its own work. If its members find it smart to establish such a supervising health commission, nothing stops the council from establishing it. The only limit is that the Security Council itself needs to act: The Charter confers rights to the Council, not to a subsidiary organ.

4 The Role of the Security Council

The UN Security Council has a mandate to maintain international peace and security (Article 24 [1] UN Charter); it is not an international Health Council. If the Security Council becomes an actor in health governance by way

60 Statement, *Record of the 7502nd meeting of the Security Council*, above Fn. 37, 8.

61 See above Fn. 56.

62 Moon, S, Sridhar, D & Pate, M A et al., "Will Ebola change the game? Ten essential reforms before the next pandemic. The report of the Harvard-LSHTM Independent Panel on the Global Response to Ebola" (2015), 386 *The Lancet*, 2204 (2216).

of states relying on its powers, health governance shifts into the direction of security. Resolution 2177 (2014) may be seen as a first step towards a securitization of health.[63] Yet securitization of health only makes sense in cases of worldwide pandemics or similar cases where the stability of an entire region is at stake. For health issues without a security implication, the Security Council is not competent to act.

Even in cases comparable to Ebola 2014, any increased importance of the Security Council comes with a price as well. Ownership of health governance is taken away from local actors or even specialized such as the WHO and conferred to the most powerful organ of the international community in New York City. In the regions concerned, however, ownership and legitimacy matter. Relying on the Security Council would increase concerns with regard to both issues.

IV The Human Right to Health as Catalyst

1 The Human Right to Health

Bringing all together is the human right to health. Despite the difficulties surrounding this right – after all, being healthy does not solely or primarily depend on state's behaviour, but on one's physical and mental preconditions[64] and due to the scope of the human right being limited – its importance can hardly be overstated. Nevertheless, when states drafted the International Covenant on Economic, Social and Cultural Rights (ICESCR)[65] and its Article 12, States were aware of the broad definition of health as well as the impossibility to safeguard a perfect health for everyone.[66] Consequently, Article 12 ICESCR guarantees a human right to the "enjoyment of the highest attainable standard of physical and mental health" (Article 12 [1] ICESCR).

Article 12 (2) ICESCR insinuates several steps that State Parties shall take to achieve the full realization of the right enshrined in Article 12 (1). Among those steps are the "prevention, treatment and control of epidemic,

---

63 See the contribution of *Ilja Richard Pavone*, "Ebola and Securitization of Health: UN Security Council Resolution 2177/2014 and its Limits" in this volume.

64 Wolff, J, *The Human Right to Health*, 2012, 27.

65 International Covenant on Economic, Social and Cultural Rights, 1966, 993 UNTS 3, thereinafter ICESCR.

66 Gostin, *Global Health Law*, above Fn. 9, 251.

endemic, occupational and other diseases" and the "creation of conditions which would assure to all medical service and medical attention in the event of sickness". However, under Article 2 (1) ICESCR it has to be taken into account that a State is obliged to undertake steps to "progressively [achieve] the full realization of the rights recognized" by the ICESCR. Hence, Article 12 (2) ICESCR complements[67] the individual human right to health with obligations of State Parties.[68]

In this sense, Article 2 (1) ICESCR "limits" the human right to health to a relatively weak and abstract obligation of progressive realization.[69] States may thus differ in their approach to the full realization due to specific domestic factors.[70] To shape the substantial obligations, some specific areas of concern have been identified in the General Comment. Among them are not, however, substantial obligations regarding emergency situations.

2 Obligations to Respect, Protect and Fulfil

State Parties to the ICESCR are under an obligation to ensure the human right to the highest attainable standard of health. The General Comment has interpreted Article 12 ICESCR to include obligations to respect, protect and fulfil.[71] In particular, a state is under the obligation to refrain from interfering directly or indirectly with this right, to protect individuals from interference by other actors and to adopt appropriate measures towards the full realization of the human right to health.[72] Of outmost importance is international assistance and cooperation, as laid out in Article 2 (1) ICESCR.

In addition to bilateral cooperation and multilateral cooperation through the WHO, the UN General Assembly is also tasked with promoting international cooperation in the field of health (Article 13 [1][b] UN Charter). In doing so, each state is expected to contribute to the maximum of its capacities.[73] How international cooperation can be achieved is, of course, a matter for each specific case.

---

67 Meier & Mori, "The Highest Attainable Standard", above Fn. 1, 101 (113).
68 See Tobin, J, *The Right to Health in International Law*, 2012, 75, 225 et seq.
69 Critical Meier & Mori, "The Highest Attainable Standard", above Fn. 1, 101 (115).
70 Ibid.
71 General Comment No. 14 (2000), *The right to the highest attainable standard of health*, UN Doc. E/C.12/2000/4, August 11, 2000, para. 33.
72 Ibid., para. 33.
73 Ibid., para. 40.

3 States Obligations Ratione Loci

The ICESCR does not provide an explicit threshold of application, unlike the International Covenant on Civil and Political Rights (ICCPR), where Article 2 [1] ICCPR obliges State Parties to undertake to "respect and to ensure to all individuals within its territory and subject to its jurisdiction the rights recognized in the present Covenant". A comparable provision is found in Article 2 [1] ICESCR where states agree to undertake to take

> "steps, individually and through international assistance and co-operation, especially economic and technical, to the maximum of [their] available resources, with a view to achieving progressively the full realization of the rights recognized in the present Covenant by all appropriate means, including particularly the adoption of legislative measures".

Any reference to the applicability ratione loci is missing.[74]

One can make the case and argue for applicability only in a State Party's territory. If the "right to health" is correctly the somehow weaker human right to the enjoyment of the highest attainable standard of physical and mental health (Article 12 [1] ICESCR), it could follow that it has no international dimension. Moreover, if a state cannot provide perfect health to everyone on its territory, how can a state than achieve this goal abroad? Providing health care is a domestic matter and states are under no obligation to provide healthcare abroad.

This view has its merits. However, interpreting the human right to the mere supply of hospitals, doctors, medicine and the like falls short of treaty law.[75] After all, Article 2 [1] ICESCR includes an undertaking of international assistance and cooperation. International assistance and cooperation has naturally an international dimension. By being under the treaty obligation to render assistance, states may not hamper efforts by other states to achieve health. One needs to keep in mind that international assistance may be rendered on the state's own territory.

4 The Role of Human Rights Law

Taken all together, human rights law may act as a catalyst in health law as part of health governance. The present author proposes to put the human

---

74 See the contribution of *Elif Askin*, "Extraterritorial Human Rights Obligations of States in the Event of Disease Outbreaks" in this volume regarding the extraterritorial applicability of the ICESCR.

75 *Elif Askin* is making a more straightforward approach in the present volume.

right to health at the very heart of health governance, which may lead to improved interaction between different branches of law. This may be achieved by the following reasoning.

If one takes into account, first, that travel and trade restrictions are detrimental to the fight against Ebola, second, that the Director-General repeatedly recommended to lift travel and trade restrictions, and third, that such measures are taken by a state on its territory, then Article 12 (1), (2) ICESCR is affected by such measures. In short, the obligation to progressively realize the rights enshrined in the ICESCR in cooperation with other states as well as the obligation to assist other states in their endeavour to provide the human right to health is violated by restrictions taken despite a temporary recommendations to the opposite.[76] Even if states are not under an obligation to render assistance without being asked for it,[77] impeding assistance is not in the ambit of the ICESCR.[78]

The Security Council should embrace the human right to health. It is unfortunate that the Council ignored this right during the recent Ebola-outbreak. If taken seriously, human rights may lead the WHO and the Security Council to cooperate more closely and combat outbreaks more effectively and efficiently.

V Conclusion

Does it make sense to modify and adapt the IHR (2005) in light of the recent crises? Does it make sense to create legally binding effects for the WHO's temporary recommendations? Does it make sense to engage the Security Council?

---

76 An international dimension of Article 12 (2) ICESCR is also identified by General Comment No. 14 (2000), *The right to the highest attainable standard of health*, above Fn. 71, para. 38 et seq.; and General Comment No. 3 (1990), *The Nature of States Parties' Obligations*, UN Doc. E/1991/23, December 14, 1990, para. 13. Critical to the General Comment Saul, B, Kinley, D & Mowbray, J, *The International Covenant on Economic, Social and Cultural Rights: Commentary, Cases, and Materials*, 2014, 139 et seq. Others identify this international dimension also, see Wolff, *The Human Right to Health*, above Fn. 64, 32; Tobin, *The Right to Health in International Law*, above Fn. 68, 325 et seq.

77 Saul, Kinley & Mowbray, *The International Covenant on Economic, Social and Cultural Rights*, above Fn. 76, 139.

78 Likewise Tobin, *The Right to Health in International Law*, above Fn. 68, 331 et seq. See also General Comment No. 14 (2000), *The right to the highest attainable standard of health*, above Fn. 71, para. 39, 41.

The assessment by the WHO's internal review may lead one to assume that it simply does not matter. Law does not cure anyone. The non-binding nature of temporary recommendations may not have had any impact on the Member States unwillingness to adhere to them. In this way, creating legal effect may be theoretically possible but would probably not matter much during the next epidemic. A more sophisticated approach may be better suitable to enforce compliance, i.e. a re-interpretation of the law. Also, engaging the Security Council is a good idea only for epidemics with negative impacts on a region's security. Relying on the Security Council would take ownership of health governance from the actors in the field and confer it to the powerful actor in New York City. Thus, legitimacy concerns with regard to the Security Council are well founded. It makes sense to focus on human rights law, which protects against the exercise of international public authority and which would lead the WHO and the Security Council to cooperate more closely.

Governance Beyond the Law

The Limits of the International Health Regulations: Ebola Governance, Regulatory Breach, and the Non-Negotiable Necessity of National Healthcare

Susan L. Erikson[*]

Abstract

If international regulation is the answer to epidemic disease containment, the 2014 Ebola outbreak in Sierra Leone would have come under control quickly. The health ministry, bi- and multi-lateral organizations, and Non-Governmental Organizations (NGOs) in Sierra Leone are rife with regulation, recommendation, and best-practice standards. The fragmentation of the health sector in many poor countries following economic liberalization, though, has led to what some anthropologists have qualified as "republics of NGOs"; each NGO has its own set of standards and regulatory affects, most often donor interest-driven. National and international law imposes another set of obligations. In Sierra Leone this has created healthcare service and response that is more of an ad hoc healthcare *assemblage* and *medicoscape* than a healthcare *system*. In many impoverished countries, the contemporary moment is one in which health regulations – the documents themselves – sometimes stand in as emergency response-ready mechanisms, not just for local administrators but also and even more so for members of the international community. That is, until there is an epidemic threat, when disease can and does move into realms of human experience beyond regulation and rule of law. This article focuses on one document, the International Health Regulations (IHR),[1] to show how despite good

---

* Dr., medical anthropologist who has worked in Africa, Europe, Central Asia, and North America. During a first international affairs career, *Susan L. Erikson* worked for or with government departments and agencies on issues of international development, foreign policy, and trade. As an academic at the Faculty of Health Sciences, Simon Fraser University (slerikson@sfu.ca), *Susan L. Erikson* combines her practical work experience with research on the relations of power informing global health scenarios. She has been working in Sierra Leone since the mid-1980s. All websites last accessed November 30, 2016.

1 This article refers to the WHO, *International Health Regulations (2005), 3th edition*, 2016, available at http://bit.ly/2mhqVK8.

international intentions, the bureaucratic energies devoted to making and maintaining the document and its regulations are over-done and disproportionate compared to the dearth of international political moxie needed to support Sierra Leonean national healthcare system-building in an age of global zoonotic disease migrations. In sum, while the IHR are important to the global health community aspirationally, the larger on-the-ground problem is that, first, there must be a national healthcare to plug them in *to.* The IHR operate as important guidelines, but do not meet the measure of regulations.

I Method

In March 2014 when news of Ebola infections first reached Sierra Leone,[2] the author was in-country leading an ethnographic research team in the capital city, Freetown. Although the author and her team were studying a different topic – the use of health data – the team was respectively embedded in and witnessed the local health sector's initial efforts to manage the Ebola outbreak. The research employed anthropological theory and method; fieldwork-informed ethnography is the disciplinary expertise of the author. The research team spent a combined total of 14 months in 2013 and 2014 in Sierra Leone collecting data, conducting over 75 interviews. In addition to the recently collected research data, the contribution is informed by nearly a decade of the author's professional experience working in Sierra Leone and Washington, DC, in the field of international development prior to becoming an academic.

In the last several decades, anthropologists and other social scientists have expanded their scholarly attentions from village and ritual life to everyday habits and practices. Fieldwork experiences are as likely to take place in global institutions as they are in rural outposts. Data collection is as likely

2 Although the Ebola outbreak primarily affected three West African countries – Sierra Leone, Liberia, and Guinea – the author has worked as an international development worker and more recently as a university researcher and anthropologist only in Sierra Leone. It is from that expert perspective that the article is written. Sierra Leone, Liberia, and Guinea have different historical, colonial, and contemporary trajectories and engagements in the world system, and this evidenced in the governance of the respective Ebola outbreaks. Although the IHR are intentionally universal in their design, the on-the-ground governance of Ebola was not universal and was shaped by former colonial engagements and particularist contemporary national healthcare configurations.

to include observations of bureaucrats and executives as it is ritual specialists. Data analyses, in the case of this article, incorporates a theoretical science and technology studies orientation that examines international artifacts of bureaucratic and political impact and control, thus making documents, regulations, standards, and laws subjects of scientific inquiry in their own right. As such, this article moves outside legal paradigms and employs the conventions of anthropological method and analysis for its conclusions.

II Introduction to the IHR

This article contextualizes and explains the ways that IHR[3] are limited in some places in the world. In this author's observation, this is not because countries intentionally defy international regulations, but rather that the IHR are too far removed from on-the-ground public health realities of particular geographies. The disconnect had and continues to have serious consequences for disease governance. As witnessed in 2014-2015, the spread of Ebola was unregulatable,[4] simply beyond the rule of law.[5]

1 IHR as a Legally Binding Agreement, in Theory

The IHR is an international treaty among 196 States Parties, which voted and approved the document most recently at the 2005 World Health Assembly. The IHR have accomplished an important achievement in that they offer a cooperative template of measures to deter "naturally, accidentally, or deliberate [sic] released infections from spreading internationally".[6] The template imposes a "reciprocal responsibility – the obligation of all nations to detect, report, and contain public health threats, in order to

3 See above Fn. 1.
4 See also Wilkinson, A & Leach, M, "Briefing: Ebola – Myth, Realities, and Structural Violence" (2014), *African Affairs*, 1.
5 "Rule of law" is a term used throughout this article. This term refers to its customary legal interpretation as an international legal principle in which laws rather than arbitrary action govern the people of a nation-state. In this article, the notion of "rule of law" also refers to the contemporary need for uniform legal principles and their enforcements for state and non-state actors.
6 Fischer, E, Kornblet, S & Katz, R, "The International Health Regulations (2005): Surveillance and Response in an Era of Globalization" (2011), *White Paper, Stimon Center Washington, DC*, 3, available at http://bit.ly/2mRC5a1.

protect lives and livelihoods worldwide"[7] – on all 194 World Health Organization (WHO) member nations plus Liechtenstein and the Holy See.[8] Article 2 states:

> "The purpose and scope of these Regulations are to prevent, protect against, control and provide a public health response to the international spread of disease in ways that are commensurate with and restricted to public health risks, and which avoid unnecessary interference with international traffic and trade."[9]

2 The WHO as Principal Implementation Agent

The principal agent for assuring global health security is the WHO, a United Nations (UN) organization endowed by its Member States with the authority to respond to public health events requiring "immediate action".[10] Following the International Sanitary Regulations that emerged from a 1892 European conference, new international health regulations were revised by WHO member nations first in 1969, and then more recently in 2005. The WHO is the world body tasked with 1) regulating, 2) identifying and naming, and 3) possessing the emergency powers to ensure global health security when the world confronts a public health emergency.[11]

3 IHR as the Primary Document Governing Global Health Security

The IHR is inarguably necessary and important to achieving measures of global health security, and there is little doubt that the IHR – as a document – succeed in setting forth international bureaucratic standards for public health emergencies of international concern. Therein lies a problem: In many impoverished countries, the contemporary historical moment is one in which health regulations – quite literally, the documents themselves –

---

7 Fischer, J & Katz, R, *International Health Regulations 101*, 2012, 4, available at http://bit.ly/2mhQIC0.

8 WHO, *International Health Regulations (2005)*, above Fn. 1, Appendix 1, 59.

9 Ibid., 10.

10 WHO Constitution, as cited in Kamradt-Scott, A, "WHO's to blame? The World Health Organization and the 2014 Ebola Outbreak in West Africa" (2016), 37 *Third World Quarterly*, 402. Kamradt-Scott is citing Articles 21 and 28 of the WHO Constitution.

11 Ibid., 402; WHO Constitution, Article 21, as cited in Acconci, P, "The Reaction to the Ebola Epidemic within the United Nations Framework: What Next for the World Health Organization?" in Lachenmann, F, Röder, T J & Wolfrum, R (eds.), *Max Planck Yearbook of United Nations Law*, 2014, 408.

sometimes stand in as response-ready mechanisms, not just for local administrators but also and even more so for members of the international community. That is, until a health emergency hits. The more difficult, necessary and fundamental task of global health security is the building of emergency clinical response capable of thwarting the spread of disease. Such an infrastructural-intensive remedy is sine qua non.

However, the research informing this contribution found that time and again, in offices in Freetown, documents and readiness checklists *stood in for* actual preparedness. These substitutions were not a product of malice or deception but rather of the contemporary ad hoc non-systems health governance structures described below. The "system-making of no system" has been taken up by various medical anthropologists, who have described the ad hoc assemblages of care in poor countries as "medicoscapes",[12] and "republic[s] of NGOs",[13] and the grand challenge of real health system building.[14] In the lead up to the 2014 Ebola outbreak and after, global governors have relied too much on these documents for governance.

4 Acknowledged and Unacknowledged Limits of the IHR

a Issue of Enforcement

When people, including the Director-General of the WHO, talk about lessons learned from the West African Ebola outbreak, they frequently reference the IHR as authoritative and legally binding.[15] For an international regulation to be authoritative as a rule of law, there needs to be aa) a clear definition of a breach, ab) a clear explanation of what will happen should

12 Hörbst, V & Wolf, A, "Globalisierung der Heilkunde: Eine Einführung" in Hörbst, V & Wolf, A (eds.), *Medizin und Globalisierung: Universelle Ansprüche – lokale Antworten*, 2003, 3.

13 Schuller, M, *Killing with Kindness: Haiti, International Aid, and NGOs*, 2012.

14 Pfeiffer, J & Chapman, R, "The Art of Medicine: An Anthropology of Aid in Africa" (2015), 385 *The Lancet*, 2143 (2143-2144).

15 See for example "The IHR [...] are the only internationally-agreed set of rules governing the timely and effective response to outbreaks of infectious diseases and other public health emergencies. If its legally-binding obligations on States Parties are not being met, change is urgently needed." In Chan, M, "WHO Director-General Addresses the Review Committee of the International Health Regulations Focused on the Ebola Response", August 24, 2015, available at http://www.who.int/dg/speeches/2015/review-committee-ihr-ebola/en/.

any party fail to fulfill their responsibilities, and ac) enforcement means in the case of a breach.[16] The IHR does not include such items.

Nation-states, according to the IHR, for example, are obliged to report infectious disease outbreaks to the WHO within 24 hours.

> "Each State Party shall assess events occurring within its territory by using the decision instrument in Annex 2 [decision tree]. Each State Party shall notify WHO, by the most efficient means of communication available, [...] within 24 hours of assessment of public health information."[17]

aa Definition of a Breach

The IHR does not define a breach of the obligations. Rather, it relies on "shall" language, leaving treaty ratifiers in question as to what constitutes "have not yet", "did not", or "will not".[18] Article 13 of the IHR, put in force with the 2005 ratification, specifies that there is a state obligation to "develop, strengthen and maintain" government capacity to respond to public health risks:

> "1. Each State Party shall develop, strengthen and maintain, as soon as possible but no later than five years from the entry into force of these Regulations for that State Party, the capacity to respond promptly and effectively to public health risks and public health emergencies of international concern [...]."

However, if a state cannot build capacity in five years (from 2005), extensions are possible:

> "2. [...] a State Party may report to WHO on the basis of a justified need and an implementation plan and, in so doing, obtain an extension of two years in which to fulfil the obligation [...].
>
> [...] the State Party may request a further extension not exceeding two years from the Director-General [...]."

---

16 The argument here is a grassroots on-the-ground common sense argument, which may cause consternation for legal technicians. For regulations to be binding, there must be a consequence in a breach. Otherwise the regulations are not binding. This is well understood in the everyday praxes of international affairs. Common sense should not be ignored as a prevailing logic system. It is well circulated on-the-ground and more pervasive than legal systems – local and global – and one that requires far less formal training and precedent dependency for participation.

17 WHO, *International Health Regulations (2005)*, above Fn. 1, Article 6, Notification, 12.

18 Appendix 2 includes Reservations, Understandings, and Declarations qualifying the IHR ratifications of seven countries, none of which are the three countries primarily affected by Ebola.

This is an example of the IHR document out of sync with the on-the-ground realities of WHO member nations. An article in *The Lancet* summarized the magnitude of disconnect between the obligations set forth in the IHR and *most* member countries' inability to build infrastructural capacity:

> "[U]nder the International Health Regulations (2005), the 2012 deadline [was] extended for some countries to 2014, then 2019 after Ebola struck [...] *as of 2014, two-thirds of countries had not met their core capacity requirements and 48 countries had not responded to WHO queries regarding their readiness [...].*"

The IHR did not include binding obligations for donors to provide support to poorer countries to meet these obligations, nor to fund WHO to fulfill its mandate to provide technical assistance. These shortcomings did not attract serious action or funding until the Ebola outbreak.[19]

ab Setting Forth What Happens If Parties Breach Delegated Responsibilities

The IHR does not explicate what the WHO will do in the case of a breach, nor does it take up the various natures of breaches such as were seen during the recent Ebola outbreak. What happens if State Parties do not notify? Or what if they *do* notify the WHO and the Director-General does not act, as was the cause of the April to August 2014 delay in declaring Ebola in West Africa a public health emergency of international concern?[20] Further, what of countries, like Australia and Canada, that introduced epidemiologically groundless and unnecessary travel bans, thus defying the IHR's mandate against "unnecessary interference with international traffic and trade"?[21]

---

19 Moon, S, Sridhar, D & Pate, M A et al., "Will Ebola change the game? Ten essential reforms before the next pandemic. The report of the Harvard-LSHTM Independent Panel on the Global Response to Ebola" (2015), 386 *The Lancet*, 2204 (2207 et seq.). Emphasis mine.

20 Kamradt-Scott, "WHO's to blame?", above Fn. 10, 404-407.

21 "Australia Suspends Visas for People Travelling from Ebola-hit Countries" (October 27, 2014), *BBC*, available at http://bbc.in/2mB0a4g; Branswell, H, "Ebola: Canada Suspending Visas for Residents of Outbreak Countries" (October 31, 2014), *CBC*, available at http://bit.ly/10be51A; see also WHO, *Report of the Ebola Interim Assessment Panel*, 2015, 5, available at http://www.who.int/csr/resources/publications/ebola/report-by-panel.pdf: "[...] in violation of the Regulations, nearly a quarter of WHO's Member States instituted travel bans and other additional measures not called for by WHO, which significantly interfered with international travel, causing negative political, economic and social consequences for the affected countries."

What of quasi-state owned airlines like Air France that suspended travel to Sierra Leone?[22] What of non-state actors standing in for states – in this post-privatizing era there are many providing services in an Ebola outbreak – who fail to report disease outbreaks and/or interfere with traffic and trade?[23] What about non-affected countries whose companies bought up Ebola supplies – such as the medical hazmat suits knowns as PPEs (Personal Protection Equipment) – thus shorting the distribution in West Africa where they were critically needed?[24]

Within the IHR document, language concerning a breach in responsibilities is brief, unspecific, and dependent mostly on legal mechanisms operating outside the purview of the WHO. In Article 56, in seeking the settlement of disputes *between* Member States, states are advised:

> "1. […] to settle the dispute through negotiation or any other peaceful means of their own choice, including good offices, mediation or conciliation […]."[25]
>
> "4. [States may] resort to the dispute settlement mechanisms of other intergovernmental organizations or established under any international agreement."[26]

With regard to disputes between the WHO and its Member States, there is an internal process mechanism. Its language and procedural instructions, however, are tautological. The tranche below translates, in effect, to "In the event of a dispute between the WHO and others, the matter will be submitted to the WHO."

> "5. In the event of a dispute between WHO and one or more States Parties concerning the interpretation or application of these Regulations, the matter shall be submitted to the Health Assembly."[27]

---

22 Gordon, S, "Air France Suspends Flights to Ebola-hit Sierra Leone at Request of French Government" (August 27, 2014), *Daily Mail,* available at http://dailym.ai/2mhWR11.

23 McKay, B, "Peace Corps, Aid Groups Evacuate Personnel From Ebola-Hit West Africa" (July 31, 2014), *Wall Street Journal,* available at http://on.wsj.com/2mSzHjm; Neate, R, "Mining Company at Centre of Fight against Ebola in Sierra Leone Goes Bust" (October 16, 2014), *The Guardian,* available at http://bit.ly/2lYy6nG.

24 Hinshaw, D & Bunge, J, "U.S. Buys Up Ebola Gear, Leaving Little for Africa: Manufacturers Strain to Meet Demand Amid Rising Anxiety" (November 24, 2014), *Wall Street Journal,* available at http://on.wsj.com/2mSwQqk.

25 Ibid.; WHO, *International Health Regulations (2005)*, above Fn. 1.

26 WHO, ibid.

27 WHO, ibid.

ac Enforcement in the Case of a Breach

Years before the Ebola outbreak, there was already an understanding that the IHR contained unenforceable regulations. Summary Conclusion 1 of the 2011 Report of the Implementation of the International Health Regulations report that:

> "24. The most important structural shortcoming of the IHR is the lack of enforceable sanctions. For example, if a country fails to explain why it has adopted more restrictive traffic and trade measures than those recommended by WHO, no legal consequences follow."[28]

Yet during the 2014 Ebola outbreak WHO Director-General *Margaret Chan* and others continued to insist that the IHRs are legally binding. When the immediate threat of epidemic Ebola eased, *Al Jazeera*[29] and *Reuters*[30] reported that the WHO explored sanctioning country violators of the IHR, including not only those which "mishandled epidemics", but also those countries which inappropriately banned travel.[31] World Trade Organization-like sanctions were discussed as a reprimand model, but were rejected as not fit for purpose.[32] Ultimately, violations of the IHR – including failures on the part of the WHO – were noted but not censured. *Acconci* parses further by distinguishing that "under the IHR, the WHO has the power to control and lead the conduct of its Member States in case of an epidemic, [but] lacks the power to adopt measures enforceable as law", thus qualifying the IHR as binding, but not enforceable as law.[33]

---

28 WHO, *Implementation of the International Health Regulations (2005) – Report of the Review Committee on the Functioning of the International Health Regulations (2005) in relation to Pandemic (H1N1) 2009*, 2011, 13, available at http://apps.who.int/gb/ebwha/pdf_files/WHA64/A64_10-en.pdf.

29 Bode, L De, "WHO Wants Sanctions Against Countries for Mishandling Epidemics" (October 22, 2015), *Al Jazeera*, available at http://bit.ly/2mhZnEm.

30 Miles, T, "States Could Be Sanctioned for Public Health Failings: WHO Boss" (October 20, 2015), available at http://reut.rs/2meWAu9.

31 Fidler, D P, "Ebola Report Misses Mark on International Health Regulations" (2015), *Chatham House Expert Comment*, available at http://bit.ly/2lSS2Yk.

32 Ibid.

33 Acconci, P, "The Reaction to the Ebola Epidemic within the United Nations Framework", above Fn. 11, 423.

b Issue of Post-Westphalian Global Governance: WHO's State Problem

The fundamental organizational unit of the WHO is the nation-state. In the 21st century, this is a fairly antiquated organizational model, one with some remaining but clearly diminished utility. WHO global health governance, though, "does not operate in a post-Westphalian environment",[34] a point elaborated on below for Sierra Leone. The contemporary governance moment is one that is both organized by the nation-state and non-state actors.[35] In many poor countries – which are often post-colonial, sometimes postwar, usually marked by earlier decades of heavy economic lender intervention – healthcare happens, but in a decentralized, ad hoc way. The austerity conditionalities of the 1980s and 1990s promoted by the World Bank and International Monetary Fund (IMF) paved the way for privatization of healthcare services. Those conditionalities required state pullback, as private sector, market-driven healthcare was expected to remedy the healthcare needs of poor countries. Results were mixed, but largely negative for the world's poorest countries.[36]

In the case of Ebola governance, those very states whose governments were required to downsize have been widely criticized for their inadequate government healthcare oversight and administration. Yet the size and functionalities of those government were not chosen by Sierra Leoneans, but rather imposed by the global banking community. WHO's state problem is rooted in the contradiction that while much is expected of nation-states, and even as the IHR obligations continued to make states central to its regulatory structures, in many of the poorest countries in the world nation-state health governance functions have been gutted *by design* at the hands of global financial institutions.[37]

---

34 Katz, R & Fischer, J, "The Revised International Health Regulations: A Framework for Global Pandemic Response" (2010), 3 *Global Health Governance*, 14.

35 See for example, Sharma, A & Gupta, A, *The Anthropology of the State: A Reader*, 2006; Ferguson, J, *Global Shadows: African in the Neoliberal World Order*, 2007; Mbembe, A, *On the Postcolony*, 2001; Roitman, J, *Anti-Crisis*, 2014.

36 Pfeiffer, J, & Chapman, R, "Anthropological Perspectives on Structural Adjustment and Public Health" (2010), 39 *Annual Review of Anthropology*, 149.

37 Benton, A & Dionne, K Y, "International Political Economy and the 2014 West African Ebola Outbreak" (2015), 58 *African Studies Review*, 223.

c Issue of Mission Creep and Confusion

Mission creep is a term that has been used to categorize an expansion in an organization's purpose, such as has been found for some military interventions[38] and international financial institutions.[39] But the WHO is guilty of that too; the IHR is an exemplar of a regulatory mechanism that takes up the right to this expansion uncritically. As cited earlier, IHR's purpose and scope includes the dictum to "avoid unnecessary interference with international traffic and trade"; the 2005 reforms of the IHR specifically added these two maxims on traffic and trade. Yet, the control of international traffic and trade are beyond the regulatory authority of IHR, not only in a pragmatic sense, but also in a bureaucratic one. The safeguarding of aviation falls to a UN specialized agency, the International Civil Aviation Organization, which is tasked with cooperative international regulation; the safeguarding of shipping falls to the International Maritime Organization, a separate UN agency. Trade falls within the jurisdiction of the World Trade Organization, an organization outside the UN family. As such, the IHR are a set of regulations designed to fail; neither the document nor the originating UN agency, the WHO, have jurisdiction over the domains of the document's own purpose and scope.

III A brief Background to Sierra Leone's Contemporary Political Economy of Health

1 European Occupation and Colonial History

Prior to first recorded contact between indigenous upper west coast Africans and European (Portuguese) explorers in the 15th century, the region now called Sierra Leone was home to multiple politically independent ethnic groups. Coastal regions of Sierra Leone, including the area now known as Freetown, were occupied by the British as early as 1695.[40] By 1787 the British staked claim to the region, and in 1808, Sierra Leone became a

38 Cushman, J H, "Mission in Somalia is to Secure City" (October 10, 1993), *New York Times*, 2.

39 Einhorn, J, "The World Bank's Mission Creep" (2001), 80 *Foreign Affairs*, 22.

40 Griffith, T R, *Sierra Leone: Past, Present and Future*, 1881, vol. 13:82, 58.

British crown colony, with an administrative system of British colonials appointed by British King *George III*. By 1880, colonial control extended only about 50 miles inland, with several up-country outposts. Notable fights for local sovereignty include 1790[41] and 1898[42] conflicts with British authority. The divide-and-conquer administrative strategy of the British – setting ethnic groups against one another during the slave trade and colonial eras – set the stage for political rivalries at independence in 1961 which are still evident in contemporary Sierra Leonean politics.

2 Independence and Postcolonial History

Sierra Leone is among those countries that since its 1961 independence from its colonial ruler has experienced brief stretches of indigenous democratic governance, with longer lengths of time at the hands of one-party rulers. Immediate post-independence commitments to democratic governance gave way to indebted, donor-dependent administrative fragmentation. As the country struggled to find its political feet as a democracy during the 1960s and into the 1970s, across the Atlantic in Washington, DC, the World Bank and IMF were establishing the habit of making development moneys available to poor countries (via Structural Adjustment Programs – SAPS) with conditionalities that encouraged privatization.[43] Into the 1970s, 80s, and 90s, Sierra Leone was among those countries with rulers who were quick to accept loan conditions that devalued local currency and incentivized privatization of public services. Long-term commitments and the investments required to build a healthcare system from the bottom up were not incentivized, and were in fact actively discouraged by international development bank lenders.[44]

---

41 Ibid., 59.

42 Abraham, A, "Bureh, The British, and the Hut Tax War" (1974), 7 *The International Journal of African Historical Studies*, 99.

43 Pfeiffer & Chapman, "Anthropological Perspectives", above Fn. 36, 149-165.

44 For an overview, see also Kentikelenis, A, King, L & McKee, M et al., "The International Monetary Fund and the Ebola Outbreak" (2015), 3 *The Lancet Global Health*, e69.

3 War

In the years leading up to the 1991-2002 war, the privatization of previously state-owned infrastructures in Sierra Leone ensued. It was at this stage that an NGO-ification of Sierra Leonean healthcare began to establish – that is, health care services when available were increasingly offered by an uncoordinated hodge-podge of mostly foreign donor-driven NGOs. Sierra Leonean government and some NGOs tried to keep programs and facilities going, but everyday life during the war was too precarious for the kind of sustained efforts that build a healthcare system capable of serving most of the people most of the time. The war was horrific and devastating. Prior to the Ebola outbreak, the war was "the most destructive event in modern Sierra Leonean history";[45] in general conversations, Sierra Leoneans commonly marked time "before the war" and "after the war". Now conversations are temporally designated before, during, and after both the war and Ebola.

4 Postwar Sierra Leone

The immediate postwar years were marked by severed hardship in Sierra Leone: inflation, continuing and intermittent school and hospital closures, and food shortages. It was a time of isolation from the global community. By January 2014, however, conversations with all kinds of Sierra Leoneans, from health administrators to people on the street were peppered with newfound hope. In 2013 *Forbes* had named Sierra Leone the second Best Investment country in the world. President *Koroma* was fond of saying that: "Sierra Leone will be a middle-income country by 2035." And then Ebola hit. Major industries shut down or left. Wealthy diaspora Sierra Leoneans who had returned after the war again dispatched themselves and their families to Europe and North America.

---

45 O'Kane, D, "Towards 'Audit Culture' in Sierra Leone? Understanding 'Quality Assurance' and the University of Makeni" (2014), 155 *Max Plank Institute for Social Anthropology Working Paper*, 7.

5 An Ad Hoc Health Assemblage in a Time of Ebola

By the time Ebola hit Sierra Leone in March 2014, the NGO-ification of healthcare was long established. The state drawback required by the IMF as a condition of receiving development loans had been on-going for almost two full decades.[46] People still looked to "Papa Govment" for healthcare, but the everyday reality was that healthcare in Sierra Leone was by 2014 more of an ad hoc healthcare assemblage than a healthcare system. The effects for rural Sierra Leoneans can involve "long, uncomfortable, and expensive journeys, navigating Kafka-esque bureaucracies".[47]

Assemblage[48] is a term that aims to capture "the actual configurations" of technological, scientific, political, and economic forms that come together in a particular place. Its markers include regulations and bureaucratic interventions like the IHR, targeted to shape human action and behavior. Sierra Leone's healthcare assemblage is a product of intermittent care that resulted from post-independence governance and foreign aid conditionalities.

The NGO-ification of the health sector means that each NGO imposes its own set of standards and regulatory affects. Whether or not these affects actively create, maintain, or disrupt successful, health governance depends on how well or poorly matched the regulatory standards are to purpose. It matters who writes the documents. Do they know the country? Do they understand village life? Do they source and eat local food? Have they traveled using public transportation? Have they gone through the paces of receiving health care in country? Do they understand the complexities of the very political vernaculars being negotiated in the governance of zoonotic disease? There is a vast range of scientific rigor and biomedical knowledge in the documents coming into Sierra Leone from the outside. In addition, it is common to find political and systems ignorance about Sierra Leone written into documented standards to which Sierra Leoneans are held.

At times of great stress to any given assemblage, as in the case of a disease outbreak, the global political economy of the on-the-ground health failures in impoverished countries is revealed. In the case of Sierra Leone, that

---

46 Kentikelenis, King & McKee et al., "The International Monetary Fund and the Ebola Outbreak", above Fn. 44, e69.

47 Ferme, M, "Hospital Diaries: Experiences with Public Health in Sierra Leone" (2014), *Cultural Anthropology,* available at http://bit.ly/2lYrOoq.

48 Collier, S J & Ong, A (eds.), *Global Assemblages: Technology, Politics, and Ethics as Anthropological Problems*, 2005.

political economy implicates non-West African nationals and international institutions.[49] For example, IMF structural adjustment programs have "required reductions in government spending, [prioritized debt repayment] [...] absorbing funds that could be directed to meeting pressing health challenges".[50] The IMF placed wage caps on government jobs, while NGOs offered salaries far exceeding those caps.[51] This contributed to "internal brain drain", with public health practitioners opting for employment in the private rather than public sector. Additionally, the IMF advocated decentralized healthcare in Sierra Leone,[52] which complicated coordinated responses during the Ebola outbreak. "The IMF and organizations like it have played an important role in creating a political environment in which the epidemic could emerge."[53] Consequentially, documents play a major role in this environment, a topic to which attention is now turned.

IV The Non-Negotiable Necessity of Health Sovereignty

Health sovereignty is the inalienable right of a nation-state, no matter how impoverished, *to decide* how it will manage available resources to fight disease outbreaks within its territorial boundaries. Health sovereignty is the idea that nation-states possess in the first instance the supreme political authority to protect the health of its people, not external agency, donors, or philanthropies. The WHO agrees to this in theory, and references such sentiments in documents:

> "Health is considered the sovereign responsibility of countries, however, the means to fulfil this responsibility are increasingly global. The International Health Regulations (2005) constitute the essential vehicle for this action."[54]

---

49 Benton & Dione, "International Political Economy and the 2014 West African Ebola Outbreak", above Fn. 37, 223-236.

50 Kentikelenis, King & McKee et al., "The International Monetary Fund and the Ebola Outbreak", above Fn. 44, e69.

51 Ibid.

52 International Development Association and the International Monetary Fund, *Sierra Leone: Enhanced Heavily Indebted Poor Countries (HIPC) Initiative Decision Point Document*, 2002, 13, available at https://www.imf.org/external/np/hipc/2002/sle/sledp.pdf.

53 Benton, A & Dione, K, "5 Things You Should Read Before Saying the IMF is Blameless in the 2014 Ebola Outbreak" (January 5, 2015), *Washington Post*, available at http://wapo.st/2mBd1n2.

54 WHO, *Report of the Ebola Interim Assessment Panel*, above Fn. 21, 5.

As with other international documents that aim to universalize action, the IHR draw on Westphalian notions of the state, which originate in territorialities. "The state" in this imaginary is able to govern people and implement policies, programs, and laws. Further, in this envisioning, state agency and authority are relatively unchallenged, and each state is assumed capable and unhindered in its pursuits of disease management.[55] This conceptualization is the ideal; the real is far more diverse and complex. The limits of ideal state forms have been realized as the weight of old political forms have become strained by internal contradictions and external hypocrisies.

No one cared more about ending Ebola in Sierra Leone more than Sierra Leoneans. Despite media representations to the contrary, "[o]ver 80 % of the personnel on the ground fighting [Ebola] in the country [were] Sierra Leonean".[56] An anthropologist with over 45 years of experience working in Sierra Leone noted that "Ebola is a fearsome disease, but learning how West Africans have coped with it is an antidote to fear and confusion".[57] Similarly, our research team witnessed that as early as March 2014 Sierra Leonean health ministry officials *knew what to do.* They recommended Ebola management through hot spot intervention, border management, contact tracing, and limited quarantine,[58] all of the classic public health interventions that, it must be noted, eventually did draw down the number of outbreaks.

Focusing disease hotspot intervention in the Eastern Province of Sierra Leone was among the most logical recommendations from Sierra Leoneans. The first Ebola outbreak occurred over 400 km from Freetown, the capital city of Sierra Leone. This is where Doctors without Borders (MSF) set up its first Ebola Treatment Center. Calls by some Ministry officials for government and NGO reinforcements to support hotspot intervention began in March 2014. These calls went unheeded and unrecognized not only federally as business owners and government officials in other Sierra Leonean sectors anticipated losses to the economy, but also of course internationally up to and after the World Health Organization's August 8, 2014 announcement of Ebola as a public health emergency of international concern.

---

55 For thoughtful analyses of the limits of the state imaginary, see also Das, V & Poole, D, *Anthropology in the Margins of the State*, 2004.

56 Koroma, E B, "Interview: President of Sierra Leone on the Ebola Crisis" (Dezember 10, 2014), *World Economic Forum*, available at http://bit.ly/2mxh57y.

57 Richards, P, *Ebola: How a People's Science Helped End an Epidemic*, 2016, 9.

58 Limited quarantine was imposed on people with known Ebola exposure. Individuals and geographies (rural villages), for example, were placed under quarantine for 21 days, the duration of Ebola incubation.

From March 2014 until August 2014, Ebola raged in Sierra Leone virtually unmanaged and uncontained. More significantly and to the incredulity of Sierra Leonean citizens on the street, Ebola progressed westward, toward Freetown, the most densely populated area because that is where most donors – again with the exception of MSF – were willing to headquarter their early outbreak containment efforts. Ebola victims were brought to Connaught Hospital in the center of Freetown for definitive care. A treatment center was set up at a former tuberculosis sanitarium on the far western region of Freetown, which required that sick patients travel from east to west Freetown through the most impoverished and densely populated parts. Doctors, public health officials, and citizens alike argued vociferously that contagious patients should not be brought to urban centers. Yet that was where the donors wanted them. The on-the-ground realities of health sovereignty are complicated. Empirical evidence from our study shows that in the Ebola outbreak stages, Sierra Leoneans did not make, did not take, and were not empowered to make sovereign decisions about health within their borders. Sierra Leoneans, including the president, attempted to declare the Ebola outbreak as a public health emergency several months before the August 8, 2014 WHO announcement.[59]

Still, in the WHO's 2015 assessment report of the Ebola spread, the emphasis remains on the IHR *document.* Even as the report acknowledges global collective action, they cite the IHR as "an essential vehicle for this action", as below:

> "9. Whereas health is considered the sovereign responsibility of countries, the means to fulfil this responsibility are increasingly global, and require international collective action and effective and efficient governance of the global health system. The International Health Regulations (2005) constitute an essential vehicle for this action. The legal responsibilities contained in the Regulations extend beyond ministries of health, and must be recognized as obligations at the highest levels of Member States' governments."[60]

Further, the report continues to declaratively promote "shared sovereignty", a notion unlikely to be promoted for the containment of diseases in affected Member States like the United States, Germany, or Japan. As such, shared sovereignty is a notion selectively promoted as a remedy.

> "10. This Panel suggests that in the interest of protecting global health, countries must have a notion of "shared sovereignty". Through the International Health

59 Koroma, "Interview: President of Sierra Leone on the Ebola Crisis", above Fn. 56; Richards, *Ebola: How a People's Science Helped End an Epidemic*, above Fn. 57.

60 WHO, *Report of the Ebola Interim Assessment Panel*, above Fn. 21, 10.

> Regulations (2005), Member States recognized that there are limits to national sovereignty when health crises reach across borders […]."[61]

Most remarkably, however, is that para. 10 continues with an emphasis still on the IHR document, rather than on the larger structural mechanisms that would empower poor countries.

> "[…] In the Ebola crisis, there were failings on the part of the Secretariat and of Member States in upholding the Regulations. Unfortunately, a great opportunity to strengthen the Regulations was lost when the 2011 recommendations of the Review Committee on the Functioning of the International Health Regulations (2005) in relation to Pandemic (H1N1) 2009 were not fully implemented […]. The Ebola outbreak might have looked very different had the same political will and resources been applied in order to support implementation of the International Health Regulations (2005) over the past five years."[62]

Most unfortunately, emphasis on the document obscures the fact that Sierra Leoneans knew how to curb the March 2014 outbreak through public health measures like contact tracing and targeted quarantine. But Sierra Leoneans – not health ministry officials, doctors, nurses, nor citizens – did not have the sovereign power and authority to catalyze the emergency response necessary and implement hot spot interventions prudently.

V The IHR are Beyond the Rule of Law in Some Countries

> "The Review Committee considers the IHR themselves to be the *best insurance policy*."[63]
>
> "The failures in the Ebola response did not result from failings of the *IHR themselves*, but rather from a lack of implementation of the IHR."[64]

These statements are part of a 2016 WHO review of the role of the IHR in the 2014 Ebola outbreak and response. Therein lies a telling problem: that global health governance experts in good faith proffer a robust defense of the IHR "themselves", thus re-sanctioning a document that erases global historical and structural inequities and holds rich and poor countries to the same account. Bureaucratic energies devoted to making and maintaining

61 Ibid.

62 Ibid.

63 WHO, *Implementation of the International Health Regulations (2005): Report of the Review Committee on the Role of International Health Regulations (2005) in the Ebola Outbreak and Response, A69/21*, 2016, 79, available at http://bit.ly/2lY-Iax4. Emphasis mine.

64 Ibid., 9. Italics mine.

regulatory documents are disproportionate to the political energy and exertions necessary for national healthcare system-making in an age of global zoonotic disease migrations.

The IHR ignores harmful caps, limitations, and austerities on health care building in Sierra Leone. In the 68 years since the inception of the WHO and the 55 years since Sierra Leone's independence from Britain, the hard, complex work of domestic health governance has yet to be accomplished. This is a profound problem with accountabilities both within and beyond Sierra Leone federal governance. The IHR will not remedy this problem.

Invigorating political moxie[65] for poor countries to establish healthcare *systems* – rather than continuing to sustain and invest in the current ad hoc assemblages of intermittent care – is the smart upstream anticipatory remedy to increase global health security. Most health policymakers who have not worked in West Africa seem to have a hard time imagining the absurdity of imposing IHR obligations in places without strong-enough healthcare systems. But for those of us who work there and have witnessed the fortitude of Sierra Leonean healthcare practitioners, even as global policies continue to *structure* local salary caps and equipment shortages, we know that they know that the IHR are but window dressing to global structural violence.[66] International health regulations and universal standards for global health security – if they are to work in the future – depend of "how standards manage the tension[s] involved in transforming work practices, while simultaneously being grounded in those practices".[67] Standards and regulations require local reappropriation. In West Africa, global histories and habits have hindered the development of local comprehensive health care systems; non-West African nationals are deeply implicated. To this day, the work of documents like the IHR obfuscate and stand in for the more important, more difficult, more fundamental work that needs to be done of building a comprehensive healthcare system first and foremost.

The IHR depends on there being a healthcare *system* – not an assemblage or medicoscape – to plug the regulations in *to*. Building on the local successes of Ebola governance to create healthcare sovereignty in Sierra Leone

65 Erikson, S, "Getting Political: Fighting for Global Health" (2008), 371 *The Lancet*, 1229 (1229-1230).

66 Farmer, P, "On Suffering and Structural Violence: A View from Below" (1996), 125 *Daedalus*, 261.

67 Timmermans, S & Berg, M, "Standardization in Action: Achieving Local Universality through Medical Protocols" (1997), 27 *Social Studies of Science*, 273.

is "next generation" work. Global health partisans[68] are most useful to Sierra Leonean overall well-being when they work on the global scale to reduce and bring more balance to the impositions placed on small countries by international development and humanitarian industry conditionalities.

VI Conclusion: When Regulations are Actually Guidelines

Documents like IHR work well as entry points for better understanding the strengths, weaknesses, and limitations of prevailing global health governance instruments. But continuing attention and refinement of the IHR cannot be a primary act of health security for impoverished areas of the world.[69] Long before the 2014 Ebola outbreak, the global community was distracted from digging in and taking up its own systemic failures of health governance at global structural levels. One of those failures has been the inability to be realistic about sovereign unevenness of states it aims to regulate. One on-the-ground effect of this failure in Sierra Leone in 2014 was that the IHR were largely irrelevant to early Ebola containment governance. Before, during, and after the height of the Ebola outbreak, health governance in Sierra Leone has been shown to be beyond the rule of law, the international umbrella under which the IHR as a treaty resides.

This article is critical of the IHR. However, the author supports their continuance as guidelines but not as regulations. After decades of working in Sierra Leone, the author concludes that both Sierra Leone and the global community need the IHR as a helpful conceptual yardstick for disease governance throughout the world. High aims and expectations for ideal disease management are essential to the further public health work that needs to be done. The world needs such guidelines and policy windows are now open for officially changing the International Health Regulations to International Health Guidelines. The global infrastructures for emergency preparedness as well as the WHO leadership are in flux. New remedies to global health governance ailments are in play. The WHO's Health Emergencies Programme (HEP), for example, may prove to be "a comprehensive way

68 Erikson, "Getting Political: Fighting for Global Health", above Fn. 65, 1230.

69 Gostin, L, DeBartolo, M & Friedman, E, "The International Health Regulations 10 Years On: The Governing Framework for Global Health Security" (2015), 386 *The Lancet,* 2222.

[to successfully manage epidemics] 'through the establishment of one single Programme, with one workforce, one budget, one set of rules and processes and one clear line of authority'".[70] HEP needs good guidelines; the IHR are good guidelines. Practical optimists acknowledge on-the-ground limitations of the IHR. Make the IHR guidelines instead of pretending they operate as regulations and get on with the harder, more intractable concerns of global health governance.

70 WHO, *Health Emergencies Programme*, 2015, available at http://bit.ly/25dvmaA.

The Governance of Infectious Diseases. An International Relations Perspective

Christian R. Thauer[*]

Abstract

The article explores Global Health Governance (GHG) under conditions of limited statehood – i.e. beyond the nation state. Drawing on empirical examples of governance involving businesses, it analyzes the conditions under which GHG can emerge and be effective despite prevailing conditions of limited statehood. The analysis shows that selective incentives deriving from a skills-driven business model, in combination with a hegemonic role of the firm in its locality, give rise to the emergence of business-driven GHG structures. Meta-governance and norm-congruence with the designated beneficiaries of the GHG structure, and government authorities, make such GHG effective. Ultimately, the article calls for a conceptual change in international law to account for the fact that private actors may fulfill public functions in situations in which the state is limited in its ability to govern.

I Introduction

This article relates recent research in International Relations (IR) on collective goods and services provision in areas of limited statehood to current

---

* Senior Lecturer, Department of International Relations and DAAD Center for German Studies, the Hebrew University of Jerusalem. I would like to thank the Fritz Thyssen Foundation and the Deutsche Forschungsgemeinschaft (DFG) for their generous support of the research presented in this article; the Sonderforschungsbereich 700, "Governance in Areas of Limited Statehood", *Adrienne Héritier*, *Thomas Risse*, *Tanja Börzel*, *Anna Müller-Debus*, *Jana Hönke* and *Nicole Kranz* for insightful collaboration, and all their support; *Zoe Bray*, the editors of this book, and the participants of the workshop on "International Health Governance (IHG) of Disease Outbreak Alert and Response", March 3-4, 2016, at the Max Planck Institute for Comparative Public Law and International Law, for very helpful comments on earlier versions of this article. All websites last accessed December 21, 2016.

debates about Global Health Governance[1] (GHG) of infectious diseases. The main function of GHG in relation to infectious diseases is to prevent, contain and manage pandemics.[2] The current structure of GHG is conceived to fulfill this function mainly through the coordination of states' public health policies – for example in the context of the World Health Organization (WHO).[3] The respective plans address health departments and other government entities in the attempt to contain the disease at its root, mitigate its worst impacts, coordinate vaccination campaigns, and control extensive proliferation. However, in many parts of the world, states have only very limited capacities to govern,[4] and are often not capable of effective policy planning or implementation.[5] This article asks whether and how "new",[6] but "functional equivalent"[7] modes of GHG involving non-state

---

1 By *governance* this article understands the making and implementation of rules, norms, standards and decision-making procedures for the production or provision of collective goods and services, see Reinicke, W H, *Global Public Policy. Governing without Government?*, 1998, 147-148; Héritier, A, "Introduction" in Héritier, A (ed.), *Common Goods. Reinventing European and International Governance*, 2002, 1.

2 The article refers to epidemics as infectious disease outbreaks on a local population-level; pandemics are disease outbreaks that go beyond a local population and cross national borders, see Morens, D M, Folkers, G K & Fauci, A S, "What Is a Pandemic?" (2009), 200 *Journal of Infectious Diseases*, 1018; Moon, S, Sridhar, D & Pate, M A et al., "Will Ebola change the game? Ten essential reforms before the next pandemic. The report of the Harvard-LSHTM Independent Panel on the Global Response to Ebola" (2015), 386 *The Lancet*, 2204.

3 Goldin, I & Mariathasan, M, *The Butterfly Defect: How Globalization Creates Systemic Risks, and What to Do about It*, 2014. For a different approach towards GHG, see also the contribution of *Mateja Steinbrück Platise*, "The Changing Structure of Global Health Governance" in this volume.

4 For the case of countries in West Africa, see the contribution of *Edefe Ojomo*, "Fostering Regional Health Governance in West Africa: The Role of the WAHO" in this volume.

5 Milliken, J & Krause, K, "State failure, state collapse, and state reconstruction: Concepts, lessons and strategies" (2002), 33 *Development & Change*, 753; Risse, T (ed.), *Governance without a State? Policies and Politics in Areas of Limited Statehood*, 2011.

6 Héritier, "Introduction", above Fn. 1, 1.

7 Börzel, T A & Risse, T, "Governance without a State - Can it Work?" (2010), 4 *Regulation and Governance*, 113.

actors could contribute to controlling and managing infectious diseases under such conditions.[8] The article draws on the author's own and collaborators' empirical research on HIV/AIDS governance in South Africa. It thereby goes in important ways beyond previous calls to move conceptually from International Health Governance (IHG) to Global Health Governance,[9] in that it a.) makes the case for limited statehood as an important context condition of pandemic control, which has so far been mostly ignored; b.) identifies specific challenges that GHG under conditions of limited statehood has to overcome, and the conditions under which GHG is more and less likely to be effective; c.) thereby suggesting a new way of thinking about the role of non-state actors in GHG, which assigns public function roles to them.

Limited statehood is not a new phenomenon. Its relevance for GHG is, however. More specifically, two developments associated with globalization processes unleashed after the End of the Cold War elevated the degree to which GHG is affected by the phenomenon. First, connectivity between formerly only remotely related areas in the world has dramatically increased. This also particularly involves the so-called developing world, where conditions of limited statehood prevail.[10] Intensified trade and investment relations and elevated levels of mobility through, for example, air travel, have helped to increase this connectivity. With this, the risk of local infectious disease outbreaks turning into global pandemics has augmented. Second, the growth of slums, townships and shantytowns in the developing world – often driven by the uprooting dynamics of global economic development and industrialization – have created new potential hot spots of epidemic disease outbreaks. Today, about one billion people live under slum and other sub-standard living conditions according to United Nations Human Settlements Programme (UN-HABITAT).[11] The state's public policies usually do not reach these places. It is in these areas of limited statehood that poverty, lack of sanitation and lack of access to other basic infrastructure and public services combine with high population density and

8 For the case of NGOs health-related activities in Liberia, see the contribution of *Hunter Keys, Bonnie Kaiser & André den Exter*, "The Real Versus the Ideal in NGO Governance: Enacting the Right to Mental Healthcare in Liberia During the 2014-2016 Ebola Epidemic" in this volume.

9 Dodgson, R, Lee, K & Drager, N, "Global health governance. A Conceptual Review" (2002), *Discussion Paper No. 1, WHO, Centre on Global Change & Health, London School of Hygiene & Tropical Medicine*, 7.

10 Goldin & Mariathasan, *The Butterfly Defect*, above Fn. 3.

11 See UN Habitat, *Background Paper*, 2014, available at http://bit.ly/1Q60HQD.

physical closeness of human-animal relations to create the conditions that increase the likeliness of outbreaks of infectious diseases.

II Globalization and Disease Outbreaks: The Need for "New" Modes of Global Health Governance

With the end of the Cold War, globalization has changed the way global governance can and should be pursued. Before 1990, both the discipline of IR and its practice were thoroughly grounded in "methodological nationalism",[12] the belief that states are the only (relevant and legitimate) actors in international relations: internationally, they coordinate policies under conditions of anarchy; internally, they are "domestic sovereigns",[13] effective and legitimate governors in their territory.

Since 1990, two developments related to the emergence of "the global" as a political and social space[14] render these assumptions in relation to many governance issues, including GHG, increasingly anachronistic. The first development concerns a change of roles of transnational networks and private actors in world politics – a development that is reflected academically in the context of a revival of transnationalist thinking in IR.[15] Globalization has improved their strategic position vis-à-vis states. Many businesses and Non-Governmental Organizations (NGOs) are today operating on a global scale – or at least have the option to do so. Once territorially confined and on the receiving end of state-based governance, multinational corporations and global value chains, for example, now play off states competing over investments and trade flows against each other. Depending on businesses' will, states may find themselves entrapped in a "regulatory race to the bottom"[16] – or pushed in the opposite direction of regulatory upgrading and a

---

12 Cerny, P G, "The Dynamics of Political Globalization" (1997), 32 *Government and Opposition*, 251 (251-252).

13 Krasner, S D, *Sovereignty: Organized Hypocrisy*, 1999; Krasner, S D & Risse, T, "External Actors, State-Building, and Service Provision in Areas of Limited Statehood: Introduction" (2014), 27 *Governance*, 545.

14 Scholte, J A, "Defining Globalization" (2008), 31 *World Economy*, 1471.

15 Kahler, M, *Networked Politics: Agency, Power, and Governance*, 2009; Risse, T, "Transnational Actors and World Politics" in Carlsnaes, W, Risse, T & Simmons, B A (eds.), *Handbook of International Relations*, 2012, 426.

16 Chan, A & Ross, R J S, "Racing to the Bottom: International Trade without a Social Clause" (2003), 24 *Third World Quarterly*, 1011.

"race to the top".[17] Transnational networks of NGOs enjoy addressing different transnational audiences simultaneously, as this allows them to exert pressure on states and other actors, such as businesses, in varied and new ways, thereby often imposing their will on them.[18] Transnational terrorist groups, often only connected via social media, challenge the established state system through the creation of new, asymmetrical security threats. Non-state actors matter for outcomes in global politics today and have emerged as the new "global governors".[19]

The second development concerns an increase in the scope of problems dealt with in the context of global governance. This increase especially concerns so-called "behind-the-border"[20] issues – problems for which the solution requires the regulation of private actors behind national borders. Given methodological nationalism, global governance-institutions usually seek to achieve this via the nation state. But the target is (the behavior of) a private actor or group of private actors, which the state, by adopting public policies inline with global governance stipulations, is supposed to regulate. In global environmental governance, for example, cross-border pollution or CO_2 emissions are mainly caused by private actors, namely industry and consumers. Their behavior is the real target of global environmental governance. But most international agreements and norms in global environmental governance address states' public policies and regulations. The same is true for numerous other issue areas that have become part of the global governance agenda after the Cold War, from occupational health, labor rights, corporate governance, banking standards, and industry processes to public health. This increase of behind-the-border issues in global governance can be traced back to the increase of interconnectedness and interdependence, brought about by globalization processes, which define "the global" as a policy space. *Goldin* and *Mariathasan* attest to a "butterfly defect":[21] rela-

17 Vogel, D, *Trading Up: Consumer and Environmental Regulation in a Global Economy*, 1995; Börzel, T A, Thauer, C R & Hönke, J, "Conclusion: A Race to the Top?" in Börzel, T A & Thauer, C R (eds.), *Business and Governance in South Africa. Racing to the Top?*, 2013, 215.

18 Keck, M E & Sikkink, K, *Activists Beyond Borders. Advocacy Networks in International Politics*, 1998; Risse, T, Ropp, S C & Sikkink, K, *The Power of Human Rights. International Norms and Domestic Change*, 1999.

19 Avant, D, Finnemore, M & Sell, S K (eds.), *Who Governs the Globe?*, 2010.

20 Zürn, M, "Global governance as multi-level governance" in Enderlein, H, Wälti, S & Zürn, M (eds.), *Handbook on multi-level governance*, 2010, 83.

21 Goldin & Mariathasan, *The Butterfly Defect,* above Fn. 3.

tively small, insignificant, "private" acts – individually or collectively conducted – can have global consequences. Traveling by airplane with an unrecognized infectious disease could result in the outbreak of a pandemic. In the attempt to manage such butterfly defect-risks, global governance has become more "intrusive",[22] targeting more and more the everyday activities of ordinary persons and private organizations. This intrusiveness, in turn, has created a potential for conditions of limited statehood impacting global governance. If the state is not capable of public policy planning and implementation, the traditional, state-centrist approach to global governance is bound to fail in relation to behind-the-border issues. Limited statehood is no longer a mere marginal or peripheral problem. Many states, in many areas, are often somewhat limited in their ability to govern.[23] The assumption of "domestic sovereignty" is as much an "organized hypocrisy"[24] as sovereignty is as an external dimension (understood as the principle of non-intervention). Statehood is in reality rather a matter of degree, and thus usually limited. This limitation comes in different forms. It may describe the functional lack of the state's regulatory capacities in a certain policy field. A state, for example, may be "strong" vis-à-vis its society and in the international system, but may lack the ability to provide basic social or health services, or to enforce environmental laws. Limited statehood may alternatively be territorially or socially defined, such as when a state lacks the ability to control parts of its territory as "domestic sovereign" or is limited in its ability to enforce its laws vis-à-vis a certain social, ethnic or religious group. Limited statehood is, of course, not a new phenomenon. But during the Cold War, it affected mainly the periphery – the formerly so-called Third World –, whereas now, with the mentioned interconnectedness, it is a central problem of global governance. The periphery no longer exists.

As concerns the nature of limited statehood, it is important to note that it is not synonymous with anarchy. Recently, *Krasner* and *Risse*,[25] and *Lee*, *Walter-Drop* and *Wiesel*[26] showed that, under conditions of fully consolidated as well as entirely failed statehood, the state's regulatory and public

22 Zürn, "Global governance as multi-level governance", above Fn. 20.
23 Krasner & Risse, "External Actors, State-Building, and Service Provision", above Fn. 13.
24 Krasner, *Sovereignty: Organized Hypocrisy*, above Fn. 13.
25 Krasner & Risse, "External Actors, State-Building, and Service Provision", above Fn. 13.
26 Lee, M M, Walter-Drop, G & Wiesel, J, "Taking the State (Back) Out? Statehood and the Delivery of Collective Goods" (2014), 27 *Governance*, 635.

policy capacities are a valid predictor for levels of collective good and service provision in a polity. That is to say, fully consolidated statehood is associated with high levels of collective goods and services provision, whereas failed statehood – such as in an endemic civil war situation – is associated with extremely low levels. However, where statehood is limited, as in most countries, the degree of statehood is vastly decoupled from levels of governance. In other words, collective goods and services provision varies here, and it does so unrelated to the state's capacity to govern. This begs the question – if it is not the state, then who is it that governs in areas of limited statehood? International organizations, development agencies, NGOs, tribal actors, and local communities have been identified as actors that fill the governance gap.[27] Even businesses – that is, for-profit, private interest-based actors – have been found at times, under certain conditions, to be the one to take over vital governance functions in areas of limited statehood.[28] Thus, in situations in which the state is absent as a policy-maker, significant governance capacities may still exist. However, they are not performed by the states' government, but by non-state actors and actor networks. Since the global governance of infectious diseases is a case *par excellence* of behind-the-border governance, and thus heavily affected by conditions of limited statehood, it is on these governance capacities that GHG will have to draw to prevent, contain and manage infectious disease outbreaks. How this may be organized in concrete situations, and what will be the obstacles and challenges of such alternative, *trans*-national rather than *inter*-national GHG, will be discussed in the next section.

III "New" Modes of GHG – Conditions for their Emergence, and Effectiveness

An important implication of research on governance in areas of limited statehood is, as mentioned, that limited statehood is synonymous with neither anarchy nor a Hobbesian state of war of all against all, except for in

---

27 Risse, *Governance without a State?*, above Fn. 5; Krasner & Risse, "External Actors, State-Building, and Service Provision", above Fn. 13.

28 Flohr, A, Rieth, L & Schwindenhammer, S et al., *The Role of Business in Global Governance. Corporations as Norm-Entrepreneurs*, 2010; Börzel, T A & Thauer, C R (eds.), *Business and Governance in South Africa. Racing to the Top?*, 2013; Hönke, J & Thauer, C R, "Multinational Corporations and Service Provision in Sub-Saharan Africa: Legitimacy and Institutionalization Matter" (2014), 27 *Governance*, 697.

extreme cases where the state has lost its capacity to control the exercise of violence, such as in civil war situations. Instead, limited statehood, as a system of governance itself, consists of at times more and at times less stable networks of reciprocal relationships between societal actors – sometimes more, sometimes less, capable of collective goods provision. The absence of the state implies that this overall system of governance is highly de-centralized. Social systems characterized by limited statehood are thus in essence decentralized, and not (necessarily) anarchic.

In systematic comparative perspective, centralized systems (of fully consolidated statehood) are more successful as concerns collective goods and services provision. No alternative can beat full-fledged statehood in this respect: fully consolidated statehood is, across the board, strongly associated with high levels of collective goods and services provision, whereas in areas of limited statehood, levels of governance vary. However, it must be emphasized that decentralization is not an obstacle to collective service provision *per se*. It only turns into one in conjunction with what *Perrow* has coined “task complexity”.[29] Task complexity refers to the frequency and intensity of interactions and the number of actors that need to be coordinated for a governance task to be accomplished. The more frequent and intense the interactions and the higher the number of actors that need to be coordinated, the more complex the governance task, and *vice versa*. *Krasner* and *Risse* argue that task complexity is indicative of the effectiveness of governance in areas of limited statehood.[30] *Schäferhoff* has applied the concept to the analysis of global health governance.[31] His work shows that when task complexity is low, such as in the context of a one-shot vaccination campaign aimed at eradicating an infectious disease, global health governance is likely to emerge and succeed in its task even under conditions of de-centralization. However, when task complexity is high, this dramatically increases the likelihood of governance failure. Infectious diseases that cannot be contained in a simple way but require complex coordination in order to be contained and managed, are thus the litmus test for GHG in areas of limited statehood. The contributions in *Börzel* and *Thauer*, and *Hönke* and *Thauer*, show in this respect that the governance of complex behind-the-

29 Perrow, C, *Complex Organizations: A Critical Essay*, 1972.

30 Krasner & Risse, “External Actors, State-Building, and Service Provision”, above Fn. 13.

31 Schäferhoff, M, “External Actors and the Provision of Public Health Services in Somalia” (2014), 27 *Governance*, 675.

border issues is possible even under such conditions.[32] Their work will be presented below in order to define the challenges of and conditions for complex coordination in decentralized systems of governance. It draws on cases of HIV/AIDS governance in the context of South Africa prior to 2009. In South Africa, about 20 % of the population in the sexually active age group has contracted HIV/AIDS.[33] In the country's townships, where most of the people affected by the disease live, there was, before 2009, hardly any access to health care services. Township inhabitants additionally often lack access to other basic services such as sanitation, and are suffering from poverty and exposure to crime and violence. Before *Jacob Zuma* became President and rolled out the largest antiretroviral medication program in the world in 2009, the government, in particular under President *Thabo Mbeki* who ruled the country until 2008, remained irresponsibly inactive in relation to the disease.[34] Drug coverage for persons sick with AIDS was then an estimated 20 % nationwide, and much lower in the townships.[35] Thus, with respect to HIV/AIDS, the country was, before 2009, an area characterized by the absence of state governance.

Unlike a vaccination campaign, fighting HIV/AIDS requires continuous efforts and goes beyond simple medical intervention: doctors and nurses in clinics have to be trained so that they are able to diagnose the disease; they also have to acquire the skills to effectively treat it. Patients have to be persuaded to test for HIV/AIDS. Fighting the disease effectively also involves prevention measures, such as sexual education programs run in schools, at the workplace and in public. Drugs ranging from immune boosters to antiretroviral medication have to be continuously provided. The lifestyle of patients needs to be changed. In other words, the governance of HIV/AIDS is an extremely difficult task, characterized by high complexity. As will be explained further below, in many instances, attempts at HIV/AIDS governance therefore failed in South Africa. In some instances however they did

---

32 Börzel & Thauer, *Business and Governance in South Africa*; Hönke & Thauer, "Multinational Corporations and Service Provision", both above Fn. 28.

33 See UNICEF, *South Africa - Statistics,* available at http://uni.cf/2mEzVKn.

34 Nattrass, N, *The AIDS Conspiracy: Science Fights Back*, 2013.

35 Nattrass, N, *Mortal Combat: AIDS Denialism and the Struggle for Antiretrovirals in South Africa*, 2007; Soest, C von & Weinel, M, "The Treatment Controversy – Global Health Governance and South Africa's HIV/AIDS Policy" in Hein, W, Bartsch, S & Kohlmorgen, L (eds.), *Global Health Governance and the Fight Against HIV/AIDS*, 2007, 202.

succeed, as in the case of Mercedes Benz – a large German multinational car company.[36]

The firm manufactures parts of its C-class models in East London in the province of the Eastern Cape of South Africa. Like most carmakers, Mercedes' production heavily depends on employees acquiring the specific skills necessary for the C-class' production. The firm's business model is thus "asset specific",[37] which heightens the firm's interest in the wellbeing of its employees.[38] In view of the threat HIV/AIDS represented to the specific skills-dependent business model of Mercedes, the firm successfully rolled out a comprehensive HIV/AIDS workplace program in the early 2000s. In the context of the program, the firm's employees were provided with comprehensive health services, including antiretroviral medication on the level of best available science, thereby effectively turning HIV/AIDS into a chronic disease. The firm also distributed condoms and offered sex education and anti-stigmatization programs. In view of the success of its programs in terms of a generally sustained healthiness of its employees (resulting in a reduction of absenteeism, higher productivity, and lower staff turnover and losses), the multi-national corporations (MNC) decided in 2006 to organize a response to the disease with a broader focus. The firm initiated a multi-stakeholder partnership, including the National Ministry of Health of South Africa, local institutions (ranging from hospitals and schools to the municipality), the DEG (Deutsche Entwicklungs- und Investitionsgesellschaft) – a German development agency –, a local association, as well as the Border Kai Chamber of Commerce (BKCC). The aim of the project was to support small and medium-sized businesses in their efforts to draw up and implement HIV/AIDS workplace policies on the basis of the WHO guideline "Healthy workplaces: a model for action".[39] More than 26,000 persons have gained access to health care services through this supplier initiative alone, in addition to another 30,000 persons who have gained

---

36 See for the following Thauer, C R, "Coping with uncertainty: The automotive industry and HIV/AIDS governance in South Africa" in Börzel, T A & Thauer, C R (eds.), *Business and Governance in South Africa. Racing to the Top?*, 2013, 45; Hönke & Thauer, "Multinational Corporations and Service Provision", above Fn. 28.

37 Williamson, O E, *Markets and Hierarchies: Analysis and Antitrust Implications. A Study in the Economics of Internal Organization*, 1975.

38 Thauer, C R, *The Managerial Sources of Corporate Social Responsibility. The Spread of Global Standards*, 2014.

39 See WHO, *Healthy workplaces: a model for action. For employers, workers, policy-makers and practitioners*, 2010, available at http://bit.ly/2ndkTrH.

access in the context of the firms' program for workers and their extended families.[40] The project also offers training for nurses and doctors in local clinics in order to improve the public health services in relation to HIV/AIDS, coordinates with schools' sex education programs, and assists local communities affected by the disease with sponsorships.

Needless to say, a comprehensive public health response organized by the government could have been more inclusive. But given that this option was not available at the time, the alternative to this multi-stakeholder initiative would have been no governance at all. The multi-stakeholder initiative thus filled a void, with important consequences for those who benefitted from it. The case shows that complex coordination for the provision of health services is possible, even under conditions of limited statehood. But what is it that sets the case of this multi-stakeholder initiative apart from other situations in which governance structures either failed to emerge, or failed to successfully deliver health services? More generally, what are the specific challenges that GHG under conditions of limited statehood have to overcome for the creation of effective governance structures? Based on the mentioned work of firms in South Africa, which includes the systematic analysis of HIV/AIDS governance - both failed and successful, involving businesses in different industry sectors - four coordination problems for the creation of complex governance structures in de-centralized systems can be identified. The first two problems concern the emergence of institutionalized forms of GHG involving firms. The third and fourth concern the effectiveness (in terms of health service delivery) of these institutionalized forms of GHG.

1 Why and Under Which Conditions Does GHG Emerge?

Public health is a public good[41] in that the society as a whole as well as each member will benefit from the absence of diseases physically, socially and economically. The health care services necessary for the creation of this public good are costly however, in particular in the presence of a sexually

40 Lorentzen, J, "Multinationals on the periphery. DaimlerChrysler South Africa, human capital upgrading and regional economic development" (2006), 2 *Occasional Papers of the Human Research Council South Africa*, 1.

41 Cornes, R & Sandler, T, *The Theory of Externalities, Public Goods, and Club Goods*, 1996.

transmitted infectious disease, as in South Africa. In decentralized systems – that is, in the absence of a central coordinator who could, if necessary, apply monitoring and sanctioning mechanisms[42] – the free rider problem will consequently obstruct the provision of this public good. Unsurprisingly, therefore, the mentioned empirical studies found that many firms in South Africa did not engage in the fight against HIV/AIDS in any significant way. Firms are for-profit actors committed to the maximization of the wealth of their owners in a highly competitive environment. Why would they spend scarce organizational resources to contribute to the fight against a disease, given that doing so could result in competitive disadvantage vis-à-vis other firms that decide to abstain from doing so? The analysis of firm cases in South Africa, such as Mercedes in East London, shows that firms do so when they have "selective incentives"[43] – that is, incentives that selectively work for the individual firm, resulting in the calculation that the benefits it will reap from contributing to public health will exceed the costs of that contribution. *Thauer* found that this is the case when firms have made asset specific investments, that is, when they have invested significantly in training programs that teach employees specialized skills.[44] The consequence of such investments is that the firm cannot substitute employees any more easily in the labor market, but becomes dependent on them, and vulnerable to their behavior. Health and general wellbeing programs offered to these employees by the firm in the context of HIV/AIDS workplace programs are in this situation highly beneficial for the firm, as they effectively mitigate the problem of staff turnover. The mentioned HIV/AIDS program of Mercedes, for example, allowed the firm to retain its investments in employee skills.

Selective incentives, however, explain cases such as Mercedes in East London only partially. The firm decided first and with priority to offer comprehensive health services to its employees. Given the complexity of the issue of HIV/AIDS, after it accomplished this task, it began to additionally coordinate with relevant actors in the strategic environment of the firm – schools, kindergartens, hospitals, suppliers, and the business community

42 This central coordinating function has also been called the "shadow of hierarchy", see Héritier, A & Lehmkuhl, D, "The Shadow of Hierarchy and New Modes of Governance" (2008), 28 *Journal of Public Policy*, 1.

43 Olson, M, *The Logic of Collective Action. Public Goods and the Theory of Groups*, 2009, 51.

44 Thauer, *The Managerial Sources of Corporate Social Responsibility*, above Fn. 38; Thauer, C R, "Goodness Comes From Within: Intra-organizational Dynamics of Corporate Social Responsibility" (2014), 53 *Business & Society*, 483.

writ large – a collective response to the disease. In systematic comparative perspective, this outreach seems unusual. The empirical findings indicate in this respect that firms, which have invested in specific skills of employees, will offer them health care services in the context of HIV/AIDS workplace programs. But not every firm that has made such investments also goes beyond its purview to coordinate a collective response in society with external actors. The firm Crossley Carpets is an example of such a firm that relies on specific skills, but yet does not coordinate with actors in society on the issue of HIV/AIDS.[45] As an industrial textile firm specialized in the making of hotel carpets – a sophisticated product requiring complex modes of production – the firm offers extensive training programs to its employees. Even floor operators on the lowest entry level of employment in the firm have to first receive months of training before they can become operational on the factory floor. Accordingly, in order to retain these built-up skills, the firm runs a highly sophisticated and generous HIV/AIDS workplace program. However, the firm does not reach out to other actors in the community to organize collective action against HIV/AIDS. How can this finding be interpreted? From the perspective of the theory of collective goods and externalities,[46] workplace programs create a different type of good than external coordination. Workplace programs, while contributing to the non-exclusive good public health, simultaneously create an exclusive, private good for the firm, namely skills-retaining, to which firms that do not have workplace programs have no access. In a competitive environment, as in markets, excludability is a key motivation.

Different to that, external coordination contributes in the first place to public health as such – a public good from which no one can be excluded – and thus confronts the mentioned free rider obstacles. But why, then, did Mercedes still decide to initiate a multi-stakeholder initiative in East London, and what sets this case apart from Crossley Carpets that did not do so? The difference boils down to aspects related to the differences in size of the two firms.[47] Mercedes is an extremely large firm in the context of East London, employing several thousand employees. It is also part of a huge multinational corporation. Crossley Carpets, by contrast, is a smaller firm with only a few hundred employees and no ties to other larger firms,

---

45 See for the following above, Fn 38, ch. 4.

46 Cornes & Sandler, *The Theory of Externalities*, above Fn. 41; Olson, *The Logic of Collective Action*, above Fn. 43.

47 Börzel & Thauer, *Business and Governance in South Africa*; Hönke & Thauer, "Multinational Corporations and Service Provision", both above Fn. 28.

neither in South Africa nor abroad. Size matters in two ways. Firstly, there is the rather trivial fact that for a large firm such as Mercedes with extensive administrative structures and financial resources, the relative burden of organizing a multi-stakeholder initiative such as the one in East London is much lower than for a small organization such as Crossley Carpets with only a thin administrative layer and very limited financial resources. From a theory of the firm perspective, going big is a specific market strategy.[48] Integrating various value-adding processes under one roof comes with the advantage that the organization has significant resources at its disposal to build up the respective administrative capacities for the management of external risks. Large firms engage in lobbying, extensive public communication, buy up competitors, and engage in corporate social responsibility activities in order to influence and shape their strategic environment. Small firms, by contrast, have the advantage that they can react to external changes flexibly and through innovation. From this perspective, the prospect that general public health-levels in South Africa may further deteriorate means for a small firm such as Crossley Carpets that it may have to change its business model and become less skills driven – or leave the country. By contrast, a large firm such as Mercedes will try to influence its strategic environment such that the actual deterioration is prevented. Large firms thrive on being governors in their environment; small firms survive because they avoid this burden.

Second, large firms such as Mercedes are in their local context economic hegemons. The whole economy and in particular their suppliers depend on their purchasing power, know-how and planning. The local public administration – the municipality and government districts – also depend on their economic power in terms of tax revenues and job creation. In the case of Mercedes, this hegemonic position is particularly strong as the firm has very close relationships with its direct suppliers, involving mutual asset specific investments.[49] The suppliers thus have made investments specifically in order to be able to trade with Mercedes. Mercedes, in turn, depends on these investments and extensively controls operations and procedures in the suppliers' factories. The multinational is thus able to take on the role of a central coordinator in the setting of East London, including the possibility to

48 Williamson, O E, "The logic of Economic Organization" in Williamson, O E & Winter, S G (eds.), *The Nature of the Firm: Origins, Evolution, and Development*, 1993, 90.

49 Héritier, A, Müller-Debus, A & Thauer, C, "The Firm as an Inspector: Private Ordering and Political Rules" (2009), 11 *Business and Politics*, 1.

monitor and, if necessary, sanction unwilling suppliers and public agencies. Small firms, by contrast, do not enjoy such a central position and lack power vis-à-vis other firms and public agencies. Large firms such as Mercedes are thus able to effectively mitigate the free rider problem, and thus to overcome the obstacles to external cooperation for collective action.

GHG structures within firms thus emerge in the event of asset specificity; asset specificity in combination with a large size of a firm create the conditions in which firms seek to initiate health governance structures beyond their purview. But under which conditions are these governance structures also effective?

2 Effective Implementation: A Matter of Legitimacy

The effectiveness of health governance networks such as the one of Mercedes Benz in East London described above is, as concerns its ability to actually deliver health services, not at all self-evident. The higher the level of complexity of the governance task, the more actors have to be continuously coordinated, and so conflicts of interest are likely to emerge, subsequently undermining the effectiveness of service delivery.[50] Indeed, on at least two levels, GHG by firms confronts norm and power clashes that can render the provision of health services ineffective. One concerns the interaction with local communities, the other government agencies of the host country of the governance network.

Firm-based GHG, such as HIV/AIDS workplace programs, is usually oriented towards international norms and standards. HIV/AIDS workplace programs, for example, cite WHO guidelines. However, these may clash with norms, culture, tradition, routines and power structures in local communities, which are, however, the designated beneficiaries of GHG.[51] In the case of HIV/AIDS workplace programs in South Africa, many firms offering sophisticated workplace programs to their employees are, for example,

50 The assumption of this argument is that the more actors are involved in close and re-iterated cooperation, the higher the likelihood of value, norm, and power conflicts.

51 Hamann, R, Kapelus, P & Sonnenberg, D et al., "Local Governance as a Complex System. Lessons from Mining in South Africa, Mali and Zambia" (2005), 18 *Journal of Corporate Citizenship*, 61; Idemudia, U & Ite, U E, "Corporate–community relations in Nigeria's oil industry: challenges and imperatives" (2006), 13 *Corporate Social Responsibility and Environmental Management*, 194.

frustrated by low participation rates in these programs.[52] Often, employees resist the programs on account of the stigmatization associated with the disease in their community. HIV/AIDS, prevention and treatment programs put established gender relations, sexual identities and traditional power structures (such as the status of traditional healers) into question. They also clash with local power structures. In townships, traditional healers have important positions. They see their social status and income threatened by the company programs, and therefore sometimes actively advocate against health services offered by firms. In consequence, persons who have contracted HIV/AIDS remain at times untreated, which renders the HIV/AIDS workplace programs of companies ineffective. However, there are also examples of firms that managed to mitigate these norm and power conflicts. A case in point concerns BMW in South Africa. The firm produces parts of its 3-series in Rosslyn and Midrand, in the Gauteng province.[53] As in the case of Mercedes, BMW's business model is specific skills-based, thus influenced by concerns with asset specificity. As a consequence, in South Africa the firm runs an extensive HIV/AIDS workplace program that offers comprehensive health services to its employees. This program is more successful than most other HIV/AIDS workplace programs in the country. The firm managed to drastically reduce absenteeism and losses. According to the project manager and local NGOs, one reason for the program's success is that the firm has realized that the acceptance of the program in the local communities where its employees live is key for its efficacy. When the firm started the program, very few employees were willing to enroll in it, which limited the program's effectiveness. It was then that the HIV/AIDS program manager recognized the extent to which the firm's health activities clashed with local community norms and power structures. In particular, local healers in the townships conceived of the company program as a potential threat to their own authority, power and economic wellbeing in the township economy and society. Most employees, however, routinely consulted these local healers. The advice they received from the healers at the beginning of the roll-out of the program seemed to have discouraged them from enrollment. To change this, the manager of the firm's HIV/AIDS program invited the local healers to the headquarters of the company to coordinate the firm's

---

52 For the following, see Bray, Z & Thauer, C, "Utopian Spaces, Dystopian Places?: A Local Community-Based Perspective on Corporate Social Responsibility" (2016), 11 *Nature and Culture*, 278.

53 See for the following Thauer, C R, "In Need of Meta-Governance: Business Networks of Transnational Governance" (2015), 48 *Israel Law Review*, 189.

program, which is based on Western medicine, with the advice traditional healers give to employees and their families. She offered the healers a deal: She would in the future routinely refer employees to them for nutrition and general healthy lifestyle advice. This offer signaled acknowledgment of and respect for the social status and work of healers, and guaranteed that they would not lose business. In return, she asked the healers to encourage employees to enroll in the company program for medical advice, and to refrain from a lifestyle that could undermine or clash with the medical treatment the firm provides. Through this strategy she managed to secure the buy-in of most traditional healers in the company program, so that they today recommend that employees enroll in the program, which makes the firm's fight against the disease so successful. The example shows that GHG confronts norm conflicts, potentially even with the designated beneficiaries of governance. These conflicts can be managed, although they may not always result in conflict resolution. The traditional healers still have a different approach to medicine than the occupational health manager and factory doctor of BMW. Rather, what was achieved was coordination on the basis of acceptance of these differences. There is no guarantee that this can always be achieved. However, the case shows that GHG is in practice, on account of the numerous conflicts it runs into, bound to engage in a management of these conflicts – thus in the governance of governance ("meta-governance"[54]).

When firms take over governance functions, however, norm and power conflicts may not only emerge in relation to local communities, but also with the local, provincial or national government.[55] Two cases illustrate such conflicts. One is the mentioned case of Mercedes Benz in East London; the other is a multinational car firm in Durban. The cases illustrate different intensities of conflict of the firms' governance activities. As concerns the Durban-based case, a large Japanese multinational car manufacturer attempted to organize a collective response to the HIV/AIDS pandemic between 2001 and early 2003 – similar to the one of Mercedes later on.[56] The firm's business model is, as in the case of Mercedes and BMW, based on skills that are not easily available in the labor market. The firm thus offers

54 Ibid.

55 On the interaction between firms and governments see a recent special issue on "Corporate Social Responsibility, Multinational Corporations, and Nation States" (2012), 14 *Business and Politics*, edited by Prakash, A & Griffin, J.

56 See for details Hönke & Thauer, "Multinational Corporations and Service Provision", above Fn. 28.

training programs to employees. At the time of the governance network, however, HIV/AIDS prevention and treatment was faced not only with capacity problems on the side of the state; the attempt by the Japanese multinational was also resisted by leading figures of the early Mbeki government, who was in power during that time and opposed the so-called "international scientific consensus" on HIV/AIDS.[57] This consensus refers to the fact that HIV causes AIDS and that medical treatment prolongs the time span between the infection with HIV and the outbreak of AIDS. The South African government publicly denied the relation between HIV and AIDS, and was openly hostile toward any medical approach to the disease.[58] A key figure in the government's denial of the international scientific consensus was the health minister, Ms. *Manto Tshabalala-Msimang* who proposed garlic, lemon juice, and beetroot as AIDS remedies. President *Mbeki* himself also attacked anyone in South Africa who questioned his "denialist" position. In this context of "denialism" the Japanese multinational initiated a multi-stakeholder partnership for HIV/AIDS prevention and comprehensive treatment. Partners were the local municipality, the University of KwaZulu Natal and the local chamber of commerce. The partners successfully applied for funding with the Global Fund to fight HIV/AIDS, Tuberculosis and Malaria in 2002. The project was to be rolled out throughout the local business world and from there on to the local community in 2004, and would have provided full medical services in relation to HIV/AIDS, including antiretroviral treatment. The project was based on the norms for public health programs in relation to HIV/AIDS of the WHO and the Global Fund itself. It was therefore inevitably in conflict with the position held by the Mbeki government. When the central government realized that Durban would start the project, at the last minute it insisted on taking full control over the budget and the content of the program before the money was released by the Global Fund. As a result, the MNC and its partners withdrew, for fear of becoming involved in a project dominated by the Mbeki government, and of consequently being held accountable for the foreseeable misuse of Global Fund money. Thus this transnational governance network ran into norm and power conflicts with the national government of South Africa, which made the project and the entire network fail. In the end, no governance services

57 Nattrass, *The AIDS Conspiracy*, above Fn. 34.

58 Dugger, C W, "Study cites toll of AIDS policy in South Africa" (November 26, 2008), *New York Times*, available at http://nyti.ms/2mhR368; Robbie, J, "Don't call me Manto" (September 14, 2000), *BBC*, available at http://news.bbc.co.uk/2/hi/africa/924889.stm.

were provided. Hence, in view of this case, it seems that a clash of norms between the car firm's governance initiative and the government rendered service delivery unsuccessful.

The second case – Mercedes in East London – was however successful. How so? By 2004, the South African government had come under international and domestic pressure for its ignorance toward the disease and its failure to fight it effectively.[59] In particular, the civil society pressure group Treatment Action Campaign (TAC) organized broad public resistance against the Mbeki government's policy. The TAC and increasing international isolation forced *Mbeki* into an agreement imposed on him by his own party, according to which he had to abstain from any public debate on HIV/AIDS. The TAC also pressured the cabinet to draft a new government program, which resulted in the "Operational Plan for Comprehensive HIV and AIDS Care, Management and Treatment for South Africa". In addition, the Constitutional Court ruled that the government had to provide antiretroviral drugs to prevent the infection of newborns. The ruling established the international scientific consensus toward the disease as the only acceptable one in South Africa. So, when U.S. President *Clinton* offered a team of experts to help the country put together a national treatment plan, *Thabo Mbeki* agreed, and a team was sent in 2004 to implement the Operational Plan.[60]

From this time on, the South African government accepted, and even supported, international help to fight HIV/AIDS. The second case of Mercedes Benz in East London reflects this new context. Mercedes' multi-stakeholder initiative made the strategic decision to also include the National Ministry of Health, so as to assure the buy-in of the national government. The initiative was successful in that it did organize health service delivery in East London. When compared to the previous case, the precondition for this effective rollout was that the South African government had moved from "denialism" to a position closer to the international "scientific consensus", on which Mercedes' program was built – and that Mercedes made a conscious decision to actively involve the national government from the very start of the project. The two cases illustrate the importance of aspects of legitimacy for the success of GHG.

---

59 Dickinson, D, "Fronts or front-lines? HIV/AIDS and big business in South Africa" (2004), 55 *Transformation: Critical Perspectives on Southern Africa*, 28.

60 Nattrass, *The AIDS Conspiracy*, above Fn. 34.

IV Conclusion: Implications for the Governance of Infectious Diseases

This article argued to move from International (IHG) to Global Health Governance (GHG) – more specifically, to move to a governance concept that includes private actors and actor networks in infectious disease outbreak response planning and management. Conditions of limited statehood and their relevance for the governance of health risks make this a necessity: township and slum conditions, for example, combine poverty, lack of sanitation and access to basic infrastructure and public services with high population density and physical closeness of human-animal relations – which increase the likelihood of infectious disease outbreaks. In these high-risk areas the state is often incapable of policy planning and implementation. Health governance should thus be conceptualized and planned beyond the state so as to be able to contain and manage a disease outbreak under such conditions. While it is yet unclear how this could and should be done precisely, the article showed that there are already empirical precedents of GHG that could helpfully inform future more systematic thinking about the legal and administrative planning of infectious diseases beyond the state – how it can and should be organized.

The article showed in this respect that in contexts of limited statehood it is often private actors that fill the policy-void. The article demonstrated this by looking at firms as governance providers in areas of limited statehood. Firms are unlikely private actors to provide governance, given their profit-seeking nature. Still, in South Africa, they have made significant contributions to the governance of HIV/AIDS. The case of HIV/AIDS governance in South Africa is particularly indicative for the potential of new modes of health governance. The governance of the disease is a highly complex task; South Africa has for a long time had a government that was openly hostile to any attempt to fight it medically. Irrespective of these generally adverse conditions, new, alternative modes of GHG involving firms emerged in order to fight the disease. More specifically, the article reported that firms, which have invested heavily in specific skills of employees, emerge as health governors in the face of the HIV/AIDS epidemic. Such firms offer sophisticated health care services to their workforces and families inside the firm, thereby contributing to public health as a public good. What is more, they also act as primary coordinators in their localities by organizing collective action against the disease beyond their own workforce. Firms such as Mercedes, BMW and others have tried to organize such a collective response in their respective localities.

As in any attempt at GHG, governance by firms is not always or automatically effective. In some cases the designated beneficiaries of firms' health governance – employees who have contracted HIV/AIDS – were unwilling to enroll in their health programs. In other instances, the South African government undermined the efforts of firms to take on central coordination functions in the fight against HIV/AIDS. The article also reported examples in which firms experiment with meta-governance mechanisms to deal with, manage and overcome these norm and power conflicts they confronted in their attempt to provide governance services. At times, these meta-governance mechanisms were capable of improving the effectiveness of GHG.

The call to move from IHG to new modes of GHG is thus not to imply that all problems of effective health governance could easily be resolved. In this respect, it is important to recall that, as the article explained, nothing beats fully consolidated statehood in terms of public goods provision. Service provision by business is also not entirely unproblematic. New modes of GHG involving firms, for example, are unlikely to be as inclusive as GHG via fully functioning statehood. Firm activities' inclusiveness is from the outset limited. In South Africa, firms' governance programs are, for example, not necessarily located where they would be needed the most – such as where infection rates or poverty are highest and public services and the general infrastructure are at their lowest – but simply where the firms are located. But since fully functioning statehood is not available in most parts of the world, including in those parts where new infectious diseases are likely to emerge in the future, such as under township and slum conditions, new modes of governance including private actors is all GHG will be able to draw on in the event of infectious disease outbreaks. The article showed that GHG is principally possible under such conditions even when the governance of an infectious disease requires a highly complex set of governance interventions. More case studies and analyses beyond the HIV/AIDS case in South Africa are needed to arrive at a more generalizable, yet more fine-tuned understanding of GHG in areas of limited statehood. This means, however, from a normative-legal perspective, that GHG may need to rethink international law in order to account for the fact that under conditions of limited statehood, private actors may fulfill public functions and roles.[61]

61 Clarke, L, *Public-Private Partnerships and Responsibility Under International Law: A Global Health Perspective*, 2014.